THE NEW DIRECT MARKETING

HOW TO IMPLEMENT
A PROFIT-DRIVEN DATABASE
MARKETING STRATEGY

*A HANDBOOK FOR DIRECT MARKETING COMPANIES AND
USERS OF DIRECT MARKETING METHODS*

THE NEW
DIRECT MARKETING

HOW TO IMPLEMENT
A PROFIT-DRIVEN DATABASE
MARKETING STRATEGY

DAVID SHEPARD ASSOCIATES, INC.

With Individual Contributions by
Rajeev Batra, Ph.D.
Andrew Deutch
George Orme
Bruce Ratner, Ph.D.
David Shepard

BUSINESS ONE IRWIN
Homewood, Illinois 60430

Sponsoring editor: *Susan Glinert Stevens, Ph.D.*
Project editor: *Karen J. Murphy*
Production manager: *Diane Palmer*
Jacket design: *Michael S. Finkelman*
Compositor: *Graphic World, Inc.*
Typeface: *11/13 Times Roman*
Printer: *R. R. Donnelley & Sons Company*

Library of Congress Cataloging-in-Publication Data

The New direct marketing : how to implement a profit-driven database
    marketing strategy : a handbook for direct marketing companies and
    users of direct marketing methods / David Shepard Associates, Inc.
        p.   cm.
    ISBN 1-55623-317-5
        1. Direct marketing—Data processing.   2. Marketing—Data bases.
    3. Data base management.   4. Direct marketing—Statistical methods.
    I. David Shepard Associates.
    HF5415.126.N48   1990
    658.8′4—dc20   90–30591
                                                                        CIP

Printed in the United States of America
        3   4   5   6   7   8   9   0   DO   7   6   5   4   3   2   1

To my father, who always asked,
"So what do you talk about all day?"

D.S.

PREFACE

A walk through the DMA library would suggest that the last thing the world needs is another book on direct marketing. There are the handbooks, the DMA manuals, and the individual books written by the top names in the field: Tom Collins and Stan Rapp's *MaxiMarketing*, Martin Baier's *Elements of Direct Marketing*, Bob Stone's *Successful Direct Marketing Methods*, Ed Nash's *Direct Marketing*, Katie Muldoon's *Catalog Marketing*, Jim Kobs' *Profitable Direct Marketing*, Rose Harper's *Mailing List Strategies*, and Joan Throckmorton's *Winning Direct Response Advertising*, to name just a very few of the many exceptional titles dealing with the business of direct marketing.

So why this book? Because the process of direct marketing has changed significantly within the last five years. The computer and statistical analysis play a far larger role in the marketing process than they did five years ago and their importance is increasing. Strategies and tactics leading direct marketers have talked about for years are now just starting to happen on a large scale. The promise of one-on-one marketing, of market segmentation, of true relationship marketing is now being implemented.

It's common knowledge that our business is growing rapidly in part because firms that had never considered direct marketing as part of their marketing mix are now taking a hard look at our business and they like what they see. But the traditional direct marketing business is also changing and nearly as rapidly. The old ways of doing business are being *supplemented* by an array of new techniques that make direct marketing, which has always been the most precise of marketing disciplines, even more precise, even more powerful.

This book, then, is about the *new* direct marketing. It assumes a working knowledge of the basics of direct marketing, and it studiously attempts not to duplicate the material presented in prior books such as those mentioned above. Of course, it is impossible not to duplicate some material, but where we do so we hope we have taken the subject matter further than it has been taken before.

In Chapter 1, we attempt to put the rapid changes that have recently affected direct marketing into perspective. Why are so many new companies looking at the benefits of database marketing and how and why are traditional direct marketing companies changing their basic operating practices? This subject is, of course, the domain of *MaxiMarketing* and so our coverage of this huge topic is intentionally brief.

Not surprisingly, this book is a reflection of our consulting practice. Much of our time is spent building and enhancing marketing databases, and the tasks involved in this work are the subjects of Chapters 2 through 8. These chapters deal with the capture and acquisition of data and the hardware and software issues associated with the development and implementation of a marketing database.

We strongly believe that direct marketers must become much more familiar with these subjects if they are to play a meaningful role in the development of their firm's marketing database. These issues are simply too important to be left solely to the judgment of MIS professionals, which in our experience is all too often the case. However, to participate constructively in decisions having to do with the development of a marketing database requires at least a working knowledge of the data processing and database management issues involved. Thus, in these chapters, we've attempted to provide the non–data processing professional with an overview of issues that are critical to the process of building and implementing a marketing database.

A consequence of the mass of data stored in our marketing databases is, perhaps ironically, an inability to deal with this much potentially useful information. In the "old" direct marketing days, there was limited information, and techniques such as RFM sufficed. Today, there is simply too much data for simple techniques such as RFM to deal with appropriately. Thus, the need for direct marketers to understand the basics of statistical analysis and modeling. Chapters 9 through 13 of the book deal with these subjects in some depth. The specific topics covered deal with the tools used for both predictive modeling, such as response analysis, and segmentation modeling: multiple regression, AID/CHAID, logistic regression, and factor and cluster analysis.

Frankly, from a purely statistical perspective, some of these topics are very advanced; however, we've attempted, we hope successfully, to present the essence of these subjects from the perspective of a direct marketer who needs to understand how and when to use each of these tools to improve marketing performance. Even the reader who studies the material carefully won't become a statistician, but will be much better at managing statisticians and interpreting the results of statistical analysis and statistical models.

Essentially, that is what we've tried to do throughout this book: help marketers understand both the applications and the implications of the technical issues of database marketing.

In Chapters 14 through 18, we attempt to place the new direct marketing into an economic perspective. The new direct marketing is more expensive than the old direct marketing and it needs to be cost-justified. Of course, before you can understand the new economics you must start with an understanding of the old economics. Consequently, this section of the book includes an analysis of the traditional measures of direct marketing performance. With that topic behind us, the balance of this section begins with a microlevel economic evaluation of predictive and segmentation models, and ends with a discussion of comprehensive macrolevel financial business models.

As will become evident to the reader who is the least bit sensitive to differences in writing styles, this book has five principal authors. George Orme is principally responsible for Chapter 1, Andrew Deutch for Chapters 2 through 8, Bruce Ratner for Chapters 9 through 12, Rajeev Batra for Chapter 13, and David Shepard for Chapters 14 through 17.

A few words of thanks. First, to Dick Montessi and the DMA who, four years ago, let us develop a course on Statistical Analysis for Direct Marketers. The structure of the statistical section of this book owes much to the development of that course over the years. Then, a special thanks to our clients, who have broken ground with us in developing the strategies and programs alluded to throughout the book. And finally, a thanks to our wives for their patience and support during the writing of this book, despite the months of evenings and weekends that they gave up.

DSA

CONTENTS

SECTION 4 STATISTICAL ANALYSIS AND MODELING

VENDORS AND TRADE NAMES

Vendor	Trade Name
Acxiom	Infobase
Ansa Software	Paradox
Apple	
Ashton-Tate	dBase III Plus
	dBase IV
Borland International	Reflex: The Database Manager
CACI	ACORN
Cincom Systems, Inc.	Supra
Claritas, Ltd.	PRIZM
Compaq	
Computer Associates	CA-Datacom/DB
	CA-Universe
Computer Corporation of America	Model 204
	MarketPulse
Condor Computer Corp.	Condor 3
Cosmos, Inc.	Revelation
Data General Corp.	DG/SQL
Digital Equipment	VAX DBMS
Donnelley	ClusterPlus
	CONQUEST
	Affluence Model
Easel	
Equifax Marketing Services	EQUIS
Fox Software	FoxBASE
Gupta Technologies, Inc.	SQLBASE
Hewlett-Packard	Image/3000

Vendor	Trade Name
IBM	DB2
	SQL/DS
	VSAM
	IMS
	VM
	DOS
	MVS
	CICS
Information Builders, Inc.	FOCUS
Informix Software, Inc.	INFORMIX
Infosystems Technology, Inc.	RUBIX
Inmagic, Inc.	INMAGIC
Innovative Software, Inc.	The Smart Database Manager
Lotus Development Corp.	Lotus 1-2-3
Metaphor	Metaphor
Metromail	
Micro Database Systems, Inc.	MDBS III
	Knowledgeman/2
Microrim, Inc.	R:BASE 5000
Motorola	
MRI	
National Decision Systems	VISION
National Demographics & Lifestyles	Lifestyle Selector
National Information Systems	Accent R
Perkins & Elmer	
Prime Computer, Inc.	DBMS
	Prime Information
Relational Technology, Inc.	INGRES
R. L. Polk	
SAS Institute, Inc.	SAS
	System 2000
Select & Save	
Smart Names	
Software A.G.	Adabas
	Natural
SRI	VALS
Toshiba	

Vendor	**Trade Name**
Transunion	
TRW	
Unisys Corp.	Mapper
United Software Systems & Services Corp.	CLIO
Wang	
Zenith	

SECTION 1

AN OVERVIEW

CHAPTER 1

AN OVERVIEW OF THE NEW DIRECT MARKETING

INTRODUCTION

There is a marketing evolution taking place in America.

We have seen companies shift from a strictly *product*-driven marketing emphasis to a much more *customer*-driven emphasis.

We have seen marketing move from a primary concentration on identifying and exploiting opportunistic product "gaps" to a process that goes beyond mere product advantages, focusing on target audiences, individual customer preferences, consumer demographics, and lifestyles.

We have seen a shift in marketing budgets as marketers, facing slower population growth and increasing competition, have resorted more to promotion than to advertising as a way to motivate customers to purchase their products.

We have seen marketers strive to improve marketing performance by "targeting" products and services to specific audiences and, in some cases, by developing new media in order to break through the clutter and differentiate both their brand and their company from the competition.

And more recently we have seen major companies begin to recognize consumers as *individuals* in an attempt to establish stronger customer relationships and "de-massify" their marketing efforts.

Consequently, we have seen an increasing number of major consumer products companies investing large sums to convert traditional product redemption name and address files into massive consumer databases, using the most highly advanced database marketing techniques to enhance these files and make them readily accessible to promotion and brand management.

Given all of the above, it is clear that the marketing playing field has changed. It is also clear that one of the critical issues in the future for all marketers, general as well as traditional direct marketers, will be their ability to get closer to their customers and discover additional ways to involve the consumer in the marketing process.

One way marketers have begun to do this is with marketing databases. Hardly a day goes by that we do not hear or read something about the power of a marketing database.

In their book *Maxi-Marketing,*[1] Stan Rapp and Tom Collins do a superb job of discussing both the transformation that has taken place as a result of new technology, and the new strategic direction in advertising and promotion that has emerged. They point out that:

> Every established norm in advertising and promotion is being trans-
> formed. . . . We are living through the shift from selling virtually everyone
> the same thing a generation ago to fulfilling the individual needs and tastes
> of better-educated consumers by supplying them with customized products
> and services. The shift [is] from "get a sale now at any cost" to building and
> managing customer databases that track the lifetime value of your
> relationship with each customer. As the cost of accumulating and accessing
> data drops, the ability to talk directly to your prospects and customers—and
> to build one-to-one relationships with them—will continue to grow.

But to truly maximize their opportunities in this new age of marketing, companies will have to be able to creatively implement programs that do not just capture the consumer's imagination, stimulate trial, and nurture loyalty, *but increase revenues and grow profits.*

Essentially, this means marketers will have to understand both the methodology and the economics of database marketing. In some cases, this means marketers will have to learn what data is important to their database. They will also need to expand their knowledge about how a database works, including what is involved in storing data, accessing data, manipulating and analyzing data, and ultimately turning data into valuable, strategic information. It also means they will have to apply new thinking, embrace new marketing methods, and focus on the strategic implications of using such methods and approaches in today's highly competitive and splintered marketplace.

This is why we have written this book. Our purpose is not to add to what has already been written regarding the changing marketplace, or the

---

[1] S. Rapp and T. Collins, *Maxi-Marketing* (New York: McGraw-Hill Inc., 1987).

database marketing evolution, but to provide a practical guide on how to profitably use database technology and new, innovative direct marketing methods to become smarter, more efficient and effective marketers.

Essentially, it is a handbook for direct marketing companies and users of direct marketing methods.

It is important to note that direct marketing used to be something only direct marketing or direct mail companies did. However, as name and address files were expanded to include huge amounts of marketing information, and as companies began to see the potential marketing benefits that would result from building databases of customers and prospects, the scope and technical complexity of the tasks required to implement marketing programs increased dramatically. Consequently, the term *database marketing* became a more accurate description of the processes involved, and it replaced the term *direct marketing* among both traditional and nontraditional practitioners.

Yet for many people, the word *database* has a very strong data processing connotation. In fact, while it is true that advanced computer software, including database management systems and hardware, are required to perform the most sophisticated database marketing programs, we intentionally chose not to title this book Database Marketing in order to emphasize the broader nature of the new direct marketing. Simply stated, the data processing resources are only one part of the new direct marketing equation that, when all parts are working together, can dramatically improve the marketing effectiveness of both traditional and nontraditional direct marketing practitioners.

In this first section, we will define the new direct marketing, and discuss the five key components that make up the new direct marketing. We will also highlight ways in which the new direct marketing is being applied by different types of marketers and provide a framework for using it to develop marketing strategies and programs.

In Section 2, we will discuss how to gather and use both primary and secondary data to identify customer and prospect profiles.

In Section 3, we will outline the key considerations and criteria that need to be evaluated in order to select the best combination of hardware and software for any given situation. We will discuss how to select a database management system as well as how to decide whether the entire database marketing process should be done in-house, or can best be handled using a combination of internal and external resources.

In Section 4, we will discuss the statistical techniques that are used to analyze data, create and profile market segments, and predict outcomes such as response rates and sales. We will also provide sufficiently detailed explanations of the processes, including modeling performance standards, to help marketers not only appreciate the power of the techniques but become much better users and buyers of statistical services.

In Section 5, we will look at the economics of this new direct marketing and discuss the financial implications of these new methods as they pertain to both traditional and nontraditional direct marketing principles and practices.

But right now we need to define exactly what the new direct marketing is, and how companies are using it to enhance their marketing effectiveness.

THE NEW DIRECT MARKETING: WHAT IS IT?

The new direct marketing is an information-driven marketing process, managed by database technology, that enables marketers to develop and implement customized marketing programs and strategies.

In order to be able to implement the new direct marketing, you need to know how to:

1. Identify and gather relevant data about customers and prospects.
2. Use database technology to transform raw data into powerful and accessible marketing information.
3. Apply statistical techniques to customer and prospect databases in order to: analyze behavior; isolate relatively homogeneous market segments; and score and rank individuals in terms of their probability of behaving in a variety of predictable ways (responding, buying, returning, paying, staying or leaving, and so on).
4. Evaluate the economics of gathering, manipulating, and analyzing data, and capitalize on the economics of developing and implementing data-driven marketing programs.
5. Creatively act on the marketing opportunities that emerge from these processes to develop individual customer relationships and to build business.

Given the above elements, the new direct marketing is much broader in scope than what has been traditionally regarded as either direct marketing or database marketing. In the past, direct marketing has been distinguishable from other marketing disciplines because of its emphasis on initiating a direct relationship between a buyer and a seller, a relationship that until recently centered primarily on the exchange of goods and services. However, in today's marketing environment, exchanging information is becoming almost as important as exchanging goods and services. With rising costs, crowded supermarket shelves, and overstuffed mailboxes, smart marketers are not just efficiently consummating a sale, they are also providing a chance for customers to communicate with them.

As a result, programs are being implemented to develop information about an individual. In some cases, marketers are actually establishing ongoing "dialogs" with customers that go well beyond acknowledging a customer relationship or nurturing customer loyalty.

Such dialogs make use of in-package surveys, special questionnaires, opinion polls, and annual tracking studies as well as point of sale (POS) programs that automatically reward shoppers with discounts while electronically recording what they are purchasing.

Significantly, such dialogs facilitate the gathering of information that has relevance and value to both consumers and marketers.

For consumers, these dialogs not only provide a mechanism to register preferences regarding merchandise and method of purchase, but also allow consumers to help mold new products and services based on their interests, lifestyles, and purchase patterns. Additionally, these dialogs enable consumers to continually make known their perceptions and attitudes about a company's products and services. Thus, they offer consumers the chance to play a more active, ongoing role in the buyer-seller relationship and help create a stronger affinity between consumers and companies.

For marketers, they produce more timely and accurate information about usage and buying habits. For example, they enable companies to track individual usage behavior and identify individual purchase habits so that marketers can precisely account for a specific brand's share of a consumer's total category purchases.

Consequently, marketers are able to use the information to develop *customized* marketing strategies and programs for *individuals* or small groups of customers, and no longer have to settle for one single solution or program to best fit their complex marketing situation.

Aside from capturing information, the new direct marketing also enables marketers to more easily use the information. Until now, customer data and product data were usually only "linked" after countless hours of analysis and extrapolation. Even the most sophisticated marketers had a tough time matching product sales and individual customer performance.

But now, using the new direct marketing, marketers can first marry product sales and data concerning individual customer attributes and characteristics, and then, using statistical techniques such as those discussed in Section 4, develop ways to quantify market size and market demand for products or services.

Simply stated, companies that are able to marry *individual* customer information with standard industry measures of product movement on an ongoing basis can more accurately and quickly evaluate opportunities and precisely identify who is buying what, how often, and why. They can relate this information to other types of products their customers are also buying, and know which elements within the marketing mix are most likely to motivate such consumers to switch or stay with a given brand.

Strategically, then, the new direct marketing is based on the premise that not all customers are alike, and that by gathering, maintaining, and analyzing detailed information about customers and prospects, marketers can identify key market segments and optimize the process of planning, pricing, promoting, and consummating an exchange between sellers and buyers that satisfies both individual and organizational objectives.

THE NEW DIRECT MARKETING AND CONSUMER PACKAGED GOODS

In consumer packaged goods marketing, the primary considerations have usually been place and promotion. That is not to say that these marketers have not attempted to develop unique and distinguishable products, or that they haven't capitalized on pricing advantages when available.

But the key element in the success of many traditional consumer packaged goods marketers has been their ability to gain and utilize superior distribution position. Simply stated, as long as they had enough places that offered their products, marketers could increase or decrease the advertising weight and promotion mechanisms depending on the desired volume of product movement.

Additionally, depending on where a product was in the product life cycle and its relative market share, these marketers could offer broader, more extensive product and price ranges to stave off possible competition, attract a wider audience, and stimulate trial among consumers who may otherwise be reluctant to purchase.

However, with all the changes that have taken place in the consumer packaged goods marketing arena, including the fragmentation of media, the proliferation of products, and the splintering of the mass market, consumer packaged goods marketers are no longer able to rely on what has worked in the past.

In many instances, to sustain profits and achieve higher volume by accelerating consumption patterns among loyal customers, these marketers have resorted to discounting as a way to motivate people to buy or try their product.

While previously, advertising accounted for as much as 65 percent of a company's marketing expenditures, in many instances promotion expenditures have overtaken advertising as the largest single item in marketing budgets.

Moreover, as marketers have been allocating more and more dollars to promotion, and in many cases to coupon activities, their results have been steadily decreasing. According to the Manufacturers Coupon Control Center, in 1985, 179.8 billion coupons were distributed and 6.49 billion were redeemed, producing a redemption rate of 3.6 percent. In 1986, with over 202 billion coupons distributed, only 7.3 billion were redeemed, resulting in a similar redemption rate of 3.6 percent. Even more important, the average dollar amount the manufacturer redeemed per coupon increased from $.34 in 1986 to $.37 in 1987. Thus, marketers are paying more money for coupon redemption and getting less in return.

Another development that has signficantly changed the playing field in the marketing arena is the use of bar code scanners at the supermarket counter. These highly sophisticated machines not only help to expedite the check-out process but also provide retailers with instant information about which products are moving and at what price.

As such, they are dramatically altering the balance of power and knowledge between retailers and manufacturers. Manufacturers have traditionally been the most knowledgeable about how well their products were selling. But with today's optical scanning capabilities, retailers are now armed with product movement information at the store level, instantly. Consequently, in some instances, retailers know more about what is selling than the manufacturers who pride themselves on their marketing knowledge.

This information has led to the increased use of *slotting allowances,* a promotion cost that retailers now charge manufacturers as a cost of doing business. In essence, with so many companies seeking to grow share by increasing the number of products and varieties they offer, the supermarket shelves are no longer large enough to accommodate all available items. In response to the quantity of products available, retailers have had to become more selective about what they stock. Retailers now use bar code information to allocate how much space they will offer a given brand, and to determine exactly what that space is worth. If an item does not give the retailer the right return, then the retailer charges a slotting allowance as a way to compensate for lost revenue. Significantly, according to Donnelley Marketing, such allowances now account for as much as 44 percent of a promotion budget, up from 34 percent just a few years ago.

What's more, retailers are going beyond simply using the scanning capabilities to help with space allocation and inventory management; they are also using it *to record a customer's purchases.*

Thus, retailers are able to effortlessly carry on an ongoing information exchange with their customers that provides them with superior knowledge of their customers' shopping habits, brand preferences, precise purchase behavior, and product usage. Such information also allows them to become more active marketers and begin to develop customized promotions and offers to different groups of customers.

However, a number of manufacturers are also creating marketing databases. Their databases will be fueled by the data they are able to obtain as a result of their own consumer information exchanges, which will utilize any two-way communication channel including in person, face-to-face exchanges between consumers and manufacturers' marketing representatives, and exchanges that are facilitated by telephone and mail. In some instances, the mechanism to initiate such information exchanges will be an in-pack questionnaire, an on-pack survey, or an end-of-aisle rebate offer. Or it could be a print ad, a Free-Standing Insert (FSI), or a TV commercial with a toll-free number.

Thus, both retailers and manufacturers are actively seeking the names and addresses of their customers. Significantly, by using the five elements of the new direct marketing discussed earlier in this chapter, they will be able to create customer profiles for different types of customers and accurately determine market penetration and usage within and between such customer segments.

As a result, marketing in the future will change dramatically. For consumer packaged goods marketers, the most likely course of action will be the use of their database resources and capabilities to help integrate their overall marketing efforts. This will result in better market analysis, better targeting, and better program planning and execution. Consequently, they will be able to more accurately measure within a matter of weeks how well a new campaign is working in a certain region or against a certain brand, and whether they have been able to reposition the brand or extend its life.

OTHER APPLICATIONS AND ADVANTAGES OF
THE NEW DIRECT MARKETING

Another advantage of the new direct marketing is that it allows marketers to know more about various types of customers and prospects, and to "grade" prospects by determining, as Lester Wunderman says, if a prospect is willing to buy, able to buy, and ready to buy your goods or services.

A good example of this methodology is the way some automotive manufacturers encourage prospects to qualify themselves during the initial stages of the information exchange process. These automotive advertisers often ask the prospect to indicate when they are planning to purchase, so that prospects can be gauged in terms of their readiness to buy. They also ask what the consumer is currently driving, and for how long, so that a consideration set — the competitive makes and models the consumer is also likely to be considering aside from the company's product — can be developed. Then the advertisers use this information to develop a superior competitive position to highlight the benefits of their own makes and models customized to the needs and wants of the prospect.

The new direct marketing can help marketers to reach the consumer with the right product and the right offer at the right time.

One example that illustrates this point is negative option book and record clubs. Some clubs, instead of sending the same set of options to all members, are customizing their option offers, based on a member's previous selections and purchases, as well as demographic and lifestyle information captured through previous communications.

Two outcomes have resulted from this customization. First, these clubs are seeing a reduction in attrition because members are receiving selections that are better suited to their tastes and interests. Second, members are buying more books.

Thus, such customizing not only helps to minimize the expense of sending offers that are not appropriate for certain customers or prospects, but it also helps to enhance the company's relationship because it encourages the customer to feel that "this company understands me and knows what I like, what I am interested in."

The new direct marketing is more than just using a marketing database to selectively target offers to customers and prospects. It is a way of marketing that allows marketers to continually incorporate new information and results back into the database.

Each time marketers get a response, it is recorded in the database so that future strategies and executions can be developed using the collective results of previous efforts. This means companies can allocate marketing resources based on current, up-to-date results including a comprehensive performance history for each customer.

Consequently, marketers are able to develop highly targeted customer acquisition and marketing retention programs, and more importantly, profitably customize the sequence and flow of marketing communications.

Using the new direct marketing, leading catalogers have found that they can regulate the number of times they promote to a customer. By selectively targeting, they can also *customize* which version of the catalog a customer receives — the complete catalog or a "mini–special interest" catalog. As a result, they have been able to help offset continually rising costs, and more importantly, maximize profits.

The new direct marketing can also be used by enterprising third-party marketers to bring together companies and customers.

American Express recently created a program that illustrates this point. They used a bill insert promotion to let cardmembers know that buying a new car has "never been easier." They promoted the fact that cardmembers could use their American Express card to charge their down payment, and listed over 25 import and domestic manufacturers where the card would be honored.

The cardmembers were asked to indicate which vehicles they would like to know more about and American Express would arrange for *information* and literature to be sent from the manufacturer. Over 100,000 responses were generated.

Aside from demonstrating how the card can help automotive manufacturers produce qualified leads for their vehicles, this effort also enabled American Express to use the information to identify the characteristics of cardmembers who were interested in certain types of cars. Using statistical modeling, they were able to create profiles of who responded for which type of cars and then segment their entire file accordingly.

As a result, American Express can now develop cooperative marketing programs with key manufacturers to help them target to American Express cardmembers who will most likely respond to a manufacturer's promotion, and offer special incentives to charge the down payment for their new purchase on the American Express card.

This is an excellent example of how using the new direct marketing can help everyone win. Consumers win because they can conveniently choose which cars they want to know more about. The automotive manufacturers win because they receive qualified leads. American Express wins because they have expanded their card usage by increasing the number of places that honor the card and the number of ways cardmembers can use the card.

What makes it work is the ability to establish a two-way communication with the consumer through a variety of channels.

As noted earlier, the purpose of such communication is not just to generate a sale but also to manage a relationship and develop greater customer allegiance and brand equity.

Engendering customer loyalty has become vital to many companies. Good customers are too valuable and too hard to find for companies to risk losing one by being passive, indifferent, or indistinguishable from the competition.

Bob Stone, in his classic book *Successful Direct Marketing*,[2] points out that the heart of building and maintaining customer loyalty is *customized persuasion*. Stone goes on to say that based on the premise that all customers are not created equal—approximately 80 percent of all repeat business for goods and services comes from 20 percent of a customer base—proponents of customer loyalty programs target specific marketing efforts to the most fertile 20 percent of their database. It is interesting to note, from an historical perspective, that while book clubs such as Book of the Month Club and The Literary Guild have been offering dividend or' bonus points as a means of rewarding purchases for as long as anyone can remember, airlines were among the first nontraditional direct marketers to recognize the opportunity to provide rewards to help retain the loyalty of selected customers. Essentially, they realized that the more a customer purchases their product and the greater the rewards, the greater the incentive would be to keep purchasing their product. As a result, airline frequent flyer programs have become the standard in terms of such customer loyalty programs.

And, of course, hotels that are dependent on frequent travelers and repeat business have also initiated reward programs for more frequent customers.

---

[2] B. Stone, *Successful Direct Marketing*, 4th ed. (Chicago: NTC Publishing Group, 1988).

Other categories of business also have adapted similar concepts. Telecommunications companies such as MCI, AT&T, and Sprint all offer incentives to stimulate usage. In some cases, they also offer special discounts on merchandise as a result of points that can be accrued based on the amount of service used over a given period of time.

Financial service companies have also used rewards to differentiate their credit cards from the pack. Citicorp's Citi-Dollars and the Discover card's annual rebate of up to 5 percent on purchases are but two examples.

Significantly, many of these companies have found that, aside from constantly keeping in touch with their members, one of the keys to success is targeting promotions and bonus offers based on previous purchases, calling patterns, or destinations, as well as the member's stated preferences. Just as in the case of the negative option selections that were noted earlier, here, too, it seems that the customer wants to be recognized for his or her individuality and treated accordingly.

In the future, it will be the companies that can gather, store, and use such information to their competitive advantage by developing new strategies and carefully targeted programs that will benefit the most from the new direct marketing.

The new direct marketing also involves a wider range of communications with customers or prospects. For smart marketers, every contact with a customer is an opportunity for the exchange of information. While such an event in and of itself might not produce a sale, the cumulative effect of such communications definitely has an impact on customer attitudes and loyalty. As such, managing the communications mix and developing a customer contact strategy have become important considerations of the new direct marketing.

SUMMARY

Over the years, regardless of whether they were operating in a direct marketing environment or the mass marketing arena, one of the major responsibilities of marketers has been to develop strategies that take advantage of the products or services that offer the best opportunity of achieving a company's overall business goals.

Today, in an information marketing environment, marketers can execute this responsibility with more precision than ever before. Marketers are analyzing more relevant and timely customer level information. They are correlating customer level data with traditional measures of off-the-shelf purchases. They are creating ongoing customer dialogs to funnel relevant information to the marketing database. They are enhancing their databases with survey, demographic, psychographic, and lifestyle data. They are using highly sophisticated mathematical segmentation and predictive models. They are identifying who is buying what, and how often. They are measuring which elements within the marketing mix are motivating consumers to make a purchase decision to switch or stay with a given brand. In short, today's information-driven marketers have all the tools necessary to develop new products and new marketing strategies in ways unheard of just a few years ago. And it's only going to get better as more companies come to understand the power of the marketing database in an information-driven economy.

SECTION 2

SOURCES OF DATA

CHAPTER 2

SOURCES OF MARKETING DATA

The new direct marketing requires vast amounts of data from a variety of sources: internally developed performance or customer behavior data, and external geo-demographic, psychographic, lifestyle, financial, and survey data. All of these data sources are critical elements of the new direct marketing. Data makes it possible to identify the characteristics associated with our best, worst, and marginal customers. Data provides the basis for segmenting customers into relatively homogeneous groups with similar characteristics, attitudes, or needs. Data is the key to all predictive models. Data is essential to identifying people on prospect files and on rented lists whose characteristics are similar to those of our best customers.

CUSTOMER DATA

Performance or customer behavior data, which includes all relevant sales and promotion history data, is, of course, the most important data that direct marketers have about their customers. Examples of this type of data are shown in Table 4–1 of Chapter 4, Section 3.

Direct marketers have consistently found that performance data or customer data is the most relevant data when it comes to building reliable predictive models. Recency, frequency, and monetary value data are no less important in the new direct marketing than they were in classical or traditional direct marketing. But in the new direct marketing these data elements are combined, in new ways, with additional data sources that allow today's direct marketers to be more efficient and more profitable.

Sections 2 and 3 of this text should be read in tandem. This section discusses data, what it is, and how it is gathered and organized.

Section 3 will focus on how customer data gets into the marketing database, how it is used in the modeling process, how model scores are used to select customers and prospects from the database, and how the database is used to analyze promotion results. We will continually reinforce the point that the marketing database itself is a tool — it is the engine that makes the new direct marketing possible. But data is the fuel that provides the marketing database with its power.

While performance data is the most important type of data we have about customers, it is not available in equal measure for all customers. Older customers will have a much richer data history in our database than will new customers.

Prospects — those people to whom we have promoted in the past but who have not yet purchased from us — will have no performance data at all, other than a history of the promotions we have sent. Some firms do not maintain files of prospects because the cost of maintaining the information would be prohibitive. An example of this situation would be a magazine publisher that sends millions of direct mail pieces as part of annual or seasonal promotion efforts to which the only available, or meaningful, response would be the purchase of a subscription. This is essentially a black-and-white case — the prospect either responds or does not and there is no meaningful gradation of responses. For other types of direct marketing situations such as lead generation, cross-selling, and most back-end marketing activities, where marketers are developing and managing a relationship, there are often numerous levels of communication with customers between promotion and conversion that do have meaning.

Consider the case of a lead generating financial services firm that offers a variety of investment programs. Because leads or prospects may not be in an immediate position to invest their funds, the financial services marketer may have to make a considerable investment — in both time and money — to nurture the relationship before the prospect turns into a customer. The dialog between the financial services firm and the prospect may begin as the result of direct mail, direct response media such as print, broadcast, or FSI, or word of mouth passed along by satisfied customers. Once the dialog has been established, the marketer can use the promotional process to nurture the relationship with the prospect. If used strategically, this dialog may help to gather data about the prospect that will contribute to conversion at a later date. For example, during the relationship building or "courtship" process, the marketer may learn that the prospect has a child who will enter college in two years. The marketer can instruct the database to contact the prospect with an appropriate message at that time.

Additionally, the marketer may use the promotional dialog to learn about the prospect's savings and investment goals such that promotions for the right products can be sent to the right prospects at the right time.

In packaged goods businesses, the dialog may be initiated by a customer responding via an in-store display, a rebate coupon, in-pack or on-pack surveys, or direct response media opportunities. Once the customer has responded, the manufacturer uses the information to nurture customer loyalty and maintain or increase share.

Thus, in the new direct marketing, all information is important, not just the types of data that we previously associated only with postacquisition customer performance. As such, the data gathering process may begin prior to purchase.

Therefore, careful attention must be paid to how we communicate to customers and prospects, when we communicate with them, and what data we are attempting to capture at each stage of the relationship building process.

PRIMARY AND SECONDARY RESEARCH DATA

In addition to customer behavior data, two other sources of data are critically important to the new direct marketing.

- **Primary research data** — data that is provided directly by individuals (customers, prospects, and even nonprospects) about themselves.
- **Secondary research data** — data that is acquired about customers and prospects from third-party sources.

For the purposes of this book, we have divided secondary data into four main types — demographic, psychographic, behavioral/lifestyle, and financial. While social scientists have a number of complex taxonomies that they use to classify data by type, and therefore may disagree with the classification used in this text, we find that it is one that marketers will generally consider to be appropriate for working purposes. One reason for our use of the preceding classification is that it describes the types of data that can be purchased commercially and appended to customer and prospect files. Therefore, we consider our taxonomy of secondary data to be practical and workable for marketers. In Appendix I, we have included listings of the data elements that appear in a number of the major commercially available databases. Certainly other databases exist and readers are advised to consult the Direct Marketing Association for a more complete census of data suppliers. However, the listings provided will give the reader a very good idea of the data overlay sources available.

The remainder of this chapter will focus on primary and secondary research data. The following portion of this chapter will discuss customer or performance data in detail in the context of building a customer database.

Primary Research Data

Primary data consists of data that is obtained directly from the source. It is generally captured through surveys, interviews, focus groups, or other direct interactions with individuals. The use of primary data has increased dramatically over the past few years, and with the advent of bar code scanners, home shopping, interactive television, and other electronic media, the number of channels through which primary data can be collected will increase exponentially.

Primary data consists of two major types:

- Individual level demographic data such as age, income, and home value.
- Attitudinal and behavioral data.

In the past, primary data was often the province of market research, and was used primarily to provide direction for marketing programs that addressed large groups of customers and prospects. Demographic data was used to get a better "fix" on the characteristics of the larger market, and attitudinal data was used to provide a sense of which issues were important to various groups of customers, and therefore should be emphasized in promotional materials.

Market researchers use primary data to identify new product opportunities or new segments within the customer file. This is usually done by sending surveys to a representative sample of customers or prospects to determine what products and services they are interested in but do not currently purchase from the firm sending the questionnaire. In this way, primary data gathered through market research surveys can lead to the development of products that are either new to the firm or, in some cases, new to the industry.

Although the primary data that is gathered by market research surveys has always been valuable for the directional guidance it provides, in the past it has had certain limitations for database marketing. That is, while market researchers for a financial services firm could tell their marketing counterparts that 20 percent of the company's prospects were males between 40 and 45 years old, who earn between $50,000 and $75,000, and are interested in investing in mutual funds, they were unable to identify the specific individuals who comprised the 20 percent. So while the information about the firm's prospects was interesting in that it described a fairly large segment within the file (20 percent) that the firm would like to promote, the opportunity was not actionable because the individuals whose characteristics matched the desired profile could not be identified by name.

More recently, the collection and manipulation of primary data at the individual level has been expanded to involve not only market research but to become an increasingly important component of the mainstream marketing process. One reason for this is the improved price performance of database technology that enables many companies to capture and manipulate large amounts of data at the individual customer and prospect level.

Perhaps a more important reason for this trend is the recognition that nontargeted mailings are becoming increasingly expensive and that strategies to decrease the cost per order are essential. By collecting primary data for individuals on the customer and prospect files, marketers in a wide variety of businesses are able to include this data as a central component of the market segmentation process.

A number of innovative marketing programs that rely on gathering, analyzing, and manipulating data have been reported in professional journals. One example was the use of survey simulators to predict direct marketing response.[1] This approach used surveys to gather data about the characteristics of individuals within the target audience and to link these characteristics to the rate and manner in which people indicated they would respond to a promotion. Green and Moore theorized that people with similar individual characteristics would have similar attitudes and that by "quantifying" a dry run of a promotion, which linked attitudinal data to data about individual characteristics, the results of a rollout could be predicted. By using survey data in this manner prior to mailing, they were able to help their client focus promotion dollars on the campaigns that had the greatest potential of success based on the characteristics of the target audience.

---

[1] Michael E. Green and Erard Moore, "Using Survey Simulators to Predict Direct Mail Response," *Journal of Direct Marketing Research* 1, no. 2, Spring/Summer 1987.

Another innovative approach described how VALS data was linked to PRIZM data in order to reduce the target audience for a mortgage insurance product and increase the cost-effectiveness of using appended data.[2] VALS, an acronym for Values And Lifestyles, offers marketers a classification of customers and markets based on psychographic characteristics. VALS categories consist of four major categories: need-driven, outer-directed, inner-directed, and integrated. Within these categories are a number of VALS types including such groupings as achievers, emulators, societally conscious, belongers, sustainers, and survivors. Customers are assigned to VALS categories based on their answers to a 30-question survey.

PRIZM, a product of Claritas, L. P., is an acronym for Potential Ratings in Zoned Markets, and provides a classification of neighborhood types based on census data, market geography, marketing, and media databases (such as Simmons) and mathematical models (notably cluster analysis). PRIZM enables marketers to assign customers and prospects to neighborhood types based solely on their address.

Both of these examples are notable because they employed as part of the mainstream marketing process research concepts that would normally be limited to the market research effort. This approach was a cost-effective way to reduce the size of the target audience to those people who were most likely to respond.

Segmentation Analysis

The assumption underlying all segmentation analyses is that a single customer or prospect file consists of a small number of relatively homogeneous market segments; and that each market segment consists of individuals whose attitudes toward your products or services are similar to others within the same segment but different from those in the other segments. Presumably, if you knew to which segment an individual belonged, and if you knew the attitude of that segment toward your product or service, you would market to the individuals within that segment differently than you would market to individuals within other segments. The issues are, then, to: (1) confirm that the segments exist, (2) determine the attitudes and characteristics of each segment, and (3) figure out a

---

[2] Nancy J. Olson, Keith Ricke, and Pamela Weisenberger, "Using VALS to Target Market through Package Segmentation," *Journal of Direct Marketing Research* 1, no. 2, Spring/Summer 1987.

cost-effective way to assign all individuals on your customer or prospect database to the correct segment.

To follow the recommended approach, marketers determine what their information objectives are and then work with their own market researchers (market research firms or researchers retained or employed by their advertising agency) to develop survey instruments that will generate the answers desired. Surveys are then mailed to a respresentative sample of a larger group; for example, customers, prospects, and nonprospects, or heavy, medium, and light users of a particular product. The survey will generally consist of a large number (dozens or even hundreds) of attitude questions as well as behavior and demographic questions. Attitude questions will probe for attitudes toward the general category or product area, or may probe for attitudes towards a particular company or individual brand. For example, "how do you feel about investing through the mail?" "what is your tolerance for risk?" "how do you make up your mind to invest in a particular investment?" "how do you keep informed?" "what is your opinion about banks, stockbrokers, insurance agents, and so on?" Behavior questions will get at the decisions you have actually made: "are you invested in stocks, bonds, mutual funds, real estate?" "do you use a stockbroker, investment adviser, subscribe to financial newsletters, and so on?" And, finally, the demographic questions will be the usual ones regarding age, income, occupation, wealth, and so forth.

Once the responses to the survey are received, statistical techniques (see Chapter 13, "Segmentation Analysis," for more information on the techniques themselves) are used to assign all responders to a small number (three to six) of relatively homogeneous segments. If the principal basis for the segmentation is the attitude questions, as is frequently the case, then members of each segment will have attitudes toward the subject in question that are similar to others within the same segment and dissimilar to those in other segments. The tradition in segmentation studies is to assign each segment a name that is representative of the predominate attitude of the group toward the product or service offered. For example, in financial services analysis, one is likely to find such groups as: the *new-money risk takers,* the *new-money schizophrenics,* the *old-money conservatives,* or the *hard-pressed savers.* As you can tell from this naming scheme, the group's attitude toward investing has been combined with the group's ability to invest to provide a more meaningful description of the group.

As we said before, this kind of segmentation study has been used by general marketers for years to gain insights into the composition and needs of individual market segments. However, in order for this information to be truly useful for direct marketers, we need a cost-effective technique for assigning all customers or all prospects to the appropriate segment. And sending a full-blown segmentation survey to everyone on a multimillion-name database is simply not cost-effective.

There are at least two ways in which direct marketers can assign customers or prospects to the appropriate segment. The first method involves analysis of all of the questions asked in the survey to discover a relatively small number of questions that do a very good job in assigning individuals to segments. It is not unusual to discover that the answers to 6 to 10 questions can result in nearly the same assignment (70 to 80 percent correct assignment) as the full-blown questionnaire. If this is the case, then an abbreviated form of the complete survey can be sent to a much larger universe of names.

Of course, even sending an abbreviated survey to a large number of names can be very expensive. Therefore, before this approach is executed, the recommended approach is to attempt to determine if segment membership can be accurately predicted by correlating known customer data with survey data in a model that would assign a probability of segment membership to each individual on the database. The exact procedure would entail building some form of regression model in which segment membership would be the variable to be predicted, and customer data and any available overlay data would comprise the independent predictor variables. (The reader will find material about regression models and other statistical techniques in the chapters of Section 4.)

In practice, some combination of both methods might work best. For example, suppose a segmentation study discovered four segments within the customer database, with one segment being particularly important. Let's further assume that a mathematical model that predicted membership in this particular segment was strong but certainly not 100 percent accurate. In this case, an abbreviated survey might be mailed to all customers with a higher than average probability of membership in this key segment. In this way, more data would be gathered about a key market segment without the expense of mailing to everyone on the database.

Response rates to surveys will depend on the strength of the relationship between the company and its customers, and may vary from less than 10 percent to better than 50 percent. Some companies, to improve response rate to surveys, will include premiums ranging from extra chances in sweepstakes, to price discounts, to cash. The expected response rate is critical to the design of the survey. In general, most segmentation studies require at least 3,000 to 5,000 responses. If the survey response rate is 50 percent, this means sending out 10,000 or so surveys. On the other hand, if the expected response rate is in the area of 10 percent, then a much larger number of questionnaires must be mailed, and the issue of nonresponse bias becomes important. That is, if only 10 percent complete the survey, how representative can these 10 percent be of the entire universe of customers or prospects? The answer is probably not very representative and care must be taken to insure the reliability of results. One way marketers sometimes evaluate the reliability of results in situations such as these is to use a telemarketing survey to confirm answers to key questions.

Using Segmentation Results

Marketers will generally take a number of action steps based on the responses to an abbreviated survey mailed to an entire database or a large segment of the database. Prospects who do not respond at all may be excluded from further promotions based on the assumption that prospects who are unwilling to respond to an abbreviated survey are unlikely to respond to a promotion.

Using a questionnaire to gather primary data about the target audience is done for a number of reasons. The problem often is that, while models may tell us something about a prospect's willingness and ability to purchase based on similarities between the prospects' personal and financial characteristics and those of current customers, models often do not have access to data about the readiness of prospects to purchase. So while predictive models based on internally available data can reduce the target audience, and models that include appended data can further improve the base models, the economics of the promotion still may not work. One reason may be that the information needed to further target the audience based on readiness and individual attitudes about purchasing is often unavailable unless marketers have already been in direct communication with customers and prospects.

One way of capturing the necessary information is to shift from one-step to two-step promotions in which the first step is an inexpensive, simplified attitudinal and behavior survey. This approach will capture data that will help marketers to understand the readiness and willingness of customers to purchase and can also improve the economics of the promotion by limiting the number of expensive pieces that will ultimately be mailed. Examples comparing the economics of one-step versus two-step promotions are contained in Section 5, "The Economics of the New Direct Marketing."

Another benefit of using a questionnaire as the first step in a two-step process is that some of the people who respond but do not initially convert may provide other valuable information about themselves that will help the marketer in future efforts. The marketer can capture this information in the database and instruct the system to mail a promotion piece at a more appropriate time. This concept of contacting prospects at a time when they are ready is an extension of marketing based on "magic moments."

Magic moment marketing is a well established concept in the insurance industry. This is the notion of mailing a life insurance upgrade or cross-sell promotion to policyholders on their birthdays or at a preset number of days prior to policy renewal. The policyholder's birthdate and effective dates of coverage are maintained in the database and the database is instructed to "wake up" and send a certain promotional piece at a preset number of days prior to the event. This is but one example of how an information-oriented communication with customers and prospects can yield valuable results that may extend beyond the promotion at hand. Although this section describes situations in which modeling alone may be unable to improve conversion performance to the point where it is economically viable, there are many situations in which modeling alone *will* be sufficient and the addition of primary data, from an economic perspective, will not be necessary. However, as marketing efforts become more and more personalized and marketers attempt to establish and maintain true one-to-one relationships with their customers, the inclusion of primary data in the marketing process will become increasingly common.

Secondary Data

While primary data provides unique information about people's attitudes, expectations, and personal behavior, it is not always available to marketers at the initial stages of a targeting process. In many cases, data from secondary sources can be a cost-effective way of enhancing the strength of models.

As stated above, secondary data is defined as data that is acquired from third-party sources rather than provided by the individuals themselves. Secondary data includes data from U.S. Census sources as well as commercially developed databases.

We stated that in this text, secondary data is classified into four types:

- Demographic.
- Psychographic.
- Behavioral/lifestyle.
- Financial.

Each of these types of data is available, in varying degrees, at both the geographical level and the individual level. Geographical data is based on various levels of small-area geography including census tracts, ZIP codes, block groups, and postal carrier routes.

A question that is always asked is whether one should operate at the ZIP code or block group level when using geo-demographic data. Obviously, ZIP code data is readily available and easy to use. To use block group data requires "geo-coding" your file so that each address on the file becomes associated with a block group and/or census track. Generally, this process costs a few dollars per thousand and adds some time to the data appending process.

On the surface, it would apear that the smaller geographic unit would offer superior predictive precision. However, because there is known to be considerable error between either area's average income, age, or educational level and the true values belonging to individuals within either the ZIP code or the block group, the practical consequence of using the block group over the ZIP code might not be as large or as severe as one would expect.

The answer to this question also depends on the task at hand. If one were actually renting a small number of names (50,000 to 100,000) whose income need would be greater than, say, $100,000, then we would probably recommend using block group data. On the other hand, if one were renting a million or more names, or if one were simply overlaying a database for profiling purposes, ZIP code level data may be satisfactory. The correct answer, however, is to pose the specific question to the vendor and perhaps test both methods to see which works best for you.

Table 2–1 shows the approximate number of each standard geographical unit in the United States at which demographic data are available.

Geography-Based Demographic Data

Geography-based demographic data is produced through a series of statistical calculations that are applied to U.S. Census data.

TABLE 2–1

Unit	Number of Units	Approximate Number of Households per Unit
Residential ZIP Codes	36,000	2,400
Carrier routes	210,000	400
Block groups	250,000	340

It is sold under a number of product names by various companies such as Donnelley (ClusterPlus), Claritas (PRIZM), National Decision Systems (VISION), CACI (ACORN), and others. A description of the major clustering products is contained in Appendix I.

The calculations that produce geo-demographic data consist primarily of two types:

Descriptive — Calculations of cross-tabulations (categorical), average values (means), and ranges (minimum, maximum) are performed for various geographical units that are captured by the U.S. Census. These are broken down by ZIP codes (both five digit and nine digit), by block groups, and sometimes at the postal carrier route level. The smaller the geographical unit, the more precise the measure is assumed to be.

Inferential — Once the profile of each neighborhood is calculated using the descriptive techniques described above, other techniques, notably cluster analysis, are applied to the neighborhoods so that ZIP codes, block groups, or carrier routes that have similar characteristics are "clustered" into neighborhood "types." These neighborhood types have similar profiles in terms of average home value, average income, family size, home type, occupation, age, presence of children, and so on.

Geo-demographic data vendors sell the notion that "birds of a feather flock together," which assumes that individuals will, for the most part, reflect the characteristics of the neighborhoods in which they live. While this will generally be true in terms of home value, it may not be true for other characteristics.

In a typical suburban neighborhood other than a new development, immediate neighbors may have bought their homes at different points in time. Depending on when the home was purchased, the purchase price may vary dramatically. In suburbs of large cities, for example, a four-bedroom house may have cost $30,000 in the 1950s, $60,000 in the 1960s, $120,000 in the 1970s, and $360,000 in the 1980s. So current home value alone may not be as precise an indicator of income, net worth, and lifestyle as we might imagine.

Table 2–2 shows the individual level demographic characteristics of six neighbors in a typical suburban neighborhood, all of whom have homes of similar value.

As can readily be seen, the ages, incomes, and family sizes of each neighbor are dramatically different. Census data would be based on averages, and as you can see, the age of only two neighbors is close to the average age and the income of only one neighbor is close to the average income. The life stage and lifestyle of each of the neighbors are similarly different, and importantly, the differences are not likely to be picked up by geography-based data.

Another point to consider about geo-demographic data is that neighborhoods change and data gets old quickly. Areas that are undergoing transition — in whatever direction — may be missed, and false assumptions about neighborhoods might be made. In many urban areas, gentrification, or the influx of young, relatively upscale professionals, into old, sometimes run-down areas, has changed the characteristics of many neighborhoods.

Young, two-career families have, in many cases, traded proximity to work — and shorter commutes — for the space and comfort traditionally associated with suburban living. Townhouse developments or renovation of existing brownstones and inner-city apartments have lured many relatively wealthy people into areas that were previously economically disadvantaged.

While the impact of these trends may be well-known locally, a national marketer may not be aware of them for a number of key markets, and may therefore invest inappropriately in a direct marketing campaign for one of two reasons:

1. A marketer may forgo promoting to people in a certain neighborhood because out-of-date geo-demographic data may not accurately report the neighborhood's ascendancy. In this case, an uninformed marketer may forgo a good opportunity.
2. A marketer may be up-to-date on changes that are in progress but may market to holdovers from the neighborhood's previous status rather than to the newly arrived group. In this case, by targeting to the wrong people in an area, the marketer may spend promotional dollars on people who are unlikely to respond. This situation can

TABLE 2–2
Neighborhood Comparison

Neighbor	Age	Marital Status	Home Value (in thousands)	Household Income (in thousands)	Number of Persons in Household
Allen	75	Married	$300	$400	2
Baker	86	Widowed	300	11	1
Corcoran	38	Married	300	125	3
Doyle	59	Married	300	52	6
Everett	38	Married	300	85	5
Freeman	50	Married	300	65	5
Average	58			$123	

be improved through the use of additional screens, often involving combining data from a variety of sources.

In either case, promotional investments based on geo-demographic data alone may lead to disappointing results. However, for companies that have not previously used any external data, geo-demographic data is likely to be quite helpful.

In some industries, geo-demographic data may be a very cost-effective means of describing neighborhoods. In one case, a cable television multisystem operator (MSO) used Claritas's PRIZM data to find out how similar the neighborhoods in a new franchise were to neighborhoods in which the MSO had previously had successful marketing campaigns for premium services. In neighborhoods that were similar in terms of their PRIZM cluster types, marketing programs that were similar to successful ones used in different cities were tested in a new market. The results in the new market were very highly correlated with the results in the original city and the test significantly outpulled the control.

Individual-Specific Demographic Data
National databases are a very important component of the secondary data market. Several companies in this business, including R. L. Polk, Donnelley, Metromail, Smart Names, Select & Save, Wiland, Acxiom (Infobase), and others, have compiled household lists of names and addresses and a great deal of individual-specific data for the vast majority of U.S. households. Each of the major vendors of individual-specific data compiles its lists in a slightly different way.

The R. L. Polk Company compiles its lists from a number of public record sources but most notably from state motor vehicle registration information. At present, Polk provides direct marketers with motor vehicle registration data for 35 states. At one time, more states participated, but recent concerns and legislation concerning privacy have curtailed access to some states. This data consists of the make, model, and year of automobiles currently owned by individuals and includes previous ownership of vehicles as well. Value of individual autos and total value of autos by household are also indicated.

A number of other primary data elements, as well as computed data elements such as income, are added to the base file. In many cases, imputed income is based on a combination of the individual's age, home value, occupation, automobile ownership and ownership pattern, neighborhood type, and other factors.

While R. L. Polk originally compiled its data from state motor vehicle registration departments and from its own city directory business, Donnelley and Metromail originally compiled their data through their telephone directory and city directory businesses. Over the years, each of these companies has expanded its sources to include additional public record agencies, private list compilers, list owners who use their facilities for other computer processing, and through new primary name acquisition businesses (e.g., Donnelley's Carol Wright).

While many of the variables that are included in data of this type are similar to geo-demographic data in content, they differ in one critical aspect—all data is specific to the named individuals rather than a set of geography-based summaries. That is, if the individual-specific age data says that John Smith of 123 Elm Street, Anytown, USA, is 37 years old, you can rest assured that the specific John Smith in question is 37 years old. It does not mean that he lives in a block group or ZIP code in which the average age is 37, although this might also be the case.

In the case of some variables, for example, age and the presence of children, implicit data may be used. And in cases where the specific age of an individual is not known, age may be stated in terms of the range that is most probable based on a number of other variables that are known with certainty. For example, if it is known that a household includes children under the age of five, it will be inferred that the children's mother is not older than 45 and that the father is not older than 50. While there will certainly be cases in which this inference is inaccurate, for the majority of cases, this inference, in combination with known data elements, will be reasonably close.

National Databases as Sources of Names

Marketers use national databases in several ways. One way is simply to use the national database as a source of names. The marketer would specify characteristics of people that are desirable for a particular promotion. The national database company's account executive would then work with the programming staff to produce a customized selection of names from the firm's national database file.

While national databases that include individual-specific data may be a valuable source of names, many marketers find that rented lists belonging to mail-order businesses outperform names selected from national databases. In most cases, this is because the source of the rented list will be an indication of two important factors:

1. People whose names are on the list are direct mail responsive.
2. The content of the magazine or the nature of the catalog or other business that is the source of the list may provide clues about the person's interests.

However, there are notable examples of marketers finding great success using national databases as sources of names. One case that comes to mind concerns an automobile company (Company A) that was planning an offensive campaign with the objective of stealing market share from its principal competitor (Company B).

Company A developed an expensive mailing package that was sent to owners of Company B's cars who were at the stage of the car ownership cycle during which people begin to contemplate the purchase of their next car. The source of the data on car ownership and stage of the ownership cycle was the R. L. Polk database. The direct mail package was designed to look as though it were a direct communication from the local Company A dealer, and included a generous test drive offer.

For the example cited, the Polk file was extremely valuable as a source of names to Company A specifically because the file contained automobile data. While this example shows how a national database was used as a source of names for an automobile promotion, there are numerous examples of applications that are not primarily automotive related and that use national databases quite differently.

National Databases as Sources of Data for File Enhancement

Many direct marketers find that they have insufficient data about people on their customer files to make strategic marketing decisions. In order to develop customer profiles and hopefully be able to segment their files, additional data concerning age, income, wealth, home value, automobile ownership, presence of children, mail-order responsiveness, and so on may be very helpful.

In this case, compiled lists are very useful primarily because of their nearly total coverage of U.S. households. Match rates between house files and compiled lists typically are in the range of 45 to 65 percent, and among home owners or mail-responsive individuals, frequently higher. Readers should note that an overall match rate of 45 to 65 percent does not mean that all matching names have values for all data elements. On individual data elements, match rates are typically much lower, often in the range of 5 to 10 percent.

Psychographic Data

Psychographic data deals with people's attitudes, mores, and perceptions rather than with the externally observable characteristics, like average home value, classified under demographic data. Marketers use psychographic data to identify groups of people who share common values about such diverse subjects as lifestyle, products, politics, religion, and criminal justice.

Marketers tend to use psychographic data when they are planning to launch a campaign or introduce new products into communities where they do not have previous experience. The cable television industry makes extensive use of psychographic data when deciding whether it should promote pay services that feature R-rated or PG-rated movies. In addition to age and lifestyle characteristics, HBO was responding to the psychographic characteristics of its audience when it introduced the Cinemax service. Unlike the more mainstream HBO, Cinemax offered movies that contained little or no sex or violence.

Geography-Based Psychographic Data

As in the case of demographic data, psychographic data can be developed or purchased at the geographic or individual-specific level. To develop geography-based psychographic data for its own customer file, a marketer would purchase data such as VALS (presented earlier in this chapter). VALS data would be overlaid onto the customer file — or a representative sample if the file is very large — and the marketer would statistically analyze the relationship between customer types and their associated VALS categories. The marketer may find that its best customers tended to come from the societally conscious and belongers categories. If this were the case, then the marketer would want to promote its products to more people who were classified as societally conscious and belongers.

To do this efficiently, a marketer could take the approach described earlier in this chapter of linking VALS data to an existing geography-based product like Claritas or Donnelley's ClusterPlus. Then, the marketer would look for cluster groups that had a disproportionately high percentage of people who were classified as societally conscious and belongers.

Individual-Specific Psychographic Data

As in the case of demographic data, psychographic data can be developed or purchased at the individual-specific level. As described above, marketers can overlay their customer files with VALS data, and simply market differently based on the VALS categories to which individual customers are assigned.

As an alternative to using a commercially available source like VALS, marketers develop their own psychographic profiles of their customer files. This is done by sending psychographic questionnaires to current customers and analyzing the relationship between their psychographic characteristics and purchase behavior. Then, based on the result of the survey, the marketer could promote differently to current customers who fall into different attitudinal groups.

Similarly, prospects can be assigned to psychographic groups either by using a VALS or custom-developed survey approach. The VALS approach would work in the same way as VALS is used for marketing to current customers. For a custom-developed psychographic survey, questionnaires would be mailed as part of the promotion stream to prospects. Based on their responses to the questionnaire, prospects would be assigned to attitudinal groups; then the marketer would use creative messages that are most appropriate for their concerns and interests to promote products that most interest them.

For example, a financial services marketer might offer different products and use different creative messages when promoting to prospects who are sophisticated investors than when promoting to prospects who are risk averse.

Behavioral/Lifestyle Data

The commercial development of behavioral/lifestyle data grew out of a recognition that geo-demographic data or compiled lists often could not describe differences in personal interests and leisure time activities sufficiently to satisfy the informational requirements of marketers.

A number of the vendors of geo-demographic data have added value to their databases by combining their geo-demographic clusters with market research data. Claritas, for example, combined its geo-demographic cluster data with Simmons market research data. This product enables client companies to link the general buyer behavior characteristics that have been captured on a neighborhood basis by Claritas with the actual purchase performance of their customers.

Other vendors of data have similarly combined their geo-demographic files with data from Simmons, VALS, MRI, and other sources to add power to their data. One of the newest of these is the Affluence Model, offered by Donnelley as a means of predicting the affluence of individual households. This product works alone or in combination with Donnelley's CONQUEST desktop market analysis tool, and with ClusterPlus, which is Donnelley's neighborhood segmentation system.

By combining geo-demographic data with purchase behavior and other consumer data, marketers increase the odds that they are placing their advertisements in print or electronic media that they know have significant reach among people whose characteristics match the profile of their current customers.

In direct mail, the same approach can help to identify prospects based on a combination of their neighborhood type and their buyer behavior characteristics. A number of other vendors that have combined their geo-demographic databases with market research data are listed in Appendix I.

Vendors of lifestyle data approach the capture and management of behavioral information in a different way. One of the most innovative companies in this field is National Demographics and Lifestyles: The Lifestyle Selector (NDL) which was established in the 1970s and was recently acquired by R. L. Polk Company.

NDL's data are compiled in a unique and fascinating way. The company provides warranty card processing services to a number of manufacturers. This service, which had long been considered a burden by many manufacturers, is highly automated by NDL. The manufacturer attaches warranty cards to its products, which are then sent to NDL for processing. NDL then provides the warranty information to the manufacturers in machine readable form. A second "warranty" card is attached to the manufacturer's products. The second card, which looks like the warranty card, is actually a demographic and lifestyle questionnaire that is used to gather individual-specific demographic and lifestyle data about the purchasers of the products. A description of the data captured by NDL is contained in Appendix I. Manufacturers are provided with lifestyle data about the purchasers of their own products, and NDL adds the lifestyle data it has captured to its own proprietary database.

NDL then uses the data in a number of ways. One way is to offer a service in which list owners can send their customer files to NDL for data appending and list profiling. In this way, list owners can begin to develop an understanding of the lifestyle characteristics of their own customers beyond what they may have known or inferred based on product purchases and original list source.

Once a list profile has been developed, list owners can rent from NDL additional names of people whose lifestyle characteristics are similar to those of their currently successful customers.

A second approach is for marketers to send rented lists, with the approval of list owners, to NDL for screening, selecting only those names that have the desired sets of lifestyle characteristics or those that have the highest scores, according to predictive models.[3]
NDL's research staff can develop these models for a marketer, or the marketer can develop the models internally, depending on staff capabilities and cost. The downside to this approach is that appending data and scoring rented lists can rapidly become an expensive proposition.

A third approach is for marketers to take the lifestyle profile that they have developed for their house lists and apply it to their own prospect files. Again, this can be done on a categorical or a statistical modeling basis. In the former, a cross-tabulation approach would be used to select prospects who fall into the same categories as currently successful customers. In the latter, scoring models would be applied to the prospect file so that only those prospects who had the highest scores based on degree of similarity with lifestyle characteristics (and most likely, with other internally available data such as list source and geography) would be promoted.

Yet a fourth approach would be to use the lifestyle profile as a guideline for sources of other rented names. If, for example, a company's

---

[3] The ethical issues are well covered in the Direct Marketing Association List Practices Information Task Force's *List Practices Handbook* (New York: Direct Marketing Association, 1988), which readers are urged to consult.

best customers all had indicated an interest in tennis, golf, and camping, a marketer might increase list rentals oriented to those interests.

Financial Data

Financial data providers are list compilers of a special type. Unlike the Polks, Donnelleys, and Metromails of the industry, who obtain their data from a variety of sources, financial data providers all get their data through service bureaus that they either own or for whom they perform clearinghouse services.

Among the largest providers of financial data are Equifax Marketing Services, TRW Target Marketing Services, and Trans Union. Each of these companies has access to data concerning credit card purchases, installment loans, applications for credit, and payment history for virtually every household in the United States. The type and extent of financial data available to marketers from each of these companies changes frequently, so marketers interested in using financial data are urged to independently contact representatives of each firm for detailed information.

Taking the geo-demographic data concept of "birds of a feather" a step further, financial data can help to further differentiate members of a potential market based on their actual financial performance. Marketers can send their house lists to any of the vendors listed above, as they would to any of the providers of other types of secondary data, and the vendor will produce a financial profile of customers on the file. For example, marketers may learn that their best customers tend to have:

- More than six revolving credit accounts.
- At least four bank cards.
- Average revolving credit balances in excess of $500.
- Very few payments that are more than 30 days late.
- At least two department store credit cards.

This information would be provided as averages or indexes for groups of people. It would not be made available at the individual consumer level.

Armed with this information, marketers could send their prospect lists to financial data vendors so that prospects whose financial characteristics were similar to those of their customers would be identified and promoted, while those whose characteristics differed might be promoted less frequently or not at all. Additionally, marketers might rent the names of people who had similar financial characteristics to their best customers.

Some marketers have worked with financial data vendors to develop predictive models of how names on the financial data files would perform in their businesses based on their financial characteristics. Then, names from rented lists are passed against the scored file so that names that are unlikely to perform well can be screened and either promoted differently or not at all.

This approach enables marketers to avoid mailing to people who are unlikely to be interested in, or unlikely to pay for, their products. By the same token, it can help marketers to find the "needles in the haystack" — those people who actually have the financial means and track record to be promoted for certain products but who live in neighborhoods that models based on geo-demographic data alone might exclude from promotion.

In order to make data more accessible to marketers, and to remain within the ethical and legal standards that govern the use of individual specific data, some of the vendors of financial data have developed clusters and financial lifestyle overlays that are similar in concept to the neighborhood and lifestyle clusters developed by vendors of other types of secondary data. These can be appended to a company's customer or prospect file, and the company can then either develop its own scoring models, or simply use the overlays as categorical selection criteria. Equifax, for example, has a series of product offers in this category, including the EQUIS Financial Clusters and Equifax Power Lists that incorporate various shopping psychographic and credit activity indexes. A description of the EQUIS Financial Cluster is included in Appendix I.

How to Obtain Secondary Data

In order to obtain secondary data, we suggest that readers contact the companies listed in Appendix I of this text or, as suggested previously, contact the Direct Marketing Association to obtain a complete list of recommended member organizations in that field. As in the case of service bureaus and software vendors discussed later in this text, it is always a good idea to ask the vendors for references and to spend the time required to learn from other companies' experiences prior to committing your own firm's resources.

SECTION 3

BUILDING
A DATABASE
MARKETING SYSTEM

A WORD ABOUT BUZZWORDS

We have attempted to restrict our use of technical buzzwords in this section to the minimum required to explain key points and to familiarize readers with the terminology they will hear from their own MIS groups and from vendors. In order to demystify these terms, from time to time a series of "Buzzword Boxes" will provide easy-to-understand translations of terms.

Like the classification of data types that we developed in Section 2, the definitions of technical terms contained in this book are likely to differ from the orthodox definitions of academics and data processing industry leaders. However, as in the case of data, we have attempted to use practical definitions that will help marketers to understand the technical terms they are likely to encounter in making decisions about DBMS products they will use as part of the new direct marketing.

CHAPTER 3

AN OVERVIEW OF KEY ISSUES TO CONSIDER BEFORE COMMITTING TO A DATABASE MANAGEMENT STRATEGY

INTRODUCTION

The core of any database marketing venture is the marketing database itself. Identifying the functional requirements of the database and selecting the database management system product that will best fit the needs of the organization are critically important tasks requiring the joint participation of the marketing and MIS groups. Yet, in many companies, the two groups have difficulty working together effectively toward a common solution because their objectives are so frequently in conflict. Whereas the marketing group wants immediate access to all data and data relationships, the MIS group is responsible for delivering systems that can be updated within existing windows and provide satisfactory on-line response time.

In order for the two groups to work together effectively, a number of questions must be resolved before serious progress toward a solution can occur.

The intent of this section is to give both marketing and MIS professionals a solid understanding of the issues involved in selecting computer hardware and software resources and the questions that should be considered about the marketing database prior to launching the project.

WHY EVERYONE IS CONVERTING TO DATABASE MARKETING

Over the past few years, many marketers have come to the conclusion that they need more information about today's customers in order to market to them more effectively and to aid them in finding tomorrow's customers.

BUZZWORD BOX 1
Generations of Languages

In the world of mainframe computing, there are currently four "generations" of languages. First-generation languages speak directly to the computer in machine language.

If you would like to see what machine language looks like, the next time your PC is at the C prompt, type TYPE COMMAND.COM. The resulting gibberish of odd lines and happy faces will be meaningless to you. Fortunately, it is meaningful to your computer.

These languages are actually combinations of 1s and 0s that are read directly by the computer as positive and negative pulses of electricity. While machine language is extremely difficult for mortals to understand, it is actually the most efficient way for computers to process instructions.

While you will probably never, in your entire life, have to write programs at the machine language level, it is useful to note that special programs called *compilers* actually reexpress your easily understandable programs written using menus, English-like prose, and point-and-click methods in machine language.

Second-generation languages like Assembler are a step closer to languages that humans can understand than are machine languages. They are "machine"-like in the words and syntax they employ but are not quite as great a stretch for programmers as writing in machine language. There are actually some "relics" from the 1960s who can still write programs in Assembler and, in fact, more programs than you might expect are written in Assembler. It is an extremely efficient language for very large, data intense programs because it can be compiled into machine language and made to run very efficiently.

Third-generation languages like COBOL and FORTRAN were invented to make life easier for programmers, and in fact, they do. One reason is that these languages have programming routines built into them, so that programmers can write in a kind of shorthand, knowing that the COMMAND level instructions in COBOL will perform fairly complex functions for them.

Third-generation languages are compiled into machine language but because they are even further removed from the simple 1s and 0s that the computer is comfortable with than second-generation languages, a price is paid in processing efficiency. So while third-

BUZZWORD BOX 1
(continued)

generation languages help to improve the productivity of programmers, they actually lower the productivity of computers. But, based on the decreasing cost of computers and the increasing cost of programmers, this trade-off in efficiencies is one that most companies are prepared to make.

Fourth-generation languages (4GLs) like FOCUS, NATURAL, USER LANGUAGE, or SQL use very simple "verbs" and syntax, and can be used both by programmers and end users. The apparent simplicity of the 4GLs provides a great deal of power to programmers or nonprogramming end users but at a great price. Because they are written at such a high level, they can be incredibly inefficient for computers to process.

There is an unsubstantiated rumor that several of the fourth-generation languages were developed, and are secretly owned by, manufacturers of hardware because the inefficiencies inherent in fourth-generation languages make it necessary for companies to buy larger, more expensive computers. All of the database management system (DBMS) products that we refer to in this book have fourth-generation languages as part of their product offering. However, many of the DBMS products themselves are written in Assembler in order to increase processing efficiency.

Procedural Languages

Procedural languages like COBOL or FORTRAN provide detailed instructions to programs in a line-by-line manner. A procedural language would include commands within programs like:

```
GO TO LINE 24
ADD THE QUANTITY SHOWN IN FIELD X
TO THE QUANTITY IN FIELD Y
STORE THE SUM IN FIELD Z
THEN GO TO LINE 30
```

A fourth-generation language would use English-like prose to accomplish the same purpose, and would include commands like:

```
FIELD Z = FIELD X + FIELD Y
```

While traditional third-generation applications have been adequate for supporting transaction-oriented, single-event-driven businesses, direct marketers today require greater access to individual-specific information about their customers and a clear understanding of the total relationship those customers have throughout their productive lifetime with the company.

DATABASE MANAGEMENT SYSTEMS

The term *third generation* refers to the type of systems that are typically written in procedural languages like COBOL and use either flat files or VSAM file structures to store data. This is in contrast to fourth-generation environments that include database management system (DBMS) software and fourth-generation language programming and productivity tools (4GLs) that are nonprocedural and include verbs and syntax that look like English words and are therefore more readily understood by people who are not data processing professionals.

Database management systems store data in "tables" that are a little like the spreadsheets we are used to seeing in PC products like 1-2-3™ from Lotus. Tables consist of columns and rows; the columns are data fields, and the rows are records. DBMS products generally include "dictionaries" in which the data elements are defined in terms of their format (e.g., character, numeric), their field length (i.e., the number of positions to the left and right of the decimal point for numeric values), and the programs in which they appear.

Dictionaries are extremely important when it comes to modifying table structures to add, modify, or delete variables. The presence of data dictionaries makes the modification process very efficient because changes need to be made only one time in the dictionary. The dictionary, in turn, notifies each program that is affected by the change.

In typical third-generation environments, access to information about customers is limited to the data structures and paths that we have defined in advance. So, if we *knew* that we were always going to examine performance by state of residence, or by the individual's original list source, we could design the application to provide us with this data very quickly. However, if our selection criteria were to change, major modifications to programs, reports, inquiry screens, file structures, libraries, and other aspects of the system would be required. In a

BUZZWORD BOX 2
SQL

SQL is an abbreviation for Structured Query Language, the ANSI accepted standard language for relational database technology. Although the name may initially seem as intimidating as all the other unfamiliar acronyms of computer technology, the language itself is fairly simple in concept. SQL (pronounced SE-QUEL by true techies) consists of a very small number of verbs. Because it is a high-level language (fourth generation), each of these verbs packs a lot of power. An example of SQL code is shown on page 48.

Suppose we had a relational database table called CUSTOMER that contained the following data elements: customer number, customer name, address including city, state, and ZIP code, purchase amount, number of purchases, and number of promotions. An extract of this database is shown below.

Customer Table

Customer Number	State	Purchase Amount	Number of Purchases	Source Code	Number of Promotions
1347	TX	$ 54	6	04	07
0259	NY	126	10	03	15
3268	AR	27	5	01	06
2139	TX	95	4	02	07
0134	NJ	182	12	04	12
0865	AR	315	17	02	06
0932	TX	191	9	04	11
1136	OK	88	8	03	15
2437	MT	113	12	04	09
4521	LA	43	6	08	07

third-generation environment, these changes require programmer intervention, which is both time-consuming and expensive.

It would be naive to assume that changes to the marketing database will not be required over time. In fact, we should assume that changes are going to be required on a frequent basis, especially during the early years of the application. Answers to queries will suggest other questions. The

---

BUZZWORD BOX 2
(continued)

If we wanted to create a file of customers who were from Texas and had purchase amount in excess of $60, we could write the following program in SQL:

```
CREATE VIEW TEXAS__BUYERS (CUST#, STATE, PURCHASE$)
AS SELECT CUSTOMER.CUST#, CUSTOMER.STATE,
CUSTOMER.PURCHASE$FROM CUSTOMER
  WHERE STATE = 'TX'
  AND PURCHASE$ > 60;
```

While the language may seem a bit foreign, consider how few verbs were required to produce the desired "view" of the data. CREATE VIEW TEXAS__BUYERS tells the database to create a new table called TEXAS__BUYERS. The items in parentheses (CUST#, STATE, PURCHASE$) are the elements we wish to include in the new table. The SELECT statement tells us which data elements we wish to extract from the existing table called CUSTOMER. The two WHERE statements, STATE = 'TX' and PURCHASE$ > 60, specify the conditions that must be met by any records that are to be included in our new table.

Once this table is created, any number of analyses can be conducted.

---

more familiar marketers become with data, the more demanding they will become in terms of the frequency and level of complexity of their queries. They will learn that some questions are asked more frequently than others but will not know which those are until some experience with the application has been gained. The flexibility of looking at data in a virtually unlimited number of ways is a primary reason why direct marketers have embraced relational database systems as the underlying technology for marketing database applications.

Fourth-generation database management system products are specifically designed to support the types of changes common to database marketing applications with relative ease and with relatively little expense. In addition, the power of the fourth-generation languages that are associated with the database management system products enables

BUZZWORD BOX 3
File Structures: Flat Files, VSAM Files, and Database Structures

To understand the differences in file structures, think of a spreadsheet created by 1-2-3™ from Lotus®. In the spreadsheet, the rows are records and the columns are fields. The spreadsheet is a file. In a flat file, no additional intelligence of organization is included beyond the record level. To know the range and average amounts of purchases contained in the file, a marketer would have to perform some data processing operations.

In 1-2-3, the range could be specified and the system could calculate the minimum, maximum, or average levels for any field. Additionally, the file could be sorted in ascending or descending sequence for a primary and secondary sort field. If a marketer using 1-2-3 wanted to know the range and average purchase level of customers who live in Texas, a simple approach would be to sort the file by state as the primary key and then by purchase amount as the secondary key. It would then be relatively simple to calculate the range and average purchase levels for the Texans.

In many ways, 1-2-3 functions like a simple database management system. If only the mainframe world were as conceptually simple! Unfortunately for marketers, many of whom are extremely facile with products like Lotus 1-2-3, the data processing complexities of direct marketing require mainframe systems that, for the most part, are nowhere near as user friendly as end users would like.

In a mainframe environment, a file like the 1-2-3 file described above would be considered a flat file. It is flat because there is no hierarchy of organization that would make it easier for the end user to get the information faster. In order to answer a question like the purchases by Texans described in Buzzword Box 2, it would be necessary to search every record in the file sequentially in order to be certain that we had not left out any Texans.

In order to make life a little simpler, IBM developed a product called VSAM, which is an acronym for Virtual System Access Method. This product enables programmers to establish "indexes" or "keys" by which specified fields can be accessed more readily. For example, if STATE were an indexed field in a VSAM file, it would be much easier to answer the Texas query. When the query was entered, the program would use the VSAM file structure to lock in on the STATE field, and within the STATE field would examine only the Texans.

BUZZWORD BOX 3
(continued)

VSAM enables programmers to establish indexes on a number of different fields at the same time. Thus, if we knew in advance all of the fields that we would like to be able to reach through indexes, and rarely made any changes to this design, a very efficient application could be developed using VSAM file structures rather than the more complex and expensive database management system products.

However, most end users do not know what their requirements will be in the future, and marketers especially must acknowledge that their data requirements are going to change continually over time. Therefore, it is the functional requirements of marketers, rather than a technical limitation of VSAM, that makes DBMS technology essential for the new direct marketing.

---

most end users to formulate queries, design and generate reports, and navigate their way around the marketing database without the expense or time delays associated with applications that require programmer intervention.

So it is little wonder that so many direct marketers are developing marketing databases using this technology. In some cases, they are replacing their transaction systems at the same time but we will describe later on why this may be unnecessary or even undesirable.

HOW TO SELECT A DATABASE MANAGEMENT SYSTEM

While there are literally hundreds of computer hardware systems and database management system software packages to choose from, the decision process that all companies need to go through should address the following issues that fall under the general heading of functional requirements:

- What do we want the marketing database to do?
- What kinds of questions must it be able to answer?
- What types of statistical analyses will be performed and what will be

the role of the database in supporting statistical analysis and implementing the results of modeling?
- What are the turnaround time requirements for various types of functions? That is, which functions must be performed in seconds, which in minutes, which ones overnight?
- How current must data be?
  a. For which functions do we need real-time data?
  b. For which functions will last night's, last week's, or last month's data be adequate?
- What data are needed to perform the required functions? To a large extent, the way in which required queries and reports are defined will determine the data elements that are needed.
- How will the database be created?
  a. Normalizing data.
  b. Scrubbing.
  c. Householding.
- What data elements are available in existing systems?
  a. If data elements that are needed in the database are not currently available in existing systems, how and where should the data elements be created?
  b. Should existing systems be modified to produce additional data elements?
  c. Should the marketing database produce the additional data elements?
  d. How will data from existing systems and from external files be brought into the database?
  e. What file transfer or updating routines need to be developed:
    - In existing systems?
    - In the database?
- What data elements from external data files might we wish to append to the database?
- Are the firm's existing hardware resources capable of supporting the database marketing application?
  a. What is the firm's existing hardware environment?
  b. Is capacity an issue?
  c. Will compatibility be an issue?
  d. Who should address the issues?
- Is the firm's existing software environment capable of supporting the database marketing application?

    a. What is required?
    b. How much will it cost?
    c. How long will it take?
    d. What is the firm's existing software environment?
    e. Is the proposed software compatible with the existing environment?
    f. Is a conversion/modification required to support the marketing database?

- Should the entire database marketing process be done in-house or should a combination of internal and external resources be considered?

The answers to these questions will define the functional requirements of the application. *Functional requirements* is the technical term for the tasks that the database must perform. Once these have been defined by the marketing end users, data processing professionals will translate the functional requirements into design and programming specifications that programmers will use to develop the database applications.

The functional requirements are, in turn, used by the MIS department to evaluate whether the various software products already in-house, or those under consideration, can support your company's needs. Other issues, such as hardware and software growth potential, functional limitations, connectivity, platform independence, and relational status will help to reduce the number of products under consideration.

Finally, the comfort level of your MIS group with particular vendors and the "fit" of the various products into your existing computer environment will lead you to a final selection. A detailed discussion of each of the issues follows in the remaining chapters of this section.

CHAPTER 4

WHAT DO WE WANT THE MARKETING DATABASE TO DO?

Many companies decide to develop a marketing database because the customer files that are currently maintained by their firms do not provide adequate information to support the marketing function. This inadequacy is generally attributable to one of two causes:

- The data that is captured is not sufficient to answer the firm's marketing questions.
- The form in which the data is currently captured and maintained makes the data inaccessible to marketers.

In the former case, it is unlikely that the database approach will be able to solve the company's information problems because the data needed is simply not captured. In order to capture different, or additional, information, existing systems would have to be extensively modified and often redesigned.

This can be a very expensive proposition for companies that are in a third-generation systems environment because changes to programs and file structure — such as adding or deleting data fields — take a great deal of time to do. It is especially true for marketing applications because the kinds of information and the amount of data that marketers will want to capture will continually evolve over time, and each evolution will require the same types of changes.

Companies whose access to data is limited by the format in which data is captured and stored, rather than by the data that is captured, have more options. Typically, lack of access to data as a result of the form in which data is captured and stored occurs when customer files are transaction-based rather than customer-based. The result is that detailed data about customer purchases and customer source is often fragmented among numerous files. A marketing database application can accept data from the company's transaction-based systems and consolidate the data into customer-oriented information.

METHOD AND FREQUENCY OF UPDATING DATA

Companies that currently capture data in third-generation, transaction-oriented systems generally need to address three issues concerning the method and frequency of updating data to the marketing database: (1) level of detail of data; (2) update or replacement; and (3) frequency of update or replacement.

Level of Detail of Data
Will data be brought into the database at the detailed transaction level or at some level of summarization? If the data does not enter the database at the detailed transaction level, then marketers will not be able to analyze relationships in the database at this level of detail.

   While it is only logical that you can't view data at a lower level than it exists in the system, try explaining that to the marketing group six months after the project is completed.

   Although it may be desirable to have data available at the lowest possible level of detail, there are cost and operational considerations to weigh. Detailed transaction level data will, in virtually all cases, require more data storage and a longer update processing window than summary data.

Update or Replacement
Will data actually be updated in the database or will the system "replace" the current database tables with a more current snapshot? If the update is to be done in the database, then more complex programming will be required so that the application can actually find previous records, then do adds, changes, and deletes to the existing tables.

   Alternatively, if the update is done in the transaction system, and the database tables are to be replaced by fresh information, it may be necessary to modify the existing transaction system so that data at the detailed level will be available to the database. The extent to which this is necessary will depend on the level of detail that the transaction system currently maintains. For example, if customer 0001 had $100 in sales from six purchases at the time of the last update, and has $160 in sales resulting from nine purchases in the current update, what was the value of each purchase during this period? Were there three equal purchases of $20? Were there two purchases at $10 and one at $40? The answers to these questions may determine the type of promotion the marketer wishes to send. If the detailed transaction level data is not made available to the database, then the ability to differentiate customers at this level may be lost.

Frequency of Update or Replacement

The frequency of update or table replacement is generally driven as much by operational processing windows as by marketing's information needs. Both replacement and updating are time-consuming processes. The frequency of updating or replacement will determine how well the database represents the actual customer master file. If promotional decisions (for example, who should be mailed what) are based largely on buyer behavior, most marketers will want information to be as current as possible to avoid excluding active customers from promotion.

SCOPE OF THE MARKETING DATABASE APPLICATION

Once the decision is made concerning the method and frequency of loading the marketing database, the next step in the process is defining the scope of the application. For some firms, the marketing database is used solely as an analytical tool that consolidates, maintains, and analyzes data that is captured by the firm's other systems, including fulfillment, order entry, inventory, accounts receivable, and so on. For others, the marketing database is designed to provide the data entry and other facilities necessary to support the complete information requirements of the firm rather than analytical functions alone.

An advantage of limiting the scope of the marketing database to analysis is that the marketing database is much simpler to develop and maintain, requiring less time and fewer resources, and does not require disrupting the firm's other existing systems. For many companies, existing systems run very efficiently, and it is questionable whether a fourth-generation version of the applications would offer improved performance.

Companies generally define the scope of their marketing database applications at one of the following levels: (1) analysis tool only; (2) modification to existing systems; and (3) fully integrated database system.

Analysis Tool Only

At this level, the functions of the marketing database are limited to inquiries and reporting based on data currently available in existing transaction systems. This approach is attractive because it requires the minimum investment in programming resources since it has the smallest scope and is the least complex of the options.

By consolidating individual transactions, this approach can provide many insights about customer behavior. Naturally, the extent of analysis will be limited to the level of detail currently being captured in the transaction systems and loaded to the database. Obviously, you cannot analyze data that you don't have. A major limitation of this approach can be the selection, mailing, and tracking of promotions if the promotion process is driven by other applications. In this case, careful consideration must be given to getting data from one system to another.

Modification of Existing Systems to Provide Better Data

At this level, the existing transaction systems are modified so that enhanced, updated data can be provided to the marketing database. This approach will also provide more information to marketing than option 1, the analysis tool approach, but it requires an investment in programming resources in support of existing third-generation systems. And because marketing's requirements are likely to be a moving target, at least in the early years of the database, the investment may be substantial and ongoing.

Modifications in a third-generation environment are generally more time-consuming, and therefore more expensive, than similar modifications in a fourth-generation, DBMS environment.

Fully Integrated Database System

With this approach, a fully integrated transaction and marketing system that is driven by fourth-generation database technology is developed. For many companies, this is the ultimate goal because it provides "seamless integration" between the transaction and analysis systems. Each system could be separately optimized in terms of processing efficiency and system performance, and all future requests for data could be filled with minor modifications to the system.

As compared to options 1 and 2, this approach assumes replacement of all current applications related to the marketing database, including the order entry, fulfillment, and possibly inventory, accounts receivable, and other systems.

While the ideal approach for some companies may be to develop a totally integrated customer fulfillment and marketing database system, they must realize that this cannot happen overnight. Accordingly, many companies assign project priorities such that the first phase of the marketing database application will provide improved access to marketing information but will limit the scope of the initial system to include only those applications that can be developed within an acceptable time period.

From a corporate political and cultural perspective, it may be necessary for the marketing database to prove its value before funding for the development of additional applications will be approved. Many firms in this situation opt for development of a marketing database in phases, setting inquiry and reporting capability as the first goal, followed by updating and integration with other systems at a later date.

Even if a company's existing systems are operating in a satisfactory manner, the company may still wish to migrate to a DBMS environment for productivity reasons. Among the advantages of programming in a fourth-generation, database environment is the reduction in time required to develop and modify applications.

In general, initial application development is considerably faster (at least 40 to 60 percent) using fourth-generation language tools in a database environment than in a conventional third-generation environment. Subsequent modifications to applications are at least three times faster in a fourth-generation database environment.

While much of the emphasis in this section is on the development of fully integrated, fourth-generation applications, we are not suggesting that efficient, smoothly functioning transaction systems be thrown out and replaced merely because they are based on third-generation technology.

Many firms have had considerable success in maintaining existing transaction systems and developing interfaces from these applications to the marketing database. As long as the required data is available in a timely manner, and the existing systems are part of the firm's strategic technology plan, there may be no reason to replace an existing transaction system. After all, if it isn't broken, there may be no reason to fix it.

CAPTURING, STORING, AND MANIPULATING DATA

The database must be able to capture, store, and manipulate customer, transaction, and external demographic data.

Capturing Data

The first requirement of a marketing database is that it must be able to capture data from a variety of sources. Customer and transaction data, and externally purchased or calculated demographic data, must be brought into the system and stored in a manner that is accessible and actionable for marketing purposes. Order entry data may come from the company's order entry system, from an order entry module that is part of the marketing database, or from third-party sources if external service providers are being used.

All traditional direct marketing companies already have some sort of order entry capability. Whether data entry is performed internally or as an external function at a service bureau does not restrict the database's ability to capture this key data. However, companies that use external service bureaus to handle telephone inquiries or to key coupon responses need to develop procedures by which the service bureau provides the company with a tape (or transmission, depending on data volume) of each day's activity. These are loaded, either daily or less frequently, to the company's database.

Some of the elements in the database will change infrequently. For example, a customer's name or address, unless entered erroneously in the first place, is unlikely to change more than once a year. Often, these elements will be unchanged throughout a customer's relationship with the firm.

Other elements that do not change include:

• Unique Customer ID.
• Original Source/Key Code.
• First Purchase Date.
• First Purchase Amount.
• Sex.

Because these elements change rarely, they can be maintained in tables that are rarely updated. However, in order to link information about customer performance to demographic or other information about individual customers, a link must be established between customer data and the performance data. The link between the customer table and other tables within the database is usually the CUSTOMER ID.

Transaction tables are updated every time the transaction file is loaded to the database. Transactions are logged to all customer records that have had activity during the intervening period, whether the transaction was a purchase, return, payment, adjustment, change of address, or other transaction type.

The decreasing cost of data storage has made it affordable for many companies to maintain a great deal of detailed customer performance data on-line, which facilitates subsequent analysis. However, for some companies, the volume of transactions that can be maintained on-line is limited by performance considerations,[1] and, in some cases by the number of available disk access storage devices (DASD).

For that reason, companies often restrict the detailed transaction history that is maintained on-line to either a specified number of transactions or else a specified time period. That is, a company may decide to maintain on-line either the most recent *n* transactions for a customer or all transactions for a customer within a specified period of time, for example, the past 12 to 18 months.

External demographic data may be either individual specific or geography-based and would be added to the file if the marketer found that these external data elements added sufficient strength to modeling efforts to justify the expense of acquiring and storing the data.

Sources of external data used by many direct marketing companies include such vendors as Metromail, R. L. Polk, NDL, Donnelley, Equifax, TRW, Claritas, and Acxiom (Infobase). Sources and types of external data and the appending process are discussed in more detail in Section 2 of this text.

Storing Data

As stated above, data must be stored in a manner that makes it accessible and actionable for marketing purposes. While many companies capture all the data needed for marketing analysis in their transaction systems, the data are often captured and stored in a form that makes it inaccessible for marketing analysis and implementation of programs.

Most often, this is because transaction-based systems store data in a way that is designed to support quick response time at the account level. Consequently, information about individual customers, as compared to individual accounts, tends to be fragmented across a large number of files.

For many companies, if a customer has multiple accounts, the individual is treated as multiple customers. This fragmentation precludes developing an understanding of the total relationship a customer has with the firm, and thus, personalized communications and long-term, one-to-one marketing relationships are difficult, if not impossible, to establish and maintain.

---

[1] The larger the database, the more time required for query response, updating, and so on. While the effects on response time can be ameliorated to some extent through good logical and physical design, some degradation in response should be expected.

In a database environment, data are stored in a series of tables. All the records for a single customer can be consolidated under a master CUSTOMER ID, and what would be independent, unrelated records in a third-generation system can be structured as repeating, related records in a fourth-generation, database environment.

A unique CUSTOMER ID serves as the linking field and the DBMS software keeps track of the records that are related.

In a DBMS environment, tables are linked by repeating key fields in related tables. In the example in Table 4–1, shown later in this chapter, the CUSTOMER ID is the data element that appears in the CUSTOMER table and is repeated in the PURCHASE table. Similarly, for a catalog business, an ITEM table that contained detailed information about all the items sold by the company, including such items as the cost, price, source, and an item description, would be linked to both the CUSTOMER table and the CATALOG table so that we would know which items were purchased by which customers and which items appeared in which catalogs.

In most transaction-based systems, it would be very difficult to learn this information unless the file had originally been structured to report it. In order to obtain this information, we would first have to assemble all the necessary data into one file and then perform a number of sequential record searches to create a series of file extracts that would address each part of the query. A *sequential search,* as the term implies, means that each record on the file would have to be read to determine whether the record met the specified criteria.

As an example of the indexed versus sequential search process, consider a telephone directory for a large city, in which the names are listed in alphabetical order by last name. Each "record" in the listing includes the customer's name, a street address, and the telephone number. If we wanted to find a specific customer and we knew the customer's last name, we could go to the section of the directory that included the first letter of the customer's last name and would narrow the range of our search by using the guide words at the top of each page until we found the record we sought. It is fairly efficient to find customer records in this way because the directory file has been indexed on the customer last-name field.

Now, suppose that we were not interested in knowing the customer's last name, but instead wanted to know how many people had telephone numbers that ended with the numbers 7654. In order to get an accurate count, it would be necessary to read every record on the file. If we wished to do further analysis about the people who had those numbers, we would create a new file in which all the records that met the criterion were filed. If we wanted to know which customers on the file had telephone numbers ending with the numbers 7654 *and* lived on Elm Street, we would perform a subsequent sequential search *within the extracted file* of people whose telephone numbers ended in the desired number.

If we knew which set was smaller—the customers who live on Elm Street or the people whose telephone numbers end in 7654—we would perform the more restrictive search first so that the second search would have fewer records to consider. This technique may be employed in either a third-generation or a fourth-generation environment if the counts by each criterion were known in advance.

A typical marketing query might ask, "which customers purchased during the period in question?" Then, for customers that did purchase, a second query might ask, "what did the customers purchase?" In many cases, the query may be seeking purchasers of specific items, or developing a count of people by purchase category.

Based on the telephone directory example above, it should be easy to picture the steps required to learn the desired customer purchase information in a third-generation environment. The telephone directory example is obviously much simpler than the kinds of questions marketers ask. But the example is useful because it demonstrates the process we would go through in a typical query *and* because the number of records in a large city's telephone directory (approximately 1 million records) is similar to the number of records in a medium-sized company's customer file. The bulk of the telephone directory helps us to visualize the size of the files that the application would have to search to produce our answers.

By comparison, database environments are designed to assemble this type of information much more efficiently and many of the searches could be done within indexed versions of the files rather than by reading the actual records themselves. Indexes are described in Buzzword Box 4.

Manipulating Data

Most database management system products have the ability to perform arithmetic and Boolean algebraic functions. This capability is essential both for creating new variables that are calculated from existing variables and also for selecting records that meet certain conditions. For example, a marketer who is interested in knowing whether new customers perform differently from old customers would select two groups based, at least in

BUZZWORD BOX 4
Indexes

Indexes in data processing are very much like the indexes readers are familiar with that appear in books. In books, the index indicates the page on which a particular subject, name, or term appears. In database systems, indexes "point" the programs to the desired data and provide an efficient means of getting there without having to read the actual records themselves.

One of the most important elements, and one of the major differences between the various commercially available database management system products, is the way in which indexes are structured.

If, for example, we wished to easily locate all the people who live in the state of Massachusetts, we would build an index by state. Then, rather than searching sequentially through all of our customer records, which might be arranged in CUSTOMER ID or alphabetical sequence, our search would begin by going to the STATE index, locating the record numbers of all customers whose entry in the STATE index was MA, creating a temporary file of those records, and then posing whatever further queries we had about those customers to this Massachusetts-only subset of the file. Because the file had been reduced to include only the relevant set of records, subsequent processing would be much more efficient.

Indexes become even more important to ease of access and good performance when we formulate complex queries that require data from a number of different tables or files (we use the two terms interchangeably). If the data fields in question have been indexed, we may be able to answer the query entirely by consulting indexes rather than reading actual records.

For example, suppose that we wanted to know the number of people who live in New York, Massachusetts, and Connecticut that purchased products 123, 456, or 789. If address and purchase information were maintained in separate tables, this query could be processed by reading the STATE index and the PRODUCT index, selecting the records of only those people who live in the three states indicated, and selecting the records of only those people who purchased products 123, 456, or 789. The two extracted index files would then be joined on the CUSTOMER ID field, and the resulting set would provide the desired answer.

BUZZWORD BOX 4
(continued)

If we knew that this type of query would be asked frequently, we would probably design the application such that both data elements appeared in the same table. This would improve response time because the join would be eliminated.

One of the most challenging issues for database designers is determining which fields in a table should be indexed, and how tables in the database should be related. In order for the database to successfully support marketing, marketers must provide the system's designers with a great deal of guidance and direction concerning which queries are most important and which data elements are related to each other. The resulting database design will optimize the data capture, storage, and manipulation requirements to achieve the maximum benefit for marketing.

As another example, suppose we wanted to know the number of Texans on the file who had total purchase amounts in excess of $60. To get this information, we would identify Texans within the STATE index, and then do an index search for purchase amount. We would then create a "found set" within the index of records that met the desired conditions. Tables 4–1 through 4–5 show how this works.

Table 4–1 repeats the CUSTOMER table shown in Buzzword Box 2. In Table 4–2, the original file has been indexed by CUSTOMER NUMBER within STATE.

If a query were made to find the number of Texans that had total purchases in excess of $60, the database would search the index of the STATE file until it found the Texans, then perform all further processing within the found set of Texans. (See Table 4–3.)

Because we are only interested in knowing the range and average purchase levels for Texans (for this specific query) the found set would include only the relevant pieces of data. (See Table 4–4.)

While we did not specifically request the CUSTOMER NUMBER, this will normally be carried so that our link to the actual Customer and Purchase tables can be maintained.

The result of the query, based on the found set, would be the count, which equals 2. (See Table 4–5.) Therefore, we know that there are two Texans on the file who have purchases in excess of $60.

While it may appear, in this example, that the database worked very hard to answer a simple question, consider how well this approach would work with multiple conditions and very large files.

TABLE 4–1
Flat File

Customer Number	State	Purchase Amount	Number of Purchases	Source Code	Number of Promotions
1347	TX	$ 54	6	04	07
0259	NY	126	10	03	15
3268	AR	27	5	01	06
2139	TX	95	4	02	07
0134	NJ	182	12	04	12
0865	AR	315	17	02	06
0932	TX	191	9	04	11
1136	OK	88	8	03	15
2437	MT	113	12	04	09
4521	LA	43	6	08	07

TABLE 4–2
A File Indexed by Customer Number within State

Customer Number	State	Purchase Amount	Number of Purchases	Source Code	Number of Promotions
0865	AR	$315	17	02	06
3268	AR	27	5	01	06
4521	LA	43	6	08	07
2437	MT	113	12	04	09
0134	NJ	182	12	04	12
0259	NY	126	10	03	15
1136	OK	88	8	03	15
0932	TX	191	9	04	11
1347	TX	54	6	04	07
2139	TX	95	4	02	07

part, on the dates that the customers were acquired. In order to select customers based on date ranges, the database must support date arithmetic.

Similarly, Boolean algebraic operators such as AND, OR, GREATER THAN, LESS THAN, EQUAL TO, IF THEN ELSE, and INCLUSION/ EXCLUSION operators are a key part of most database management system products. These operators make it possible for marketers to pose queries such as, "count the customers who came from Source X, between April 1 and May 15, who live in New York, New Jersey, or Connecticut, and who bought products 123 and 456 but not 789."

TABLE 4–3
The Found Set of Texans

Customer Number	State	Purchase Amount	Number of Purchases	Source Code	Number of Promotions
0932	TX	$191	9	04	11
1347	TX	54	6	04	07
2139	TX	95	4	02	07

TABLE 4–4
The Reduced Found Set of Texans

Customer Number	State	Purchase Amount
0932	TX	$191
1347	TX	54
2139	TX	95

TABLE 4–5
The Found Set of Texans Who Have Purchases in Excess of $60

Customer Number	State	Purchase Amount
0932	TX	$191
2139	TX	95

In the above example, the marketer is asking the database to:

- Select customers by source.
- Perform date arithmetic.
- Select by state, using an OR operator.
- Select by product, using the AND and BUT NOT operators.

While most marketers would consider this query to be a perfectly straightforward example of the information they routinely need to make marketing decisions, the data processing required to answer the query is quite complex. In a third-generation environment, the AND/OR and BUT NOT operations would be difficult to perform even if the file were structured to support the informational needs of the query. In a database environment, the flexible file structure, combined with the availability of the logical operators, makes it much easier to support the query.

USER–FRIENDLY ENVIRONMENTS

The marketing database must provide a user-friendly environment in which marketing end users can inquire, analyze, and report about customers, products, promotions, and transactions without requiring programming intervention by data processing professionals.

Since the advent of the personal computer in the early 1980s, end users who have little or no programming experience have become used to performing analytical tasks independently of their company's data processing professionals. Despite the fact that many end users have had to invest time and energy in rekeying data from mainframe reports into their PC-based systems or in developing complex downloading procedures, they view the PC-based analysis as a major productivity asset compared to the time and difficulty of getting the same information through their MIS group. This experience has both benefits and drawbacks.

On the positive side, end users have, in many cases, overcome their fear of computer technology and have become used to the flexibility and relatively quick turnaround that personal computers provide. On the negative side, many end users have come to expect their company's mainframe computer systems to provide the same relative ease of access to data and quick turnaround as their PC-based systems. They don't take into consideration the complexity of the questions they are attempting to answer or constraints posed by file structures that were designed to support the performance requirements of other aspects of the company's business (for example, customer service). These factors have combined to create a level of expectations that is often unrealistic in a third-generation environment. In a fourth-generation environment, however, this expectation level is often attainable.

End users who are familiar with microcomputer tools such as spreadsheets, databases, or graphics programs have become used to working with menus, icons, pop-up screens, point-and-click mouse devices, guided modes of operation, and on-line help screens that assist them in performing complex data analysis tasks. Because of the power of these tools, many end users are entirely unaware that in order to perform the desired tasks, the PC-based products are actually writing complex computer programs in the background.

In a fourth-generation environment, the same types of user-friendly tools — menus, icons, pop-up screens — are available to help end users write extremely powerful programs even when they have no knowledge whatsoever of the programming languages involved. Queries, which are actually complex computer programs, can be saved and reused, or modified to suit the needs of other end users. Queries that are used on an ongoing basis can be stored and "secured" by limiting access to authorized users. Even the alterations can often be made in English or natural language terms, or by returning to menu screens and modifying the existing query using menus and point-and-click techniques.

Some state-of-the-art systems combine the power of mainframe processing with the ease of use of PCs in ways that are transparent to end users, that is, end users can simply indicate the functions they wish to perform and are unaware of which tasks are being performed in the mainframe and which in the PC.

In a well-designed marketing database, end users can gain access to data about customers, products, promotions, catalogs, transactions, or other data in a virtually unlimited number of ways simply by using menu screens or by selecting previously generated reports or queries. Regularly occurring reports such as daily response to a promotion can be set up such that each end user can get an individual report that supports his or her unique information needs.

These highly individual reporting capabilities are referred to as *views* of the data. While end users often think only in terms of their own desktop device providing the information they seek, it is actually the database engine that makes this limitless variety of views possible.

AD HOC QUERIES

One of the most important tasks of the database is to facilitate the dialogue between statistical analysis and the subsequent implementation of model results. The first part of this process is to make the selection of names for statistical analysis according to any set of ad hoc defined criteria an easy task for marketing end users.

For companies that perform statistical analysis in-house, the analytical work is done either in a mainframe or a PC environment. If the work is to be done in a mainframe environment, the task of the database is to

---

BUZZWORD BOX 5
Productivity Tools

Developers of database management systems have long realized that in order for their products to be truly successful, they would have to put the power of sophisticated data processing in the hands of end users who are not data processing professionals. This goal becomes more difficult if the end users have no knowledge of programming whatsoever.

An initial response was to provide *menus,* that is, tables of processes that could be selected by positioning the cursor over the item or by keying the first letter of the word and hitting the enter key. Users of Lotus 1-2-3 will be very familiar with this concept.

More recently, software and hardware developers have offered *mouse* devices as an alternative and often easier means of selecting menu items. Mouse devices are small machines that control a targetlike cross-hair image on the screen. The end user moves the mouse over a flat surface until the cross-hairs are positioned over the desired menu item and then presses a button on the mouse. This process selects the menu item in exactly the same way that cursor movement or keying the first letter of the desired item would. Some software products include *icons,* which are visual image representations of the functions offered on the menu. The mouse is positioned over the desired icon and the user points and clicks to make a selection.

---

extract a file that contains the desired number of names and the specified data elements and produce an output file in the form that the statistical analysis product requires. If the analysis is going to be done in the same mainframe environment where the database resides, extract files are either stored on DASD or on magnetic tape.

If the analysis is to be done on a PC and the file is relatively small, the file will most likely be downloaded using the company's standard PC-to-mainframe communications link, for example, an IRMA, PCOX, or similar communications protocol.[2] If the analysis file is larger, or if the

---

[2] In order for PCs to communicate with mainframe systems, a communications board is required. The most common of these are IRMA or PCOX boards.

analysis work is going to be done using third-party computer facilities, the analysis file is generally stored on magnetic tape.

The decreasing cost of CD–ROM technology, which uses the same type of CDs that are used for recorded music to store massive amounts of data in PC-readable format, has made this technology attractive for a number of high-volume purposes. A good example of this would be storing encyclopedia data that can readily be retrieved using PCs.[3]

SELECT NAMES BASED ON MODELING SCORES

Implement the results of models developed through statistical analysis by executing scoring equations, storing scores, and providing a facility for selecting customers, based on their scores, for specific direct marketing programs.

Once models have been developed using statistical analysis software products like those mentioned above, the database is used to implement the results of the models. This process includes:

- Incorporating the model equations into the language used by the database system (or in some cases, COBOL or FORTRAN, for more complex mathematical functions if the database system's fourth-generation language does not support mathematical functions efficiently).
- Executing the scoring equation within the database so that all records that meet the conditions specified for the sample group will be scored using the scoring equation. (See Section 4, "Statistical Analysis and Modeling.")
- Storing the scores produced by the scoring equation in the database.
- Sorting the file in descending sequence by score.
- Dividing the file into a number of equal-sized groups (frequently 10 groups or *deciles*).
- Assigning the customer records to their appropriate deciles, based on their scores.
- Storing the decile score for each customer record along with its raw

---

[3] CD–ROM technology is also sometimes referred to as WORM, for Write Once, Read Many. Since data is stored on these devices using laser technology, the process has been given the somewhat whimsical name "Burning the WORM."

score, the name of the model, and the date on which the model was run.

- Providing a facility for selecting names based on the decile, or raw score, which they were assigned by the scoring model.

In this way, the database completes the dialogue that it began earlier when it was used to select names for modeling by:

- Scoring the names in the file.
- Assigning records to their appropriate deciles.
- Providing the facility to select names for marketing activities.

CHAPTER 5

SUPPORT OF AD HOC QUERIES
AND STATISTICAL ANALYSIS

WHAT KINDS OF QUESTIONS SHOULD THE
MARKETING DATABASE BE ABLE TO ANSWER?

One of the most important issues to address when designing a marketing database is to define the kinds of questions the database must be able to answer. The more specific the marketing group can be during this stage, the better, because the answers to these questions will help to define the logical and physical design of the system as well.

By logical design, we mean the data elements that are going to be included in the database and the way the elements in the data tables relate to each other. As part of the physical design, the system designer then groups the data elements that we believe logically belong together into physical tables, so that elements that are likely to be involved in queries will be included in the same tables. This will improve response time for queries and limit the amount of seek time that the system must spend looking for the location of data elements that are part of a query. *Seek time* is the time required for the system to find the right file and data needed to answer the query.

Physical design also refers to the size of files. The placement of data on physical devices (generally, DASD) is considered "tuning" and is not technically part of the physical design of the system. However, it is sometimes included under this definition anyway because the DBA and system designers are responsible for tuning the application to run as efficiently as possible. Proper placement of data helps to reduce the time that will be required to get data from DASD into the computer. So you can see that response time is affected both by the logical and physical design of the system as well as the placement of data and other tuning issues.

BUZZWORD BOX 6
Logical and Physical Design

According to C. J. Date, the conceptual or logical database design consists of identifying the entities that are of interest to the enterprise and the information that is recorded about those entities. In other words, each firm must decide which of the data elements contained in its various applications will be contained in the database, and define the relationships between those data elements. Generally, this is the job of the database administrator, but it is done in conjunction with the user sponsors.

The physical design of the database, again according to Date, is the definition of the storage structure and associated mapping of the system. In other words, the physical design of the database consists of determining which data elements should be contained in which tables, and how the tables are related to each other by primary and secondary key fields.

Key fields are the data elements that appear in more than one table and serve as a link, both logical and physical, between tables.

Source: C. J. Date, *An Introduction to Database Systems,* vol. 1, 4th ed. (Reading, Mass.: Addison Wesley Publishing, 1986).

In general, a marketing database should be able to readily answer any questions dealing with customer performance, for example:

- How many people responded to a campaign?
- What was the response rate by cell?
- How did this compare to the expected response rate by cell?
- Are the results significantly different from what was expected?
- What is the comparative performance of various list sources?
- Should some list sources be excluded from future mailings based on past performance?
- Is there a regional variation in response?
- Based on two years of performance, who are our best and worst customers on the back end?
- What is the profile of our best customers on the back end in terms of list source, initial purchases, payment mode, subject cluster, product type, external demographics, and so on?

BUZZWORD BOX 7

CPU

The central processing unit (CPU) is the heart of the computer. This is where the work gets done. In a PC, the CPU is defined in terms of the RAM (random access memory) and the processing speed. For example, a 386/25 machine with 2 MB of RAM refers to a PC that has an 80386 chip that has a processing speed of 25 megahertz and two megabytes of core memory that the computer can use for processing. In a mainframe environment, RAM is referred to as core memory or internal memory, and processing speed is generally quoted in a measurement called MIPS (millions of instructions per second).

Channel

Channels are the electronic paths that are used to get data into and out of the CPU. If data cannot efficiently get into and out of the CPU, processing will slow down. This is like having a car with a very large engine capacity that has a clogged fuel line. Although the engine could make the car go very fast, it is unable to do this processing if it cannot get the fuel it needs.

Channel capacity and channel contention are major concerns to system designers who are responsible for the efficiency of processing.

Disk Drive (DASD)

Disk drives are the most common form of external memory, or data storage, in on-line computing environments. Companies store data on the disk drives that they know they will need frequently. Programs issue commands called *calls* that tell the system which data files are needed for the process in question. The CPU then sends a message over the channel to find the data that the program needs. In a PC environment, there is generally only one disk drive and one channel over which data enters and leaves the CPU.

Seek Time

When the request for data is made by the program, the command goes through the channel to the disk drive(s) to find the data that is requested. The time that is required for the request to find the right data and bring it back to the CPU is referred to as *seek time* since the program is seeking the data. System designers attempt to design systems initially

---

BUZZWORD BOX 7
(continued)

such that seek time will be minimized. However, as a system is used and more and more data is stored, the initial efficiencies of physical data storage tend to erode, and a conscious effort must be made to reposition data in ways that will produce greater efficiencies of operation. This function, called *tuning,* is generally the responsibility of the database administrator.

Channel Contention

If the physical storage of data on DASD is not done in an efficient manner then, in mainframe systems, channel contention will develop. Channel contention is analogous to a clogged highway or artery in which too many blocks of data are attempting to get through a constrained space. In data processing, the result is that one block of data must wait until the passageway is clear. End users will experience delays in response time as a result.

   In a PC environment, there is generally only one disk drive and one channel. Seek time in a PC environment is reduced by storing files in directories or subdirectories so that the number of files that must be searched prior to loading data is minimized. In a mainframe environment, where there are multiple disk drives and multiple channels, efficiency is increased by physically designing systems such that data likely to be used in the same queries are distributed across a number of DASD units and channels. In this way, channel contention, that is, the number of data requests that are attempting to get through an individual channel at the same time, is reduced.

- How does the profile of the segment in question compare to other customer segments?
- Do new customers have characteristics that are similar to key groups of current customers?
- Based on customer characteristics, can we select customers who are expected to perform well and treat them differently?
- How early in a customer's relationship can good (or bad) customers be identified so that we can treat them differently?

PROFILING

One of the most basic — and critical — tasks of the marketing database is to provide profiles of customers or prospects on the file. There are many situations in which marketers may wish to segment customers based on their characteristics, not necessarily on their performance in terms of a dependent variable such as purchase amount. Marketers may wish to know how their customer base breaks by age, sex, region, source, or any number of other characteristics.

In order to make this data accessible, the database must be designed to support the creation of profiles according to any set of criteria on demand. This will facilitate the process of defining new segments within the file.

Marketers will also want the database to define segments of the file based on performance. In this regard, the database can help marketers to identify who their best customers are today, identify where they came from, and help them to find other customers like them in the future.

Similarly, we may wish to pose queries about products purchased so that patterns of customer purchasing can be identified. A product analysis can help to identify which products can most successfully be cross-sold and, in combination with customer purchase patterns, may help to identify which customers are the best prospects for cross-selling promotions.

STATISTICAL ANALYSES

What types of statistical analysis will be performed and what will be the role of the database in supporting statistical analysis and implementing the results of scoring models?

The types of statistical techniques that marketers most commonly perform are described in detail in Section 4, "Statistical Analysis and Marketing." The role of the database is to help select names for modeling, implement the results of the modeling process by scoring names and assigning them to the appropriate decile, and selecting names by decile and other criteria for marketing programs.

This chapter will describe some of the objectives of the modeling process and how the database is involved in implementing modeling results.

Most companies use statistical analysis for two principal reasons: (1) segmentation and (2) predictive modeling.

Segmentation

Segmentation techniques are used to identify and profile groups of customers whose characteristics are similar. If the objective is to segment customers based on their performance, then the procedure is to group people according to their performance characteristics and then develop profiles of each performance group. Typical segmentation variables are performance measures such as recency, frequency, and monetary value of purchases; types of products purchased; or types of promotions responded to.

By linking this data with customer performance data, marketers can analyze who buys what and use the profiles of customers in each segment as a means of finding other customers like them.

Once the segments have been created, individual customers will be assigned to segments and these assignments will be recorded in the database. This makes subsequent selection of individuals for promotion based on the segmentation criteria relatively simple.

Predictive Modeling

Based on previous purchase history, again based on recency, frequency, and monetary value, models can be developed to predict who is most likely and least likely to purchase at the next opportunity. This scoring model would be used to determine who should be promoted and what they should be promoted with. More detailed information on this topic is contained in Section 4.

Once scoring models have been executed and customers assigned to deciles, this information is recorded in the database so that subsequent selection of customers who have the highest probability of responding to a promotion is easily accomplished.

End users would use a selection menu in which they would indicate which scoring model they wish to use and either a specific cutoff score or a desired number of names to select. The database would then perform the selection and produce an output file to the specific medium. This would either be a file, a magnetic tape, or mailing labels. A file could either be used for further analysis, or in many cases, the file could be combined with a patterned letter file to produce personalized mailings.

TURNAROUND TIME

What are the turnaround time requirements for various types of functions? That is, which functions must be performed in seconds, which in minutes, and which ones overnight?

The answers to these questions will evolve over time as marketers become more familiar with their companies' database systems and begin to develop a sense of how frequently certain types of queries are made. In a database environment, using indexes and summary files, the speed with which queries are answered can be modified quickly and easily.

It is a natural tendency for marketers to request that all information, in any combination, be available immediately at all times. The relative importance of various queries should be weighed, however, because system performance does not come free of charge, and quick response time often requires an increased investment in computer hardware.

This will generally mean an increased number of DASD units (each costing about $2,000 per month), increased channel capacity, and most often, increased CPU capacity (similar to adding memory cards to a PC), both in terms of processing power and memory. This can become expensive very quickly, so a selective approach, based on priorities, is urged.

Generally speaking, marketers will want to get quick responses to simple queries, for example, the number of people from source X who purchased more than four units within the past six months. A query of this type should generally be available within 30 to 60 seconds.

The importance of quick turnaround for queries of this type is that marketers will formulate new questions based on the answers they receive, and maximum productivity is achieved if response time is quick enough to maintain the marketer's train of thought. Although turnaround time of minutes, rather than hours or days, for queries of this nature may seem rapid today, many studies of interactive productivity have shown that when computer response time exceeds 20 seconds, an end user's mind begins to wander. This may involve doing desk work, returning telephone calls, or initiating other activities that distract the end user from the set of queries at hand.

In an inverted file database structure like Model 204, Datacom/DB, or ADABAS, queries that involve quick counts, as in the example above, are typically handled within a few seconds, even on databases containing several million records. Complex, ad hoc queries are likely to take much

---

BUZZWORD BOX 8

Summary Files

Summary files are files that have been created by extracting and summarizing data from one or more tables in the database. Their purpose is to provide quicker response time for counts according to groupings that we know in advance are going to be important and will be accessed frequently.

A typical case where summary files would benefit system performance would be a situation where a number of different tables must be joined together in order to bring data together for queries or reports. If, for example, we always want to know the counts of products purchased by state and source of purchaser, we would probably want to create a summary file to speed up this process. A fully "normalized" database would maintain data about customers and products purchased in separate tables.

Normalized

In a relational database environment, data are normalized as much as possible. Normalization means that each piece of data will appear only once, so that data redundancy will be minimized if not eliminated. One of the functions of the DBMS product itself is to "navigate" through the tables to find the required data.

---

longer to produce. This is especially true if multiple database tables have to be joined together to produce the desired information.

Here, the trade-off becomes one of frequency of queries versus system performance. If the query is going to be asked on a very frequent basis, it may be appropriate to develop tables that contain all of the required data elements and pay the price in additional data storage and update time. If the query is going to be asked infrequently, overnight response using the table structure already in existence may be adequate. Standard management reports are likely to continue to be produced on an overnight, weekly, or even monthly basis.

In order to improve the response time for complex queries, databases must be designed such that all the data elements required to answer the queries are contained in a single table, or at most, a small number of tables.

BUZZWORD BOX 9
Types of Database Products

Hierarchical

The oldest and fastest (in certain circumstances) type of DBMS products were hierarchical. In these products, a series of defined paths (not unlike the VSAM description) is established, and data access and processing are very fast. Hierarchical systems are commonly used for banking, airline reservations, and other applications that require very-high-speed processing and rarely change the paths of data storage or retrieval.

Inverted File

Inverted files are like hierarchical database structures except that they work from the bottom up rather than from the top down. This enables programmers to design systems that will allow access to virtually any field within the system from any other point. High-speed access from point to point is enhanced by creating indexes that link key fields. Examples of inverted file systems are Model 204, IDMS/R, Adabas, and CA's Datacom/DB. Inverted file systems are very commonly used for direct marketing applications because their combination of processing speed and flexibility is well suited to this environment.

Relational

Relational systems are essentially collections of relatively simple tables that the user combines and extracts information from in an endless number of ways. These are the most flexible of all database management systems, but because of their flexibility, they are not as fast as inverted file or hierarchical systems. In practice, direct marketers tend to design inverted file applications that are relational in concept, and relational applications that are structured like inverted files for improved performance.

Unfortunately, structuring a database such that all the data elements are contained in a single or small number of tables will generally result in increased update time. Some companies get around this problem by creating separate databases for marketing analysis and operations.

An increasing number of companies that have very large customer databases are moving in the direction of representative sample databases for analysis. These files can be used to perform analysis efficiently yet provide statistically significant estimates of the actual distributions of records on the customer file.

Marketers must work together with their MIS groups to determine whether the importance of certain queries and the frequency with which they are made justifies the resulting impact on system performance and the additional costs of data storage that may ensue. In fact, the more that marketers know about how the technology works and the issues that their MIS professionals must resolve in designing an application, the more control they can exercise over the quality and functionality of the marketing database system. In recognition of this fact, many vendors of DBMS software, as well as universities and professional associations, offer courses in DBMS technology that are oriented to end users.

CHAPTER 6

DATA RELATED ISSUES

CURRENCY OF DATA

How current must data be to support marketing's information requirements and what impact will this have on the database update schedule?

For some functions, real-time data may be required, while for others, last night's, last week's, or last month's data may be adequate. Practical decisions must be made concerning the required frequency of updates because as databases become large, the time required for update processing grows very quickly.

Many marketers initially believe that they require access to real-time data in order to make marketing decisions. While many companies engineer their computer systems to provide real-time data for customer service, real-time data is rarely needed for marketing since most analyses examine trends across large groups of customers and over long periods of time.

In many companies, there is a priority conflict between analytical users of data, like marketers, and operational or production users of data, like customer service or data processing operations. In general, if a company has only one system in operation to support both analysis and operations, and if the two functions are being operated simultaneously, then conflicts in processing priority are inevitable. This is one of several reasons that a number of direct marketing companies create separate databases for each function. Then, each application can be separately tuned such that each one will operate at optimal efficiency.

From a data standpoint, this separation requires that separate files of data be maintained for each application, and this means that more money will have to be spent for data storage. However, data storage is relatively inexpensive. For example, the space required to store 2 million records, each containing 1,000 bytes (characters) of data, ranges from about $1,500 to $2,000 per month. Even with the additional space required to store indexes for the files, the cost will only be about $3,000 per month.

The potential disadvantage of this approach is that marketers will not have up-to-the-minute, or real-time, data in their file. Marketing's data will be accurate only through the time that the marketing database was last updated. For many companies, key files are updated daily, twice a day, or in some cases, on a real-time basis. For some data, pertaining to customers, list sources, items, or departments, the data itself does not change on a daily basis, except when new records are added.

Purchase or return transaction data, on the other hand, may change several times during the course of a day. A large-sized catalog company, for example, could have anywhere from 50,000 to 100,000 customer transactions per day. While these transactions are extremely important to the company's business, real-time transactions are rarely critical to the kinds of analysis that marketers are likely to do. For calculation of trends, distribution by list source, or the comparative performance of items or product type, it is not necessary to have real-time data.

The following update schedule is typical for many companies:

Nightly updating
  Purchase and return data for current customers, including total sales, by:
    Department.
    Item/SKU.
    Product type.
  Customer data, including new customers and customer change-of-address data.
  Performance by list source during a campaign.
Less frequent updating (often done quarterly)
  Address correction from external sources.
  Assignment of customers to product groups.
  External demographic data about customers.
  Performance index by demographic or ZIP cluster.

WHAT DATA IS NEEDED TO PERFORM THE REQUIRED FUNCTIONS?

In order to answer the questions listed in Chapter 5, most of the data elements shown in Figure 6–1 would be needed. Figure 6–1 describes how tables in a relational database are linked by key data elements.

In a relational database structure, there is a minimum of duplicated data. This is done to improve processing speed and to reduce the expense of data storage. In a well-designed database system, the only duplicated data elements (fields) will be those that are used to form the logical connections between tables. An example is shown in Figure 6–1:

FIGURE 6–1

	Table I Customer Data	Table II Purchasing Data	
Data Elements	Customer ID Name Address Demographic Data	Customer ID Purchase Date Catalog Number Product Code Item Code	Repeating Records

Figure 6–1 contains two tables. Table I contains CUSTOMER data including a unique CUSTOMER ID, NAME, ADDRESS, and DEMO-GRAPHIC DATA. DEMOGRAPHIC DATA, for example, age, income, home value, lifestyle, car value, and so on, is usually obtained from external sources and is appended to the file.

Table II contains PURCHASE DATE, CATALOG NUMBER, PRODUCT CODE, ITEM CODE, and CUSTOMER ID. All of the data elements except CUSTOMER ID are related to a specific purchase. Based on this data, we would know the DATE, CATALOG, PRODUCT, and ITEM CODES for any individual transaction. These are repeating records because each transaction for an individual customer will generate a new record. The CUSTOMER ID field in Table II is not recurring because the individual customer does not change.

However, by including the unique CUSTOMER ID in Table II, all of the detailed information about the customer that is contained in Table I is available to us. In this way, we have avoided the inconvenience and expense of repeating all of the individual specific data in Table II. The CUSTOMER ID is the link between the two tables, and by joining the tables together, we could examine, in detail, the purchase behavior of individual customers. By organizing the data in this way, processing efficiency is achieved while information remains readily available.

The descriptions of data elements in each table and their links to other tables will demonstrate how the relational database structure makes data accessible and actionable for marketing purposes.

Figure 6–2 is a series of tables that would appear in a typical marketing

FIGURE 6–2
Data Tables

Customer Table	Repeat Purchase Table	Item Table	Catalog Promo Table	Print/FSI Promo Table	Broad-cast Promo Table	Catalog Source Table
			Key Fields			
Customer ID	Customer ID	Item Code	Catalog Number Item Code	Key Code	Key Code	Catalog Number Key Code Offer Code
			Nonrecurring Fields			
Name	Purchase IDs	Item Cost	Date Mailed	Ad Code Release	Ad Code On Air	Duplication Rate
Address	Actual	Subject Code	Quantity	Date	Date	versus
Match Code	Catalog Number	Product Code	Mailed	Media Cost	Air Time	House File
Prior Name	Attributed Catalog	Descrip-tion	Item Price Percent of	Circulation Offer	800 Phone Number	Quantity Ordered
Prior Address	Number Purchase		Page Page Num-	Code Production	Production Costs	Quantity Mailed
Individual Demo-graphic	Date Purchase		ber and Position	Costs Fixed	Fixed Vari-able	Costs Broker ID
Data	Amount		Key Code	Vari-able	Total Cost	Creative Code
Original Source	Payment Mode		Offer Code Test Code	Total Cost	Description	Test Code
Code	Ordering Mode		Production Costs			
Date of First Pur-chase			Fixed Variable Total Cost Description			

Print/FSI Source Table	Medium Table	Offer Code Table	Deciles Table	Model Table	Purchase Item Table
		Key Fields			
Key Code Offer Code	Medium Code Key Code	Offer Code Catalog Number	Customer ID Model Code	Model Code	Item Code Purchase ID
		Nonrecurring Fields			
Circulation Creative code Test code Description Costs	Major media code(s) Description	Description	Model score Date of scoring Decile code	Model name Model de- scription	

Customer Table

Data Element	Description
	Key Fields
Customer ID	A unique customer identification code that, once assigned, will always remain associated with that customer. This is used to link the Customer table with a number of other tables in the database and to help identify repeat customers who may have been archived from the system because of inactivity.
	Nonrecurring Fields
Name	Customer's current name.
Address	Customer's current address.
Match Code	A match code based on the customer's current name and address. This code makes customers who are already on the database easily identifiable when new orders or inquiries are received. Match codes are associated with the unique Customer ID.
Prior Name	Some marketers like to carry at least one prior name on the database.
Prior Address	Similarly, some marketers like to carry one or two prior addresses on the file for ease of identifying customers who have moved.
Individual Level Demographic Data	Through modeling, many marketers have found that demographic data, for example, individual age, income, lifestyle, home value, and so on, is useful in predicting response to a particular promotion and lifetime value of customers. A number of fields are usually made available for storing this data in the Customer table, even though the specific data elements that will fill these fields may not be known at the time the database is created.
Original Source Code	This field links individual customers with their original source. Although it would also be possible to link customers by source via the Purchase table, there are many instances in which it is desirable to determine the number or the characteristics of customers who come from a particular source without having to sort through their purchase behavior. Also, since the Original Source Code will not change, it makes sense to maintain this as one of the static fields in the Customer table.
Date of First Purchase	While the Purchase table will capture dates of all future purchases, the Date of First Purchase defines a class of purchasers, and is therefore often maintained separately.

Repeat Purchase Table

Data Element	Description
	Key Fields
Customer ID	The unique customer ID is the link between purchases made and the customers who made them.
	All of the Following Purchase Data Elements Are Recurring with Each Purchase or Return Transaction
Purchase ID	The purchase ID identifies individual purchase or return transactions so that detailed information about purchases could be obtained if desired.
Actual Catalog Number	The catalog number (catalog) that the customer bought from.
Attributed Catalog Number	In situations where the Actual Catalog Number is unknown, an Attributed Catalog Number is calculated, usually based on the most recent catalog that contained the purchased item that was mailed to the customer prior to ordering.
Purchase Date	For all subsequent purchases, the date of the purchase is maintained in the Purchase table.
Purchase Amount	For each purchase, the Purchase Amount is maintained.
Payment Mode	An indicator is often maintained to show whether a purchase was made using cash or a credit card. This data may be important in the future when selecting customers for certain promotions.
Ordering Mode	An indicator is maintained to show whether an order was placed by mail or by telephone.

Item Table

Data Element	Description
	Key Fields
Item Code	This field links the Item table with other tables including Purchase, Product, and Catalog, and through them with customers.
	Nonrecurring Fields
Item Cost	The cost of an item to the cataloger.
Subject Code	The subject with which each item in the table is associated.
Product Code	The product type with which each item is associated.
Description	A free-form description of the item.

Catalog Promotion Table

Data Element	*Description*

Key Fields

Catalog Number	Each catalog has a unique identification number.
Item Code(s)	Item Code field links specific items purchased to the Catalog from which they were purchased. Because prices and costs of items may vary depending on quantities ordered or special promotions, each combination of Catalog Code with Item Code is able to support unique prices and costs. This data is carried in detail in the Item table.

Nonrecurring Fields

Date Mailed	Each catalog has a unique value for Date Mailed, which will be maintained in the database.
Quantity Mailed	The mailing quantity of each catalog is maintained for subsequent analysis.
Item Price	The standard (or default) price for an item. This may change for special offers or for certain catalogs. The combination of Item Code and Catalog Code is linked with a unique price.
Percent of Page	Indicates the percent of page in a catalog given to a specific item.
Page Number and Position	Indicates the page of the catalog on which the item appeared and the position of the item on the page.
Key Code	Links Catalog Number to specific mailing source(s).
Offer Code(s)	Provision for unique codes to describe the offers being conducted in a specific catalog.
Test Code(s)	Provision for unique codes to describe the offers being conducted in a specific catalog.
Costs	Costs associated with mailing.
Production Costs	For each catalog mailing, costs, including list rental, postage, and detailed production, are maintained so that Return on Promotion can subsequently be calculated.

Fixed Costs
    Color Separations
    Type
    Mechanicals
    Creative
  Variable Costs
    Printing
    Lettershop
    Lists
    Postage
    Return Postage	

Total Costs	Total of all fixed and variable costs associated with production and distribution of catalog.
Descriptive Data	
Number of Pages	The number of pages in the catalog is maintained.
Free-Form Description	Free-form text describes the seasonality, theme, coloration, or other relevant data about the department.

Print/FSI Promotion Table

Data Element	Description
Key Fields	
Key Code	Links to other tables.
Nonrecurring Fields	
Ad Code	Unique ID for each ad.
Release Date	The date on which the periodical issue will be released.
Media Cost	Cost per page for print, cost of production, and distribution for FSIs.
Circulation	Circulation of periodical or guaranteed distribution volume for FSIs.
Offer Code	As in direct mail, specific offers can be tested in other media.
Production Costs	Costs associated with print or FSI promotions. For
Fixed	each promotion, costs.
Color Separations	Costs include production, creative, and other fixed
Type	costs, as well as variable costs such as printing
Mechanicals	and distribution.
Photography	
Creative	
Variable Costs	
Printing	
Media	
Response Cost	Inbound coupon or telephone response cost.
Lettershop	
Postage	
Return Postage	
Total Costs	Total of production, response, and media expenses.

Broadcast Promotion Table

Data Element	Description
Key Fields	
Key Code	Links to other tables.
Nonrecurring Fields	
Ad Code	Unique ID for each ad.
On Air Date	Date on which promotion airs.
Air Time	Media cost for airtime used.
800 Phone Number	In-bound response costs.
Production Costs	
Fixed	Costs of developing broadcast promotion including creative, talent, studio expenses, and so on.
Variable	Airtime, response expenses, and so on.
Total Costs	Total of production, airtime, and response expenses.
Description	Free-form description of ad content.

Catalog Source Table

Data Element	Description
Key Fields	
Catalog Number	Unique catalog ID that source is being used for.
Key Code	Specific use of a particular medium, for example, the *New York Times,* November 9 issue.
Offer Code	
Nonrecurring Fields	
Duplication Rate versus House File	Many direct marketers have found that the density of the duplication rate between the house file and an external source is predictive of response the next time that the source is used for promotion.
Quantity Ordered	Number of names considered for promotion from a source.
Quantity Mailed	Net number of names mailed after merge, purge, suppression, and so on.
Costs	List rental.
Broker ID	Unique identifier for each list or media broker.
Creative Code(s)	Different creative packages are constantly being tested. This code links sources with the specific creative packages they are being mailed.
Test Code(s)	Within an offer or creative package, a variety of tests may be used in each mailing. The Source table captures a code that identifies the specific test people are being subjected to.

Print/FSI Source Tables

Data Element	Description
Key Fields	

Data Element	Description
Key Code(s)	This unique identifier links the Source table with the Print/FSI Promotion table so that the cataloger will know which sources received which promotions.
Offer Code(s)	A unique identifier that links specific offers with the sources to which the offers were mailed.
Nonrecurring Fields	
Circulation	For print sources, this is the number of guaranteed names that will have direct visual access to an ad. Response is calculated against the Circulation Number in much the same way that response rate is calculated against Quantity Mailed for direct mail promotions.
Creative Code(s)	Different creative packages are constantly being tested. This code links sources with the specific creative packages they are being mailed.
Test Code(s)	Within an offer or creative package, a variety of tests may be used in each mailing. The Source table captures a code that will identify the specific test people are being subjected to.
Free-Form Description	Free-form text that identifies the list source in detail.
Costs	Costs in relevant units, for example, per page, black and white versus color versus four-color bleed.

Medium Table

Data Element	Description
Key Fields	
Medium Code(s)	Specific periodical or newspaper, for example, the *New York Times, Time.*
Key Code(s)	Specific use of a medium for a particular promotion or subset of a promotion.
Nonrecurring Fields	
Major Media Code(s)	Indicates whether medium is a rented list, broadcast, space, and so on, and for space, the type of medium, for example, magazine, newspaper.
Description	Free-form description of medium.

Offer Table

Data Element	*Description*
	Key Fields
Offer Code(s)	Identifies a specific offer that may include discounts, special premiums, and so on.
Catalog Number	Ties specific offers to specific department numbers.
	Nonrecurring Fields
Description	Free-form description of offer.

Deciles Table

Data Element	*Description*
	Key Fields
Customer ID	Provides link to Customer table and Customer data.
Model Code	Unique code for each scoring model.
	Nonrecurring Fields
Model Score	Score produced by model.
Date of Scoring	Date model was used to score names in Customer table.
Decile Code	Indicates the decile that customers or prospects are assigned to by the various models.

Model Table

Data Element	*Description*
	Key Fields
Model Code	Unique code for each scoring model. Link to Decile table.
	Nonrecurring Fields
Model Name	Name of each scoring model.
Model Description	Free-form description of each scoring model.

Purchase Item Table

Data Element	Description
	Key Fields
Item Code	Links purchases to the items purchased. There may be several items purchased in one transaction.
Purchase ID	Links to Repeat Purchase table so that data about purchase transactions can be related to items purchased.

FIGURE 6–3
Examples of Summary Information

By Customer
  Total Purchases.
  Total Orders.
  Total Mailings.
  Product Frequency (how many times a product code ordered).
  Subject Frequency (how many times a subject code ordered).
By Source
  Key Code (Specific Mailings).
  Total Sales.
  Total Costs.
  Profit Calculations:
  1. CPM.
  2. CPO.
  3. Average Sales.
  4. Sales Per Thousand Pieces Mailed.
  5. Profit Per Thousand Pieces Mailed.
  6. Average Lifetime Value for Customers.
By Department
  Total Sales.
  Total Costs.
  Profitability Measures:
  1. CPM.
  2. CPO.
  3. Average Sales.
  4. Sales Per Thousand Pieces Mailed.
  5. Profit Per Thousand Pieces Mailed.
  6. Average Lifetime Value for Customers.
By Item
  Item Number.
  Total Sales.
  Total Usages (Departments).

database for a catalog company. Each table consists of a set of data elements, each of which is described. While this list is not meant to be exhaustive, it should provide a good idea of the kinds of data that most companies try to capture.

Figure 6–3 is an illustration of data that would be stored in summary form in a typical marketing database.

SUMMARY INFORMATION

The database will be used to produce a number of summary reports. These will be available in hard copy (paper) as well as on-line. A number of intermediate calculations are required to produce these reports, and the structure that has been suggested for the database will make these easier to produce.

It is virtually certain that the data elements and data relationships that are captured, maintained, and produced in the database will change over time. Also, many of the inquiries and reports that marketers will want to develop have not been thought of thus far. As stated earlier, the principal advantage of relational database management systems is that they make it easy to add, delete, or modify data elements or relationships. These features will become increasingly important over time.

CHAPTER 7

CREATING THE MARKETING DATABASE

NORMALIZING THE DATA

While this process may sound as simple as inserting a diskette into a floppy drive on a PC, loading the database is actually one of the most time-consuming and challenging tasks facing marketers and MIS professionals in the development of their marketing database applications. This is because loading the database has an impact on both the logical and physical design and truly lies at the heart of the database system.

Before the database can be loaded, the relationships between data elements (or fields) must be defined. Figure 7–2 shows how two tables in a marketing database have been linked by the CUSTOMER ID field in a "normalized" manner.

One of the principles underlying relational database technology is that data will be normalized into logical groups. To carry forward the example shown in Figure 6–1, let's assume that we began with a single file in which we maintained records for a number of customers. Each record, in unnormalized form, contains the data elements (fields) shown in Figure 7–1.

Each customer's ID is followed by a detailed list of the purchases the customer made. Some customers might have 1 purchase, others may have 5, and others may have 10. If we wanted to know whether a specific individual purchased a particular item, we would first have to find a CUSTOMER record and then search the purchases made until we had exhausted that customer's items.

If we were to move the items purchased into a separate table, in which the CUSTOMER ID and the items purchased were maintained, we could

FIGURE 7–1

CUSTOMER ID
CUSTOMER NAME
CUSTOMER ADDRESS
DEMOGRAPHIC DATA
PURCHASE DATE(S) $1 \ldots n$
CATALOG NUMBER(S) $1 \ldots n$
PRODUCT CODE(S) $1 \ldots n$
ITEM CODE(S) $1 \ldots n$
ITEM NAME(S) $1 \ldots n$
CATALOG NUMBER(S) $1 \ldots n$
CATALOG NAME(S)

---

increase the efficiency of this search by searching only the Purchase table to determine whether the relevant CUSTOMER ID and the specific item coincide in the same record. (See Figure 7–2.)

Creating two separate tables that are linked with the common CUSTOMER ID as the key field (linking field) meets the requirement of *first normal form.* This is a relational database definition that means that repeating groups have been eliminated by making a separate table for each set of related attributes, and giving each table a primary key. In this case, the CUSTOMER ID is a primary key in each table and the ITEM CODE is a primary key in the PURCHASE table.

The second step in the process, termed *second normal form* in the relational database world, requires that redundant data be eliminated. If an attribute depends on only part of a multivalued key, it is removed to a separate table. In this case, the ITEM CODE and ITEM NAME appear in the PURCHASE table. Because the ITEM NAME would appear each time that the ITEM CODE appears, it is redundant.

Consider for a moment what would happen if the ITEM NAME associated with a particular code were changed. In the present configuration, that would require making the change in the record of every customer that purchased the item. In order to make the database more efficient, we would create a third table that would allow us to capture all the desired information but in a more organized way. (See Figure 7–3.)

To achieve *third normal form,* the catalog name must be removed to a separate table because it does not add explanatory power to the PURCHASE table beyond that provided by the CATALOG NUMBER. Accordingly, a fourth table, as shown in Figure 7–4, will be created to resolve this problem.

FIGURE 7–2
First Normal Form

Customer Table	Purchase Table
CUSTOMER ID	CUSTOMER ID
CUSTOMER NAME	ITEM CODE(S)
CUSTOMER ADDRESS	ITEM NAME(S)
DEMOGRAPHIC DATA	CATALOG NUMBER(S)
	CATALOG NAME(S)

FIGURE 7–3
Second Normal Form

Customer Table	Purchase Table	Item Table
CUSTOMER ID	CUSTOMER ID	
CUSTOMER NAME	ITEM CODE	ITEM CODE
DEMOGRAPHICS	CATALOG NUMBER(S)	ITEM NAME
	CATALOG NAME(S)	

Depending on the levels of data available, the normalization process can be continued beyond that shown in this example. The intent of the process is to organize data into its lowest level of granularity such that no further elemental level can be reached. The reason for going through this process is that the database cannot provide data at a lower level than that which was entered. While marketers may find that a certain level of summarization is adequate for the purposes of today's analysis, there is no way to know that this level of analysis or the relationships being analyzed will continue to be the same in the future. By establishing the data elements that will enter the database in their most normalized form, this problem will be avoided in the future.

CONSOLIDATING RECORDS

Another difficult, time-consuming, and often expensive step in the database loading process is record consolidation. For many firms, customer records are captured in a transaction-oriented system, and multiple records for each individual and for each household may exist on the file.

FIGURE 7–4
Third Normal Form

Customer Table	Purchase Table	Item Table	Catalog Table

CUSTOMER ID
CUSTOMER NAME
DEMOGRAPHICS
	CUSTOMER ID
	ITEM CODE
	CATALOG
	    NUMBER(S)
		ITEM CODE
		ITEM NAME
			CATALOG
			    NUMBER(S)
			CATALOG
			    NAME(S)

Before these records are loaded into the database, they should be put through a merge/purge process, and in some cases, a "scrubbing" process (described later in this chapter), so that the marketer will have the clearest idea possible of how many customers there are and what their relationships to each other may be.

In a single-product company, if unique CUSTOMER IDs or MATCH CODES are used in the fulfillment system, it is likely that only one record will exist for each customer. However, for many companies, particularly in financial services, a single customer may have a number of different relationships. If the data processing systems of the firm are account-based rather than customer-based, it is very likely that the company will be unaware of the customer's total relationship with the firm and each product group will be unaware of the customer's relationships with other parts of the firm.

For these reasons, it is essential that a merge/purge process be executed prior to loading names into the database. Most often, merge/purge processes are performed on a name and address basis. The more sophisticated merge/purge software products use a number of algorithms to predict the probability of two records belonging to the same person. Users can set the criteria to be tighter or looser, as required, and the algorithms within the program will suggest which customers are duplicates and which are unique.

The merge/purge process may be equally important for the Prospect file, since there may be a history of prior inquiries and related promotions. For many companies, the number of previous inquiries that a prospect has made is a very strong predictor of eventual conversion. For customers, there may be prior inquiry information about products other than those currently owned by the customer. If so, this data may provide additional guidance of how to market in a cross-selling campaign.

SCRUBBING

For some companies, particularly those in the financial services industry, registration information may be imbedded in the customer record as part of the name and address. An example is shown in Figure 7–5 in which we begin an examination of account information for Anthony and Julia Smith, who have a number of different relationships with City Federal.

In Figure 7–5, we see that City Federal is the trustee for an IRA account that is owned by Anthony and Julia Smith as joint tenants. Before we could match this customer record against a customer record like that shown in Figure 7–6, we would first have to strip out registration information that is unrelated to name and address.

Scrubbing software would recognize that City Federal, ITF, and JTTNT are all terms that are not names or addresses of individuals. It would strip out this data and prepare a new record that would much more readily be matchable using merge/purge software.

HOUSEHOLDING

Once the file is scrubbed, some additional steps must be taken if we want to accurately and efficiently market to households. Suppose that Anthony Smith had a separate IRA from his wife Julia, and that the mortgage for the home where they reside is in Julia's name alone. In order for City Federal to understand the full extent of the Smith's relationships with the

FIGURE 7–5

City Federal ITF
Anthony Smith Julia Smith JTTNT IRA
123 Elm Street
Anytown, USA

FIGURE 7–6

Anthony and Julia Smith
123 Elm Street
Anytown, USA

bank, and their household relationship, the bank would have to go through all of the steps shown above.

Only after the normalization process, scrubbing, matching, and householding have been completed can the database be loaded. The next step in the process is to determine whether the desired data elements are available in existing systems or whether they will have to be obtained from other sources.

ARE THE REQUIRED DATA ELEMENTS AVAILABLE IN EXISTING SYSTEMS?

Once the required data elements have been defined, the next step is to review the data elements that are currently captured by existing systems. For most companies, it is not the lack of data but rather the fragmentation of data that makes loading and updating the database awkward.

An evaluation needs to be made as to whether it is cost advantageous to load each of the various files to the database and consolidate them there, or to write programs that will consolidate currently fragmented data prior to updating the database. This is a question both of cost benefit and strategic direction for the firm.

If data elements that are needed in the database are not currently available in existing systems, how and where should the data elements be created?

- By modifying existing systems to capture and/or produce additional data elements.
- By capturing and/or producing additional data elements within the marketing database itself.

For companies that have existing in-house fulfillment systems, the data elements that are required to enter and ship orders, record transactions to accounts receivable and inventory, and provide basic accounting reports are generally in place. Unfortunately, the data elements that are needed for transactions are rarely stored in a way that makes them accessible for marketing analysis.

For most companies, if the strategic direction of the firm did not include the long-term support and enhancement of the existing transaction systems, there would have to be an overwhelming economic advantage to investing programming dollars in existing systems to produce data for the marketing database. Alternatively, the investment can be made in the marketing database system. The cost of each approach should be estimated, and the decision should be based both on the current programming investment required and the company's strategic technology plan.

HOW WILL DATA FROM EXISTING SYSTEMS AND FROM EXTERNAL FILES BE BROUGHT INTO THE DATABASE?

Depending on the frequency of data updates, as described in Chapter 6, the cost of developing a full-scale updating capability within the database should be compared to the cost of periodically replacing database tables with newer "snapshots" of data from the transaction system.

The advantage of data replacement is that data updates would be done before the data was brought into the marketing database and the database can therefore be designed to include a simpler set of functions. This simpler application may cost considerably less to develop and be operational much sooner.

The disadvantage is that changes within the transaction file would have to be inferred and, as a result, the accuracy and integrity of data in the database might be compromised. This is because many transaction systems do not maintain detailed information in the form that is needed for marketing analysis.

In many transaction systems, once an order has been recorded and a shipment has been made, detailed information about items purchased may be maintained only in summary form for the entire Customer file, or at best, by segments of the file, rather than at the individual customer level.

In many cases, summary information at the individual customer level may be limited to such items as total sales, total number of purchases, or categories of purchases. As a result, the comparison of one month's snapshot to the following month's snapshot will often provide inexact information. We would have to assume that a difference in total sales from one month to the next was the result of a purchase or a return.

However, if there was more than one purchase in a month, or a purchase and a return, we would be looking at a net result only and would not understand the full dynamic of the customer's actions. Any analysis based on incomplete data would necessarily be flawed, and the confidence with which a marketer could act would be similarly limited.

If, on the other hand, the existing transaction systems *do* capture and maintain detailed data at the individual customer level, snapshots of the transaction file may be a satisfactory method of loading data to the marketing database.

Regardless of the updating approach taken, the accuracy of data and the validity of analysis will be dependent on the ability of the marketing database to relate individual customer actions to marketing actions.

EXTERNAL DATA

Many companies have found that external data from sources like Donnelley, Polk, Infobase, and Equifax is very valuable for segmenting the CUSTOMER file and developing profiles or predictive modeling. In order to determine whether external data has predictive or segmentation value for a company, many data vendors will make arrangements so that companies can append their data and compare the results of models that include external data with the results of models that include in-house data alone.

The economics of data appending will then determine whether the improvement attributable to appended data justifies the cost of using it on a production basis. A detailed presentation of the economics of this analysis is presented in Section 5, "The Economics of the New Direct Marketing."

In order to use external data on a regular basis, once the initial analysis is completed, the database must have a facility that will allow easy extraction of records to be appended with external data and an efficient means of loading appended records back into the database. Then, selections of records can be made based on values of externally appended data in combination with other factors maintained in the database.

CHAPTER 8

HARDWARE, SOFTWARE, AND RELATED VENDOR ISSUES

What is the firm's existing hardware environment? Most firms that are considering the development of database marketing systems already have a mainframe computing environment. However, increasing numbers of companies are developing database marketing systems in midframe or even microcomputer environments.

A number of software vendors have products that will run in any of the three environments, while others are limited to only one or two. A discussion of software issues appears later in this chapter, and a listing of software products for each of the three computing environments is contained in Appendix II.

While the selection of a database management system product to be used as the base software for the marketing database will be driven primarily by the *functional* requirements of the marketing group, there are a number of very important technical issues that must be addressed as part of the selection process, and that should involve the active participation of the company's MIS management.

HARDWARE ISSUES

Mainframe Computers

The mainframe computer hardware environment at most companies falls into one of two categories:

- IBM.
- Non-IBM.

IBM has about a 60 percent share of the mainframe installations, with the balance going to Unisys, the larger Wang systems, IBM plug-compatibles (e.g., Amdahl), and clusters of midframe computers (e.g., Digital Equipment). For the purposes of this discussion, we will focus on the IBM mainframe environment and separately discuss the midframe computers, whether configured in clusters or as stand-alone machines.

The IBM mainframe world is currently divided into three classes of CPUs (central processing units). The largest class covers the 30XX machines, which include older machines such as the 3033s, the more recent 308Xs (including 3083s and 3081s), and the newest, most powerful class of IBM mainframes, the 3090s.

While these machines are the largest computers available for most commercial applications, their capacity is not limitless. Memory and processing power can be added on but incremental growth for IBM machines is relatively expensive. MIS management, like any other corporate management, attempts to scale the available capacity of computer resources to the known and anticipated resource level required. Unless major growth is expected in the immediate future, few MIS directors would want to incur the expense of significant excess computer capacity.

In typical data centers, optimal system performance is achieved when 65 to 75 percent of available CPU capacity is being consumed. At this level of use, applications get the processing power they need to provide generally acceptable response time for on-line transactions while sufficient capacity remains available to support the requirements of background transactions and the operating system.

Midframe Computers

Increasing numbers of companies are finding midframe computers to be a cost-effective alternative to mainframe computer systems. This is especially true for companies that configure several midframe computers into clusters that can easily rival or exceed the capacity of mainframe computers at a lower total cost. In addition, midframe computers can be configured such that if one CPU within the cluster goes down, work can be redirected to continue processing in other parts of the cluster. This is one reason that midframe clusters have been adopted by a number of companies for whom continuous uptime is a critical issue. Companies in fields as diverse as financial services and publishing have based their technology strategies on midframe clusters.

Another reason that this approach has increased in popularity is that the cost of incremental growth is often considerably less than comparable growth in a mainframe computing environment. If additional processing requirements develop, the firm can simply add an additional CPU to the cluster, thereby increasing CPU processing power and memory with a stand-alone unit.

A third reason for recent growth in this segment is that midframe computers are often thought of as departmental machines. Because each unit is relatively inexpensive and can support a number of users ranging from fewer than 8 to more than 100, depending on the size of the cluster, the purchase price of midframe computers is often within the annual computing budget of a single large department, rather than requiring a capital investment that would require corporatewide approval and would normally go through the MIS department. In decentralized companies, this factor alone may drive the hardware acquisition decision.

For some companies, developing a marketing database in a stand-alone, midframe computer environment may make far greater economic sense than expanding its mainframe computer environment solely to support the new application. Depending on the capacity available in the firm's existing mainframe computer environment, the approach selected will often be a function of the incremental cost required to support the incremental benefit that the anticipated marketing database will bring.

Vendors who have a strong presence in the midframe marketplace include Digital Equipment (DEC), which is by far the leader in this segment; Data General; Hewlett-Packard; Stratus; Perkins & Elmer; Prime; and Wang. While IBM is a major player in the midframe marketplace with its System 38, AS400, and 9370 systems, it is nowhere near as dominant as it is in the mainframe environment.[1]

Microcomputers

Microcomputer processing power and storage capacity are increasing at such a dramatic rate that the line between large, multiuser microcomputers and small midframes has grown very fuzzy. The advent of microcomputer networks has increased potential processing power and storage capacity by such an extent that large networks easily rival the power of midframe

---

[1] The IBM 9370 is a family of midframe-sized and -priced computers that use IBM mainframe operating system software.

computers and begin to approach the power of small mainframe configurations as well.

While companies now have a much wider range of hardware choices for their marketing databases, the issues of cost, technical support, data integrity, updating, and system management have become increasingly complicated.

The major players in the microcomputer marketplace have become household words — IBM, Apple, Compaq, Toshiba, Zenith, Motorola, and so on. All the major microcomputer products that are being used for database applications are IBM compatible, including the newer products from Apple.

Regardless of which hardware decision is made, companies that are evaluating database management systems to support their database marketing applications should keep one thought in mind: *All database management systems require a great deal of computer capacity.* This should not be surprising, especially when you consider all the work that they do. Remember the ease of use, menu-driven screens, pop-up windows, and all the other tools that enable marketing end users to directly access information about their customers without having to rely on the intervention of data processing professionals. As in all resource allocation considerations, there is no such thing as a free lunch.

All the productivity and user-friendly features that we want in a database management system can only be made available by including large numbers of very complicated computer programs as part of the packages.

The trade-off for increased access to data and increased productivity on the part of end users is increased cost of CPU hardware and, often, of data storage as well. Companies must evaluate the additional benefits that will accrue to the firm as a result of increased end user productivity in the context of increased computer hardware expenses and in terms of the firm's strategic technology plan.

For marketing-driven firms, this evaluation usually comes out on the side of the database management system. In any event, marketing and MIS management must be prepared to discuss the issues based on overall benefit to the firm.

When selecting a database management system (DBMS), marketing and MIS executives must consider whether the systems under consideration are consistent with the firm's existing operating environment and whether other applications that will provide or receive data from the database can readily do so.

For example, if a company planned to install a DBMS that required IBM's MVS[2] mainframe operating system and would operate only under CICS,[3] and the firm currently used the VM[4] or DOS[5] operating systems and did not have CICS installed, then a great deal of preliminary preparation work (and expense) would have to take place prior to installing the DBMS software.

The best way to avoid problems related to system compatibility is to include the MIS management in the evaluation process.

Generally, MIS managers can assess the system compatibility and resource requirements of a DBMS product within a few minutes of discussion with the technical support staff of the vendor.

An additional step that we strongly recommend is that a company's MIS managers schedule site visits with their technical counterparts at firms that are currently operating the various products under consideration, to review both hardware and software issues. The other firms' technicians can readily describe the impact on system resources, relative efficiency, update requirements versus on-line performance, technical support requirements, and all the other aspects of system performance that are expressed in the private acronyms of MIS professionals.

Inclusion of the MIS team in the DBMS selection process is critically important to the success of the marketing database for a number of reasons:

- If the addition of the DBMS system will require additional hardware (or software) resources, the MIS group must plan for, and in many cases, budget for, the additional resources.
- By conferring with their technical colleagues at other companies, the MIS group will be able to contribute to a more accurate understanding of how well the software will fit the needs expressed by the marketing group.
- The technology world is still relatively small, and products that have developed bad reputations for system performance or companies that have poor histories of technical customer support will be

---

[2] MVS, which is short for Multiple Virtual Systems, is one of IBM's mainframe operating systems.

[3] CICS is IBM's on-line teleprocessing monitor.

[4] VM, which is short for Virtual Machine, is another of IBM's mainframe operating systems.

[5] DOS, short for Disk Operating System, is an earlier IBM mainframe operating system. Many companies still operate their computer systems using DOS. While many DBMS manufacturers have versions that will run under the DOS operating system, the number is not as great as under MVS or VM. Therefore, the selection of products is more limited.

identified to the MIS group within a small number of telephone calls.
- Most importantly, a successful implementation of a database marketing system will depend on the level of support given by the firm's in-house MIS staff. Even if the application is developed by external programming consultants, the internal MIS group must "buy in" to the selection if the application is to be successful in the long term.

SOFTWARE ISSUES

Existing Database Management System Software

Some companies may already have a database management system in place. If this is the case, then the marketing group and the MIS group should first consider whether the company's existing systems can support the additional functional requirements that the marketing group has defined. To the extent possible, it is preferable to use resources that are in place. For one thing, it reduces the initial cost of developing a marketing database. For another, the programming skill set that has already been developed on other projects can readily be applied.

Types of DBMS Products

DBMS products fall into three general categories:
- Hierarchical.
- Inverted file.
- Relational.

Appendix II contains a listing and description of database management system products by type.

Hierarchical Systems
The first DBMS products, for example, IBM's IMS, used a hierarchical structure. Hierarchical databases are designed for efficiency in high-volume transaction environments. While they are much more flexible than non-DBMS systems, their structure can often constrain the flexibility required for the types of ad hoc queries that marketing end users typically require.

Hierarchical systems were designed primarily to support limited analytical flexibility while providing support for high-volume transaction applications. As a result, many companies use hierarchical DBMS products to support customer service, airline or hotel reservation, or financial applications. While these DBMS products offer greater analytical and reporting flexibility than traditional third-generation systems, they are not designed to support the multiplicity of views or the ad hoc query requirements of today's database marketing applications.

IBM's DB2 and SQL/DS products, and Computer Associates' IDMS/R, were developed partly to bridge the gap between today's requirements and the hierarchical DBMS products that are ideal for large-volume transaction environments. A number of utility programs have been developed that make it relatively easy to load data from hierarchical systems to relational database environments.

So, while existing hierarchical DBMS products themselves may not be ideal for database marketing applications, companies that are already using them for order entry, customer service, or other transaction-oriented applications may find that their hierarchical systems, when used in combination with other DBMS products, provide a great deal of the information that is required for marketing.

Inverted File Systems

If the company's existing database has an inverted file structure, for example, Computer Associates' Datacom/DB, Computer Corporation of America's Model 204, or Software A. G.'s Adabas, the marketing group would find that these software products are especially well-suited for database marketing applications. In fact, a number of major direct marketing companies, including General Foods, Scudder Stevens & Clark, Random House, R. L. Polk, Wiland, and Metromail, currently have database marketing applications that are based on these software products.

One major difference between these products is that CCA's Model 204 and Computer Associates' Datacom/DB are designed to run exclusively in IBM or IBM-compatible environments, whereas Adabas is designed to run on IBM, DEC, and a variety of other vendors' hardware. Companies that do not currently have IBM environments should be cognizant of this fact when they evaluate products.

Inverted file systems are popular for direct marketing applications because they are very good at providing quick counts of records that meet specified conditions. In order to produce quick counts, inverted file systems have a facility for creating index versions of the data stored in their files. If queries can be answered by index-only processing, that is, not actually reading raw data records, counts can be produced for databases of several million records in a matter of a few minutes at most. In many cases, query responses are returned in seconds.

In order to take full advantage of the power of index-only processing, marketers must be very conscious of which variables are important enough to be indexed, and which data relationships should be predefined to the system. While there is a natural tendency among marketers to create indexes for every variable field, this approach will result in significantly slower updates and data loads.

Developing a true understanding of the trade-offs involved in designing the database to be efficient for both processing and updating requires years of experience. That is one reason that many firms hire consulting systems analysts and designers who have several years of hands-on experience with the database product they selected. Consulting expertise during the early stages of the database design process can literally save years of development time and processing headaches.

Relational Systems

For the last few years, data processing circles have heralded relational database technology as the wave of the future. Relational technology is based on the premise that data redundancy should be minimized and that the most logical arrangement of data within a database is in a series of tables that can be logically joined by key fields.

From a logical standpoint, this makes a great deal of sense. From a practical standpoint, logical joins, if done on a dynamic basis, have proven to be an inefficient way to link data for the types of queries that are typical for direct marketers.

As a result, relational databases that are going to be used for the kinds of quick counts that were described above tend to be designed such that they look like inverted files. If quick counts are a requirement, relational databases are generally structured as one large file in which virtually all fields are indexed.

In some cases, summary files that already contain counts known to be important may be produced as part of the regular production process so that key pieces of information for the firm are prepared in advance. The query process can then function more like a "look-up table" and avoid actually counting records.

While the ability to perform quick counts is not an essential function for all database users, it is particularly important to direct marketers. For this reason, you would expect the number of direct marketing users whose systems are based on relational database systems to be small. However, this is not actually the case.

There are several reasons why relational database technology has been used for database marketing. One is that the way in which relational databases are structured, using a process called *normalizing,* is very similar to the way in which marketers visualize their data. Data elements are organized into logical tables and are linked by common data elements. An example of this process is shown in Figure 6–1 of Chapter 6.

The utility and dictionary functions available within relational database product families make it relatively easy to extract the desired data elements from the numerous, often fragmented, files in which they are currently captured, and load the data elements into logical groupings that are more appropriate for the kinds of questions marketers tend to ask. Once the data has been loaded into the relational table format, all of the queries and reports that marketers require can readily be produced.

Another reason for using a relational database is that IBM, which controls about 60 percent of the mainframe computing marketplace in the United States, has made the strategic decision to support relational technology. In order to stimulate usage of its relational products, IBM has placed its DB2 and SQL/DS products in thousands of data centers that are committed to the IBM product line.

Because the cost of database management system software is relatively high, and because technical support staff are expensive, it is only natural that companies that already have a database management system in-house would want to develop new applications using whatever system is in place.

One of the criticisms of DB2 has been that it is difficult for end users who are not data processing professionals to use. For that reason, a number of products have been developed to bridge the gap between the kinds of menu-driven, PC-based screens that end users are comfortable with and the database management system itself.

Some user-interface products, for example, Natural/SQL, are add ons to the product lines of other mainframe DBMS products—in this case, Software A. G. Oracle also has a number of user-friendly tools that can readily be used in conjunction with DB2. Because the Oracle database product itself is written in SQL, any programs written using its products will, by definition, be compatible with an SQL product environment like DB2's.[6]

In order to make access to information that is contained in DB2 databases even easier, a company called Metaphor has introduced a combination hardware and software solution. Their software product, which is also called Metaphor, will run on IBM-compatible equipment or on its own hardware.

Metaphor's screens consist of a series of menus and icons that resemble Apple's MacIntosh, Microsoft's Windows, or other products that are the staples of the point-and-click approach to end-user computing. All of these products tend to lower the resistance that computerphobes have toward using technology.

What is special about Metaphor is that it enables end users to have access to data that may be stored in a number of different tables and to perform very complex data analysis tasks without requiring any knowledge of programming or systems. All they need to do is point the Metaphor mouse at the appropriate icons on the screen and click. Once a listing of the available database files is displayed, end users select the desired files by pointing and clicking the mouse. A display of the fields contained within the table is readily available, and end users can select fields from within tables, combine these with fields selected from other tables, and dynamically create the database needed to solve the marketing questions they have in mind.

Another relational product that has had phenomenal success in the last few years is Oracle, a relational database developed and marketed by the Oracle Corporation. Oracle's success has come about for two primary reasons:

- It is an exceptionally good relational database product.
- Oracle is committed to platform independence (see definition below).

In widely publicized tests over the past few years, Oracle has outperformed DB2 both in processing speed and also in flexibility for end users.

---

[6] SQL is the abbreviation for Structured Query Language, which is the ANSI standard language that underlies all relational database management systems. (See Buzzword Box 2 in Chapter 3.)

Perhaps more importantly, Oracle has from the beginning been committed to the concept of platform independence. That is, Oracle's products are developed in such a way that they can be used on virtually any computer hardware and with virtually any operating system. It is one of the very few products that can be used on the full range of IBM mainframe machines, the full line of DEC midframes, and virtually any IBM-compatible microcomputer.

This flexibility is ideal for companies that use DEC or other midframe equipment as departmental machines, since programs can be written in any of the environments and then be run in any of the other environments without changing a single line of program code.

If properly designed, relational database systems can be very well suited for the requirements of database marketing, and in some cases, if the marketing database is to be linked with other applications that the company is running, it may be cost-effective for firms to go with a single-vendor, single-DBMS strategy. Again, the company's strategic technology plan is a very important component of the DBMS selection process.

Customized Applications for Direct Marketing

A number of DBMS manufacturers have ventured into the realm of application development—generally targeted to specific industries. Oracle, for example, has developed a number of applications for financial services users. IBM's DBMS software has been used as the core of a number of database-oriented applications including payroll and personnel systems. Vendors have developed versions of their products that have DB2 as the core database system. It is likely that this pattern will continue into the future as more and more database-oriented applications are developed.

An application system that is particularly noteworthy for direct marketers is MarketPulse, a generic database marketing system that the authors of this text helped Computer Corporation of America (CCA) to develop. (CCA is the company that developed Model 204, mentioned earlier in the discussion of inverted file systems.)

The MarketPulse application takes advantage of the high-speed data retrieval and processing aspects of Model 204 but, in addition, provides a series of menus and screens that are relevant to the types of queries, reports, and data organization that are the core of most direct marketers' information requirements. MarketPulse is designed such that it can simply be "dropped in" at companies that do not currently have the Model 204 database installed. In this situation, MarketPulse will simply operate as a stand-alone application.

With the optional Easel-based PC front end, marketers can use MarketPulse on a purely functional basis, selecting the data elements and relationships that they are interested in without ever having to write a line of code or even know whether the work they are doing is taking place on the mainframe, within the PC workstation, or a combination of the two. The underlying database structure of MarketPulse manages all of the "navigation," that is, the links between the screens the user sees, the computer programs that are doing the work, and the data required to answer the users' queries.

MarketPulse is noteworthy for two reasons:

- It is the first such system to be available on a licensed basis that is specifically designed to support marketing users.
- The emergence of a data- and function-driven system that operates independently of the end user's knowledge of computing is fast becoming the dominant mode of end-user computing for the future.

Summary

This discussion was intended to provide marketers with a sense of how database management system technology can be used to support the information needs of marketing and to provide both marketers and MIS professionals with an understanding of the issues that must be addressed in order to insure successful implementations of marketing database applications.

A small number of vendors' products were mentioned as representative examples of current trends in DBMS technology. For a more complete listing and description of the products offered by a number of different vendors, please see the Product Directory that appears in Appendix II.

INSIDE DEVELOPMENT VERSUS EXTERNAL VENDORS

Should the entire database marketing process be done in-house, or should a combination of internal and external resources be considered?

In-House Development

There are three principal reasons why it is preferable to do the entire job of developing a marketing database in-house: (1) cost, (2) control, and (3) customization.

Cost
There is always a perception that is less expensive to develop applications in-house because the programmers on staff are part of a fixed cost budget. This assumption must be validated, however, based on the existing workload of the in-house staff; if they are fully occupied supporting other projects, the incremental cost of new programmers must be compared to the cost of using external resources.

Control
A more important consideration for many companies is the issue of control. For most direct marketing companies, the customer list is the lifeblood of the business. Any use of external facilities must, by definition, create additional risk exposure for the integrity and confidentiality of a company's data. In order to maintain control of critical data while using external resources, companies must first assess the risk, and then manage that risk through procedural and contractual measures in conjunction with the external service provider.

Customization
Customization is one of the most important reasons to consider doing the project in-house. No matter how committed an external service provider is to the company's project, no one understands a firm's data as well as the people who work with it every day. Consequently, a system that is developed by an external service provider is likely to fit the more general needs of numerous clients rather than providing the same level of customized screens, menus, and reporting capabilities that an internally developed application would offer.

External Vendors

There are two principal reasons to consider using external resources when developing a marketing database: (1) experience and facilities, and (2) speed.

Experience and Facilities
If the company does not have a DBMS product in-house, or if a different DBMS product is being used for the marketing database, time (and therefore money) must be invested in getting the MIS staff up to speed on the product before any application development work can begin.

Meanwhile, the application development process will remain stalled until the marketing group and the MIS group have developed a functional requirements document, discussed design issues, and in many cases, reinvented the wheel a few times before the MIS group is ready to get down to serious application development work. While all this preparatory work is going on, the marketing group *still* does not have the access it requires to data, and marketing decisions are being made based on the same quality of information that was available before the application development process began.

One of the most important benefits an external service provider can offer to a company at this point in its application development process is the experience and the facilities that will enable the marketers to load their current data into a database format, get immediate access to their data so that better marketing decisions can be made, and give them a chance to develop some hands-on experience with database technology. This hands-on experience will have direct benefits when it comes to defining the functional requirements of their own applications.

Speed
Marketers often cannot wait until the application is completed internally to make their critical marketing decisions. By using external facilities, marketing decisions can be made in a timely manner, based on much better information; as a result, higher quality decisions are likely to result.

A Combination Approach

It doesn't have to be an either/or decision. Many companies find that the most successful approach is to use external services for those functions that are most efficiently done externally, while concentrating their development activities on internal resources. For some companies, it is actually more efficient to use external services for the full range of database marketing services, and, at a later date, bring the application in-house. Several vendors will assist client companies in making this transition, and will often continue to provide services such as NCOA, lettershop, or creative services.

The important point to remember is that using external services and internal resources are not mutually exclusive approaches. The specific mix of services depends on the company, its available resources, and the development timetable.

SECTION 4

STATISTICAL ANALYSIS AND MODELING

THE OBJECTIVE OF THIS SECTION

The objective of this section on statistical analysis and modeling is to provide the reader with an understanding of the basics of statistical analysis, segmentation, and predictive modeling so that he or she can confidently use the quantitative techniques available to today's database marketers.

Most customer and prospect databases are simply too large to be used effectively without the aid of statistical models. While it is certainly possible to use database technology to select names that meet particular individual level criteria, for example, "select all married males who purchased product X within the last 30 days," it is not possible to run large direct marketing businesses solely on this basis.

Direct marketers need to be able to manage customer files on the basis of either predictive or segmentation models. Predictive models are useful in identifying individual customers or prospects who are expected to respond or behave significantly better or significantly worse than some economic criteria, and therefore, should either be included or excluded from particular marketing programs. Segmentation models identify groups of people with similar characteristics, needs, or attitudes so that marketing programs can be customized to meet the needs or requirements of the groups or individual segments.

However, in order to understand and use predictive and segmentation models, a basic understanding of some fundamental statistical principles is required. Obviously, no one book, much less one or two chapters of a book, can turn a person into a statistician. However, it is our belief that direct marketers need to be better users of statistical methods in order to be on the cutting edge of database marketing, and we hope that a study of the material in these chapters will make the reader a much better user.

GETTING STARTED

This section will cover an enormous amount of material. We'll start slowly with the basics of data analysis, and move on to hypothesis testing or tests of significance. Most direct marketers are concerned with the traditional questions of sample size and statistical significance; this material has been covered in almost every text on direct marketing. However, we repeat some of this material here because the same principles having to do with change and sample variation (generally associated with list testing—"did list A do better than list B?" "did the test package really beat the control?") also apply to model building.

After this basic review, we'll get into the fundamentals of model building. We'll start slowly with a presentation of correlation and simple regression analysis, and then move on to multiple regression analysis, the workhorse of predictive modeling within the direct marketing business. In recent years, the appropriateness of the ordinary regression technique has been questioned and we'll review the arguments for and against regression and provide the reader with a detailed outline of the steps that need to be taken when regression is used as the primary modeling tool. Finally, we'll discuss the alternative techniques to regression modeling and suggest an approach to predictive modeling that uses all of the tools available to direct marketers today.

CHAPTER 9

THE BASICS OF STATISTICAL ANALYSIS

THE PROCESS OF DATA ANALYSIS

Data analysis is a process. It starts with observations of an event, a behavior, or an outcome that are first encoded into data (called variables), then analyzed, and eventually turned into information. (See Figure 9–1.)

ILLUSTRATION 1

An example will illustrate the process.

Let's consider a catalog marketer who sells woodworking tools and supplies. Catalogs are mailed four times a year to all customers. The company has 1 million names on its customer file (database). For each customer on the database, there is a fairly complete history that includes dates of all purchases, items purchased, purchase dollar amounts, and a code indicating the source from which the name was originally acquired.

The cataloger would like to know if "new" customers buy more than "old" customers. Classifying new customers as anyone whose first purchase was made within the last 12 months, and an old customer as anyone whose first purchase was made over a year ago, the mailer's analyst draws a sample of 100,000 names and calculates the following:

5,000 orders were received in the last month.

3,000 orders (60 percent) were from new customers.

2,000 orders (40 percent) were from old customers.

Even in this simple example, the analyst was involved in a fairly complicated and very structured process. First, observations of customer

FIGURE 9–1

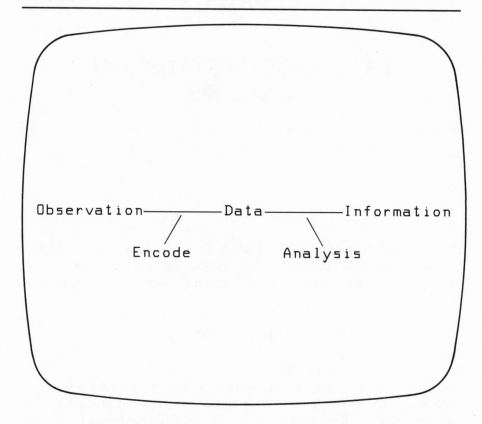

Observation————————Data————————Information

            Encode   Analysis

purchasing were encoded based on dates of first purchase, thereby creating the variable CUSTOMER TYPE with two values, new and old. Similarly, purchase data was encoded into the variable PURCHASE with two values, yes and no.

Finally, the resultant variables were analyzed by calculating the percentages of new and old customers among the total number of buyers in the period analyzed. The resulting information is that new customers accounted for 60 percent of sales volume and old customers represent 40 percent of sales volume.

Let's examine the process in more detail and discuss what else could have been done. The analyst transformed the observations into *categorical* data; that is, observations were classified into two distinct and nonoverlapping categories or groups. For CUSTOMER TYPE, a customer is either new or old; for PURCHASE, a customer either did purchase or did not purchase.

Data at this gross level of detail provides no discrimination among the customers within either group. For example, a customer whose first purchase is 11 months old is "equal" to a customer whose first purchase is 11 days old.

Similarly, customers who purchased any item, regardless of amount, are considered equal. Clearly, information is *lost* when using categorical data.

The analyst could just as easily have created *scalar* data or *continuous* data, which provides more information. The PURCHASE variable could take on actual purchase amounts as its values. This new PURCHASE variable is scalar, by definition, because it satisfies the required condition: the four operations of arithmetic ($+$, $-$, $\times$, and $/$) can be meaningfully performed on the variable's values.

For example, the sum of two purchases may be added together — $5 and $2 equals $7 — which is a meaningful number. In contrast, if CUSTOMER TYPE, a categorical variable, is coded 1 for new customers and 0 for old customers, adding the two category numbers together results in a number that is obviously not meaningful.

If this scalar PURCHASE variable had been used, the analyst might have found that the average purchase amount among new customers was two or three times larger than the average among the old customers. This information adds to the understanding of the new-customer group. Not only do new customers purchase more but their purchases are worth more.

Hopefully, this short walk through the data process conveys the intended impression that the process of analyzing data requires a feeling for the data. However, since we never really know whether or not we have the right feeling, we need more tools to help us get that feeling, to help us better understand what we are about to analyze.

PICTURES OF DATA: STEM AND LEAF

Actually, we can see what the data looks like — in a picture the statisticians call *stem-and-leaf.*

The stem-and-leaf picture is easy to draw, either by hand or computer, and easy to understand. Since it's easier to illustrate the method of construction than it is to describe it, let's go to an illustration.

ILLUSTRATION 2

Consider a small sample of a mailing consisting of 20 observations of purchase dollar amounts. Ranking the dollar amounts from low to high, we have:

5 6 7 8 10 12 14 15 17 18 20 30 40 45 47 50 50 50 66 90

Each number can be broken up into two parts: a stem and a leaf.

The stem is the first part of the number. In this case, since we are dealing with two-digit numbers, the stem is the digit representing the 10's position. The leaves are the unit digits.

Thus, the data can be first expressed as follows:

		Stem	+	Leaf
5	=	0	+	5
6	=	0	+	6
7	=	0	+	7
8	=	0	+	8
10	=	1	+	0
12	=	1	+	2
14	=	1	+	4
15	=	1	+	5
17	=	1	+	7
18	=	1	+	8
20	=	2	+	0
30	=	3	+	0
40	=	4	+	0
45	=	4	+	5
47	=	4	+	7
50	=	5	+	0
50	=	5	+	0
50	=	5	+	0
66	=	6	+	6
90	=	9	+	0

Accordingly, the stem-and-leaf picture of purchase amounts in dollar units looks like this:

Stem	Leaf
0	5678
1	024578
2	0
3	0
4	057
5	000
6	6
7	
8	
9	0

The stems are written vertically. The leaves are put on the stems horizontally in rank order, and if necessary they are repeated according to the actual number of occurrences (e.g., 50 occurs three times, resulting in stem 5 with three 0 leaves).[1]

At a glance, we can see the overall *shape* of the variable PURCHASE. The shape of the variable is dependent on *wild observations* (e.g., 90), *gaps* (70 through 89), and *clumps* (10 through 18) in the data.

Why this emphasis on the shape of the data? The answer is that traditional statistical techniques such as regression, which will be the focus of this section, work better if the shape of the data (or variables) conforms to a specific profile. If the data does not match this profile, then either certain techniques (like regression) should be used with caution, or the data must be "massaged" or reshaped to fit the desired profile.

The desired profile is the well-known bell-shaped curve, formally referred to as the *normal curve* or *distribution*. Figure 9–2 shows a stem-and-leaf display of normal data and Figure 9–3 shows a traditional graph of the normal curve.

The normal distribution is important to many traditional statistical methods. However, in order to understand its importance, two other basic

---

[1] When we are working with numbers having more than two digits, we must decide on the appropriate break for the stem and leaf. This depends on the data at hand and the objective of the analysis; therefore, rules of thumb for splitting the data cannot be made. However, let's consider the two possible breaks for data in the hundreds. One break is between the 100's and 10's positions, in which case we ignore the units digit. For example, 345 = 3 plus 4. This stem-and-leaf display implies the stem is multiplied by 100 and the leaf is multiplied by 10.

The second possible break is between the 10's and unit's positions. For example, 345 = 34 plus 5. This implies the stem position is multiplied by 10 and the leaf is multiplied by 1.

FIGURE 9–2

0	13
1	009
2	3333
3	1111112
4	11112223346
5	112223334566
6	0003345699
7	444445
8	3333
9	5

FIGURE 9–3
Probability Distributions

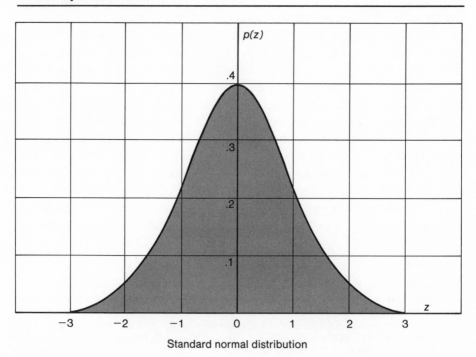

Standard normal distribution

Source: Thomas H. Wonnacott and Ronald J. Wonnacott, *Introductory Statistics for Business and Economics,* 2nd ed. (Santa Barbara: John Wiley & Sons, Inc., 1977), p. 92.

concepts must first be understood. So let's present these basics and then discuss the role the normal distribution plays in data analysis and statistical model building.

NUMERICAL SUMMARIES

The two basic concepts are the *center* of a set of numbers of data, more commonly known as the *average,* with which everyone is familiar, and the *spread* or variation in the data set, a concept which few of us who aren't statisticians think much about, if at all. As it turns out, there are three ways to find the center and several alternatives to measure spread.

Center of Data

ILLUSTRATION 3

Let's consider the following set of 9 numbers, or observations:

$$1\ 2\ 3\ 5\ 5\ 5\ 7\ 8\ 9$$

The sum of these nine numbers is 45. The sum of the observations (45) divided by the number of observations (9) is called the *mean,* which is the everyday average. In this case, the mean is 5.

It is also true, in this case, that the mean is equal to the number in the center or middle of the set of numbers. The number in the center of a set of numbers ranked from high to low (or low to high) is called the *median.* Thus, in our example, the median equals the mean.

If we look closely at our set of 9 numbers, we will see that one number, the number 5, appears more frequently than any other number. The number that appears most frequently in a set of numbers is called the *mode.* Thus, in our example, all three measures of center are equal.

Variation within the Data

The notion of variation is more complicated but equally important. For example, three persons with incomes of $49,000, $50,000, and $51,000 could all be meaningfully described as coming from a fairly homogeneous group with a mean income of $50,000. But three persons with incomes of $25,000, $50,000, and $75,000 are clearly not alike even though their mean income is also $50,000.

To assess variation, we can use several summary measures.

Range

Going back to our simple example, we see that the numbers go from a high of 9 to a low of 1. We can measure the variation by the distance or difference between the high and low numbers. In this case, the difference or range is equal to 8.

Differences about the Mean

We can measure variation by observing the differences of the numbers about their center, say, the mean. The set of differences about the mean of 5 are:

$$-4 \ -3 \ -2 \ 0 \ 0 \ 0 \ 2 \ 3 \ 4$$

Thus, we can summarize the differences by using the sum of the differences, or the mean of the differences. In either case, the value is zero.

$$\text{Sum:} \quad -4 + -3 + -2 + 0 + 0 + 0 + 2 + 3 + 4 = 0$$

$$\text{Mean:} \ \frac{-4 + -3 + -2 + 0 + 0 + 0 + 2 + 3 + 4}{9} = \frac{0}{9} = 0$$

Intuitively, a numeric summary intended to represent variation should equal zero only when there is no variation, which is clearly not the case here. The pluses and minuses, in this case, cancel each other out and cause the zero. Although for a different set of numbers this canceling out might not be a problem, we'd rather use a measure that is not sensitive to this problem. To avoid this problem, we must eliminate the minuses. There are at least two ways to do this.

Absolute Difference

Use only the absolute value of the difference; that is, ignore the sign and use only the value. Accordingly, the set of absolute numbers is:

$$4 \ 3 \ 2 \ 0 \ 0 \ 0 \ 2 \ 3 \ 4$$

The sum and the mean of the differences are 18 and 2, respectively.

Squared Difference

Use the square of the difference, which produces a positive number. (Remember, a negative number times a negative number results in a positive number.) Accordingly, the squares of the differences are

$$16 \ 9 \ 4 \ 0 \ 0 \ 0 \ 4 \ 9 \ 16$$

The sum and mean of the squared differences are 58 and 6.4, respectively.

Thus, for summary measures of variation for the set of the nine numbers 1, 2, 3, 5, 5, 5, 7, 8, and 9, we have:

   8.0 = Range.
   0.0 = Either sum or mean of the difference about the center.
   18.0 = Sum of the absolute difference.
   2.0 = Mean of the absolute difference.
   58.0 = Sum of the squared difference.
   6.4 = Mean of the squared difference.

Aside from the effects of the canceling out issue, all the measures work the same way: the larger the value, the greater the variation.

To assess which of two or more sets of numbers has the greatest variation, we select *one* summary measure and calculate its value for all sets. The set with the largest numerical value has the greatest variation. Why have we taken you through all this? First, to demonstrate that the objectivity of data analysis can be affected by the subjectivity or preference of the analyst. Second, and more importantly, to introduce you to, and provide you with, a basic understanding of three very important measures that are used in a variety of statistical applications.

- **Total sum of squares** – the sum of the squared differences, used in all regression theory.
- **The variance** – the sum of the squared differences divided by the number of observations.
- **Standard deviation** – the square root of the variance.

The concept of variation, expressed in terms of the standard deviation, is integral to the understanding of *confidence intervals* and *tests of significance* – formal statistical procedures for determining with what level of confidence we can assert that the findings of a study are real or due to chance (i.e., what the statisticians call *sample variation*). This is our next topic.

CONFIDENCE INTERVALS

ILLUSTRATION 4

Returning to our catalog example, let's assume our analyst is now interested in knowing the average purchase dollar amount of the customers on the house file. The analyst draws a sample of 75 customers and calculates the mean purchase amount, which turns out to be $68. This mean value seems small, so another sample of 75 is drawn and the mean turns out to be $122. Although the analyst knows that the means will vary from sample to sample due to the nature of randomly selecting different groups of customers, the analyst feels the two means are too far apart to provide an indication of the true mean purchase amount. Accordingly, the analyst draws another 38 samples of 75 customers and calculates the mean of each sample.

The analyst creates a stem-and-leaf display of the *sample means*. The shape of the distribution of sample means looks normal. (See Figure 9–4.) The variation and standard deviation of the 40 sample means can be calculated using the following formulas:[2]

$$\text{Variance of sample means} = \frac{\text{Sum (each sample mean} - \text{average of all sample means)}^2}{\text{Number of samples} - 1}$$

$$\text{Standard deviation of sample means} = \text{Square root of the variance of sample means}$$

Note: It is customary to refer to the standard deviation of sample means as the standard error of the sample mean, and we will follow that custom from this point on.

In this case, the variance among the 40 sample means turns out to be 166.75 and the standard error is 12.91.

At this point, the analyst is prepared to consider $94.85 as the true mean purchase amount, that is, the average that would have been discovered if all customers on the database were included in the calculation. How confident should the analyst be in this mean of means?

---

[2] A statistical note: when working with a sample, not the entire population, which is almost always the case, the variance is calculated by dividing by the number of observations minus 1.

FIGURE 9–4

Stem	Leaf
12	22
11	24
10	00222268888
9	0222444446688
8	00224466
7	048
6	8

Mean = 94.85
Median = 94.00
Variance = 166.75
Standard error = 12.91

The analyst knows that the mean is affected by the variation of the data on which it is calculated. That is, if the variation is small, the mean is more representative of the true mean than if the variation is large. Thus, if the variation of the mean of the means is small, the analyst would have more confidence in the mean of means representing the true purchase amount. On the other hand, if the variation is large, then we would have less confidence.

Now, the analyst has three important pieces of information:

1. The shape of the data appears to be normal.
2. The mean of means is $94.85.
3. The standard error is $12.91.

In order to put the pieces together, to establish a sense of confidence about the assertion of the true mean purchase, the analyst needs one of the fundamental rules (statisticians call them theorems) of statistics.

Theorem 1

About 95 percent of the time (95 out of every 100 sample means) the true mean purchase amount lies between plus or minus 1.96 standard errors from the mean of the sample means.

Thus, we can create a *95 percent confidence interval* around the mean of $94.85, which includes all values between the mean plus 1.96 standard errors and the mean minus 1.96 standard errors.

In our example, we have:

$$1.96 \text{ times the SE} = 1.96 \times \$12.91 = \$25.30$$
$$\text{The mean plus } 1.96 \text{ times the SE} = \$94.85 + \$25.30 = \$120.15$$
$$\text{The mean minus } 1.96 \text{ times the SE} = \$94.85 - \$25.30 = \$69.55$$

Thus, the 95 percent confidence interval includes all values between $69.55 and $120.15.

The theorem also allows for varying the levels of confidence, though 95 percent is a widely used standard. By increasing the confidence, the interval becomes wider; and conversely, by decreasing the confidence, the interval becomes narrower. For example, the factor for a confidence interval that would include 99.7 percent of all observations is calculated by multiplying the standard error by 3.0 rather than 1.96. The factor for 90 percent confidence interval is 1.64.

Where do these factors — 1.64, 1.96, and 3.0 — come from? The normal distribution! When a variable is normally distributed or nearly normal, we have the following facts (see Figure 9–5):

90 percent of the observations or values fall between plus and minus 1.64 standard deviations.

95 percent of the observations fall between plus and minus 1.96 standard deviations.

99.73 percent of the observations fall between plus and minus 3.0 standard deviations.

The center or middle value is the mean of the variable.

In practice, we do not have to draw many samples to construct a *confidence interval for a mean*. We work with only one sample. However, to describe this one sample approach, we need to have another way to calculate the standard error of the mean.

Standard error of the mean = Standard deviation from a single
  sample, divided by the square root of *n*, the number of observations

We use the following example to illustrate the one sample approach.

ILLUSTRATION 5

Let's say we want to know the mean age of all customers on a house file; that is, the true mean age. The file is too large to calculate the mean directly, so we pull a sample of 30 names from the house file and draw an inference from the data contained in the sample. (See Figure 9–6.)

FIGURE 9–5
Areas under the Normal Curve for Various Standard Deviations from the Mean

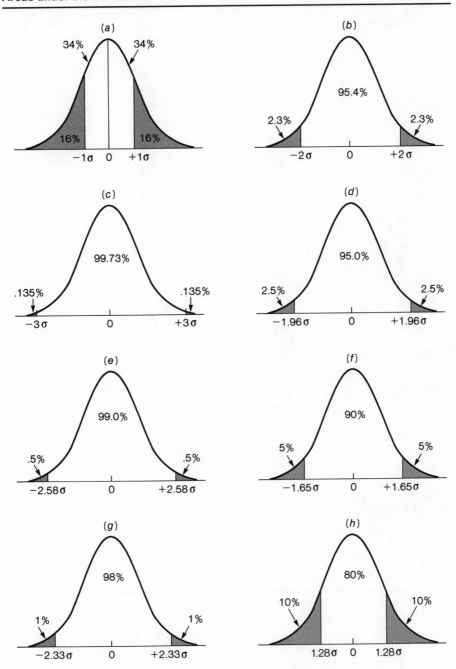

Source: Sam Kash Kachigan, *Statistical Analysis* (New York: Radius Press, 1986), p. 61.

FIGURE 9–6
Sample from House File

Observations	Age	$(x - \bar{x})$	$(x - \bar{x})^2$
1	45	0.967	0.934
2	45	0.967	0.934
3	45	0.967	0.934
4	65	20.967	439.601
5	45	0.967	0.934
6	36	− 8.033	64.534
7	45	0.967	0.934
8	56	11.967	143.201
9	62	17.967	322.801
10	43	− 1.033	1.068
11	34	− 10.033	100.668
12	54	9.967	99.334
13	57	12.967	168.134
14	59	14.967	224.001
15	47	2.967	8.801
16	38	− 6.033	36.401
17	38	− 6.033	36.401
18	32	− 12.033	144.801
19	23	− 21.033	442.401
20	28	− 16.033	257.068
21	47	2.967	8.801
22	49	4.967	24.668
23	58	13.967	195.068
24	61	16.967	287.868
25	26	− 18.033	325.201
26	32	− 12.033	144.801
27	34	− 10.033	100.668
28	36	− 8.033	64.534
29	38	− 6.033	36.401
30	43	− 1.033	1.068

Average	44.03		3,682.966
n	30		
$n - 1$	29		
Variance			126.9988
Standard deviation			11.26937
Standard error			2.057497
95% confidence			1.96
Range = + or −			4.032694
Range =			40.00063
			48.06602

We have the following pieces of information:

- The sample size, n, = 30.
- The sample mean age, $\bar{x}$ = 44.03.
- The sum of squared differences = 3,682.966.
- The variance equals the sum of squared difference divided by $n - 1$, which equals 126.9988.
- The standard deviation is the square root of the variance and the square root of 126.9988 = 11.26937.
- The standard error of the mean equals the standard deviation divided by the square root of n. The square root of 30 is 5.477. Therefore, the standard error is equal to 11.26937/5.477 = 2.0574.

We want to use the sample mean to estimate the true mean age, with 95 percent confidence. For this, we need another theorem, which reads very similarly to Theorem 1.

Theorem 2

About 95 percent of the time (95 out of every 100 samples) the true mean lies between plus or minus 1.96 standard errors from the sample mean.

Accordingly, we can say that the sample mean age will differ from the true mean age by less than 4.03 (1.96 × 2.0574) years with 95 percent confidence. That is, we can assert with a confidence of 95 percent that the true mean age lies between:

$$44.03 \pm 4.03$$

or:

$$40.00 \text{ and } 48.07$$

Confidence intervals apply not only to means but also to percentages or, in the case of direct marketing, to response rates.

CONFIDENCE INTERVALS AND TESTS OF SIGNIFICANCE FOR RESPONSE RATES

The theorem needed to calculate the 95 percent confidence interval for response rates is very similar to the theorem for means.

Theorem 3

About 95 percent of the time (95 out of every 100 samples) the true response rate lies between plus or minus 1.96 standard errors from the sample response rate,

where:

$$p = \text{Sample response rate}$$
$$n = \text{Sample size}$$
$$\text{Standard error} = \text{Square root of } p \times (1 - p) \text{ divided by } n$$

Let's consider an example.

ILLUSTRATION 6

Our cataloger wants to test 1,000 names selected at random from a new list. However, in order to break even, the list must be expected to have a response rate of 4.5 percent on a rollout mailing. The cataloger wants to be 95 percent certain that the list test will hold up on the rollout.

Prior to mailing the list, the cataloger could calculate a confidence interval based on the number of pieces mailed (1,000) and the desired level of confidence (95 percent). Using the formula:

$$\text{Confidence interval} = \text{Expected response} \pm 1.96 \times \text{SE}$$

or:

$$\text{CI} = p \pm 1.96 \times \text{SE}$$
$$\text{CI} = .045 \pm 1.96 \times \sqrt{[(.045) \times (1-.045)/1{,}000]}$$
$$\text{CI} = .045 \pm 1.96 \times \sqrt{(.04298/1{,}000)}$$
$$\text{CI} = .045 \pm 1.96 \times 0.00656$$
$$\text{CI} = .045 \pm 0.0128$$
$$\text{CI} = .0578 \text{ to } .0322 \text{ or } 3.22\% \text{ to } 5.78\%$$

Based on this confidence interval, a statistician would say that any response rate between 3.33 and 5.78 percent will support the hypothesis that the true response rate *is* 4.5 percent. However, this does not mean that the true response rate is definitely 4.5 percent. Therefore, the cataloger would say that any response rate within the confidence interval would support the conclusion that the true response rate *may be* 4.5 percent. If a response rate is achieved that is outside the interval, the cataloger is prepared to accept the conclusion that the true response rate is not 4.5 percent.

The list is mailed and pulls a 3.5 percent response. Based on the confidence interval we just calculated, we can conclude that the true response rate may be 4.5 percent. On the other hand, we now have more information. We have an actual 3.5 percent response rate on a test mailing of 1,000 pieces. Therefore, we could calculate a confidence interval based on this information.

$$p = .035$$
$$(1-p) = 0.965$$
$$n = 1,000$$

Standard error = Square root of $(.035 \times .965)/1,000 = .006$

$$.035 - (1.96 \times .006) = .035 - .012 = .023$$

$$.035 + (1.96 \times .006) = .035 + .012 = .047$$

Thus, we can be 95% certain that the true response rate lies in the interval between 2.3 to 4.7 percent. Of course, the confidence interval around 3.5 percent had to include the desired 4.5 percent response rate because the confidence interval around the 4.5 percent response rate included 3.5 percent.

How do we interpret this new information? Again, if 4.5 percent were *not* included in the interval, we could say with 95 percent confidence that the true response rate was not 4.5 percent. But, as we said before, and it bears repeating, the converse is not true. Even though 4.5 percent is included in the confidence interval, we cannot say with 95 percent confidence that the true response rate is 4.5 percent, but we can say that the true response rate may be 4.5 percent, and that the list deserves to be tested again.

This phenomenon of a test result being different from the true result is often associated with the concept of *regression to the mean*. More often than not, regression to the mean is referred to in the context of a list that tests well but does not do as well when rolled out in larger quantities. What's happening here is that part of the high response is due to chance or sample variation. For example, a list with a true response rate of 4 percent on a test of 5,000 names might pull as high as 4.5 percent just due to chance. However, when rolled out in large quantity, in all likelihood the list will respond closer to its true mean of 4.0 percent. In statistical parlance, the performance of the list will regress back to its mean. Since direct marketers usually don't retest lists that fall below a cutoff rate, the reverse side of this phenomenon is seen less frequently. We don't often see lists that initially tested poorly do well on larger rollouts because we don't do larger rollouts on lists that initially don't test well. Hopefully, this discussion will cause marketers to give more thought to lists whose cutoff rate is within the confidence interval of the test result — and to be cautious when a test result is above the break-even point.

A clear implication of this analysis is that the size of the confidence interval is related to the number of pieces mailed. Remember, the confidence interval is equal to the response rate plus or minus 1.96 standard errors. And the standard error is calculated using the equation:

$$SE = \sqrt{(p \times (1-p))/n}$$

In the case where the response rate is 3.5 percent, $(p \times (1-p))$ will always be equal to $(.035 \times .965)$ or 0.034, no matter what the size of the sample. Therefore, the larger the sample, the smaller the standard error. If $n = 1,000$, then the standard error is $\sqrt{.034/1,000}$ or .005811. If n were 10,000, then the standard error would be $\sqrt{.034/10,000}$ or .001837, and so on.

Following this example, it is clear that if we have some idea of how large an error we are prepared to tolerate, and if we have some idea of the expected response rate, we can use the above information to solve for the number of pieces to mail.

For example, if we think the true response rate is 3.5 percent, but we want to be 95 percent certain that our test mailing will tell us if the true response rate is between 3.3 and 3.7 percent, we are in effect saying that we want 1.96 times the standard error to be equal to .002 or 0.2 percent — because 3.5 percent plus or minus 0.2 percent is equal to 3.3 to 3.7 percent. Statisticians use the term *precision* to describe the amount of error we are willing to tolerate on either side of the expected response rate.

Therefore, in this example:

$$\text{Precision} = .002 = 1.96 \times SE \text{ (standard error)}$$

Then, solving for SE we get:

$$SE = .002/1.96 = .001020$$

and

$$SE = \sqrt{(p \times (1-p)/n)}$$

Thus,

$$.001020 = \sqrt{(p \times (1-p)/n)}$$

and, substituting .035 for p and .965 for $(1-p)$, we get:

$$.001020 = \sqrt{(.033775/n)}$$

and, squaring both sides of the equation, we get:

$$0.00000104 = .033775/n$$
$$n = .033775/.00000104 = 32{,}437$$

In general, then, the rule for determining the number of pieces to mail (at the 95 percent level of confidence) is equal to:

$$n = \frac{(p) \times (1-p) \times 1.96^2}{\text{Precision}^2}$$

where:

$$p = \text{Expected response rate}$$
$$\text{Precision} = \text{One half the 95 percent confidence interval}$$

ILLUSTRATION 7

Suppose the cataloger mailed not only one new list but two new lists, and suppose the second list consisted of 1,200 names and pulled 4.5 percent. Are the true response rates for the two lists unequal? Can we declare with 95 percent confidence that the true response rates are different?

What are we really asking? If we believe the two lists have the same true response rate, then we are in effect saying that we think the difference between the two true response rates is equal to zero, and the difference we observed is due to chance.[3]

In this case, the difference in response rates is equal to 1 percent (4.5 − 3.5 percent). So then we are really asking, "how likely is it to find a difference in sample response rates of 1 percent, when there is no difference in true response rates?"

If this test of the two lists were repeated many times, there would always be differences between the lists, but statistical theory tells us that

---

[3] In statistics, the argument that there is no difference between two percentages (two response rates in direct marketing language) is referred to as the *null hypothesis*. When a statistical test indicates that there is no difference between response rates, a statistician would say that we accept the null hypothesis; and conversely, when we find a statistically significant difference, a statistician would say that we reject the null hypothesis.

the differences would be approximately normally distributed – and if the two lists had the same true response rate, the average or mean difference would be zero.

Our discussion of the normal distribution told us that in any normally distributed population, 95 percent of all observations would fall within a range equal to 1.96 standard errors, and that 90 percent of all observations would fall within range of 1.64 standard errors. In the latter situation, 5 percent of the observations would be below 1.64 standard errors from the mean and 5 percent above 1.64 standard errors from the mean. In situations where we want to be 95 percent sure one number is greater than another, not just different but greater, we use 1.64 standard errors as our factor to determine statistical significance.

Now the question of whether 4.5 percent is different from 3.5 percent starts to come into sharper focus. The question can now be restated to read, "can we be 95 percent certain that an observed difference of 1 percent is more than 1.64 standard errors away from a mean value of zero?" Well, if 1.64 is the benchmark, all we have to do is divide 1 percent by the correct measure of the standard error and see if the result is more or less than 1.64. If it is more than 1.64, we will say that this difference couldn't be due to chance and we'll declare the difference to be statistically significant. If the result is less than 1.64, we'll say the difference may be due to chance and we will not declare the lists to be different.

It is algebraically cumbersome to calculate the standard error of a difference between two response rates. The reader shouldn't worry if he or she gets lost. The concept is important, but we'll try the algebra anyway.

First, we must estimate the true response rate, given the two results and the number of pieces mailed on both sides of the test. In effect, we calculate a weighted average response rate.

Remember, the first list test was mailed to 1,000 persons and the response rate was 3.5 percent.

$$p1 = .035$$
$$n1 = 1,000$$

The second list test was mailed to 1,200 persons and the response rate was 4.5 percent.

$$p2 = .045$$
$$n2 = 1,200$$

The average value, called p, is equal to:

$$p = \frac{p1 \times n1 + p2 \times n2}{n1 + n2}$$

$$p = \frac{.035 \times 1,000 + .045 \times 1,200}{1,000 + 1,200} = \frac{89}{2,200} = .04045$$

The standard error of p equals

$$SE = \sqrt{(p) \times (1-p)} \times \frac{n1 + n2}{n1 \times n2}$$

$$SE = \sqrt{(.040450) \times (1 - .040450)} \times \frac{1,000 + 1,200}{1,000 \times 1,200}$$

$$SE = \sqrt{.03881379} \times \frac{2,200}{1,200,000}$$

$$SE = \sqrt{.03881379 \times .001833}$$

$$SE = \sqrt{.00007159}$$

$$SE = .0084355$$

Now we divide the observed difference by the standard error of the difference:

$$.01/.0084355 = 1.185 < 1.64$$

Since the observed difference divided by the standard error of the difference is less than 1.64, we can say that the difference is not statistically significant at the 95 percent level of confidence.

What if the same response rates were achieved but the quantity mailed on each side of the test were 5,000? Without going through all of the arithmetic, the answer is that the observed difference of 1 percent would be divided by a standard error that would now equal 0.003919 and the result of 2.55 would be greater than 1.64, so we would say that there is a statistically significant difference in response rates. Again, the point is that the larger the sample size, the more confident one can be in one's results. No real surprise, but a factor that will come up again and again as we move into statistical modeling.

The questions of statistical significance and sample size can be answered through the formulas presented in this chapter; however, to make life a little easier for our readers, we've included in Appendix III three Lotus 1-2-3 programs that automatically calculate confidence intervals, sample size, and test for statistical signficance. Sample screens and the cell formulas supporting each screen are included.

TESTS OF SIGNIFICANCE – TWO TYPES OF ERRORS AND POWER

We hope the relationship between confidence interval and significance testing is apparent by now. In a test versus control situation, if the test result lies within the confidence interval of the control, then the finding is that the test is not different from the control. If the test result lies outside the confidence interval of the control, then we say the test result is significantly different from the control.

Implicitly related to both confidence intervals and significance tests are two kinds of errors. Recall that we state our findings with a confidence level of less than 100 percent but typically greater than 95 percent. Thus, if we are confident 95 percent of the time, what about the other 5 percent of the time? The other 5 percent of the time we make errors. Statisticians call them Type I and Type II errors.

To understand Type I and Type II errors, let's think about them in our test versus control situation, and let's assume that the observed test result is greater than the observed control result.

A *Type I* error occurs when we

Reject the null hypothesis H when it is true.

The null hypothesis states that there is *no* difference between reponse rates. Therefore, when we reject the null hypothesis, we are in effect accepting the conclusion that the difference in observed rates is significant. So, if we make a Type I error, and reject the null hypothesis when it is true, we therefore are also making the error of believing that (in our test/control situation) the test result is greater than the control result, and we would therefore act to replace the control, when in fact the control should be maintained.

The probability of making this kind of error is defined by the alpha level you establish. The alpha level is equal to 1 minus the confidence level. A decision to work at the 95 percent confidence level means that you have established a 5 percent alpha level. Having established a 5 percent alpha level, you are in effect saying that 5 percent of the time you may be making this kind of error. If you want to be even more sure of not making this kind of error, reduce alpha to, say, 1 percent. This will have the effect of increasing the confidence interval of the control, thereby requiring an even higher test response before the observed response rate can be declared to be statistically different—in this case, greater.

A *Type II* error occurs when we

Accept the null hypothesis when it is false.

Again, in a test versus control situation where the observed test result is greater than the control result, acceptance of the null hypothesis when it is false means not recognizing a test that really beat the control.

Now we would also like to make the chances of making a Type II error as small as possible. But here's the catch—the probability of making a Type II error, called beta, is mathematically related, in a complicated way, to alpha. As alpha decreases, beta increases. So if you want to make the probability of making a Type II error small, you have to make alpha, the probability of making a Type I error, large.

What do you want to do as a businessperson? Suppose you have a good solid business, with a control offer that makes money. You run a test of a new offer and it appears to beat the control. But what if this is one of the situations in which acting on the test results will result in implementing a Type I error? You never know when this is happening! Clearly, as a prudent businessperson, you don't want to roll out a test that is really not better than your control. One approach is to set a low alpha, between 1 percent and 5 percent, if the economics of the situation warrant such care, and don't worry about making a Type II error.

To summarize, in most situations you want to be conservative—if you are going to make an error, you don't want to accept a difference as significant when it is not. In statistical terms, therefore, you want to minimize the probability of making a Type I error. Beyond lowering alpha, this can be accomplished by increasing sample size, not surprising since we know that confidence intervals are reduced when sample size is increased. It is even possible to state statistically how certain you are of not making a Type II error. This is called the *power* of the test. The mathematics are complicated but the point to remember is that the power of the test increases as sample size increases.

CHAPTER 10

RELATIONSHIPS BETWEEN VARIABLES

With some of the fundamentals of statistical analysis behind us, we can now begin to study the *relationship between variables,* which is the subject matter of statistical modeling. Simply stated, two variables are related if they move together in some way.

Variables can be related in varying degree from strong to weak, including a perfect relationship or no relationship at all. With a strong relationship, knowing the value of one variable will tell us a lot about the value of the other variable; knowing everything, we have a perfect relationship. With a weak relationship, knowing one variable will tell us little about the other variable; knowing nothing, we have no relationship at all.

ILLUSTRATION 8

Let's return to our cataloger, who just tested a mailing of two different catalogs (A and B) to both new and old customers. The mailer wants to know which customers, new or old, buy more from which catalog, A or B.

To address this query, our cataloger's analyst pulls a small sample of 100 names to see if there is a relationship between customer type and catalog received.

The sample results are in Table 10–1.

From Table 10–1, we see that all new customers buy only from Catalog A, and all old customers buy from only Catalog B. In terms of percentages, we have:

1. 100 percent of new customers buy from A and 0 percent from B.
2. 100 percent of old customers buy from B and 0 percent from A.

TABLE 10–1

| | Customer Type | | | | | |
Catalog	New	Percent	Old	Percent	Total	Percent
A	50	100%	0	0%	50	50%
B	0	0%	50	100%	50	50%
	50	100%	50	100%	100	100%

TABLE 10–2

| | Customer Type | | | | | |
Catalog	New	Percent	Old	Percent	Total	Percent
A	500	50%	500	50%	1,000	50%
B	500	50%	500	50%	1,000	50%
	1,000	100%	1,000	100%	2,000	100%

Apparently, there is a perfect relationship between the variables CUS-TOMER TYPE and CATALOG.

It is interesting to plot the percentages of Table 10–1. In Figure 10–1, the percentages are plotted with a vertical axis of percent of customers buying from Catalog A and a horizontal axis of CUSTOMER TYPE. We see a line with a steep slope, which tells us in some obscure way that the relationship is perfect.

Although the analysis seems convincing, the analyst wants to validate the finding with another somewhat larger sample. The results of a second sample of names are shown in Table 10–2.

The findings of Table 10–2 look drastically different than the findings of Table 10–1.

1. 50 percent of new customers buy from A and 50 percent from B.
2. 50 percent of old customers buy from B and 50 percent from A.

Clearly, there is no relationship between the CUSTOMER TYPE and CATALOG; for every new customer buying from B there is an old customer buying from A.

In Figure 10–2, the plot for the percentages of Table 10–2 shows us a horizontal line, or a line with no slope, which, following the logic of the plot in Figure 10–1, tells us there is no relationship.

FIGURE 10–1

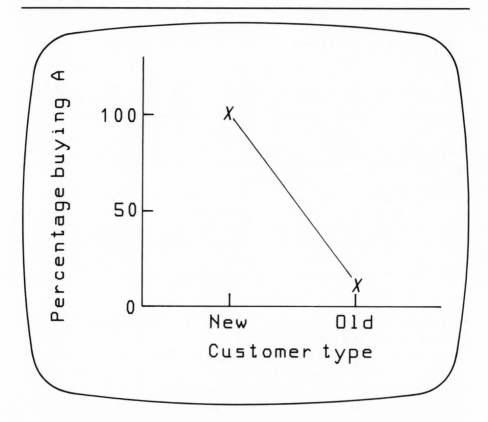

The analyst, somewhat disturbed by the two conflicting sample results, pulls a third and much larger sample to obtain a truer picture of the house file. The sample results are in Table 10–3.

From Table 10–3, we have:

1. 84 percent of new customers come from A and 16 percent from B.
2. 13 percent of old customers come from A and 87 percent from B.

The corresponding plot is in Figure 10–3. The slope of this line is between the slopes of the perfect line (in Figure 10–1) and the no relationship, horizontal line (Figure 10–2). It would seem that the closer this line's slope is to the perfect line's slope, the stronger the relationship; and conversely, the more this line's slope conforms to the no relationship line's slope, the weaker the relationship. How do we measure this relationship between CUSTOMER TYPE and CATALOG? Between any two variables?

FIGURE 10–2

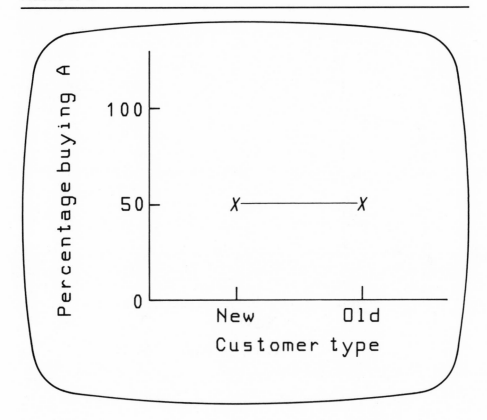

TABLE 10–3

Catalog	Customer Type				Total	Percent
	New	Percent	Old	Percent		
A	110,300	84%	11,500	13%	121,800	56%
B	20,700	16%	76,600	87%	97,300	44%
	131,000	100%	88,100	100%	219,100	100%

CORRELATION COEFFICIENT

As you may suspect, there are statistical measures to indicate the degree of relationship between two variables. The most popular measure is the *correlation coefficient (r),* which is the workhorse of many statistical

FIGURE 10–3

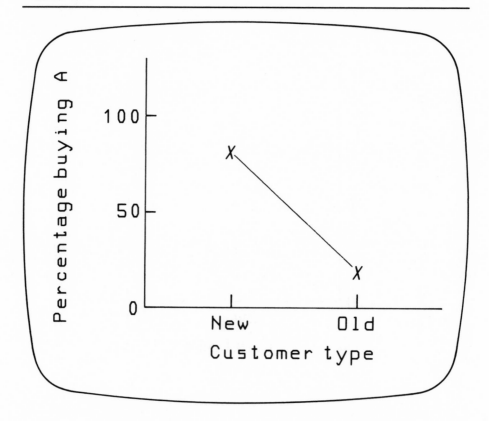

theories, applications, and analyses. The correlation coefficient is used either directly or indirectly in statistical work ranging in complexity from 2 × 2 tables (like Tables 10–1 to 10–3), to simple regression models, to multiple regression models, factor and cluster analyses, and more.

For categorical variables, the correlation coefficient *r* takes on values ranging from 0 to 1, where:

0 indicates no relationship
1 indicates a perfect relationship
Values between 0 and 1 indicate a weak to moderate to strong relationship

as depicted in Figure 10–4.

Returning to Table 10–3, our analyst calculates the correlation coefficient using a formula that applies to categorical variables and

FIGURE 10–4
Strength of Relationship as _r_ Goes from 0 to 1

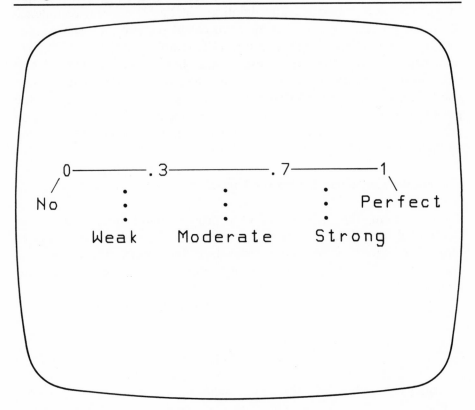

determines that $r = .702$. Accordingly, the relationship between CUS-TOMER TYPE and CATALOG is strong.

Descriptively, we declare the relationship as strong; but is the relationship significant? Again, the analyst may choose to call the finding significant or not important based on experience. Or the analyst can defer to the objectivity of tests of significance, which address the issue of whether or not the finding of $r = .702$ is due to chance (sample variation) or is beyond chance. The former implies the finding is not statistically significant, and the latter implies statistical significance. Fortunately, all computer programs you are likely to encounter calculate the correlation coefficient and a measure of the statistical significance of the correlation for you automatically, so we won't burden you with formulas for these calculations. The measure of statistical significance is, as you might imagine from Chapter 9, related to the concept of the normal distribution and confidence intervals. However, instead of declaring the coefficient of correlation to be statistically significant at the 95 percent confidence level, the programs produce a measure called the *p*-value. The *p*-value indicates the likelihood or probability of the sample correlation coefficient occurring given that there is no true relationship between the variables. If the *p*-value is less than .05 or 5 percent, then we conclude that the true coefficient is not zero and that there is a significant relationship. If the *p*-value is greater than 5 percent, then we conclude the true correlation coefficient is zero and that there is no significant relationship between the variables.

Correlation Coefficient for Scalar Variables

To the extent that scalar variables provide more information than categorical variables, the correlation coefficient for scalar variables gives more information about the relationship. Specifically, the correlation coefficient for scalar variables indicates both the *direction* and *degree* or strength of a *straight-line* relationship.

These concepts are best explained with an illustration.

ILLUSTRATION 9

Consider two scalar variables *x* and *y*, whose pairs of points are depicted in Figure 10–5. We see that large values of *x* correspond to large values of *y*, and that the reverse is also true — small values of *x* correspond to small values of *y*. The dots or points on the graph each represent a single observation of an *x* − *y* relationship. The entire set of points is called a *scatter plot* or *scatter diagram*. Finally, one could easily imagine drawing a straight line through the points, as in Figure 10–6.

The straight line has a positive slope, that is, as *x* increases in value, *y* also increases in value. So we say there is a positive straight-line relationship between *x* and *y*.

In Figure 10–7, we have an opposite pattern of scatter points: Large values of *x* corresponding to small values of *y*. A straight line could still be drawn through the scatter points, but in this case the slope of the line would be negative. As *x* increases, *y* decreases. Therefore, we would say that a negative straight-line relationship exists between *x* and *y*.

FIGURE 10–5
Scatter Plot

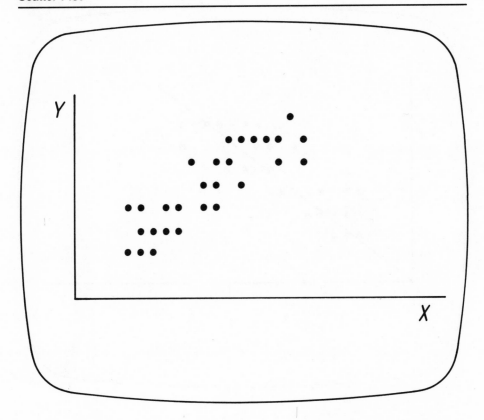

Accordingly, when working with scalar or continuous data, as opposed to categorical data, the correlation coefficient can range in values between −1 and +1 where:

> 0 indicates no relationship
> +1 indicates a perfect positive relationship
> −1 indicates a perfect negative relationship
> Values between 0 and 1 or 0 to −1 indicate a weak to moderate to strong relationship

as depicted in Figure 10–8.

FIGURE 10–6

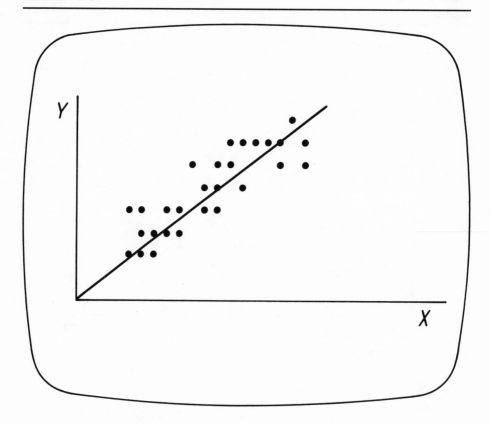

Correlation Coefficient in Practice

There are two basic issues when working with correlation coefficients in practice. First, are the data straight or linear? Pictorially, can the relationship between the x variable and the y variable be adequately expressed by a straight line? Second, as previously discussed, is the relationship between the two variables significant?

Are the Data Straight?
The correlation coefficient for scalar variables should be used to measure the strength of a straight-line relationship. That is, the use of r is only valid when the data suggests a straight-line relationship. To the extent that the data does not support a straight-line or linear relationship, r can be

FIGURE 10–7

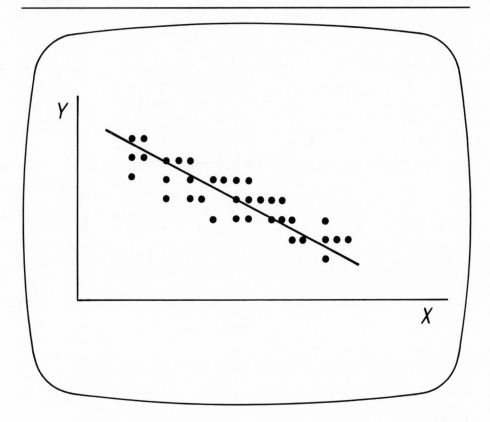

misleading. In other words, an *r* of 1 does not guarantee that the data are straight, nor does an *r* of 0 indicate that the variables are not related. Accordingly, we use scatter plots to see what the data suggests. An illustration will make this point.

ILLUSTRATION 10

Consider the four sets of *x,y* data in Table 10–4. Although the sets have equal means, variances, and correlation coefficients, the scatter plots clearly show different relationships. (See Figures 10–9 through 10–12.)

FIGURE 10–8

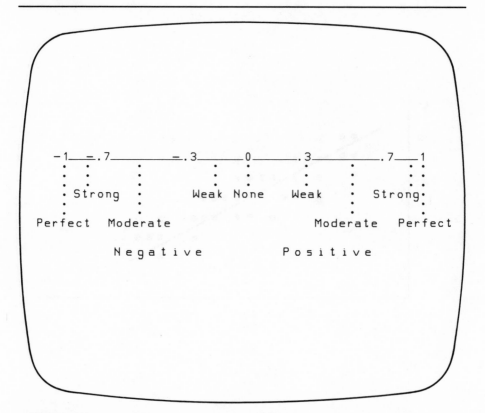

TABLE 10–4
Four Data Sets with Equal Descriptive Measures

	x1	y1	x2	y2	x3	y3	x4	y4
	10	8.04	10	9.14	10	7.46	8	6.58
	8	6.95	8	8.14	8	6.77	8	5.76
	13	7.58	13	8.74	13	12.74	8	7.71
	9	8.81	9	8.77	9	7.11	8	8.84
	11	8.33	11	9.26	11	7.81	8	8.47
	14	9.96	14	8.10	14	8.84	8	7.04
	6	7.24	6	6.13	6	6.08	8	5.25
	4	4.26	4	3.10	4	5.39	19	12.50
	12	10.84	12	9.13	12	8.15	8	5.56
	7	4.82	7	7.26	7	6.42	8	7.91
	5	5.65	5	4.74	5	5.73	8	6.89
Mean	9	7.50	9	7.50	9	7.50	9	7.50
Variance	10.96	4.12	10.96	4.12	10.96	4.12	10.96	4.12
r		.81		.81		.81		.81

S. Chatterjee and B. Price, *Regression Analysis by Example* (New York: John Wiley and Sons, 1977), p. 8.

FIGURE 10–9
Plot of Y1, X1

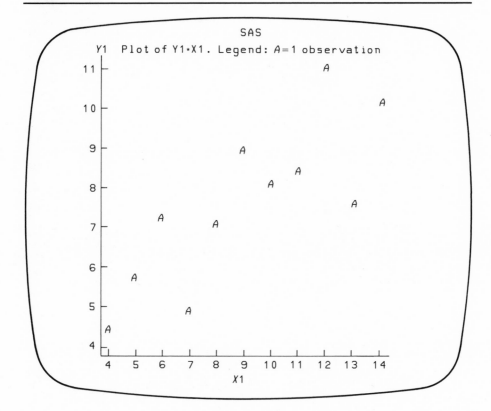

In Figure 10–9, the relationship is straight; therefore, *r* can be used confidently to assess the straight-line relationship between *X*1 and *Y*1.

In Figure 10–10, the relationship is curved down and the use of *r* is not necessarily recommended; however, certain measures can be taken to salvage the relationship. More about this later.

In Figure 10–11, the relationship appears straight except for the wild point at (13,12.74), which must be examined. If the point is a "typo-mistake," then *r* should be calculated after removing the point and the resultant *r* value can be used with confidence.

If the point is a valid but unusual observation, then either more data should be collected to firm up the shape of the relationship, or the special situation in which it occurred should be investigated, for the information surrounding the situation may be more helpful than *r* itself.

FIGURE 10–10
Plot of *Y2*, *X2*

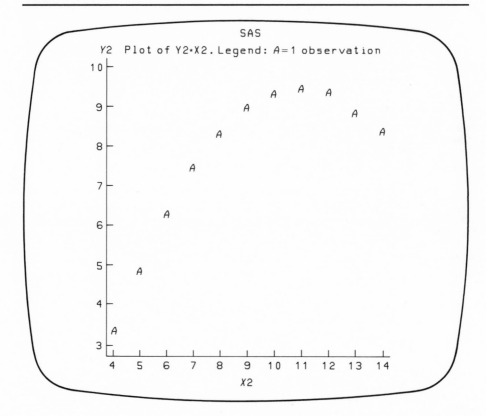

The relationship shown in Figure 10–12, which is really no relation-ship at all, is an example of how misleading statistics can be and why it is always important whenever possible to look at pictures of data, not just summary statistics.

SIMPLE REGRESSION

Now that we have a way of measuring the extent to which knowing one variable tells us something about the other variable, let's see how to extend this process to *predict* the value of one variable based on the value of the other variable, or from the value of many other variables. The technique is called *regression: simple* regression when there is only

FIGURE 10–11
Plot of Y3, X3

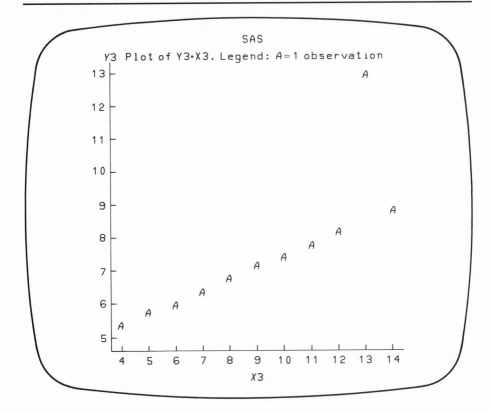

one other variable, and *multiple* regression when there are many other variables.

In statistics, the variable we want to be able to predict or forecast is called the *dependent* or *criterion variable.* The variable or variables used to make the prediction or forecast is called the *independent* or *predictor* variable(s).

The input for a simple regression is a table, where the first column consists of data for the independent variable *(X)* we always know, and the second column consists of data for the dependent variable *(Y)*, the variable we are trying to predict. The output of the regression is an equation that permits us to:

1. Explain why the values of *Y* vary as they do.
2. Predict *Y* based on the known values of *X.*

FIGURE 10–12
Plot of Y4, X4

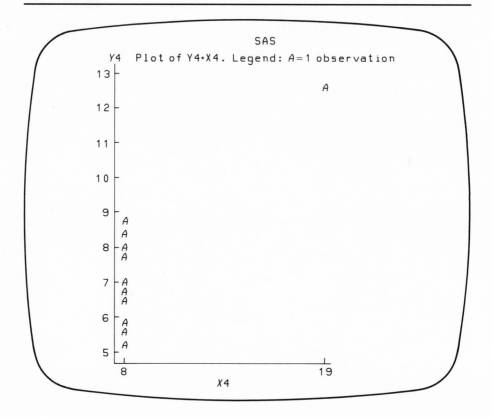

The equation is based on the relationship between X values and Y values for simple regression; and on the relationship between each X and Y, and among the Xs themselves, for multiple regression.

The Regression Line

What makes regression tick?

ILLUSTRATION 11

Let's return to our catalog example, where we learned that there was a relationship between the length of time our customers have been on the file and sales. Remember, new customers purchased more orders and produced greater sales than old customers.

If we define length of time on file more specifically as the independent variable *(X)*, the number of months since the date of first purchase, and the dependent variable, the variable we would like to be able to predict *(Y)*, as the dollar value of sales within the last month, we can build a model that will relate date of first purchase to sales.

Suppose our analyst draws a sample of 15 customer records from the house file, and puts the data into a table format. (See Table 10–5.) Let's begin our analysis with a scatter plot of the observations, where *Y* (sales) is plotted on the vertical axis and *X* (months since date of first purchase) is the horizontal axis. (See Figure 10–13.)

We would like to draw a straight line using a ruler and our eye such that it passes through the middle of the cloud of points. Our objective should be to draw the line such that a more or less equal number of points lie above and below the line. The reader will recall (we hope) from simple algebra that the equation of a straight line is:

$$Y = mX + b$$

where:

b = the point at which the line would cross the Y axis
m = the slope of the line, or the rate at which Y increases as X increases

We'll review this in more detail below.

In Figure 10–13, we draw such a line through the points and estimate that the line has a slope of 1.0 and intercept of 10.0. The "eye fitted" regression line is therefore:

$$Y = 10.0 + 1.0 \times X$$

The goal of having the line have as many points above it as below it relates to the statistical objective of minimizing the difference between the actual observations and the estimated observations referred to as the *fit*. The difference between an actual observation and a fitted point is called a *residual*. This leads to a very important identity:

An actual observation = A fitted observation + A residual

or more simply:

Residual = Actual − Fit

Recalling the canceling out problem when measuring variation, a reasonable way to measure the *goodness-of-fit* of a line, fitted by eye or by

TABLE 10–5

X Months since First Purchase	Y Dollar Sales in Past Month
3	10
3	9
3	12
5	15
5	13
5	11
7	14
9	18
9	17
9	15
13	23
13	21
13	16
15	26
15	23
15	20
19	30
19	27
19	23

formal statistical methods, would be to use the total sum of squares of residuals. Accordingly, the line or equation with the smallest total or mean *residual sum of squares* is said to have the best fit of the data.

It turns out that the most common fitting rule, referred to as *least-squares,* uses residual sum of squares as just described and produces the smallest residual sum of squares. Accordingly, the resultant equation, called the *ordinary least-squares regression equation,* produces the best fit of the data and is considered the best equation. The equation for the simple regression is:

$$Y = b0 + b1 \times X1$$

where:

b0 = A constant called the Y intercept because it is the point on the Y axis through which the regression line passes when the value of X equals 0.

b1 = the slope of the regression line, referred to as the *regression coefficient.*

Most algebra texts use the letter *m* to represent the slope but in statistics texts, *b* is used to represent this concept.

FIGURE 10–13
Plot of Y, X

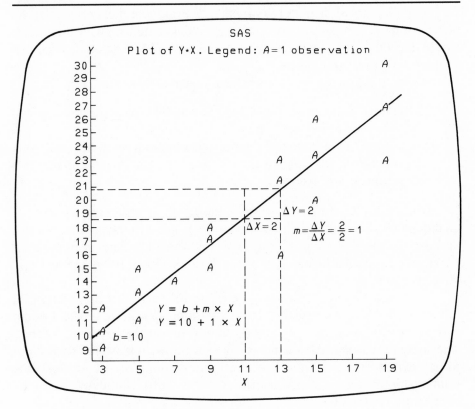

Simple Regression in Practice

Simple regression in practice is easy and fun because there are only five steps to take in order to complete the regression analysis:

1. Turn observations into data (variables).
2. Assess whether the relationship between the X and Y variables is linear or straight.
3. Straighten out the relationship, if needed.
4. Perform the regression analysis using any one of a number of computer programs.
5. Interpret the findings.

We will illustrate the steps with a new example.

ILLUSTRATION 12

Let's build a regression model to support the argument that customers who purchase more frequently also buy bigger ticket items. Accordingly, we would like a model to predict largest-dollar-item (LDI) amounts based on frequency of prior purchases.

Again, the first step is to transform observations into data.

1. We must define a period of time in which to measure frequency of purchase. Let's choose the past 12 months.
2. Find the LDI amount among customers who made only one purchase in the past year; among customers who made two purchases; and so on.

Based on a large random sample, the resulting data array consists of an independent variable X, the number of purchases in the past 12 months, and a dependent variable Y, the LDI amount. (The largest number of purchases in 12 months was 9, thus the X ranges from 1 to 9.) (See Table 10–6.)

To assess the relationship between X and Y, we review the scatter plot in Figure 10–14, which reveals that the relationship is more or less straight except for what looks like a curved relationship in the lower left corner. The curve is not too terrible, and we chose for now, at least, not to attempt to straighten it out. Thus, we feel the assumption of straight-line relationship has been met, which enables us to confidently use the correlation coefficient.

A regression analysis was performed on the data (using one of the standard statistical software packages, in this case SAS^{tm}) resulting in the following output.

Variation of Y: Variance: 792.94

Total sum of squares: 6,343.55

Correlation coefficient: $r = +0.97254$

Intercept, $b0$: -18.22

Regression coefficient, $b1$: 10.00, with p value of .001

The regression equation is:

$$Y = -18.22 + 10.00 \times X$$

The large positive value of r indicates there is a positive and strong

TABLE 10–6

X Number of Purchases	Y LDI
1	2
2	3
3	10
4	15
5	26
6	35
7	50
8	63
9	82

FIGURE 10–14
Plot of Y, X

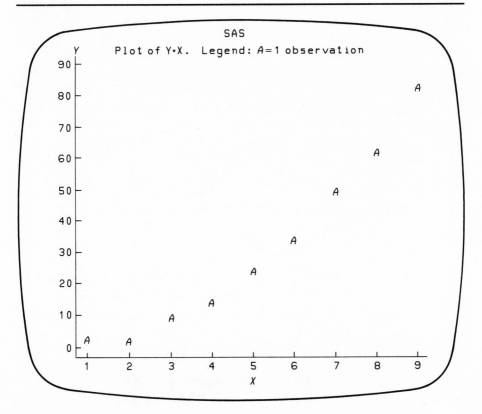

straight-line relationship between X and Y, which is consistent with the hypothesis that large sales are associated with frequent purchase.

A second and perhaps more useful interpretation of r is obtained by squaring its value and relating it to the amount of variation of Y that is accounted for by X.

This statistic r squared is probably the most popular statistic associated with the output of a regression model. r squared goes under the name of the *coefficient of determination,* and it ranges in value from 0 to 1.

In this case, r squared is .946 or 94.6 percent. Therefore, we can say that 94.6 percent of the variation of Y can be accounted for by X. (Technically, of the variation [total sum of squares] of Y, 6,343, X accounts for 94.6 percent, or 6,000.)

The intercept has limited meaning and in most cases can be viewed as a "placeholder" in the equation. When the equation is built with X values that include zero, the intercept has meaning and the predicted value of Y when X equals zero can be used reliably. In the present example, the intercept must be treated as a placeholder because the predicted LDI amount is a nonsensical negative $18.22.

The regression coefficient $b1$ represents the change in Y for every change in X. That is, every additional purchase made (in the past 12 months) is associated with an increase in average LDI dollars (Y) of $10.

Is this $10 increase significant? Maybe it is due to the sample drawn, sample variation. The p value, the probability of a value of $b1 = \$10$ occurring by chance only, is .001. Since this is less than the usual .05 level, we conclude that the regression coefficient is statistically significant and the $10 increase for every additional purchase is meaningful.

The use of the regression equation as a predictive model is easy: To predict the expected largest-dollar-item amount from a customer who has made, say, three purchases in the past 12 months, simply plug in a value of 3 for X in the equation and calculate the Y.

$$Y = -18.22 + 10.00 \times 3$$
$$= 11.78$$

Thus, the expected dollar amount of the largest dollar item made by a customer with three purchases in the past 12 months is $11.78.

STRAIGHTENING OUT THE DATA

This just about wraps up the simple regression analysis of the data. However, what about that curve in the data? Since the analysis rests on the data being straight, *perhaps* the regression results will be better—in terms of explanatory and predictive powers—if we can straighten out the data to remove the curve. We say perhaps because straightening out the data may not necessarily make things better. Straightening out the data involves transforming or reexpressing the data (variables) by means of arithmetic operations, which include taking logs, squaring, and raising to powers. The choice of which operation or combination of operations to use may involve more art than science.

Accordingly, we use the reexpression that raises Y to the ½ power, more commonly termed as *taking the square root of Y* ($\sqrt{Y}$). The effect on Y values from the square root reexpression is in Table 10–7. The range of the new values is much smaller than the original values ($9.05 - 1.41 = 7.64$ compared to $82 - 2 = 80$), and the new values are also much closer to one another than are the original values.[1]

The scatter plot of X and $\sqrt{Y}$ is in Figure 10–15. The curve is gone. The data look very straight. The new r is .99750, which is an improvement of 2.56 percent over the original r of .97254. Is this 2.56 percent improvement enough to make a difference, enough to bother with reexpressing?

Explanatory Power

An r of .99750 implies that virtually all, 99.5 percent, of the variation of the new reexpressed variable $\sqrt{Y}$ is explained by X. The 2.56 percent represents "topping the gas tank" and appears not to be a substantial improvement. Thus, reexpression here does not help in terms of explanatory power.

Predictive Power

The new (predictive) regression equation is:

$$\sqrt{Y} = .108845 + .984016 \times X$$

---

[1] The "magic" of reexpression, which is beyond the scope of this chapter, lies in the property that the reexpression preserves the order of the values. That is, the smallest original value is also the smallest new value, and the largest original value is the largest new value. The same holds true for all the values in between.

TABLE 10–7

X	Y	$\sqrt{Y}$
1	2	1.41
2	3	1.73
3	10	3.16
4	15	3.87
5	26	5.09
6	35	5.91
7	50	7.07
8	63	7.93
9	82	9.05

FIGURE 10–15
Plot of $\sqrt{Y}$, X

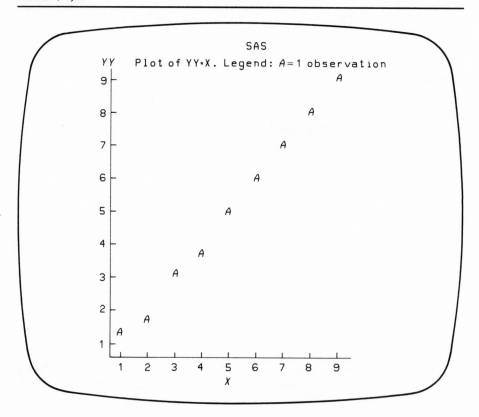

TABLE 10–8

Data			Estimated Y Original Model	Error	Estimated Value $\sqrt{Y}$	Estimated Value Y − sqrt Model	Error
X	Y	$\sqrt{Y}$					
1	2	1.41	−8.22	10.22	1.09	1.19	0.81
2	3	1.73	1.78	1.22	2.08	4.31	−1.31
3	10	3.16	11.78	−1.78	3.06	9.37	0.63
4	15	3.87	21.78	−6.78	4.05	16.36	−1.36
5	26	5.09	31.78	−5.78	5.03	25.29	0.71
6	35	5.92	41.78	−6.78	6.01	36.16	−1.16
7	50	7.07	51.78	−1.78	7.00	48.96	1.04
8	63	7.93	61.78	1.22	7.98	63.70	−0.70
9	82	9.05	71.78	10.22	8.97	80.38	1.63

TABLE 10–9

Data		Estimated Y Original Model	Error	Error Squared	Estimated Value Y − sqrt Model	Error	Error Squared
X	Y						
1	2	−8.22	10.22	104.04	1.19	0.81	0.64
2	3	1.78	1.22	1.44	4.31	−1.31	1.71
3	10	11.78	−1.78	2.89	9.37	0.63	0.39
4	15	21.78	−6.78	44.89	16.36	−1.36	1.84
5	26	31.78	−5.78	32.49	25.29	0.71	0.49
6	35	41.78	−6.78	44.89	36.16	−1.16	1.32
7	50	51.78	−1.78	2.89	48.96	1.04	1.08
8	63	61.78	1.22	1.44	63.70	−0.70	0.47
9	82	71.78	10.22	104.04	80.38	1.63	2.85
Total				339.01			10.79
Mean				37.06			1.19

To assess the predictive gain of the new regression model over the original regression model, we look to see which model predicts better, that is, produces the smallest residual. (See Table 10–8.)

An examination of Table 10–8 shows that the errors or residuals resulting from the transformed data are clearly smaller than the residuals produced from the model built on the original data. In particular, the errors around the extreme values of X are smaller. When X equals 1 or 9, the errors are very large, which is characteristic of linear regression models applied to curved data.

In Table 10–9, we calculate the sum of the residuals squared to demonstrate that the straightened model produces a much smaller sum of squares. The sum of the errors or residuals squared using the original data is equal to 339.01. The sum of the residuals squared using the transformed data, the straightened model, is 10.79.

CHAPTER 11

MULTIPLE REGRESSION

Multiple regression is used in situations where it is believed that more than one independent variable affects the dependent variable. Since, in practice, there is almost always more than one independent variable affecting the dependent variable, we almost always use multiple rather than simple regression.

The form of the multiple regression model is given by the following equation:

$$Y = b0 + b1 \times X1 + b2 \times X2 + b3 \times X3 + \ldots + bn \times Xn,$$

where:

$$X1, X2, X3, \ldots, Xn = \text{Independent variables}$$
$$Y = \text{Dependent variable}$$
$$b0 = \text{A constant again, but this time}$$
it's impossible to visualize, since the intercept is going through a multidimensional plane.
$$b1, b2, b3, \ldots, bn = \text{Regression coefficients associated}$$
with the n variables $X1, \ldots, Xn$.

Multiple regression is obviously much more complicated than simple regression. In simple (one-variable) linear regression, we always know what the two variables in the model are, and we simply decide which variable is the dependent variable and which is the independent variable. In a simple two-variable regression model, it is also fairly easy to look at a scatter plot of the relationship and determine if the relationship is linear or if the relationship needs to be straightened by the use of some transformation.

With multiple regression, in practice, the tasks are more complicated. Assuming for the moment that we know the dependent variable we want to predict (which is not always the case), we have to make the following decisions:

1. Which variables in our database should be included in the model and which should not? A direct marketing company may have literally hundreds of variables to choose from, making variable selection a difficult and time-consuming task.

2. Is the relationship between the dependent variable and each of the variables to be included in the model linear, or must transformation be performed?

3. Is the dependent variable normally distributed for all values of the independent variables? This is one of the basic assumptions of regression, needed for tests of significance. If non-normality exists, transformations can be used to induce normality.

4. Without regard to their relationship with the dependent variable, are the independent variables each normally distributed? This condition is often overlooked in practice when building regression models. We'll talk about the consequence of this later in the chapter.

5. Are there variables that affect the dependent variables that we might have overlooked because they are not "natural" variables themselves but really contrived variables made from combinations of two or more independent variables? These are called *interaction variables* and we'll talk more about them later as well.

6. When we add many variables to our models, are the independent variables themselves highly correlated, causing a condition known as *multicollinearity;* if so, what effect will this have on the reliability of the models we produce?

Despite all these complexities, the procedures for performing multiple regression are a straightforward extension of the simple regression. We'll illustrate these procedures and present solutions to all of the issues raised above through the use of a number of examples.

ILLUSTRATION 13

Let's return to our cataloger, who now believes that by knowing the age (AGE) and income (INCOME) of customers, a model can be built using these two variables to predict dollars spent in the last six months (DOLLSPENT). The analyst draws a sample from the house file and captures the three variables (see Table 11–1), and performs a multiple

TABLE 11–1

Income (thousands)	Age (years)	DOLLSPENT
$35.6	52.5	$54.1
40.9	57.2	52.4
38.6	58.0	56.1
48.7	52.9	41.4
43.9	53.0	58.0
51.2	52.5	47.1
48.1	57.4	52.5
42.0	54.5	50.8
45.9	66.3	64.9
49.8	60.2	54.0
48.9	51.1	46.4
42.5	51.7	54.7
36.4	51.8	57.1
33.3	51.3	55.4
30.6	57.8	57.7
33.5	54.7	62.8
44.4	62.6	58.7
36.5	56.3	69.9
43.0	60.3	63.2
37.4	50.8	59.1

Variation of DOLLSPENT: Variance: 4,427.65
Total sum of squares; 84,126.55
Correlation coefficient: multiple R-square = .5480
Intercept, $b0$; 351.29
Regression coefficients:
$b1$ for INCOME: -0.65 with a p value of .0020
$b2$ for AGE: .86 with a p value of .0038

regression of DOLLSPENT on INCOME and AGE, which results in the output shown in Table 11–1.

The multiple regression equation is:

$$DOLLSPENT = 351.29 - .65 \times INCOME + .86 \times AGE$$

MULTIPLE REGRESSION STATISTICS – HOW TO READ THEM

The first thing we notice about multiple regression statistics is that they look very much like the statistics associated with simple regression. We have variance and total sum of squares of the dependent variable

(DOLLSPENT). We also have an *R*-square with the adjective *multiple* to indicate multiple or many variables are being used.

The *R*-square for a multiple regression indicates the proportion of variation in DOLLSPENT "explained" by all the independent variables in the equation. In this example, *R*-square is .5480, indicating that INCOME and AGE together account for 54.8 percent of the variance in DOLL-SPENT.

It is important to note that although it is desirable to have a regression model with high *R*-square values, a large *R*-square does not necessarily guarantee a better model. Since by a mathematical necessity of the regression calculations *R*-square can never get smaller and typically increases on adding variables to the model, we can arbitrarily increase *R*-square by just loading up the model with variables until we reach a comfortably large value of *R*-square.

Clearly, such a model built on a helter-skelter selection of variables will not assure good predictions and reasonable explanatory power despite its large *R*-square. Thus, the analyst must be guided by past experience when building a regression model instead of striving for a model with a large *R*-square. There are statistical search strategies to systematically and logically add variables into a model. We'll discuss these in detail later.

The interpretation of the intercept, as in the simple regression model, must be treated as a placeholder in the regression equation since DOLLSPENT equals the intercept only when a customer has zero INCOME and is not born yet (AGE = 0), clearly a ridiculous condition.

The interpretation of the regression coefficients, however, requires careful explanation. Let's take the coefficient of AGE, .86.

.86 = the average change in DOLLSPENT associated with a unit change (i.e., every one year increase in AGE)

when INCOME *is held constant.*

By this means of control, we are able to separate the effects of AGE itself, free of any influence from INCOME.

Thus, for every one year increase in a customer's age, the predicted DOLLSPENT increases by $0.86, regardless of the customer's income. Or, in other words, if there are two customers one year apart in their ages, the older customer has an associated DOLLSPENT of $0.86 more than the younger one, regardless of their incomes.

Similarly, for the coefficient of INCOME, −.65, we can say that for every additional $100 in INCOME, there is an associated decrease in DOLLSPENT of $0.65, regardless of (controlling for) the influence of AGE.

Are these associated increases in the DOLLSPENT significant? Statistically speaking, the coefficients are statistically significant because the p values are less than the usual .05. However, if any one of the variables had a p value greater than .05, then it would be declared nonsignificant and would be deleted from the equation by redoing the regression analysis without that variable. If both variables were declared nonsignificant, there are two options:

1. Find new independent variables.
2. Use the mean value of DOLLSPENT based on the full sample of customers to predict DOLLSPENT. In other words, when good predictors cannot be found, the mean is the best predictor.

ILLUSTRATION 14

Let's go a little further with our catalog example. Our cataloger would now like to build a model to identify those customers who are most likely to buy from the catalog scheduled to be mailed next month. The cataloger wants to be sure to include the best customers in the mailing. By the same token, if those customers most unlikely to buy from the next catalog could be identified, the cataloger might exclude them from the next mailing.

In other words, the cataloger wants a model that predicts response such that each customer can be assigned a score indicating the propensity or likelihood to respond. After all customers on the file are scored, they can be ranked from most to least likely to respond. Assuming the cataloger does not wish to mail to all customers on the file, the cataloger can use the ranked file to mail as many names as desired, or as many as the budget allows.

Unfortunately, our cataloger has never tracked responses to individual catalog mailings and so isn't able to build a model based on the results of a similar prior mailing.

However, for the last year, while learning statistics, our cataloger started keeping extra data on a 10 percent sample of customers. Two of the statistics kept included the total number of pieces mailed (TOT_MAILED) and a record of the total number of orders received (TOT_ORDERS).

Our cataloger now hypothesizes that the ratio of total orders to total pieces mailed for an individual is a good measure of a person's likelihood of responding to the next planned mailing.

This seems to make sense. It may not be true, but it seems to make sense. Remember, we said the choice of a dependent variable is not always simple. Very often, the variable you want to use is not available and you have to improvise. Well, this is an example of improvising.

In any event, the decision is made to make the ratio of TOT__ORDERS to TOT__MAILED the dependent variable. To make life simpler, we'll call this new variable RESP.

Our choice of independent variables must be sure to include only variables that appear on both the Sample file and the total Customer file, so that the model can be applied to all customers. For both files, we have the following variables that we will use as the independent variables:

TOT__DOLL – Total purchase dollars to date

AVG__ORDR – Average dollar order

LAST__BUY – Number of months (from today) since last purchase

We draw two samples of 100 customer records from the 10 percent Sample file that includes these three variables. One sample will be used to build the model and the other will be used to test or validate the model.

We always need to validate a model on a fresh sample because evaluating a model using the same data that produced the model would overestimate the model's predictive power. The data for building and validating the model are in Tables 11–2 and 11–3, respectively.

Quick and Dirty Regression

The cataloger is anxious for a model, so we perform a quick and dirty (Q&D) model regressing: RESP on TOT__DOLL, AVG__ORDR, and LAST__BUY. In other words, we expect to see a regression equation that has the form:

RESP = $b0$ + $b1$ × TOT__DOLL + $b2$ ×
$$AVG\_\_ORDR + b3 \times LAST\_\_BUY$$

The SAS regression output is in Table 11–4.

TABLE 11–2
Data for Building Regression Model

OBS	TOT_DOLL	AVG_ORDR	LAST_BUY	RESP
1	265.02	26.502	0.33333	0.05952
2	242.98	15.186	0.58333	0.09195
3	109.72	13.715	0.25000	0.06400
4	1990.12	73.708	0.16667	0.14286
5	307.82	11.839	0.25000	0.14525
6	416.04	32.003	0.16667	0.07647
7	534.89	7.429	0.16667	0.40449
8	773.58	17.990	0.16667	0.23118
9	285.65	20.404	0.08333	0.07865
10	579.76	23.190	0.08333	0.13812
11	370.43	24.695	0.41667	0.06818
12	143.26	6.822	0.91667	0.13816
13	479.35	8.410	0.08333	0.32571
14	555.40	29.232	2.58333	0.09314
15	427.35	11.550	0.91667	0.20670
16	256.63	12.220	0.83333	0.13208
17	1093.74	109.374	0.16667	0.05587
18	299.78	7.687	2.16667	0.19024
19	376.52	8.011	0.75000	0.26257
20	290.97	6.191	0.33333	0.21860
21	883.51	25.986	1.66667	0.19101
22	368.94	6.961	0.83333	0.28962
23	195.42	4.248	1.08333	0.28221
24	528.11	12.282	1.33333	0.24294
25	518.19	11.515	0.75000	0.24725
26	199.56	7.127	0.08333	0.18301
27	297.07	14.146	0.75000	0.12883
28	516.24	14.340	0.50000	0.18947
29	309.82	8.606	1.66667	0.20690
30	427.30	11.245	0.25000	0.21111
31	2722.85	42.545	0.00000	0.17827
32	1556.99	16.742	0.50000	0.52542
33	463.94	14.966	0.08333	0.16848
34	260.22	12.391	1.58333	0.12651
35	191.56	9.578	1.33333	0.12121
36	518.53	16.204	1.16667	0.18286
37	229.51	17.655	1.33333	0.07738
38	1033.03	19.130	0.50000	0.24000
39	382.97	8.510	0.41667	0.25568
40	430.83	21.541	0.41667	0.10929
41	843.90	21.097	0.50000	0.21277
42	965.85	16.370	0.91667	0.21533
43	276.14	4.315	1.91667	0.32323
44	1042.32	14.477	0.25000	0.37895
45	697.28	24.044	0.00000	0.14573

TABLE 11–2
(continued)

OBS	TOT_DOLL	AVG_ORDR	LAST_BUY	RESP
46	884.73	12.120	0.16667	0.38421
47	485.09	8.222	1.16667	0.34104
48	353.24	10.093	0.25000	0.20468
49	3092.58	44.820	0.00000	0.23549
50	1519.39	41.065	1.33333	0.16667
51	640.34	14.553	0.83333	0.20091
52	1965.66	23.1254	0.08333	0.46703
53	514.83	9.7138	2.66667	0.31737
54	861.86	57.4573	0.25000	0.07979
55	260.32	18.5943	1.41667	0.10072
56	267.11	7.0292	0.41667	0.23457
57	207.75	20.7750	0.83333	0.06211
58	432.63	21.6315	0.75000	0.11173
59	583.20	25.3565	0.75000	0.12169
60	311.60	8.2000	0.50000	0.21229
61	1359.44	26.1431	1.16667	0.27513
62	456.68	11.7097	1.91667	0.20745
63	236.22	11.2486	0.00000	0.13816
64	476.55	12.8797	0.25000	0.20330
65	505.85	8.8746	0.58333	0.30978
66	845.57	31.3174	0.25000	0.14439
67	358.84	22.4275	0.75000	0.09581
68	103.93	3.8493	0.50000	0.18750
69	686.72	18.0716	0.50000	0.20430
70	586.02	10.6549	0.58333	0.25463
71	673.51	13.4702	1.25000	0.24272
72	364.15	17.3405	0.08333	0.12000
73	397.88	18.9467	0.33333	0.11351
74	2038.75	30.4291	0.16667	0.34359
75	322.07	12.8828	1.83333	0.14535
76	921.64	28.8013	1.08333	0.14545
77	686.71	16.7490	0.00000	0.20098
78	549.22	22.8842	0.33333	0.12698
79	724.27	38.1195	0.75000	0.10270
80	437.21	54.6512	0.58333	0.04848
81	256.18	8.5393	0.83333	0.18293
82	595.82	17.5241	1.25000	0.18085
83	792.00	34.4348	0.91667	0.12849
84	779.18	31.1672	0.50000	0.15625
85	859.21	13.4252	0.08333	0.28319
86	1716.75	30.1184	0.50000	0.31319
87	319.88	11.8474	0.50000	0.15882
88	627.58	14.2632	0.08333	0.24309
89	774.58	21.5161	0.16667	0.21429
90	559.81	27.9905	0.50000	0.10526

TABLE 11–2
(concluded)

OBS	TOT_DOLL	AVG_ORDR	LAST_BUY	RESP
91	597.83	11.7222	0.25000	0.28492
92	691.70	20.3441	0.00000	0.20482
93	1964.13	22.5762	0.33333	0.46774
94	158.01	7.1823	0.08333	0.14103
95	420.93	15.5900	0.75000	0.14362
96	1061.77	16.0874	1.66667	0.31884
97	335.43	23.9593	0.75000	0.08383
98	768.71	23.2942	0.00000	0.18539
99	673.18	15.6553	0.58333	0.23118
100	453.98	15.1327	0.25000	0.15075

We see a lot of output in Table 11–4, more than we previously discussed. We'll still focus on what we know: R-square, coefficient estimates and p values, but will explain the rest of the printout as we go along. In SAS, p values are shown in the column labeled Prob > |T|.

TOT_DOLL and AVG_ORDR are very significant, with p values much less than .05. LAST_BUY is not significant, with a p value of .8204. Before deciding what to do about this insignificant variable, let's review the other new statistics and measures shown in Table 11–4.

Interpretation of SAS Output

Analysis of Variance Table. Table 11–4 reports how the total sum of squares are broken up into parts corresponding to the:

Model – the sum of squares that can be accounted for or explained by the variables in the model.

Error – the sum of squares that are unexplained by the model.

Sum of squares (SS) has associated with it numbers called *degrees of freedom* (DF). DF for the model is the number of independent variables in the model; DF for the total SS is the number of observations minus 1; DF for the error is the difference between the total and model DFs.

We can obtain R-square from the ratio of sum of square explained by the model to the total sum of square:

TABLE 11–3
Data for Validating Regression Model

OBS	TOT_DOLL	AVG_ORDR	LAST_BUY	RESP
1	1679.13	40.954	0.83333	0.18062
2	574.61	22.100	0.33333	0.13265
3	586.64	19.555	0.75000	0.17143
4	513.03	10.470	0.91667	0.28324
5	1561.91	53.859	0.25000	0.15591
6	274.26	13.713	0.75000	0.11765
7	477.19	22.723	0.08333	0.12209
8	232.09	8.596	0.41667	0.15976
9	879.43	39.974	0.08333	0.09692
10	432.25	36.021	0.83333	0.07643
11	350.53	21.908	0.16667	0.09249
12	311.95	12.998	0.83333	0.13953
13	236.54	14.784	1.08333	0.09357
14	440.33	17.613	0.75000	0.13298
15	1097.03	47.697	0.66667	0.12105
16	344.67	13.257	2.16667	0.15758
17	737.44	67.040	2.00000	0.06748
18	319.66	9.133	1.00000	0.19774
19	1930.83	22.986	0.16667	0.44920
20	303.59	12.650	0.08333	0.12565
21	1009.29	59.370	0.08333	0.09140
22	1088.09	24.180	0.08333	0.24064
23	378.98	10.243	1.25000	0.22289
24	536.41	16.255	0.08333	0.19298
25	304.03	13.219	1.00000	0.12366
26	417.28	34.773	0.66667	0.06977
27	1080.00	30.000	0.25000	0.18947
28	501.70	23.890	0.66667	0.12000
29	376.15	34.195	1.00000	0.05612
30	817.06	28.174	0.08333	0.15676
31	1883.37	117.711	0.25000	0.07729
32	230.95	5.922	1.33333	0.24375
33	457.21	9.525	0.33333	0.24615
34	446.43	24.802	0.08333	0.10405
35	749.20	32.574	1.91667	0.10952
36	110.26	4.794	0.75000	0.14744
37	1664.19	46.228	0.00000	0.19149
38	183.75	12.250	0.25000	0.09934
39	249.64	7.801	0.50000	0.20126
40	196.55	16.379	1.41667	0.08955
41	852.11	23.030	0.08333	0.20330
42	914.48	35.172	0.16667	0.12322
43	892.33	21.764	0.41667	0.11549
44	2281.84	17.827	0.33333	0.47059
45	122.38	6.441	1.25000	0.11728
46	1800.32	47.377	0.41667	0.15323
47	752.08	19.792	1.16667	0.20879

TABLE 11-3
(continued)

OBS	TOT_DOLL	AVG_ORDR	LAST_BUY	RESP
48	448.52	12.122	1.25000	0.20670
49	756.85	42.047	0.00000	0.09677
50	536.83	16.776	0.00000	0.14884
51	145.07	6.307	0.16667	0.15033
52	769.18	18.7605	1.00000	0.22043
53	1092.98	52.0467	0.50000	0.11538
54	547.62	19.5579	0.50000	0.11290
55	333.49	12.8265	0.00000	0.15205
56	859.70	26.8656	0.25000	0.17778
57	426.97	11.8603	0.08333	0.20225
58	288.86	11.1100	1.91667	0.15569
59	376.68	9.4170	0.08333	0.21978
60	511.88	15.9962	0.00000	0.18182
61	1766.24	47.7362	0.00000	0.19892
62	930.93	23.2732	0.66667	0.18957
63	690.51	36.3426	2.91667	0.11446
64	554.32	34.6450	1.41667	0.08889
65	1189.95	56.6643	0.00000	0.11351
66	805.75	73.2500	0.25000	0.05238
67	227.14	16.2243	0.33333	0.07143
68	556.49	20.6107	0.50000	0.13846
69	602.23	25.0929	0.58333	0.11111
70	1156.40	22.2385	0.50000	0.27660
71	349.65	13.4481	1.41667	0.15385
72	324.02	8.5268	0.08333	0.22353
73	515.43	13.5639	2.08333	0.21839
74	347.12	26.7015	0.66667	0.07429
75	227.91	9.1164	0.41667	0.15152
76	349.74	19.4300	0.41667	0.11043
77	320.61	14.5732	1.25000	0.12571
78	447.28	16.5659	0.00000	0.14211
79	2777.47	27.7747	0.16667	0.18975
80	501.86	33.4573	0.25000	0.08621
81	1130.55	32.3014	0.25000	0.17766
82	733.18	13.5774	0.58333	0.27411
83	295.82	10.2007	1.58333	0.12719
84	1115.04	38.4497	0.25000	0.15676
85	484.19	17.2925	0.16667	0.16000
86	255.10	28.3444	1.41667	0.05844
87	234.52	18.0400	0.66667	0.07602
88	991.80	70.8429	0.50000	0.06512
89	453.94	17.4592	0.33333	0.14943
90	426.52	25.0894	0.50000	0.09189
91	513.76	24.4648	0.25000	0.11538
92	345.89	15.7223	1.75000	0.09322
93	95.99	9.5990	1.25000	0.07937

TABLE 11–3
(concluded)

OBS	TOT_DOLL	AVG_ORDR	LAST_BUY	RESP
94	854.35	32.8596	0.50000	0.13978
95	846.52	16.2792	2.08333	0.29050
96	1233.51	44.0539	0.33333	0.14973
97	1363.34	34.0835	0.08333	0.19048
98	1742.23	31.1113	0.16667	0.21374
99	389.75	16.9457	0.58333	0.12500
100	309.53	8.1455	0.08333	0.23313

$$R\text{-square} = \text{Model SS/Total SS}$$
$$= .50495/.90722$$
$$= .5427$$

The ratio of model SS divided by its DF to error SS divided by its DF is the F statistic, which is used to test the significance of all the independent variables in the model. If the p value of the F value is less than 5 percent, then the model is considered statistically significant with 95 percent confidence.

Another way to interpret the F statistic is to check to make sure the value of F is greater than 4; a value greater than 4 will correspond to a p of less than 5 percent. The reason for looking at the F statistic two ways is that when comparing two or more models to each other, each may have p values of less than .05, but an examination of the difference in the F statistic can provide a sense of which model is most significant, when all models are significant.

Also of note is the relationship between R-square and F:

$$F = \frac{R\text{-square/Number of variables}}{(1 - R\text{-square})/(n - \text{Number of variables} - 1)}$$

From this definition of F, we see that when the number of variables increases without significantly increasing R-square, the F value becomes smaller, thus decreasing the statistical significance of the model. It is also clear for the formula that F increases as the number of observations increase.

Another way of considering the effects of adding variables to the model is as follows: As we mentioned, R-square typically increases when variables are added to the model even if they are not important; thus, to

TABLE 11–4

SAS

Model: MODEL1
Dependent Variable: RESP

Analysis of Variance

Source	DF	Sum of Squares	Mean Square	F Value	Prob > F
Model	3	0.50495	0.16832	40.168	0.0001
Error	96	0.40227	0.00419		
C Total	99	0.90722			

Root MSE	0.06473	R-square	0.5566	
Dep Mean	0.19586	Adj R-sq	0.5427	
C.V.	33.05019			

Parameter Estimates

Variable	DF	Parameter Estimate	Standard Error	T for H0: Parameter = 0	Prob > |T|
INTERCEP	1	0.194386	0.01508134	12.889	0.0001
TOT_DOLL	1	0.000141	0.00001443	9.780	0.0001
AVG_ORDR	1	−0.004708	0.00051457	−9.150	0.0001
LAST_BUY	1	0.002589	0.01137582	0.228	0.8204

Variable	DF	Standardized Estimate
INTERCEP	1	0.00000000
TOT_DOLL	1	0.78196276
AVG_ORDR	1	−0.72689782
LAST_BUY	1	0.01589971

offset their unimportant contribution to R-square, we often consider adjusted R-square:

$$\text{adj } R = 1 - (1 - R \text{ sq}) \times \frac{(n - 1)}{(n - \text{number of variables})}$$

Parameter Estimates Table.   Table 11–4 reports the regression coefficients (called *parameter estimates*), their corresponding standard errors, t values (T for H0:), and p-values (Prob > $|T|$).

The t value is the ratio of parameter estimate to standard error. If the t value is less than -1.96 or greater than $+1.96$, then we conclude the true parameter or regression coefficient is greater than zero, and the variable in question is significantly related to the dependent variable, with 95 percent confidence. For a t value inside this interval, the true regression coefficient is zero and there is no relationship between the variable and the dependent variable.

Often, it is useful to know which variables in the model are most important. The parameter estimates or regression coefficients cannot be used because the units are not comparable. In our example, we have dollars (for TOT__DOLL), number of orders (for AVG__ORDR), and number of months (for LAST__BUY) with a coefficient of .000141 for TOT__DOLL versus .002589 for LAST__BUY. We cannot say LAST__BUY contributes more than TOT__DOLL in predicting RESP on the basis of the apples-to-oranges comparison of the size of the coefficients.

One way around this problem is to use standardized coefficients (standardized estimates), which are the regression coefficients converted into a common unit by multiplying the coefficient by the standard deviation of the independent variable divided by the standard deviation of the dependent variable. Thus, TOT__DOLL and LAST__BUY have standardized coefficients of .7819 and .0158, respectively, which indicate that the former is roughly 49 times more important than the latter.

More Quick and Dirty Regression

Now that our review of the regression output from an SAS program is complete, let's review the regression equation and decide what to do about that insignificant variable LAST__BUY.

The regression equation derived from Table 11–4 is:

$$\text{RESP} = .19 + .00014 \times \text{TOT\_\_DOLL} - .0047 \times$$
$$\text{AVG\_\_ORDR} + .0025 \times \text{LAST\_\_BUY}.$$

As we said before, the model includes TOT__DOLL and AVG__ORDR, and both variables are significant with p values of .01 percent. But the LAST__BUY variable has a t value of less than 2 and a p value of .82. Clearly, the variable should not be used according to either of our rules: that t should be greater than 2, or that the p-value should be less than .05. However, before redoing the model with this variable removed, let's note that the model has an R-square of 55.66 percent and an F value of 40.1. We'll want to compare these values with the values produced from a new model with only two independent variables, TOT__DOLL and AVG__ORDR. Table 11–5 shows the results of running the model with the variable LAST__BUY removed.

TABLE 11–5

SAS

Model: MODEL1
Dependent Variable: RESP

Analysis of Variance

Source	DF	Sum of Squares	Mean Square	F Value	Prob > F
Model	2	0.50473	0.25237	60.820	0.0001
Error	97	0.40249	0.00415		
C Total	99	0.90722			

Root MSE	0.06442	R-square	0.5563	
Dep Mean	0.19586	Adj R-sq	0.5472	
C.V.	32.88825			

Parameter Estimates

Variable	DF	Parameter Estimate	Standard Error	T for H0: Parameter = 0	Prob > |T|
INTERCEP	1	0.196591	0.01150215	17.092	0.0001
TOT__DOLL	1	0.000141	0.00001421	9.897	0.0001
AVG__ORDR	1	−0.004718	0.00051005	−9.251	0.0001

Variable	DF	Standardized Estimate
INTERCEP	1	0.00000000
TOT__DOLL	1	0.77937273
AVG__ORDR	1	−0.72849090

The new model has the form:

$$RESP = .19 + .00014 \times TOT\_DOLL - .0047 \times AVG\_ORDR$$

In this case, the regression coefficients did not change with the removal of the insignificant variable LAST__BUY. We see that the two variables are still significant. Their t values are well above 2, and their p values are below the .01 percent level. The F value has improved from 40.2 to 60.8, indicating that this model in total is stronger, in a statistical sense, than the prior model. And the reason for this improvement is that the R-square value has not changed appreciably; its value is still 55.6 percent, but this R-square has been achieved by a model with one less variable, and you'll recall from the discussion above that the F value tends to increase as the number of variables decreases.

So we have a good model, but should we stop here? Remember, this was a quick and dirty model; it was built with almost no examination of the data. We did not check to see if the independent variables were normally distributed. We did not check to see if the relationship between the independent variables and the dependent variables was linear or straight. We did not probe for interaction variables. We did not check for multicollinearity. We did a quick and dirty job—but we still got a pretty good model. Let's see what a better, more thorough, job would produce.

REGRESSION BUILT WITH CARE

Step 1—Examination of the Correlation Matrix

A thorough regression analysis often begins with an examination of a correlation matrix. A correlation matrix simply produces a correlation coefficient and a p value for each combination of all independent and dependent variables.

A correlation matrix of the four variables in our example is shown in Table 11–6.

In practice, the analyst will scan the correlation matrix to get an idea of which independent variables appear to be related to the dependent variable. The reason for doing this is that in most real situations, there may be hundreds of potential independent variables, and it's literally impossible to deal with all of them in a thorough fashion. So the analyst looks to include, for further analysis, only those variables that seem to have a good chance of being related to the dependent variable, that is, a good chance of entering a final regression model.

An examination of Table 11–6 indicates that the variables TOT__DOLL and AVG__ORDR both have relatively high correlation coefficients (.39032 and −.32488) with the dependent variable. The p values of both are less than .05, indicating statistical significance.

On the other hand, LAST__BUY has a relatively low correlation coefficient (.09807) and its p value is greater than .05.

At this point, the analyst looking at the correlation matrix may guess that LAST__BUY will fall out of the picture, but we'll try to salvage this variable. Maybe the variable is correlated with response, but the relationship is not linear, and this could account for the low correlation? We'll see.

Step 2—Normalization of All Variables

After deciding which variables are worthy of further consideration, the next step is to check to see if the variables in their raw form are more or

TABLE 11–6

SAS
CORRELATION ANALYSIS
4 'VAR' Variables: RESP   TOT_DOLL AVG_ORDR LAST_BUY

Pearson Correlation Coefficients / Prob > |R| under Ho: Rho=0 / N = 100

	RESP	TOT_DOLL	AVG_ORDR	LAST_BUY
RESP	1.00000	0.39032	−0.32488	−0.09807
	0.0	0.0001	0.0010	0.3317
TOT_DOLL	0.39032	1.00000	0.57381	−0.29063
	0.0001	0.0	0.0001	0.0034
AVG_ORDR	−0.32488	0.57381	1.00000	−0.15539
	0.0010	0.0001	0.0	0.1226
LAST_BUY	−0.09807	−0.29063	−0.15539	1.00000
	0.3317	0.0034	0.1226	0.0

less normally distributed. Does their shape correspond to the shape of the bell-shaped curve or normal distribution? If not, what can we do to make their shape appear normal?

In Figures 11–1 through 11–4, we see stem-and-leaf pictures of all four variables.

In each case, we see that the distributions are skewed toward the lower numbers in the stem. On the right-hand side of each figure we see something called a boxplot. The boxplot is simply an aid to answer the question, "is the distribution normal or skewed?" When the bar with the stars on each end (*------*) is in the middle of the box, the distribution is normal. As you can see, these distributions are not normal.

So we'll normalize them. Distributions are normalized by transforming the original variable into some other variable. Often, this is done by replacing the original variable with its logarithm or by taking the square or the square root of the original variable. There are lots of ways to do this and these techniques are part of the statistician's bag of tricks. It really doesn't matter which method or transformation is used, what matters is that the final shape of the variable be as normal as possible before entering the regression mode. Having said that, we should keep in mind the fact that a final regression model may have to be applied to a Customer file of millions of names, and the more complicated the model, the more difficult it may be for programmers, who are not statisticians, and who may not have the programming tools required to deal with logs, to score the database. We'll come back to this point later on in Section 5.

FIGURE 11–1
SAS
UNIVARIATE PROCEDURE

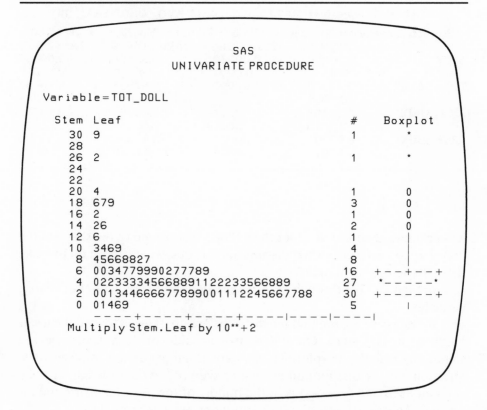

```
                          SAS
                  UNIVARIATE PROCEDURE

   Variable=TOT_DOLL

     Stem Leaf                                    #      Boxplot
       30 9                                        1        *
       28
       26 2                                        1        *
       24
       22
       20 4                                        1        0
       18 679                                      3        0
       16 2                                        1        0
       14 26                                       2        0
       12 6                                        1        |
       10 3469                                     4        |
        8 45668827                                 8        |
        6 0034779990277789                        16     +--+--+
        4 022333345668891122233566889            27     *------*
        2 001344666677899001112245667788         30     +-----+
        0 01469                                    5        |
          ----+----+----+----|----|----|
       Multiply Stem.Leaf by 10**+2
```

In Figures 11–5 to 11–8 we see the effect of transforming each variable into its logarithm. (We used logs to the base 10, but natural logs would have accomplished the same objective.) The result is that the distribution of each variable comes closer to the shape of the normal distribution. The importance of this to the final regression model will become clearer in a few minutes.

Step 3—Checking for Linearity

To check for linearity or straight-line relationships, we ask the computer program (again we are using SAS) to produce scatter diagrams of the relationships between each independent variable and the dependent variable.

FIGURE 11–2
SAS
UNIVARIATE PROCEDURE

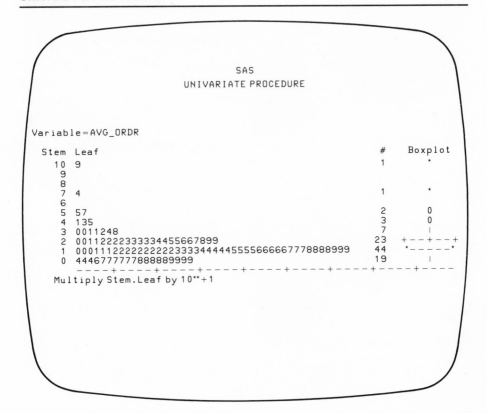

```
                            SAS
                     UNIVARIATE PROCEDURE


Variable=AVG_ORDR

  Stem  Leaf                                                    #   Boxplot
   10  9                                                        1      *
    9
    8
    7  4                                                        1      *
    6
    5  57                                                       2      0
    4  135                                                      3      0
    3  0011248                                                  7      |
    2  00112222333334455667899                                 23   +--+--+
    1  00011122222222223333444445555666667778888999            44   *-----*
    0  44467777778888889999                                    19      |
      ----+----+----+----+----+----+----+----+----+----+----
   Multiply Stem.Leaf by 10**+1
```

In Figure 11–9, we see the relationship between RESP and TOT_DOLL. The relationship isn't great but it seems to be linear and positive. In other words, an argument could be made that a straight line drawn through the points fits the points just as well as any curved line. To illustrate this observation, we've drawn a straight line through the scatter points.

Figure 11–10 plots the relationship between AVG_ORDR and RESP. The relationship is clearly negative. The negative correlation sign told us this, and the scatter plot simply describes the relationship pictorially. If we assume for the moment that the three data points that stand apart from the rest of the data points are real, not errors, then one could argue that a curved line fits the points better than a straight line and some straightening is required.

FIGURE 11–3
SAS
UNIVARIATE PROCEDURE

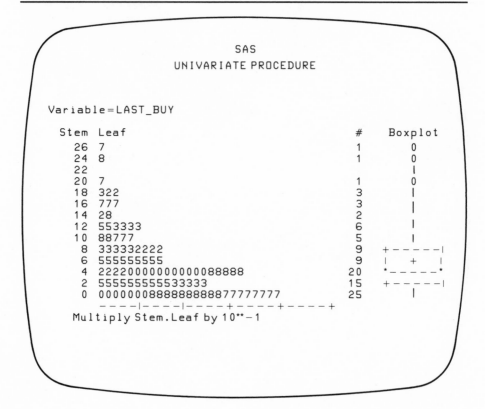

```
                              SAS
                     UNIVARIATE PROCEDURE


Variable=LAST_BUY

  Stem  Leaf                                      #     Boxplot
    26  7                                          1        0
    24  8                                          1        0
    22                                                      |
    20  7                                          1        0
    18  322                                        3        |
    16  777                                        3        |
    14  28                                         2        |
    12  553333                                     6        |
    10  88777                                      5        |
     8  333332222                                  9     +-----|
     6  555555555                                  9     |  +  |
     4  22220000000000088888                      20     *-----*
     2  555555555533333                           15     +-----|
     0  00000008888888887777777777                25        |
        ----|----|----+----+----+
     Multiply Stem.Leaf by 10**-1
```

Figure 11–11 simply reinforces the argument that there is no relationship between LAST_BUY and RESP.

At this point, the reader might be curious as to what scatter plots of the transformed variables might look like, and what effect transforming the variables has on the question of linearity.

To assist in this analysis, we should also produce a new correlation matrix using the transformed variables. The new correlation matrix is shown in Table 11–7.

If we compare the results of Table 11–6 with Table 11–7 we note some interesting things:

- The correlation coefficient between RESP and TOT_DOLL decreased from .39032 to .30066.

FIGURE 11–4
SAS
UNIVARIATE PROCEDURE

```
                              SAS
                     UNIVARIATE PROCEDURE



   Variable=RESP

    Stem  Leaf                                    #      Boxplot
       5  3                                        1        0
       4  77                                       2        0
       4  0                                        1        |
       3  88                                       2        |
       3  11222344                                 8        |
       2  556688889                                9        |
       2  00000011111112233344444                 23    + - - + - - +
       1  5555566778888899999                     19    * - - - - - *
       1  0001111222333334444444                  22    + - - - - - +
       0  5666678888899                           13        |
       0
          - - - - + - - - - + - - - - + - - - - + - - -
       Multiply Stem.Leaf by 10**-1
```

- The correlation coefficient between RESP and AVG__ORDR increased from −.32488 to −.38477 (the direction sign can be ignored).
- The correlation coefficient between RESP and LAST__BUY also increased from −.09807 to −.16945.

The decrease in correlation between RESP and TOT__DOLL suggests that we might have been better off by not transforming the data. However, even though we lost some "correlation" points from TOT__DOLL, we prefer to use relationships that are symmetrical or approximate the normal distribution because the underlying mathematics of regression analysis assumes linearity of all variables with the dependent variable, which is enhanced when the variables are as close to a normal distribution as possible. Also, models built on variables that

FIGURE 11–5
SAS
UNIVARIATE PROCEDURE

```
                          SAS
                  UNIVARIATE PROCEDURE


   Variable=LOG_TDOL

     Stem  Leaf                                    #    Boxplot
       34  49                                       2      0
       33  01                                       2      |
       32  399                                      3      |
       31  389                                      3      |
       30  1234                                     4      |
       29  033345568                                9      |
       28  0133444469999                           13   +------+
       27  011112344567788                         15   *--+--*
       26  02233344667889                          14   |      |
       25  0135567788                              10   +------+
       24  11222346678999                          14      |
       23  02679                                    5      |
       22  089                                      3      |
       21  6                                        1      |
       20  24                                       2      |
           ----+----+----+----+----+
        Multiply Stem.Leaf by 10**-1
```

do not violate these assumptions have a better chance of holding up in practice.

Another reason for sticking with variables that conform more closely to the normal distribution assumption is that, to the extent that the normality assumption is violated, the interpretation of the t and F statistics becomes difficult. In other words, the ts might not be as reliable estimates of significance as we assume them to be, and since variables are evaluated on the basis of their t scores, it's important that their interpretation be correct.

Now let's look at the scatter plots of the transformed variables.

In Figure 11–12, we see the relationship between LOG__TDOL and LOG__RESP. Compared to the raw data relationship shown in Figure

FIGURE 11–6
SAS
UNIVARIATE PROCEDURE

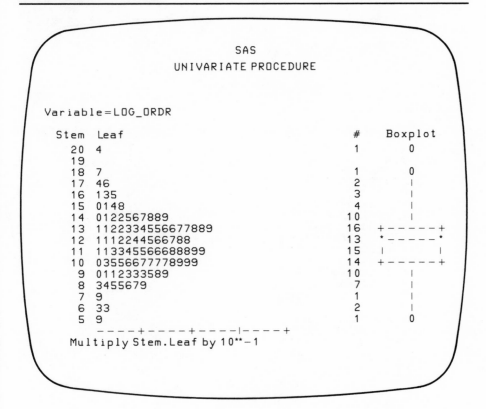

```
                              SAS
                     UNIVARIATE PROCEDURE


  Variable=LOG_ORDR

   Stem  Leaf                                      #    Boxplot
     20  4                                          1       0
     19
     18  7                                          1       0
     17  46                                         2       |
     16  135                                        3       |
     15  0148                                       4       |
     14  0122567889                                10       |
     13  1122334556677889                          16    + - - - - - +
     12  1112244566788                             13    * - - - - - *
     11  113345566688899                           15    |           |
     10  03556677778999                            14    + - - - - - +
      9  0112333589                                10       |
      8  3455679                                    7       |
      7  9                                          1       |
      6  33                                         2       |
      5  9                                          1       0
          - - - - + - - - - + - - - - -|- - - - +
       Multiply Stem.Leaf by 10**-1
```

11–9, we see that the extreme values of response are somewhat closer to the rest of the data points, which is a function of the log transformation. To the naked eye it appears that the relationship is a bit more straight, but the difference does not appear to be significant.

We see a bigger difference when we compare Figure 11–13 with Figure 11–10. Here, the transformations have clearly resulted in a straighter relationship between LOG_ORDR and LOG_RESP. This example points to a very interesting and valuable conclusion: *Reexpressing most of the time normalizes and straightens the data simultaneously.* This means that by taking care of one problem, normality, most of the time you will take care of the second problem, the linear relationship assumption of regression.

FIGURE 11–7
SAS
UNIVARIATE PROCEDURE

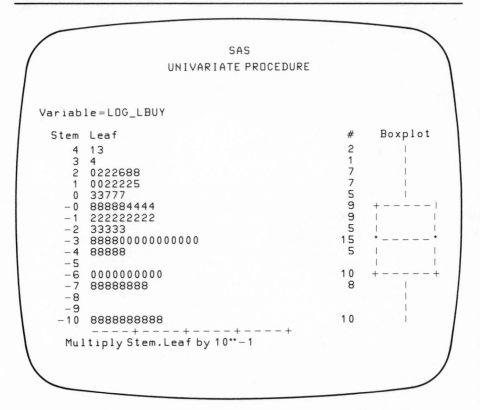

```
                               SAS
                      UNIVARIATE PROCEDURE


   Variable=LOG_LBUY

     Stem  Leaf                                      #     Boxplot
        4  13                                        2        |
        3  4                                         1        |
        2  0222688                                   7        |
        1  0022225                                   7        |
        0  33777                                     5        |
      - 0  888884444                                 9     +-----|
      - 1  222222222                                 9     |     |
      - 2  33333                                     5     |     |
      - 3  888800000000000                          15     *-----*
      - 4  88888                                     5     |     |
      - 5                                                  |     |
      - 6  0000000000                               10     +-----+
      - 7  88888888                                  8           |
      - 8                                                        |
      - 9                                                        |
      -10  8888888888                               10           |
           ----+----+----+----+----+
      Multiply Stem.Leaf by 10**-1
```

Finally, the transformation of the LAST__BUY variable, Figure 11–14, doesn't make very much difference. It's getting close to the time when we should disregard this variable from further consideration.

RERUNNING THE MODEL

Now we're ready to build the model using the transformed variables. The first model we'll try will take the form:

$$LOG\_RESP = b0 + b1 \times LOG\_TDOL + b2 \times LOG\_ORDR, + b3 \times LOG\_LASTBUY$$

FIGURE 11–8
SAS
UNIVARIATE PROCEDURE

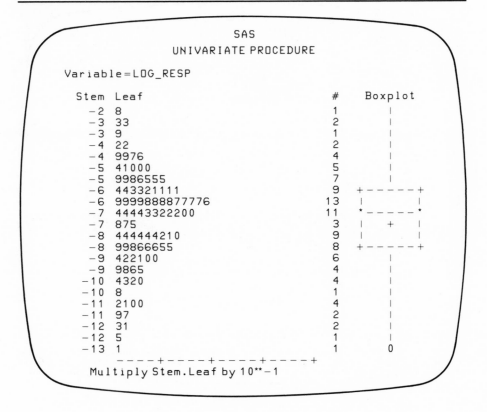

```
                          SAS
                  UNIVARIATE PROCEDURE

     Variable=LOG_RESP

      Stem  Leaf                         #      Boxplot
       -2   8                            1        |
       -3   33                           2        |
       -3   9                            1        |
       -4   22                           2        |
       -4   9976                         4        |
       -5   41000                        5        |
       -5   9986555                      7        |
       -6   443321111                    9     +-----+
       -6   9999888877776               13     |     |
       -7   44443322200                 11     *-----*
       -7   875                          3     |  +  |
       -8   444444210                    9     |     |
       -8   99866655                     8     +-----+
       -9   422100                       6        |
       -9   9865                         4        |
      -10   4320                         4        |
      -10   8                            1        |
      -11   2100                         4        |
      -11   97                           2        |
      -12   31                           2        |
      -12   5                            1        |
      -13   1                            1        0
            ----+----+----+----+----+
        Multiply Stem.Leaf by 10**-1
```

The regression printout (see Table 11–8) for this three-variable model shows a *t* value close (but still less than) 2 for the variable LOG__LBUY, and a correspondingly large *p* value. The *p* value of the transformed variable is much smaller than before but is still greater than the .05 or 5 percent rule we established for entry into a model, so we'll drop this variable and run the model again with only two transformed variables.

Rerunning the model without LAST__BUY results in the following model (see Table 11–9):

$$\text{LOG\_RESP} = -1.89 + .084 \times \text{LOG\_TDOL} -$$
$$0.959 \times \text{LOG\_ORDR}$$

FIGURE 11–9
Plot of RESP, TOT__DOLL

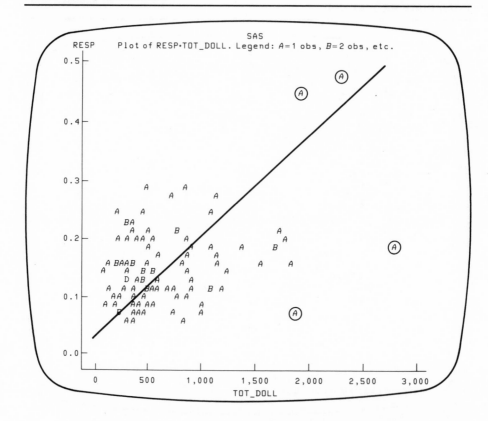

Both transformed variables are very significant, with high *t*s and low *p* values. The *R*-square for this model is 96 percent, which represents a large improvement over the Q&D model's *R*-square of 55 percent.

Based on *R*-square values, we may be tempted to say that the carefully built model is clearly better than the Q&D model because its *R*-square is larger. However, we cannot say this for two reasons.

First, a model with a larger *R*-square would be better than a competing model with a smaller *R*-square *provided* that the dependent variables were the same for both models. To compare models using different variables is, in effect, making the proverbial comparison of apples and oranges. And a transformed variable is equivalent to a different variable.

FIGURE 11–10
Plot of RESP, AVG__ORDR

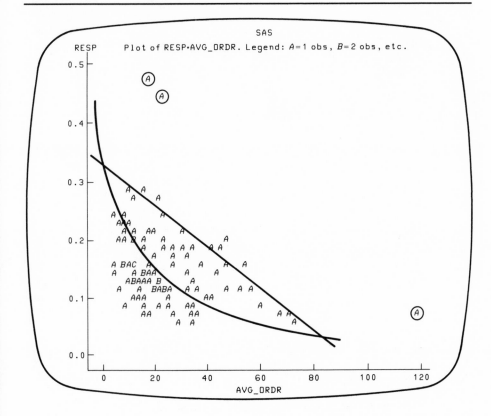

The second and more important reason for not using R-square as the ultimate measure in evaluating a model, as previously pointed out and to be repeated, is simply because it has been shown that models with large R-squares put to use under real situations or simulated conditions do not always perform better than their small R-square model counterparts.

To sum up, we have two models with the following equations:
The Q&D model:

RESP = .19 + .00014 × TOT__DOLL − .0047 × AVG__ORDR

The carefully built model:

LOG__RESP = − 1.89 + .84 × LOG__TDOL − .95 × LOG__ORDR

FIGURE 11–11
Plot of RESP, LAST__BUY

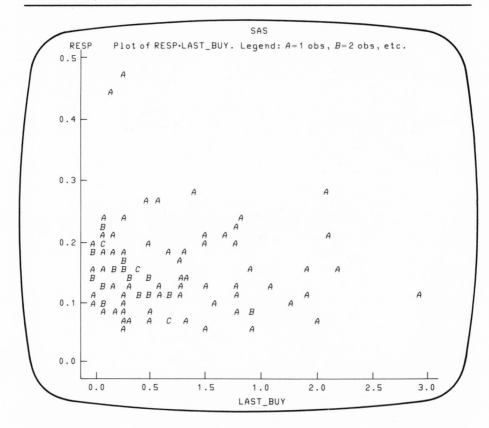

The model using log transformations has an *R*-square of 96 percent, the quick and dirty model has an *R*-square of 55 percent. It appears that the carefully built model is almost twice as good as the quick and dirty model. Is it?

VALIDATION – CHOOSING THE BEST MODEL

If we cannot rely solely on *R*-square, then how can we choose the best model? The answer lies in the validation of the candidate models under simulated conditions. That is, we apply the model to a file of names for which the dependent variable is known, and then evaluate the predicted

TABLE 11–7

<table>
<tr><td colspan="5">SAS
CORRELATION ANALYSIS
4 'VAR' Variables: LOG__RESP LOG__TDOL LOG__ORDR LOG__LBUY
Pearson Correlation Coefficients / Prob > |R| under Ho: Rho=0
/ Number of Observations</td></tr>
<tr><td></td><td>LOG__RESP</td><td>LOG__TDOL</td><td>LOG__ORDR</td><td>LOG__LBUY</td></tr>
<tr><td>LOG__RESP</td><td>1.00000</td><td>0.30066</td><td>−0.38477</td><td>−0.16945</td></tr>
<tr><td></td><td>0.0</td><td>0.0024</td><td>0.0001</td><td>0.1064</td></tr>
<tr><td></td><td>100</td><td>100</td><td>100</td><td>92</td></tr>
<tr><td>LOG__TDOL</td><td>0.30066</td><td>1.00000</td><td>0.73874</td><td>−0.28732</td></tr>
<tr><td></td><td>0.0024</td><td>0.0</td><td>0.0001</td><td>0.0055</td></tr>
<tr><td></td><td>100</td><td>100</td><td>100</td><td>92</td></tr>
<tr><td>LOG__ORDR</td><td>−0.38477</td><td>0.73874</td><td>1.00000</td><td>−0.14667</td></tr>
<tr><td></td><td>0.0001</td><td>0.0001</td><td>0.0</td><td>0.1630</td></tr>
<tr><td></td><td>100</td><td>100</td><td>100</td><td>92</td></tr>
<tr><td>LOG__LBUY</td><td>−0.16945</td><td>−0.28732</td><td>−0.14667</td><td>1.00000</td></tr>
<tr><td></td><td>0.1064</td><td>0.0055</td><td>0.1630</td><td>0.0</td></tr>
<tr><td></td><td>92</td><td>92</td><td>92</td><td>92</td></tr>
</table>

values of the dependent variable with the actual values. The model that *performs best* in the validation test *is the best.*

For validating the cataloger's two models, we use the second sample of 100 fresh names for which the response rates are known. We score each name for each model and compare predicted and actual response rates by a decile analysis. A decile analysis starts by ranking the scored file from high to low score and dividing the ranked names into 10 equal groups or deciles. The mean value of the actual dependent variable for each decile is calculated. In this case, the model with the largest mean response rate for the top two or three deciles is declared the best model.

The decile analyses for the two models are in Table 11–10. We see that the carefully built model beats the Q&D model in the top decile with a mean response rate of 29 versus 27 percent, but performs the same in decile 2 with a mean response rate of 20 percent. Thirty percent into the file, both models perform the same. Depending on how deeply the cataloger plans to mail, the 2 percent difference could represent a significant gain in dollars per response, in which case the preferred model is the one built with care. However, if the cataloger plans to use the model to mail to 50 percent of the file, not just the top 10 percent, then either model will produce the same result.

FIGURE 11–12
Plot of LOG__RESP, LOG__TDOL

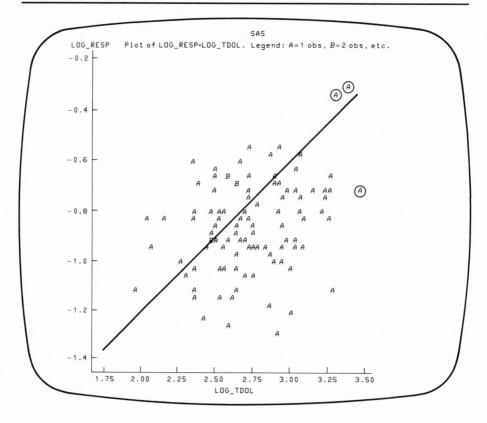

This example was intentionally designed to produce a result in which two models produce very different R-squares, but have little difference in practical results, to convince the reader to pay less attention to the R-square statistic and more attention to the validation results.

In practice, users will discover that the R-squares associated with most models, particularly response models, where only a very small percent of the population responds, are generally under 10 percent, very often under 5 percent. Nevertheless, these models can be used with confidence, provided: (1) the individual variables are significant (ts greater than 2 and the corresponding p values less than .05); (2) the F value for the entire relationship is greater than 4 or 5; and (3) most importantly, the model validates, that is, produces a meaningful

FIGURE 11–13
Plot of LOG__RESP, LOG__ORDR

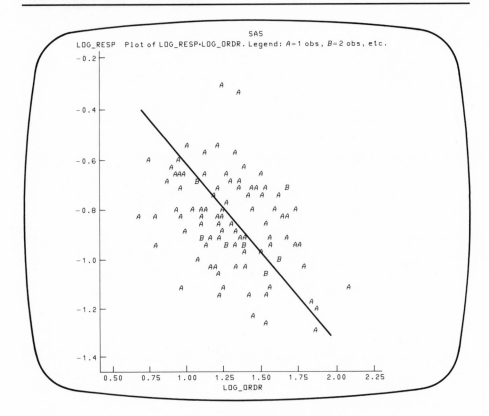

difference in decile performance when applied to a fresh validation sample.

MULTIPLE REGRESSION – SOME ODDS AND ENDS

Through our illustrations, we hope that you've obtained some feel for how multiple regression works in practice. At this point, hands-on experience with regression models will be the only way you will become proficient in the application of regression and your company will become efficient in its direct mail programs.

In Chapter 12, we will outline a how-to for building regression models. But before doing so, we would like to take care of three loose ends.

FIGURE 11–14
Plot of LOG__RESP, LOG__LBUY

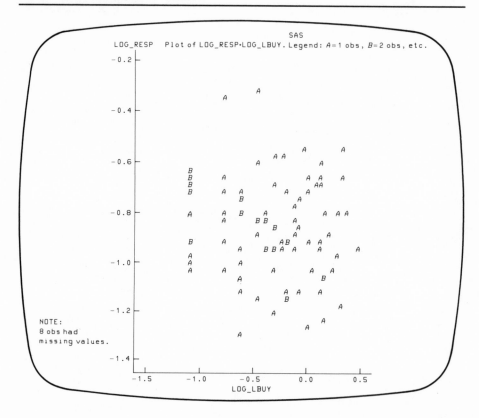

Interaction

We note that in the regression model, each independent variable is multiplied by a weight (its coefficient) and then all the weighted variables are added to obtain a score or predicted value of the dependent variable. In effect, we are saying that the regression model is an *additive* model – the independent variables in the models are said to have an additive effect on the dependent variable.

Let's recall the model in Illustration 13, where we predict DOLL-SPENT based on income and age.

TABLE 11–8

SAS

Model: MODEL1
Dependent Variable: LOG__RESP

Analysis of Variance

Source	DF	Sum of Squares	Mean Square	F Value	Prob > F
Model	3	4.60627	1.53542	1052.486	0.0001
Error	89	0.12984	0.00146		
C Total	92	4.73610			

Root MSE	0.03819	R-square	0.9726	
Dep Mean	−0.76149	Adj R-sq	0.9717	
C.V.	−5.01583			

Parameter Estimates

Variable	DF	Parameter Estimate	Standard Error	T for H0: Parameter=0	Prob > |T|
INTERCEP	1	−1.973401	0.03939574	−50.092	0.0001
LOG__TDOL	1	0.875307	0.01787217	48.976	0.0001
LOG__ORDR	1	−0.961115	0.01887344	−50.924	0.0001
LOG__LBUY	1	−0.015471	0.00991300	−1.561	0.1222

Variable	DF	Standardized Estimate
INTERCEP	1	0.00000000
LOG__TDOL	1	1.06809616
LOG__ORDR	1	−1.10992738
LOG__LBUY	1	−0.02768440

$$\text{DOLLSPENT} = 351.29 - .65 \times \text{INCOME} + .86 \times \text{AGE}$$

As the model stands, AGE and INCOME are in the model and contribute to the prediction of DOLLSPENT additively. That is, regardless of the age of a customer, the DOLLSPENT will decrease $0.65 for every thousand dollars of income. The equation tells us that if you hold age constant, there is a negative relationship between sales and income. In other words, the product line appeals more to lower income persons than to upper income persons. This may be true, but what if it's "really" true for younger people and only "a little" true for older persons?

What if the effect of income on sales is much greater than −$0.65 for younger people, but much less than −$0.65 for older people? If this is true, then the $0.65 regression coefficient is really an average that reflects the behavior of both older and younger people. Clearly, we would like to have

TABLE 11–9

SAS

Model: MODEL1
Dependent Variable: LOG__RESP

Analysis of Variance

Source	DF	Sum of Squares	Mean Square	F Value	Prob > F
Model	2	4.58193	2.29096	1124.797	0.0001
Error	97	0.19757	0.00204		
C Total	99	4.77949			

Root MSE	0.04513	R-square	0.9587	
Dep Mean	−0.76009	Adj R-sq	0.9578	
C.V.	−5.93756			

Parameter Estimates

Variable	DF	Parameter Estimate	Standard Error	T for HO: Parameter = 0	Prob > |T|
INTERCEP	1	−1.890376	0.04300760	−43.954	0.0001
LOG__TDOL	1	0.844590	0.01995868	42.317	0.0001
LOG__ORDR	1	−0.959345	0.02220746	−43.199	0.0001

Variable	DF	Standardized Estimate
INTERCEP	1	0.00000000
LOG__TDOL	1	1.12039211
LOG__ORDR	1	−1.14375208

a technique that would do better than simply average out the behavior of both older and younger people.

In regression analysis, there are a couple of ways to handle this problem. You could run two models, one for older people and one for younger people. You could create a categorical "dummy" variable to represent age and include this variable in the model. Or you could create what is called an interaction variable.

An interaction variable is needed when the additive effects of the independent variables do not adequately explain the relationship between the dependent variable and independent variables. An example we often use has to do with the sale of opera tickets. A statistical profile of opera ticket buyers would reveal that they are both highly educated and upper income. This observation could be used in building a model of opera ticket buyers. We would want both variables, education and income, to be included in the model as independent variables. However, as we all know, not all highly educated persons have high incomes, nor are all upper

TABLE 11–10
Decile Analysis – Mean Response Rate

	Careful Model		Q&D Model	
Decile	Decile	Cum	Decile	Cum
1	29.0%	29.0%	27.0%	27.0%
2	20.0	24.5	20.0	23.5
3	19.0	22.6	21.0	22.6
4	16.0	21.0	16.0	21.0
5	14.0	19.6	14.0	19.6
6	14.0	18.6	13.0	18.5
7	11.0	17.6	13.0	17.7
8	11.0	16.7	10.0	16.8
9	08.0	15.8	08.0	15.8
10	06.0	14.8	06.0	14.8
House file average response rate	14.8		14.8	

income persons highly educated. What we would like in the model, therefore, is a third variable that reflects the fact that a person is *both* highly educated and upper income. This third variable, which is the combination of the two original variables, is called an *interaction variable*.

If an analyst were building a regression model of opera ticket buyers and had correctly identified income and education as important independent variables but had failed to create the interaction variable, the regression model *would not* include the interaction variable. An analyst has to create interaction variables and include them in the set of variables to be considered by the regression program. Fortunately, interaction variables can easily be added into regression models.

Going back to our example where we believe there might be an interactive effect between AGE and INCOME, we create an interaction variable to take the suspected effect into account by simply defining a new interaction variable AGE_INCOME as the product of the AGE and INCOME: AGE_INCOME = AGE × INCOME.

Putting interaction variables into a model is easy because mechanically, all we have to do is instruct the regression program to create a new variable by multiplying two old variables together. However, in practice, finding which two variables (or even three or four variables for higher order interaction effects) is not easy. Although a working knowledge of the variables is the best guide for creating interaction variables, there is a statistical method called Automatic Interaction Detection (AID/CHAID) expressly developed for finding interaction. (We'll discuss AID/CHAID in Chapter 12.)

Multicollinearity

For multiple regression to produce good and reliable coefficients for its independent variables, there must be the absence of perfect multicollinearity. That is, none of the independent variables has a correlation coefficient of 1 with any of the other independent variables or with any weighted sum of the other independent variables. When perfect multicollinearity exists, the regression coefficients cannot be calculated. In such cases, the problem is always identified — the program literally won't run.

The real problem arises when there is high multicollinearity; however, there are some practical rules for identifying multicollinearity:

1. Multiple R-square is high and all or most of the p values are greater than 5 percent.
2. The magnitude of the regression coefficients changes greatly when independent variables are added or dropped from the equation.
3. There are unexpectedly large regression coefficients for variables thought to be relatively unimportant and/or small regression coefficients for variables thought to be relatively important.
4. There are unexpected signs of the coefficients.

Remedies for Multicollinearity

OK, now that you know what multicollinearity is, what it does, and how to detect it, here's how to alleviate the problem.

1. Try to get more observations, more data. That's right, more data. Often, multicollinearity can be a data problem rather than a modeling problem and increasing the sample size will make the problem go away. Actually, while multicollinearity is discussed extensively in texts on statistics, in most direct marketing applications where we are dealing with thousands of observations, multicollinearity is generally not a problem.

2. If you cannot get more data, try to examine all correlation coefficients to spot those with Rs greater than .90. Then, eliminate one of the two "culprit" variables.

3. Review all the independent variables to try to combine those that seem to measure the same content. For example, three variables capturing the number of hours spent listening to MTV, playing the stereo, and watching movies on the VCR can be summed or averaged to obtain a measure of passive media interest. Factor analysis, a technique we'll describe in Chapter 13, can be used for this purpose.

Selection of Variables

Perhaps the most important step in the building process is finding the right variables to include in the model. Without a relevant set of predictors, no amount of data manipulation can produce a good model.

There are three basic approaches to variable selection. The first one we recomend is by far the most important one. It's not statistically elegant but satisfies the validity test of logic and reasonableness and, accordingly, will be accepted by all. It's the selection based on knowledge of the data. Nothing replaces the analyst's experience with the data in terms of what it measures, what it suggests, and how it behaves.

The second approach helps the analyst when either his or her experience with the data is limited or the analyst cannot distinguish among a subset of very good variables. The approach of (forward) stepwise selection starts off by finding the variable that produces the largest R-square with the dependent variable. Then, given that the "best" variable is in the model, it finds the next best variable in terms of adding to the R-square. This process of finding variables that add to R-square stops when variables can no longer add to R-square according to certain statistical criteria.

This approach is helpful in paring down a large number of variables; however, it is notorious for finding subsets of variables that do not "hang" together. That is, the selected variables are difficult to justify because they appear not to be related in any logical or reasonable way to the dependent variable.

Even if a subset of variables produced by the stepwise approach hangs together well, the fact that it is declared best because it has the largest R-square is no guarantee, as we pointed out, of it being the best. In sum, the stepwise selection is only a good first step in finding the right variables.

The third approach uses a relatively new measure of total prediction error, denoted by Mallow's C(p). Using this approach, which is produced automatically by one of the procedures in SAS, we obtain many subsets or combinations of independent variables to choose from. Each combination of variables is associated with a C(p) statistic. The rule of thumb for using

C(p) is to work with sets of variables whose C(p) value is equal or less than 1 plus the number of variables in the subset. However, even though we favor this approach, selection based on C(p) is just like the first two approaches in that there's no guarantee of getting the best set of predictor variables.

If we've made variable selection into "mission impossible," that's because it sometimes seems that way. When the final model is not as strong as desired, we assume it's because we cannot find the right set of variables. Which gets us back to the need to collect better data, which was the theme of Chapter 2 on primary research data.

CHAPTER 12

RESPONSE ANALYSIS

In Illustration 14 in Chapter 11, we discussed building a regression model to predict response. The dependent variable was undoubtedly a response variable but not of the usual kind found in most DM response modeling projects. In most response analyses, the dependent variable is a categorical "dummy" variable. Each person mailed is given a score of 1 or 0 on the variable RESPONSE. A 1 means the person responded, and a 0 means the person did not respond. As we all know, the vast majority of the persons mailed unfortunately do not respond; this is the problem.

INTRODUCTION

The technique of regression analysis was originally developed for scalar or continuous dependent and independent variables. When independent variables are categorical, there are ways (for example, using dummy variables, which will be discussed shortly) to include such variables in the analysis without violating the assumptions of the technique. Use and interpretation of a regression model with categorical variables is similar to that of a model with scalar independent variables.

When the dependent variable is a categorical response variable with two levels, response yes/response no, or 1/0, the regression model is formally called the *linear probability model* (LPM). This label is appropriate because the predicted value of the response variable is interpreted as the probability of response. However, this label gives a false sense of form (linear) and correctness (probability) of the model. It turns out that the presence of a yes/no response-dependent variable violates a number of the assumptions of the regression technique, which renders questionable the model and its utility. One assumption that is violated is that the dependent variable conforms to the shape of the normal distribution. A variable that can have only two values, 1 or 0, cannot be normally distributed. If the response rates to direct marketing offers were greater than 20 percent, this violation would have little practical consequence. However, since this is rarely the case, with many of our response rates hovering around the 1 to 3 percent area, this violation of the normality assumption cannot simply be dismissed.

Without going too deeply into theoretical issues, the LPM suffers from *potentially* excluding important predictors from the final model. This can happen because the t and F statistics can give false signals, potentially causing the analyst to either include insignificant variables or exclude significant variables. In addition, the LPM often results in estimates with probabilities less than 0 or greater than 1.

Not all model builders consider these potential problems terribly serious. Knowing the subject matter, they feel it is easy to identify the important variables and put them into the model. As for the "outside" probabilities, if the number of occurrences is small (which is usually the case), they view the model as more than acceptable.

It has been shown in practice that if one is only interested in ranking a file of customers from most to least likely to respond, then the LPM and alternative techniques (such as logistic regression and discriminant analysis, which will be described shortly) all produce essentially the same ordering of a customer file.

The following are more important issues: Does each technique have access to the correct set of variables? For example, are interaction variables available to all techniques? Is each technique being used properly? Are variables being transformed to approximate normality? Are linear relationships sought out, and so on.

However, for those analysts who just do not want to use a model that is flawed, or really need to go beyond ranking the names on a file, and who need reliable probabilities of response, there are alternative techniques.

Before getting into the mechanics of these techniques, it might be helpful to clarify some terms that are used almost interchangeably but in fact have slightly different meanings. The terms are: (1) log-linear modeling, (2) logit models, (3) logit regression, (4) logistic models, (5) logistic regression.

The terms *regression* and *models* in this context mean the same thing, so we have only to define the differences among log-linear models, logit models, and logistic models.

Logit models and *logistic models* are essentially the same thing. In both cases, the dependent variable is the categorical yes/no, or 1/0, or respond/did not respond variable we work with in direct marketing. However, some of the computer programs that perform these analyses distinguish between logistic models and logit models. In statistical packages such as SAS where there is a difference, logistic models or programs are run when the independent variables include one or more continuous variables; logit programs are run when all of the independent variables are categorical. However, there are other statistical packages in which logit programs accept both continuous and categorical independent variables.

Log-linear models are used when all variables are categorical. Technically, log-linear models do not distinguish between independent and dependent variables. One can, however, take the results of a log-linear model and declare one variable as the dependent variable and run what is essentially a logit model.

Log-linear and logit models, as well as ordinary regression models, can accept interaction variables but cannot systematically identify them—they can only test them for significance. However, CHAID (which we will discuss in detail shortly) is a technique that does identify significant interaction variables that can then be used as variables in any of the three techniques just mentioned.

With that as background, let's examine logistic regression in more detail. It should be pointed out that the following material is mathematically difficult and some readers may want to skip ahead to the sections on Discriminant Analysis and CHAID.

Just remember, for most direct marketers, the bottom line with regard to logistic or logit modeling is that they are perfectly appropriate techniques and should be used provided your statistician is familiar with the techniques. Not all statisticians are. On the other hand, if, as we said, you are using modeling to rank a large file in terms of each individual's probability of responding, the rankings developed with ordinary regression are likely to be equivalent to the rankings found using these more appropriate statistical techniques.

As a practical matter, most of the work involved in modeling projects has to do with the understanding and massaging of the available data. After all this preliminary work is done, it's a relatively simple matter to run the data through all three techniques: the LPM or ordinary least squares regression, discriminant analysis, or logit or logistic regression. Figure 12–1 shows the results of such a process. As you can see, from a ranking perspective, the differences are not terribly different. More often than not we find this to be the case.

FIGURE 12–1

Comparison of Statistical Methods: OLS Regression, Logistic, and Discriminant

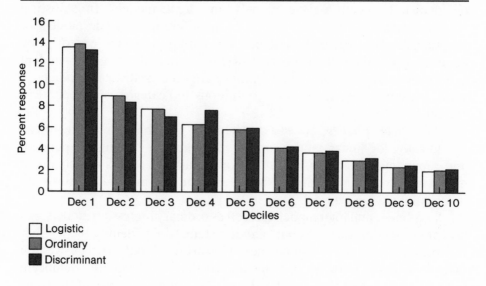

LOGISTIC REGRESSION

Concepts and Definition

The concepts that hold the logistic regression model together are:

1. Probability.
2. Odds.
3. Logit.
4. Odds ratio.
5. Log odds.

It takes a fair amount of algebra to transform raw yes/no data into a form that can be used in a logistic model. The algebra that follows is no more than a transformation but the logic of the steps taken is not intuitively obvious. The reader who wishes to follow along is welcome but again, understanding how the transformation is accomplished is not necessary to understanding how to use the results.

To begin, let Y stand for the response to a mailing, where Y equals 1 for a yes response and 0 for a no response.

Let's define the probability of a response as *p,* and therefore the probability of a nonresponse is $(1 - p)$. (If the probability of a response is 5 percent, then the probability of a nonresponse is 95 percent.)

The next concept is the concept of *odds.* By definition, the odds of a yes response are the ratio of the probability of a response divided by the probability of a nonresponse.

$$\text{odds} = \frac{p}{(1 - p)}$$

With a little algebra, the probability *p* can be expressed in terms of odds:

$$(1 - p) \times \text{odds} = p$$
$$\text{odds} - p \times \text{odds} = p$$
$$\text{odds} = p + p \times \text{odds}$$
$$\text{odds} = p \times (1 + \text{odds})$$
$$p = \frac{\text{odds}}{(1 + \text{odds})}$$

We'll use this relationship later.

If the odds of a yes response is given by $p/(1 - p)$, then the natural log of the odds of a yes response (log to the base *e*), denoted by *ln,* is:

$$ln(\text{yes}) = ln(p/1 - p) = ln(p) - ln(1 - p)$$

This difference, the natural log of a yes response, is called the *logit* of yes.

Now, let's consider another variable *X* that takes on two values, *a* and *b.* Also, assume that *Y* depends on *X,* where:

the probability of a yes response when $X = a$ is $p(a)$
the probability of a no response when $X = a$ is $1 - p(a)$

the probability of a yes response when $X = b$ is $p(b)$
the probability of a no response when $X = b$ is $1 - p(b)$

The odds of a yes response given $X = a$ is $p(a)/1 - p(a)$.
The log of a yes response given $X = a$ is:

$$ln(\text{yes given } X = a) = ln\, p(a) - ln(1 - p(a))$$

This difference is called the *logit of yes given X = a.*

The odds of a yes response given $X = b$ is $p(b)/1 - p(b)$.
The log of a yes response given $X = b$ is:

$$ln(\text{yes given } X = b) = ln\,p(b) - ln(1 - p(b))$$

This difference is called the *logit of yes given $X = b$.*
The ratio of the odds of yes for $X = a$ to the odds of yes for $X = b$, called the *odds ratio,* is:

$$\frac{p(a)/1 - p(a)}{p(b)/1 - p(b)}$$

The log of odds ratio, called the *log odds* is:

$$ln\,(\text{odds ratio}) = \frac{(\text{Logit of yes given } X = a)}{- (\text{Logit of yes given } X = b)}$$

Logistic Regression Model

All of the above algebra allows us to introduce the concept of a logistic regression model. The logistic regression model is a linear model of the form:

$$G = b0 + b1 \times X1 + b2 \times X2 + \ldots + bn \times Xn$$

where:

G = the logit of a yes response given specific values of $X1, X2, \ldots, Xn$. (Implicit in the phrase *yes response* is a categorical dependent variable with two values of yes and no)

$b0$ = the intercept, which, as in ordinary regression, can be viewed as a placeholder necessary to make the equation work well

$b1, \ldots, bn$ = logistic coefficients (to be discussed shortly)

Logistic Equation

ILLUSTRATION 15

Let's consider a sample of 20 customers from our cataloger's latest catalog mailing. The cataloger would like to build a model to predict response to this mailing for use in developing a list for future mailings of similar catalogs. The goal is to identify new customers on the file who have a high likelihood of responding to a similar program.

The 20 records consist of three variables: RESPONSE to the mailing (1 = yes/0 = no), AGE (in years), GENDER (0 = male/1 = female). (See Table 12–1.)

The variables of the model are: the categorical dependent variable RESPONSE, the scalar independent variable AGE, and GENDER, a categorical independent variable.

Up to this point, all our independent variables were scalar. Can linear models, whether ordinary, logistic, or otherwise, handle categorical independent variables? Yes.

Dummy Variables

The trick for putting categorical independent variables into any regression model is to create dummy variables. Suppose, for example, that the categorical variable is SOURCE OF ORDER, which has been coded as direct mail, print, and other. In this case, two dummy variables are needed.

TABLE 12–1

RESPONSE	AGE	GENDER
0	21	1
0	23	1
0	25	1
0	29	1
0	32	1
0	33	0
0	34	0
0	34	0
0	45	1
0	45	1
1	46	1
1	46	1
1	57	1
1	57	1
1	58	1
1	58	0
1	69	1
1	63	1
1	64	1
1	64	1

The first dummy variable, $D1$, is coded 1 if the individual's source is direct mail, and 0 if the individual's source is print or other. The second dummy variable, $D2$, is coded 1 if the individual was acquired from a print source, and 0 if acquired from direct mail or other.

Accordingly, if an individual was acquired from a direct mail source, then for that person, $D1$ equals 1 and $D2$ equals 0; if an individual was acquired from a print source, then $D1$ equals 0 and $D2$ equals 1; and, if the source were neither direct mail nor print, that is, an other, then $D1$ and $D2$ are both equal to 0. Table 12–2 shows the dummy variables for SOURCE OF ORDER.

Thus, whenever there is a categorical independent variable to be put into a model, we simply create a set of dummy variables (the number of variables in the set is equal to the number of category values minus 1).

Since the GENDER variable has only two values, which implies that only one dummy variable is needed, and it is coded 1 if female and 0 otherwise (for male), GENDER is already a dummy variable. GENDER, as is, can go directly into the model.

Running the data through a logistic regression program produces the logistic equation shown below:

$$G = -10.83 + .28 \times \text{AGE} + 2.30 \times \text{GENDER}$$

G is the logit of a yes response to the mailing given specific values of AGE and GENDER.

Let's see what G is all about. Consider a male customer age 40 (GENDER = 0 and AGE = 40); his G or logit score is:

$$
\begin{aligned}
G(0,40) &= -10.83 + .28 \times 40 + 2.30 \times 0 \\
&= -10.83 + 11.2 + 0 \\
&= .37 \text{ logits}
\end{aligned}
$$

A female customer of the same age would have a score of 2.67:

TABLE 12–2

SOURCE OF ORDER	D1	D2
Direct mail	1	0
Print	0	1
Other	0	0

$$G(1,40) = -10.83 + .28 \times 40 + 2.30 \times 1$$
$$= -10.83 + 11.2 + 2.30$$
$$= 2.67 \text{ logits}$$

Logits, with the aid of tables, can be converted into odds, which can be converted into probabilities.

Accordingly, we have:

Odds of yes response for a 40-year-old male   = .37 logits = 1.44
Odds of yes response for a 40-year-old female = 2.67 logits = 14.44

recalling from above that

$$p = \frac{\text{odds}}{(1 + \text{odds})}$$

For the 40-year-old male

$$p = 1.44/(1 + 1.44)$$
$$p = .59$$

For the 40-year-old female

$$p = 14.44/(1 + 14.44)$$
$$p = .93$$

Thus, the 40-year-old male customer has a 59 percent probability of response. The female customer has a probability of 93 percent.

Logistic Coefficients

Since G is in logits, then the coefficients are also in logits. Since we can un-log G logits to obtain odds, we can un-log the coefficients, too. Doing this will give us the meaning of the coefficients and add to the understanding of a logit.

Let's consider the coefficient of AGE, .28, that is, .28 logits. Un-logging the coefficient of .28, we have 1.32, that is, the odds of yes response is 1.32. Thus, for every one-year increase in age, the odds of a yes response increases 1.32 times. Let's see.

The G logit score for a male 41-year-old is:

$$G(0,41) = -10.83 + .28 \times 41 + 2.30 \times 0$$
$$= -10.83 + 11.48 + 0$$
$$= .65 \text{ logits}$$

The odds corresponding to .65 logits is 1.92 and the odds corresponding to .37 logits is 1.44; thus, the increase in the odds for a male when his age increases one year is 1.32 times (1.92/1.44 = 1.32).

Now that we have some idea of where logits come from, let's remind ourselves of how they are used. If everyone on a file is scored and the scores are in terms of logits, the scores, that is, the logits, can still be ranked from high to low and the traditional decile analysis can be performed. You recall that we, and others, argue that most of the time the ranking based on a logit analysis will be equivalent, from a practical decision-making perspective, to the rankings resulting from an ordinary regression analysis. On the other hand, each individual logit score can be transformed back into a specific probability of response, a probability that will always be between 0 and 1, which is not always the case in regression.

One last point. While it is one thing to find a statistician who can build a logit model, it is another thing to find computer programmers who have the skills and tools available to translate logits back into probabilities. Scoring in logits and ranking in logits is simple because to the computer, a logit is just another number. This is a similar problem to the one of presenting a programmer with an ordinary regression equation that requires the use of logs or exponential functions. The point to be remembered is to always check with data processing to make sure any solution you come up with can be implemented.

DISCRIMINANT ANALYSIS

In the preceding discussion, we mentioned discriminant analysis as an alternative to regression when the dependent variable is a categorical yes/no or 1/0 response variable. The independent variables can be either scalar or categorical with the use of dummy variables, and interaction variables can also be included, just as in multiple regression.

Discriminant analysis is a statistical technique that was developed to identify variables that explain the differences between two or more groups (e.g., responders and nonresponders of a mailing) and that classify unknown observations (for example, customers) into the groups. The discriminant model looks like a multiple regression model where the categorical dependent variable is again expressed as a sum of weighted independent or discriminant variables.

$$Z = b0 + b1 \times X1 + b2 \times X2 + b3 \times X3 + \ldots + bn \times Xn$$

The weights (the bs), called *discriminant coefficients*, are derived such that the resultant discriminant model maximizes the statistical difference among the groups. It is interesting to note that in regression, the coefficients are derived to maximize R-square. Thus, both techniques are very similar in their maximizing derivation. In addition, both methods depend on certain assumptions about the normality of the variables that go into the model.

In a simple two-group discriminant analysis, if an individual's Z score is greater than some critical value determined by experience, the individual is placed in group 1; if the Z score is less than that value, the individual is placed in group 2. The evaluation of the model is based on whether or not the model places persons into groups more accurately than would occur by chance.

However, it has been shown in practice that discriminant analysis is more sensitive to violations of normality than regression. This is particularly true when the size of the two groups is very different, as is the case in response analysis when the yes group is generally below 10 percent. Although we try to reshape the data as best we can for those situations where the best we can do in reexpression is not enough, discriminant models will not perform as well as regression models. Therefore, a conservative approach is to stick with ordinary regression or logistic regression over discriminant analysis.

AUTOMATIC INTERACTION DETECTION – AID/CHAID

Thus far, we've described and illustrated two regression methods. If the dependent variable is scalar and the independent variables are scalar and/or categorical, then ordinary regression is the appropriate method to use. If the dependent variable is a categorical 0/1 response variable and the independent variables are scalar and/or categorical, one can, in most circumstances, still use ordinary regression if the application is only to rank a file from most to least likely to respond. If good reliable estimates of probability of response are needed, then one must use the logistic regression method.

Now, we discuss two complementary methods to ordinary and logistic regression: Automatic Interaction Detection (AID) and CHAID. In an AID or CHAID analysis, the dependent variable is categorical and the independent variables must also be categorical. If an independent variable is scalar, it must be transformed into a categorical variable. This is not hard to do – the analyst simply breaks the scalar variable into ranges. For example, Sales, which is a scalar variable, can be expressed in ranges of $0 to $9.99, $10 to $19.99, $20 to $49.99, and so on.

Notice the word *interaction*. This is the same interaction as previously discussed in the context of interaction variables. AID/CHAID was originally developed for the express purpose of finding interaction variables for inclusion into a regression, logit, or log-linear model.

As it turns out, today AID/CHAID is often used as an "end" analysis rather than as a "means" to provide insight for further model building. We'll discuss the use of AID/CHAID as both a complement to regression and as a stand-alone technique.

First, let's explain the differences between AID and CHAID. AID was developed in the 1960s at the University of Michigan as a method to identify segments of a market. It defines the segments in terms of *two-level* categorical independent variables. For example, an AID "model" with two independent variables (MARITAL STATUS and COLLEGE EDUCATED), each with two possibilities (MARRIED/NOT MARRIED, COLLEGE/NO COLLEGE), can divide a market into four segments:

1. Married, with college.
2. Married, without college.
3. Unmarried, with college.
4. Unmarried, without college.

Later, two significant improvements to the method were introduced. First, multiway splits of the independent variable were allowed — no longer was it necessary for the independent variables to be limited to two-way splits. Second, the differences between end-point cells in an AID analysis were not subject to a test of statistical significance. This deficiency was eliminated with the introduction of the chi-square test for statistical significance. Thus, the addition of CH in CHAID, which stands for the chi-square test of statistical significance. Dr. Gordon V. Kass is credited with the development of the CHAID methodology.[1] Jay Magidson enhanced the basic CHAID program with a series of features that make CHAID more useful to direct marketers and produced a product called SI–CHAID™, which is now marketed by SPSS. (SI stands for Statistical Innovation, the name of Magidson's company.)

---

[1] Gordon V. Kass, "Significance Testing in, and Some Extensions of, Automatic Interaction Detection" (doctoral dissertation, University of Witwatersrand, Johannesburg, South Africa, 1976).

ILLUSTRATION 15

Let's illustrate the use of CHAID by making one last return to our cataloger, who now believes that it is possible to build a predictive response model based on knowledge of:

1. How long a customer has been on the database (HOW__LONG).
2. What part of the country the customer lives in (REGION).
3. Whether or not the customer is married (MARITAL).

A random sample of approximately 40,000 customers who received a recent mailing was drawn. The data was coded as follows:

1. HOW__LONG
   a. Less than 1 year (coded 1)
   b. 1–2 years (coded 2).
   c. 2 years, plus (coded 3).
   d. Years unknown (coded 4).
2. REGION
   a. Northeast (coded 1).   e. Midsouth (coded 5).
   b. East (coded 2).   f. Northwest (coded 6).
   c. Southeast (coded 3).   g. Southwest (coded 7).
   d. Midwest (coded 4).
3. MARITAL
   a. Divorced/separated (coded 1).
   b. Married (coded 2).
   c. Single (coded 3).
   d. Widowed (coded 4).
   e. Unknown (coded 5).
4. RESPONSE (to the last mailing)
   a. Yes (coded 1).
   b. No (coded 2).

The average response rate was 12.59 percent. Response rates by each level of the variables HOW__LONG, REGION, and MARITAL are shown in Table 12–3. In a regression model, each break will be treated as an independent variable. Not yet having heard of CHAID, the analyst runs an ordinary dummy variable regression analysis. The results of that analysis are shown in Table 12–4.

Table 12–4 depicts a result that direct marketers are becoming accustomed to seeing: a significant model ($F = 58.295$), with significant independent variables (ts range from 4.2 to 9.0, and all p values

TABLE 12–3
Results by Segments of Individual Variables (in Percents)

HOW__LONG 1 = 13.98%	MARITAL 1 = 13.66
HOW__LONG 2 = 13.40	MARITAL 2 = 12.95
HOW__LONG 3 = 11.12	MARITAL 3 = 12.21
HOW__LONG 4 = 14.24	MARITAL 4 = 5.76
	MARITAL 5 = 12.25
REGION 1 = 9.44	
REGION 2 = 13.00	
REGION 3 = 15.53	
REGION 4 = 12.85	
REGION 5 = 14.93	
REGION 6 = 11.29	
REGION 7 = 13.20	

are less than .0001), and an almost nonexistent R-square of .0071 or .71 percent.

As we said, the real proof of the usefulness of a predictive model is in the analysis of a validation sample. In Table 12–5, we apply the model to a second sample of 40,000 names and look to see how well the model "spreads" the average response rate. This is shown in Table 12–5.

The model spreads the average response rate fairly well. The best 14.4 percent of the names mailed pulled 17.1 percent, the bottom 13.9 percent pulled 8 percent, and another 9.8 percent pulled 11 percent. The question is, "can we do better?" and specifically, "can CHAID identify important interactions between the independent variables that regression did not explicitly take into account?" Remember, regression has no provision to automatically look for interactions; it has to be told that interactions exist.

THE SI–CHAID ANALYSIS OF THE SAME DATA

The SI–CHAID program begins by presenting the response rates for each segment of each variable, and then uses the chi-square test to combine segments that are not statistically different from each other. (See Table 12–6.)

Table 12–6 tells us that the SI–CHAID program has found no statistical difference among the HOW__LONG variables 1, 2, and 4, so it has combined them into HOW__LONG 124. Similarly, it has combined REGIONS 2, 4, and 7 and REGIONS 3 and 5 into two new

TABLE 12–4

Model: RESP__HAT
Dependent Variable: RESPONSE

Analysis of Variance

Source	DF	Sum of Squares	Mean Square	F Value	Prob>F
Model	5	33.00807	6.60161	58.295	0.0001
Error	40581	4595.56640	0.11324		
C Total	40586	4628.57447			

Root MSE	0.33652	R-square	0.0071
Dep Mean	0.13127	Adj R-sq	0.0070
C.V.	256.34856		

Parameter Estimates

Variable	DF	Parameter Estimate	Standard Error	T for H0: Parameter = 0	Prob > |T|
INTERCEP	1	0.149570	0.00270699	55.253	0.0000
MARITAL4	1	−0.070960	0.00784734	−9.042	0.0001
HOW_LNG3	1	−0.027374	0.00335740	−8.153	0.0001
REGION1	1	−0.034529	0.00434860	−7.940	0.0001
REGION3	1	0.028100	0.00564363	4.979	0.0001
REGION5	1	0.024340	0.00566267	4.298	0.0001

Variable	DF	Standardized Estimate
INTERCEP	1	0.00000000
MARITAL4	1	−0.04497071
HOW_LNG3	1	−0.04052533
REGION1	1	−0.04058342
REGION3	1	0.02524823
REGION5	1	0.02181160

TABLE 12–5
Ordinary Dummy Variable Regression Model

Regression Segments	Quantity	Number of Responses	Percent Mailing	Cumulative Percent Mailing	Percent Response	Cumulative Percent Response
1	2,097	361	5.2%	5.2%	17.2%	6.8%
2	3,756	642	9.3	14.4	17.1	18.8
3	12,194	1,829	30.0	44.4	15.0	53.1
4	1,948	269	4.8	49.3	13.8	58.2
5	10,975	1,339	27.0	76.3	12.2	83.3
6	3,986	438	9.8	86.1	11.0	91.5
7	5,691	450	13.9	100.0	8.0	100.0
Total	40,587	5,223	100.0%		13.1%	

TABLE 12–6

Before Merging	After Initial Merging
HOW_LONG 1 = 13.98%	HOW_LONG 124 = 14.06
HOW_LONG 2 = 13.40	HOW_LONG 3 = 11.12
HOW_LONG 3 = 11.12	
HOW_LONG 4 = 14.24	
REGION 1 = 9.44	REGION 1 = 9.44
REGION 2 = 13.00	REGION 247 = 12.96
REGION 3 = 15.53	REGION 35 = 15.23
REGION 4 = 12.85	REGION 6 = 11.29
REGION 5 = 14.93	
REGION 6 = 11.29	
REGION 7 = 13.20	
MARITAL 1 = 13.66	MARITAL 1235 = 12.94
MARITAL 2 = 12.95	MARITAL 4 = 5.76
MARITAL 3 = 12.21	
MARITAL 4 = 5.76	
MARITAL 5 = 12.25	

variables: REGION 247 and REGION 35. The five original marital variables has been reduced to two variables.

The solution of the CHAID analysis is in the form of a tree diagram, found in Figure 12–2. There are seven end segments defined by the three independent variables HOW_LONG, REGION, and MARITAL, even though there were 105 possible segments (3 times 7 times 5) before the segments within variables were combined and 16 possible segments after the segments within variables were combined (2 times 4 times 2).

Notice that of the three "main effects" variables (MARITAL, HOW_LONG, and REGION), the CHAID program determined that MARITAL with the two new levels of 1, 2, 3, and 5 versus 4 was the single best predictor of response.

Next, CHAID treats the two segments of MARITAL as the starting point for two new analyses. CHAID now attempts to split the MARITAL cell (MARITAL 1235) by either REGION or HOW_LONG. CHAID determines that MARITAL 1235 is "best" (largest statistically significant difference) divided by REGION, resulting in three new levels (REGION 1 versus REGION 2467 and REGION 35). On the other hand, the cell identified as MARITAL 4, at this point, is "best" further divided by the variable HOW_LONG with two new levels HOW_LONG 14 and HOW_LONG 23.

FIGURE 12–2

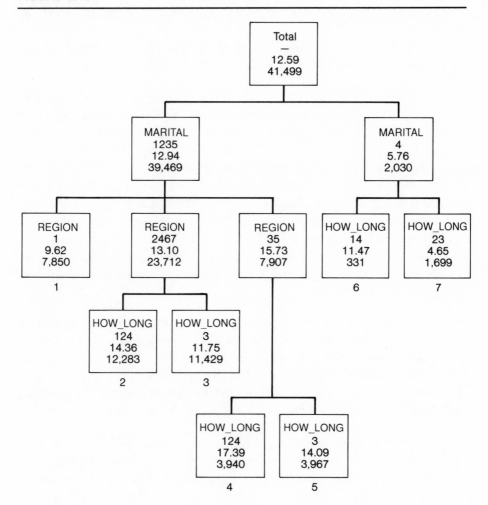

Notice how REGION 6 has been combined with REGIONS 2, 4, and 7. Originally REGION 6 could not be combined with any of the other REGIONs, but after MARITAL 4 is removed from consideration, those persons in REGION 6 look statistically similar to those in REGIONs 2, 4, and 7. This is what we mean when we say that the process is repeated from the beginning at each new level in the tree.

The two HOW__LONG segments (segments 6 and 7 on the CHAID tree) are considered end or final segments because the remaining variable

(REGION) does not provide any further predictive splitting power. The same holds true for segment 1, which cannot be split by HOW_LONG.

Thus, at this "depth" of the tree, there are three final segments defined as follows:

> **Segment 1** — customers who are either divorced/separated, married, single, or marital status unknown *and* live in the northeast region of the country. These customers have an average response rate of 9.62 percent, somewhat below the house file average of 12.59 percent, which is indicated in the top box of the tree.
>
> **Segment 6** — Widowed customers who have been on the database less than one year or the number of years is unknown; these customers have an average response rate of 11.47 percent and consist of approximately 1 percent of the file (331/41,499).
>
> **Segment 7** — Widowed customers who have been on the file two years or more. These customers have an average response rate of 4.65 percent.

The remaining two cells (defined by REGION 2467 and REGION 35) are both split by the HOW_LONG variables with the same combined levels (HOW_LONG 124 and HOW_LONG 3), resulting in four final segments. Segment 4 has the largest average response rate of 17.39 percent, significantly above the overall average 12.59 percent, and consists of a reasonable market size of 9.5 percent of the house file.

At this point, we could stop and use the results of the SI–CHAID analysis as the sole basis for segmenting the database, or use the results of the CHAID analysis as input to a regression model. If we were to stop here, we would have the model shown in Table 12–7.

As mentioned previously, many mailers will stop at this point and use the CHAID output to segment their file and mail accordingly. Others may use the CHAID output as input into a regression or a logit model, attempting to build a model with more predictive power than the CHAID model.

How does the CHAID solution compare to the dummy variable regression solution? Essentially, the results are the same. The CHAID solution appears to have identified a small, poor-performing segment of the file (4.1 percent of the names mailed that pulled only 4.65 percent) that the regression model missed, but we really can't be sure of that

TABLE 12–7
Model Based on CHAID Analysis

CHAID Segments	Quantity	Number of Responses	Percent Mailing	Cumulative Percent Mailing	Percent Response	Cumulative Percent Response
4	3,940	685	9.5%	9.5%	17.39%	13.1%
2	12,283	1,764	29.6	39.1	14.36	46.9
5	3,967	559	9.6	48.7	14.09	57.6
3	11,429	1,343	27.5	76.2	11.75	83.3
6	331	38	0.8	77.0	11.47	84.0
1	7,850	755	18.9	95.9	9.62	98.5
7	1,699	79	4.1	100.0	4.65	100.0
Total	41,499	5,223	100.0%			

without looking much more closely at a ranking of the bottom 4.1 percent of the file scored with the regression model. And that's not easy to do. Another, easier way to see what CHAID has added to our understanding is to use the results of the CHAID analysis in a regression model.

USING CHAID IN REGRESSION ANALYSIS

There are lots of ways to use the information gained by CHAID in a regression model. One way is to take advantage of what the CHAID model tells us about the breaks within the main variables HOW_LONG, MARITAL, and REGION, as well as what CHAID tells us about the important interactions among the main variables.

For simplicity let's examine just the second level breaks shown in Figure 12–2. If we use a * to indicate the interaction between two main variables we see the following:

Second Level Breaks
MARITAL_1235 * REGION_1 = 9.62
MARITAL_1235 * REGION_2467 = 13.10
MARITAL_1235 * REGION_35 = 15.73
MARITAL_4 * HOW LONG_14 = 11.47
MARITAL_4 * HOW LONG_23 = 4.65

Given these five mutually exclusive categories we can create four dummy variables and use these dummy variables in a regression equation. Since the response rate to MARITAL 1235 * Region 2467 is closest to the average response rate of 12.59 we will use this category as the neutral or base case in setting up the dummy variables.

	Dummy Variables			
Conditions	M1R1	M1R3	M4H1	M4H2
MARITAL __ 1235 * REGION __ 1	1	0	0	0
MARITAL __ 1235 * REGION __ 35	0	1	0	0
MARITAL __ 4 * HOW LONG __ 14	0	0	1	0
MARITAL __ 4 * HOW LONG __ 23	0	0	0	1

The results of a regression model using all of the dummy variables defined above is presented in Table 12–8. The significant variables turned out to be REGION 1, REGION 35, HOW__LONG 3, and the interaction variables: M4H2, M4H1, and M1R3.

Did the regression model provide the user with a better model? The answer to this question is in Table 12–9, which presents the validation results for the model built with the CHAID variables, and in Table 12–10, which compares the two regression models, the one built without the knowledge of interactions (Table 12–5) and the one just built with knowledge of interactions (Table 12–9).

As you can see from a comparison of the two models, the CHAID enhanced model does the better job at the extremes. It identifies a small group (about 5 percent) that pulls 19.7 percent, compared to a similar-sized group that pulled only 17.2 percent, and on the bottom, it identified a relatively large group that pulls only about 6 percent, as compared to a similar-sized group that pulled about 8 percent.

Are these results typical? That's a very hard question to answer. The results can be more (or less) dramatic than those shown in the example used. Certainly, when the effect of interaction does not work in the same direction for all combinations of variables, the results can be much more important. For example, take two variables — SEX and ADVERTISING COPY — each of which was split two ways — MALE/FEMALE and COPY A/COPY B. If COPY A had a positive effect on men and a negative effect on women, and COPY B worked in the reverse

TABLE 12–8

Model: RESP__HAT
Dependent Variable: RESPONSE

Analysis of Variance

Source	DF	Sum of Squares	Mean Square	F Value	Prob > F
Model	6	34.53475	5.75579	50.842	0.0001
Error	40580	4594.03972	0.11321		
C Total	40586	4628.57447			

Root MSE	0.33647	R-square	0.0075
Dep Mean	0.13127	Adj R-sq	0.0073
C.V.	256.30914		

Parameter Estimates

Variable	DF	Parameter Estimate	Standard Error	T for H0: Parameter = 0	Prob > |T|
INTERCEP	1	0.149459	0.00271559	55.037	0.0000
REGION1	1	−0.034585	0.00434798	−7.954	0.0001
REGION35	1	0.048844	0.00906417	5.389	0.0001
HOW__LONG3	1	−0.026411	0.00338888	−7.794	0.0001
M4H2	1	−0.084690	0.00883210	−9.589	0.0001
M4H1	1	−0.044651	0.01928074	−2.316	0.0206
M1R3	1	−0.028018	0.00980542	−2.857	0.0043

Variable	DF	Standardized Estimate
INTERCEP	1	0.00000000
REGION1	1	−0.04064964
REGION35	1	0.05834542
HOW__LONG3	1	−0.03910062
M4H2	1	−0.04918049
M4H1	1	−0.01165782
M1R3	1	−0.03087002

way, that is, a positive effect on females and negative on men, a model that took these two variables (SEX and COPY) into consideration but failed to look at the interactions of SEX and COPY would be incomplete and potentially misleading.

An examination of Table 12–11 indicates that a test of MALE versus FEMALE would conclude that females respond better than males. Without looking at the different effect COPY has on each SEX, one would also conclude that COPY had no effect on response when in fact COPY A increases response among women and decreases response among men. COPY B has the reverse effect; it increases response among men and decreases response among women. A regression model that had only two dummy variables, one for SEX and one for COPY, would

TABLE 12–9
Regression Model Using Information From CHAID

Regression Segments	Quantity	Number of Responses	Percent Mailing	Cumulative Percent Mailing	Percent Response	Cumulative Percent Response
1	1,976	379	4.6%	4.6%	19.7%	7.3%
2	3,554	608	8.6	13.2	17.1	18.9
3	12,202	1,830	29.4	42.7	15.0	53.9
4	3,302	466	8.0	50.6	14.1	62.8
5	10,975	1,218	26.5	77.1	11.1	86.1
6	4,034	403	9.7	86.8	50.0	93.8
7	5,456	322	13.2	100.0	5.9	100.0
Total	41,499	5,227	100.0%			

not discover this interaction effect, and could in fact produce misleading results — an incorrect ranking of the four combinations of the variables. However, a regression analysis that included an interaction variable that was the product of the two dummy variables would take the interaction into account and produce a correct ranking of the four combinations of SEX and COPY.

The lesson to be learned is that interactions can be very important and a search for interactions should be one of the first steps in the modeling process. A summary of that process follows.

TABLE 12–10
A Comparison of Regression Results

Regression Segments	Regression without Interaction Effects			Regression with Interaction Effects		
	Quantity	Percent Mailing	Percent Response	Quantity	Percent Mailing	Percent Response
1	2,097	5.2%	17.2%	1,976	4.6%	19.7%
2	3,756	9.3	17.1	3,554	8.6	17.1
3	12,194	30.0	15.0	12,202	29.4	15.0
4	1,948	4.8	13.8	3,302	8.0	14.1
5	10,975	27.0	12.2	10,975	26.5	11.1
6	3,986	9.8	11.0	4,034	9.7	50.0
7	5,691	13.9	8.0	5,456	13.2	5.9
Total	40,587	100.0%		41,499	100.0%	

TABLE 12–11
The Effect of Interaction When the Effect of Variable A Depends on the Value of Variable B

Average response rate	= 4%	
Response among men	= 3%	
Response among women	= 5%	
Response to COPY A among both groups	= 4%	
Response to COPY B among both groups	= 4%	
Response to COPY A among men	= 1%	
Response to COPY B among men	= 5%	
Response to COPY A among women	= 7%	
Response to COPY B among women	= 3%	

MULTIPLE REGRESSION: GUIDELINES FOR BUILDING A MODEL

The following are basic guidelines for building a multiple regression model.

1. Know your data, or work with someone who does. A data analyst without a working knowledge of your data is a data analyst who's going to get you in trouble.
2. Start with an examination of a correlation matrix to develop ideas about candidate variables and to check for two-variable multicollinearity.
3. Look at your data using stem-and-leaf displays. If the data is not normal, attempt to normalize it using the transformations we suggested.
4. Plot your original and transformed data two variables at a time, for all pairs of variables. Examine all the relationships to make sure they are straight.
5. Try some interaction variables, using your knowledge of the business or CHAID.
6. Select variables for inclusion into the model using all the approaches discussed: your choice of variables, stepwise selections, and models based on the $C(p)$ statistic.
7. Validate the model on fresh data.

CHAPTER 13

SEGMENTATION ANALYSIS

In Chapters 10 through 12 of this section, we concentrated our attention on predictive models. Predictive models are designed, as their name implies, to predict some outcome, for example, response to a mailing, returns, bad debts, sales volume, and so on.

In this chapter, we turn our attention to segmentation models. Segmentation models are designed to assign people or geographic areas to groups or clusters on the basis of the similarities in characteristics or attributes that describe them — rather than on the basis of some specific action such as response to a mailing.[1]

In Chapter 2, we discussed the many segmentation products available to direct marketers: PRIZM, ClusterPlus, ACORN, Vision, and so on. All of these products combine small geographic units, usually the census block group, into larger units or clusters based on similarities among the block groups. The characteristics or attributes examined in making this decision include each area's values on the many census (and other) variables collected by the Census Bureau and other government and private agencies.

In this chapter, we will discuss the two primary statistical techniques used in building segmentation models: factor analysis and cluster analysis. These techniques can be used to build customized segmentation models of customers and prospects based on survey and customer or prospect performance information, as well as segmentation models based on census data.

One of direct marketing's unique strengths as a promotional medium is its potential ability to make customized promotional offers to individual

---

[1] In Chapter 12, we treated CHAID as a tool to be used in predictive modeling. CHAID also may be used as a segmentation tool when the final step in the analysis is the CHAID model itself.

customers through the use of available or inferred information about each customer. Unfortunately, all too often, this potential capability is still not adequately utilized. Most direct mail packages are still not customized for the recipient: The same package is usually sent to every name on the mailing. True, laser technology is often used to print the recipient's name in a dozen places in the package, and the recipient's address may be mentioned in the letter—but the guts of the offer are for the most part not customized. The product, the price, the terms, and the strategy are most often identical. And yet one would expect, intuitively, that just as different recipients have different buying preferences, a mailing would work better if its offer were tailored to each individual's specific needs.

Such targeting and customization of the offer is different in concept from the kind of list segmentation and decile analysis covered earlier in the discussions of predictive modeling. Predictive modeling is used to indicate *which* segment of a list should be mailed, or how often. It does not tell you *how* that segment of the list, or that individual name, should be mailed, in terms of the kind of offer that is most likely to be successful with that segment.

DATA NEEDED FOR SEGMENTATION MODELING

In customizing offers for each segment, the direct marketer uses the data on hand about the customer. At minimum, the direct marketer knows each customer by name, address, and ZIP code, and the list the customer's name came from. If this list is a response list of some kind, the mailer knows what kind of product or service the name responded to. It is sometimes possible to negotiate even more detailed information from the list owner, such as the amount of money spent, previous buying history, and so on. Even better, if promotion and sales history is maintained on a customer database, the direct marketer will know what this customer purchased in the past, how often he or she purchased, how purchases were paid, and so forth. To this data could be added individual information from customer surveys on, for example, demographic characteristics, attitudes, and interests. Finally, actual or inferred demographic and/or lifestyle characteristics could be overlaid on the existing data; these could come from census or survey sources (see Chapter 2 on sources of primary and secondary data).

The marketer's task now is to "beat the data till it confesses" on what kind of offer to mail each customer. Since it is usually impractical, infeasible, and financially ruinous to customize the offer to every individual mailing recipient, the best we can usually do is to assign names to a relatively small number of homogeneous groups, so that the people in each group can be sent the same mailing but that different groups, clusters, or consumer segments (the three terms are used interchangeably) can then be sent different mailings.

In discussing factor and cluster analysis, the techniques that make up segmentation analysis, our objective is to provide enough information to make you, the reader, an *informed user* of these techniques — but definitely not an expert. To become an expert in these techniques usually requires several years of instruction and experience, and such expertise is more effectively "bought," rather than "made." After reading the following pages, you should know when to call for these kinds of analyses, how to conduct or manage a segmentation study yourself, how to understand the most important elements of the computer output that accompanies these procedures, and what questions to ask of an expert, if you decide to work with one.

FACTOR ANALYSIS: WHAT IT IS, AND WHEN YOU SHOULD USE IT

Factor analysis is a technique used to reduce data into a workable form so that the reduced data can then be used for some other analysis (like cluster analysis, discussed below, or in response modeling using multiple regression, discussed earlier). Technically, the output of a factor analysis can be quite revealing in and of itself, and some researchers find it unnecessary to go further. However, we will treat the output of a factor analysis as input to another procedure.

Factor analysis is usually called for when there is too much data to deal with intuitively or statistically. It may seem paradoxical to marketers who are continually searching for more and better information about their customers to talk about situations where you have too much data, yet these situations can easily occur. Leaf through an information vendor's catalog and you will often find hundreds of pieces of information available. Look through what the Census Bureau has to offer, and you will find each ZIP code or census block described on more than 150 different variables. Conduct a customer survey on attitudes, lifestyles, opinions, interests, and values, and you will probably ask 200 different questions.

Two things happen when you get a huge amount of information. First, it just becomes too much to absorb and comprehend. (There is a well-known psychological principle that says that humans cannot, at one time, hold more than seven pieces of information in working consciousness at any one time.) Second, it can become difficult to work with this mass of data, both statistically and operationally. Not only can it eat up huge amounts of computer memory, it can actually seriously distort the results of many statistical analyses, as we discussed earlier in Chapter 11 under multicollinearity. If you get, say, 150 pieces of information about a person or a ZIP code, it is very likely that some of those pieces of information will be highly related. For example, if you try to explain response rates to a mailing across different ZIP codes in terms of the average education and income levels of each ZIP code, your statistical coefficients for these two variables can get distorted because income and education are often highly related. This could then threaten the validity of some statistical analyses.

In such situations, you need factor analysis. What factor analysis does is to take your 150 different pieces of information and reduce them to far fewer, say 20 (or 10 or 30). The reduced pieces of information are now called *factors* or *components.* The bulk (say, 75 percent) of the information contained in the 150 original pieces of information is now contained in the 20 factors. So what factor analysis does is to enable you to sacrifice some of the information you began with (in this example, 100 percent minus 75 percent, or 25 percent), for the benefit of greatly improved economy of processing and parsimony of description.

As an example: Suppose you buy Census Bureau data describing every ZIP code on 150 different variables such as percent male population, percent white, percent earning above $35,000, percent with two or more cars, median monthly mortgage, percent homeowner, percent with four or more years of college education, percent in white-collar occupations, and so on. These variables represent 100 percent of the raw information. You wish to use these census data to help you analyze statistically the results of a mailing. Having read this book, you know that (1) 150 raw variables are too many to work with, and that (2) factor analysis is the way to cope with this surfeit of data. After you or your statistical analyst factor analyze the data, you will be able to describe each ZIP code in terms of its scores on (perhaps) 20 factors, instead of the 150 original variables. In doing so, you will lose — willingly — some of the richness of the original data. That is the price you will pay — sacrificing perhaps 20 to 30 percent of the raw information you started out with — for the benefit of a dramatic reduction in the number of ZIP code descriptors (from 150 variables to 20 factors) that you now have to work with.

HOW FACTOR ANALYSIS WORKS

There are actually many varieties of factor analysis techniques. The one we are describing here is more accurately labeled *principal components* analysis, and what we are referring to as factors are what finicky statisticians would call *components*. But we will continue, for our purposes, to call them factors, for that is what nonstatisticians call them.

There are essentially three key things you need to understand about how factor analysis works. First, each factor is really a composite, or combination, of original raw variables. The score of each person, or ZIP code, on each factor is thus a weighted combination of the scores of each person, or ZIP code, on each of the original, raw variables. What factor analysis does is combine those raw variables that are highly related among themselves into composite factors, thereby allowing you to let this combination replace those original raw variables. Thus, if average income levels, average monthly mortgage payments, and the percent of households with two or more cars were highly correlated in the actual data, factor analysis would combine these three into a factor (which you might label "affluence"), and you could then create factor scores for each ZIP code for this factor. (In actual practice, the factor score would use information on all the raw variables, but these three would be the ones carrying the highest weights.)

If a ZIP code had average income of $40,000, average monthly mortgage payments of $1,500, and 30 percent of households owning two or more cars, the factor analysis computer output would tell you what weights to apply to these raw numbers to create the factor score (for example, .0035, .25, and 300.17). Thus, the factor score on this factor for this ZIP code would be $.0035 \times 40,000 + .25 \times 1,500 + 300.17 \times .30$, which equals 605.0510. So in subsequent analyses you would not use those three original numbers ($40,000, $1,500, and 30 percent) but one composite factor score (605.0510). Hence, the data-reduction service of factor analysis.

Importantly, when factor analysis gives you these factor coefficients (similar to regression coefficients) called *loadings,* it does so in a manner that the factor scores you create (for the first, second, and third factor, and so on) have a zero correlation with each other. Thus, you can use them as independent (predictor) variables in a multiple regression without any danger of the problems of multicollinearity, which occurs when the independent variables are highly related to each other — and these factor scores, as we just said, are not related to each other at all because of the way we do factor analysis.

The second key idea is that factor analysis shifts the information you feed to it for analysis. Suppose we give it 150 census variables to analyze. Let us say that each of these raw variables has a value, going in, of one *information unit* each. (Statisticians call this an *eigen value.*) So we are feeding the computer a total of 150 units of information, with each raw variable having exactly one unit. What factor analysis does is a little like performing a centrifugal operation on milk to let the cream float to the top. If you think of the cream as being rich in information, factor analysis shifts the information when it creates the factors so that the first factor it creates is richest in information content, the next one a little less so, and so on, till the last one barely contains any — its information value (or eigen value) being close to zero.

In fact, the mathematics of factor analysis are such that if you feed it 150 raw variables (each with a raw information value of 1), the computer solution will initially give you 150 factors — as many as the number of variables you put in — but with this key difference: the first factors now contain most of the raw information that went in (the cream), while the rest are, from an information standpoint, trivial and unimportant. Therefore, the analyst tells the factor analysis program to retain only the first few (high–information value, or high–eigen value) factors, and to drop the rest from consideration.

While there are many rules concerning which factors should be kept and which ones dropped, one frequently used rule is to drop those factors that have an eigen value of less than 1. The reasoning here is that if a raw variable starts out with an eigen value of 1, a final factor must, after the analysis, have at least that same amount of information if it is to be worth keeping.

There are many other ways to decide how many factors to keep, however, and you and your analyst should try several, ending with one that leaves you with a factor analysis output you can most easily and intuitively interpret and implement.

For example, you might decide to keep as many factors as are necessary to retain some fixed amount of information. This might be 70 percent, 80 percent, and so on. Alternatively, you might simply decide that 5 (or 6 or 10) are the number of factors you wish to keep. If you really want to be scientific, you could apply what is called a *scree test.* In this approach, you ask the computer to give you a graph of the eigen value of the first through last factors, and try to find the factor at which the curve bends sharply — what statisticians with anatomical bents call an *elbow.* This is very often the point where subsequent factors really add very little by way of extra information (i.e., begin to have small eigen values), and so it is reasonable to stop at that factor where the elbow occurs.

Before we get to interpretation, however, there is one last idea that the user needs to grasp. Doing a factor analysis is a lot like taking a photograph with a camera. Just as you would focus the lens—by rotating it—to get a sharp (not blurred) picture on film of whatever it is that you are photographing, so also are you expected to "rotate" the factor analysis table of loadings (the output) to get a more focused interpretation of what is in the data. By focused, we mean a situation where you can look at the output table and read off unambiguously which raw variables are key to forming each factor. There are many ways to rotate the output, but one called *varimax rotation* is frequently used. Once again, you should try a few rotation alternatives to find one that yields an output table you find easiest to interpret.

RUNNING AND INTERPRETING FACTOR ANALYSIS

Let's walk through the steps you need to use factor analysis on your own, and talk about how you would interpret what you get.

Let's suppose you are managing a negative option book club. You decide that instead of mailing the same negative option selection to all of your million-member file, you would like to customize the negative option to the reading preference of the member. You are thinking of dividing your file into perhaps five segments, or clusters, and featuring a different negative option selection in your monthly mailing to each segment. What you need is information to let you create these segments. So you mail a sample of 5,000 customers a 100-question survey on reading habits, lifestyle, demographics, attitude, and interests, and get 2,500 responses. Eventually, you will use cluster analysis to create these groupings of people, but first you want to use factor analysis to reduce these 100 questions into fewer factors—so that you can later use these factor scores in your subsequent cluster analysis.

You first create a data file where the rows are the 2,500 people and the columns (or fields) are the answers to the 100 questions. A few things need to be noted here. You can only use factor analysis on data that is continuous or scalar, such as age and income. Attitude questions answered on a 5- or 7-point agree/disagree scale also meet this requirement. You cannot legitimately use factor analysis on data where people are put into categories (such as male/female). Note, also, that you should usually have many (e.g., 10 or more) times the number of rows (people or areas) than you have columns (questions or attributes). Since we have 25 times more people than we have questions to analyze, we have no cause for worry here.

Next, you pick Factor Analysis from your statistical software package's menu. In submenus, you pick Principal Components analysis. You tell the software package where your data file is and what the 100 raw variables are called, and you ask it to create *orthogonal* factors (those that have a zero correlation to each other) from those 100 variables.

In its first output solution, it will give you a table of the eigen value (remember, this was analogous to the amount of information) for each factor. There will be 100 factors since you used 100 raw variables. You notice from the table that, after the 20th factor, the eigen value drops below 1. You also note that the first 20 factors (of the 100) explain 80 percent of the variance, or raw information, that went in. You decide to ask the factor analysis program to rerun the output, but this time to keep only the first 20 factors (and retain 80 percent of the raw information). Though you are sacrificing 20 percent of the information, you are gaining the ability to work with just 20 factors instead of five times as many raw variables. (In later computer runs, you can experiment with other cutoff rules.)

You also ask the software program to rotate the output table using varimax rotation (or another one from the menu). This time around, the output contains the key table of interest, called *rotated factor loadings*. The rows here, 100 in all, are the original question variables. The 20 columns correspond to your 20 retained important factors, with the first one being the most important (it has the highest eigen value). The numbers in the table, called *factor loadings,* represent the correlation relationship between each factor (column) and each variable (row), measured from -1.00 (strong negative relationship) through 0.00 (no relationship) to $+1.00$ (strong positive relationship). Mathematically, to create the first factor's score for each of the 2,500 people, you would multiply each person's score on each of the 100 raw variables by the loading for each variable on the first factor, and add up the results. Usually the computer program will do this automatically, if you ask it to, for each of the 20 factors. You can then create a new data file of 2,500 rows (people) and 20 columns (factors) and now use this second data file, instead of your first raw data file, in subsequent modeling (such as regression and cluster analysis).

For interpretation of the rotated loadings table, however, all you have to do is look down each column (factor) and see which variables have a high loading (e.g., 0.50 or above — use your judgment) on that factor. A positive and high loading means that a high factor score is created by a high score on that particular raw variable. A negative and high loading means that a high score on that raw variable *decreases* the factor score. Since the factor score is essentially based on those raw variables that have a high loading on it, you can now give the factor a name to summarize what those high-loading variables appear to have in common. For example, if the raw variables that have a high loading on that factor all deal with aspects of religion and morality (such as attitudes toward sex on TV, prayer in public schools, and abortion), you might want to label that factor the "religious" factor. Giving names to factors is often the most enjoyable part of factor analysis, so savor this opportunity!

CLUSTER ANALYSIS: WHAT IT IS, AND WHEN YOU SHOULD USE IT

Cluster analysis, as we said previously, is used whenever you want to assign people or areas to groups such that those people within a group are similar to each other, and those in different groups are different from each other. After forming such groups (clusters) through cluster analysis, you can then create offers and packages that are tailored to each group, thus (hopefully) increasing response and profitability. This is the promise and technique of market segmentation.

Not only can people or areas be assigned to clusters but other things as well, for example, brands within a category. Any "thing" that is given a number for each of a reasonably large number of variables (such as ZIP codes rated on average age, average income, percent white population, and so on) is fair game for a cluster analysis. When we are dealing with consumers, we typically score each individual or household on demographic variables, previous purchases (what was purchased, when purchased, how much, how often, how paid), source of name, lifestyle and attitudinal data (perhaps from overlays), benefit preference data from surveys, and so on. This data is more easily handled in cluster analysis if it is of the continuous scalar type, but methods do exist for working with binary (yes/no) information as well. Thus, if your house file contains data on how each name responded in the past to different offers, that yes/no response history can also be used in certain kinds of cluster analysis to put your file into response segments.

The most common use of cluster analysis is with geo-demographic data—the kind discussed in Chapter 2 and marketed as ClusterPlus, PRIZM, Acorn, and so on. In essence, what these companies have done is to take census data on various variables by block group, update the data, add other data (such as auto registration statistics), and then use cluster analysis to create clusters of these block groups. Those block groups within a cluster are very similar to each other in terms of their scores on these variables (no matter where they happen to be geographically), and the clusters themselves are different from each other.

Thus, for example, Cluster S01 in the *ClusterPlus* scheme is described by the cluster concept of "Established Wealthy," and has (among other things) the highest socioeconomic status indicators, highest median income ($62,684), homeowners living in prime real estate areas (median home value $148,291), with high education levels (median school years 15.8), professionally employed people (55.8 percent so employed), whose children go to private schools. Towns across the country having a large proportion of people in this cluster include Los Altos, California; Westport, Connecticut; Bethesda, Maryland; Scarsdale, New York; and Highland Park, Illinois. While forming only 1.4 percent of the nation's population, people in this cluster buy disproportionately large amounts of expensive clothes, financial products, imported wines, vacations, and expensive cars, and fly more often. Not surprisingly, people in such a cluster respond more readily to high-priced offers—and packages sent to them most profitably appeal to upscale values. In contrast, people in the bottom clusters are not good targets for such offers and appeals.

These syndicated geo-demographic cluster assignments to ZIP codes or census block groups are used most often, and most easily, for name selection purposes in a mailing—to decide which names in a list you wish to mail to and which ones you wish to suppress. Yet the technology of cluster analysis is also used to classify customers or prospects, at an individual level, into benefit segments (people who value similar benefits in a product category, such as reading preference segments in a book club), or lifestyle and psychographic segments (people with similar attitudes, values, and interests).

HOW CLUSTER ANALYSIS WORKS

There are many different varieties of cluster analysis, so many that statisticians don't really know which ones are best or standard. In fact, these different varieties work in different ways and very often yield different cluster results. The practical consequence of this, and a very important one, is that you should often use more than one technique, and be satisfied only when two or more techniques yield outputs that look reasonably similar. Otherwise, you may be seeing clusters that exist only as a figment of the computer's imagination. Always ask your analysts to try more than one technique, and to demonstrate some convergence.

When you work with continuous, scalar data (such as income, years of education, age, and agree/disagree attitude scales), cluster analysis works much like the coordinate geometry that we all learned way back in high school. As we said earlier, the objective of cluster analysis is to put similar things together in a group. How do we know when things are similar? The computer calculates a statistical measure of similarity called *distance* — obviously, things that are similar are not distant, and things that have high distance (that are far apart) are not similar.

The distance between any two things is calculated much like we would calculate the distance between the two points A and B on a graph with two axes or dimensions (X and Y). If point A is located at ($X1$, $Y1$) on this map, and point B is located at ($X2$, $Y2$) on this map, coordinate geometry tells us that the distance between A and B is given by the square root of the squared total of ($X2 - X1$) and ($Y2 - Y1$). (If you don't remember, or don't care, that's OK; we are simply giving you an intuitive feel for what's inside the black box of cluster analysis.) Now, suppose we're dealing with ZIP codes instead of points. The same logic applies; the axes become the variables (such as average age, average income, or average education), and each ZIP code has a location (its score) on each axis. The computer first calculates a total distance between every pair of points (ZIP codes or people), and then uses some rule to put points that are closest to each other in the same cluster.

If you are working with binary (yes/no, bought/didn't buy) kinds of data, the methods of calculating similarity use a different approach. Suppose you market collectibles, and in the last year you mailed 10 offers to each of a million people. For each offer, some people bought, and most didn't buy. You had the good sense to record in your file how they responded (bought/didn't buy) to each of the 10 mailings. For such data, the computer will define similarity for every pair of names as the proportion of times they acted the same way (both bought, or both didn't buy) to the total number of offers mailed; if one name in the pair bought one offer while the other didn't, then that should count as dissimilar behavior.

The user has to tell the computer program which method it should use to calculate distance, which method it should use to bring close points together, and how many clusters it should create. Obviously, statisticians spend lifetimes studying which rules are best for making these method-ological decisions. We will skip the details here but will now give you some guidelines.

RUNNING AND INTERPRETING CLUSTER ANALYSIS

First, you have to create a data file in which each of the things you want to cluster (the rows) is scored on each of the variables you want it to be clustered on (the columns). These might be ZIP codes scored on various census variables. The columns might be factor scores, which (as we saw in the earlier section) are combinations of variables. (Some statisticians recommend that you *standardize* these column scores before using cluster analysis. This means each number is mathematically converted to another equivalent one, with the new set of numbers having an average of 0 and a standard deviation of 1. Most computer programs do this painlessly, on request.)

When you pull up the cluster analysis portion of your statistical software, the menu will ask you (1) which kind of program you want to use, (2) how you want distance computed, (3) which method you want it to use to put points into clusters, based on their distances, and (4) how many clusters you want it to create. It may also ask you in what shape and form you want to see the output, that is, tables or trees (called *dendograms*).

The first decision — on what kind of program — really depends on how large your data set is. Calculating and storing the distance between *every* pair of 35,000 residential ZIP codes, for example, is beyond the capacity of most computers and software. For really large data sets, therefore, you should pick a cluster analysis program that doesn't require these pairwise calculations, and works somewhat differently. Though the name may vary with the software package, such programs are often called *K-means* clustering programs (the software will usually tell you clearly that it is meant for large data sets). Smaller data sets are handled by most cluster analysis programs.

The second decision — what kind of distance measure to use — typically depends on your data as well. Binary (yes/no) data has its own types of distance measures (which not all software programs have, so check before you pick your software if you want to work with such data). If you are working with continuous, scalar data, you would normally pick Euclidean or Squared Euclidean distance measures. (Your software might recom-mend which kinds of distance measures work best with different kinds of grouping methods, discussed next. The programs for larger data sets typically have a default measure and grouping method.)

The third decision—what kind of grouping rule you want to apply to the calculated distances—offers a big array of possibilities. Statisticians again have their preferences but one called *Ward's Method* works well in many situations.

The fourth decision—how many clusters you want the program to form—is, unfortunately, the most judgmental. While some statistical packages offer ways to help you here, most often it is simply a subjective question of how many clusters you want. This, in turn, depends on your economics, the number of logical segmentation possibilities, and your production capabilities—how many customized offers or mailings you can profitably and feasibly handle.

After you indicate your choices to the computer, it will eventually give you (among a host of other output) a table in which each thing (person/ZIP code, and so on) you have clustered is given a cluster number. You can, optionally, get a tree diagram telling you the exact sequence of the clustering process; this will give you a visual idea of how the clusters and cluster members relate to each other in terms of overall similarity, and the sequence in which the method split up the total mass of things into a greater and greater number of clusters. Finally, the program may give you an average score for each cluster on each raw variable used for the clustering (if not, you can do this separately, by computing the average scores on these variables for each of the things in that cluster); you use this to profile each cluster and to understand these clusters intuitively.

One final point on validation. We have already mentioned the need to repeat your analyses using different methods to see if you get similar solutions. Another method of checking the validity of your cluster solution is to first get a cluster output on a randomly selected half of your data, and then on the other half. Check to see that the clusters look similar—trust them only if they do.

CONCLUDING EXAMPLE AND REVIEW

The example below came about as a result of what began as a simple use of one of the commercially available clustering products. An analysis of our client's mailing of an upscale product indicated that contrary to expectations, response was not coming from the very top socioeconomic clusters but from middle and lower socioeconomic clusters. The reliability of the clustering product was questioned by the client. In order to verify the analysis, we created our own clustering scheme for just New York State, based on available census data at the ZIP code level.

Forty census variables were selected (of the more than 150 available) as the raw data for summarization through factor (principal components) analysis. Each of 2,000 New York State ZIP codes was rated on these 40 census variables; this formed the raw data file. Initial analysis showed that only the first 10 of the 40 factors extracted had an eigen value (amount of information) that exceeded 1, so only these 10 factors were retained in the next round. The table showed that these 10 factors retained 70 percent of the information (variance) that originally came in with the 40 raw variables, and this was considered an acceptable trade-off.

Table 13–1 shows abbreviated varimax-rotated factor loadings for the factor analysis of New York State ZIP code data. Figure 13–1 shows the scree diagram that suggested a 10-factor solution.

Table 13–1 describes the original census variables (the rows) and gives the loadings (the numbers relating each row to each of the factor columns). For brevity, only the first 26 rows and first 3 columns are reproduced here. (The full table had 40 rows and 10 columns.) The computer would automatically create 10 factor scores for each ZIP code for use later. For interpretation, note that the first factor related highly negatively to the percentage of homeowners, percentage of households with two or more cars, percent white population, and percent born in the state where they now live. It related highly positively to the percentage of renter homes, percent homes with elevators, percent foreign born, percent Hispanic, and percent single-person households. This factor should paint an easily interpreted picture in your mind's eye. What the analysis suggests is that ZIP codes that will score high on this one factor will represent poorer urban areas.

As a contrast, the second factor is very different – almost the reverse image of the first but still urban. These ZIPs appear to represent educated, upper income professionals with children in nursery schools. Yuppies! Factor 3 scores high on two-income families, suggesting ZIP codes populated by hard-working, low- to middle-income families.

Factor scores were then derived for each of the 2,000 ZIP codes, for each of the 10 factors; this formed the new data file for later input into cluster analysis. We used a program suitable for large data sets and requested 50 clusters (to be consistent with the commercial product that was being questioned). The program output told us which of the 50 clusters each of the 2,000 ZIP codes belonged to, as well as how close each ZIP

TABLE 13–1
Varimax-Rotated Factor Loadings for Census Variables (First Three Factors)*

Raw Census Data at ZIP Code Level	Factors		
	1	2	3
1. Percent homeowners	−.91	−.05	.00
2. Percent renters	.91	.05	.00
3. Percent two-car households	−.87	.14	.14
4. Percent households with elevators	.82	.06	.12
5. Percent born in foreign countries	.71	.29	.07
6. Percent Hispanic	.68	.02	−.14
7. Percent white	−.66	−.04	.18
8. Percent single-person households	.66	−.20	.12
9. Percent born in same U.S. state	−.62	−.17	−.04
10. Percent income of $25,000+	−.21	.80	.34
11. Median household income	−.30	.78	.30
12. Percent with central air conditioning	−.10	.70	.16
13. Median monthly mortgage	.03	.69	.18
14. Median monthly rent	.09	.67	.13
15. Percent in professional occupations	.10	.62	.18
16. Percent with four+ years college education	.17	.61	.42
17. Percent who work in a place different from where they live	.01	.60	−.03
18. Percent urban population	.54	.59	.08
19. Percent educated high school+	.03	.53	.47
20. Percent of children in nursery schools	−.02	.48	−.07
21. Percent in administrative occupations	.28	.47	.15
22. Percent of English origin	−.38	−.65	.10
23. Percent of population in total labor force	.06	.28	.90
24. Percent of females in labor force	−.11	.24	.78
25. Percent of males in labor force	.18	.24	.74
26. Percent of households with two or more workers	−.35	.13	.63

*Loadings have been sorted so that factor 1 has high (positive or negative) loadings on variables 1 through 9; factor 2, variables 10 through 22; and factor 3, variables 23 through 26. Factor 1 appears to be urban Hispanics; factor 2, affluent, white-collar, suburban commuters; and factor 3, level of employment in that ZIP code.

code was to the center of that cluster. For each cluster, we then selected the one ZIP code that was closest to that cluster's center, and used that ZIP code's profile on the 10 factor scores as a proxy for the factor score profile of the entire ZIP code. Finally, we compared the resulting cluster profiles with that provided by the commercial product for these 16 center ZIP codes.

FIGURE 13–1
SPSS Factor Analysis

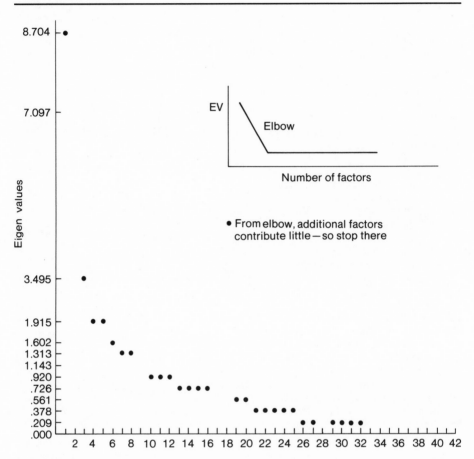

TABLE 13–2

ZIP Code	Abbreviated Commercial Description	Factor 1	Factor 2	Factor 3
10504	Wealthy	− 1.04107	2.67803	.75684
10026	Center City	2.98245	− .92635	− 1.88863
14146	Small Town	.42019	− 1.14470	3.36004

Table 13-2 shows the factor loadings for the three factors discussed above, for three entirely different ZIP codes or neighborhoods.

As you can see, there is a strong relationship between the factor scores and the vendor's abbreviated description of the ZIP code. ZIP code 10504, described as Wealthy, scores highly negative on factor 1 and highly positive on factor 2. Center City ZIP code 10026 scores highly positive on factor 1 and highly negative on factor 2. ZIP code 14146, commercially described as Small Town, scores high on factor 3, which you will recall represented areas with large percentages of two-income families.

Thus, the integrity of the commercial product was supported by our analysis. But what about the conclusion, that upscale ZIP codes were not responding as well to an upscale product as middle and low income ZIP codes were? Well, it turns out that we haven't been telling you the whole story. The key fact we omitted to tell you is that the upscale product was being promoted with the aid of a downscale premium, which did not appeal to an upscale market but did appeal to middle and lower level markets. The final result was that the premium offer was changed to an offer more attractive to the client's desired market.

THE ECONOMICS OF THE NEW DIRECT MARKETING

CHAPTER 14

AN INTRODUCTION TO
THE ECONOMICS OF THE NEW
DIRECT MARKETING

What if this chapter were titled "The Economics of Direct Marketing"? Would the contents be any different? The answer is yes. The difference between the economics of the *new direct marketing,* or, to use the more conventional term, *database marketing,* and the economics of *direct marketing* is fundamentally the same as the difference between database marketing and what is generally thought of as *classical direct marketing.*

So before jumping into equations, formulas, and P&Ls, let's spend a few minutes on the differences we see between classical direct marketing and modern database marketing, the new direct marketing. Let's also take this time to define the important differences between a *traditional* direct marketing company, which may employ both classical direct marketing methods and database marketing methods, and companies that are not traditional direct marketing companies (*nontraditional* direct marketers) but who use classical direct marketing methods and/or database marketing methods as just one part of their marketing mix. (See Figure 14–1.)

The differences are important and have much to do with the popularity of database marketing and the changes that are taking place within traditional direct marketing companies and within what is generally referred to as the direct marketing industry, as represented by the members of the Direct Marketing Association.

Traditional direct marketing companies or divisions of companies are operating units that depend entirely on acquiring and servicing customers through direct marketing methods. This definition would encompass all of the business-to-business and consumer catalogers, fund raisers, continuity,

FIGURE 14–1
A Framework for Understanding the Direct Marketing Industry

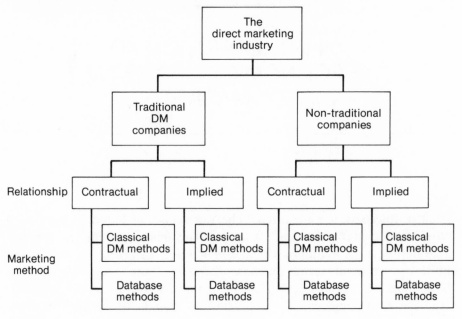

club, and subscription businesses, as well as all financial service organizations that use only direct media to acquire and retain customers. If we include direct sales as part of direct media, this definition could also accomodate firms that may not consider themselves hard-core direct marketing companies, for example, all of the direct door-to-door sales companies and cable TV firms.

Nontraditional direct marketers would include all firms that use direct marketing methods, in combination with general advertising and nontraceable sales promotion techniques such as coupons, to increase sales that are consummated either at retail or with the aid of a salesperson. This definition would include all retailers using classical direct marketing or database marketing methods to generate store traffic; all consumer products companies using targeted coupons or fulfillment offers to support retail sales; all car manufacturers, telecommunications companies, computer manufacturers, and office equipment dealers. The list goes on and on, and includes any organization using direct marketing as just one of a number of advertising, promotion, and marketing options.

IMPLIED VERSUS CONTRACTUAL RELATIONSHIPS

Traditional direct marketing organizations may, in turn, be divided into two groups: those that have contractual obligations with their customers or members and those whose relationships are only, at best, implied. As you'll see, organizations with contractual relationships have been among the slowest to employ database marketing techniques—even though these firms are at the heart of the direct marketing business. In fact, as we'll see later in this chapter and throughout this book, it has been the nontraditional direct marketing companies that have made the greatest contribution to database marketing.

Contractual relationships exist in all subscription programs, clubs, and continuities. A contractual obligation, as executed by a signed coupon or telephone call, means that both the customer and the company understand what is expected of the other. Subscribers expect to receive a year's worth of magazines and then to be renewed (even though there's no contractual obligation to be renewed or to renew); club members expect to receive offers every three or four weeks; continuity members expect to receive a shipment every four, six, or eight weeks, and so on. Contractual relationships also exist within nontraditional direct marketing companies. For example, customers who sign on with a frequent flyer (or any other frequent purchaser or user) program understand what is expected of them and what is expected from the organization sponsoring the program.

On the other hand, an implied relationship is one in which there is no obligation on either party's part to do anything in the future. For example, in a catalog situation, after the initial response on the part of a consumer to a cold solicitation, there is no obligation on the consumer's part to purchase again, or even on the cataloger's part to mail another catalog. However, most consumers will not be surprised when they receive another catalog in the mail. Some implied relationships are less obvious. For example, the flood of financial service offers that follow the establishment of a banking relationship, though not a complete shock to the knowledgeable consumer, might come as a surprise to the average person.

The extent to which relationships are contractual or implied is directly related to the decision-making discretion available to the direct marketer. In contractual obligations, there is less discretion, thus less obvious need for sophisticated decision-making tools. Conversely, when there is no contractual obligation, much more care needs to go into the decision of to whom to mail, what to mail, and how often to mail. Thus, the reader should not be surprised to discover, later in this chapter, that database-driven decision making, or database marketing, is more likely to happen when there is an absence of a contractual relationship or even a strongly implied relationship.

CLASSICAL DIRECT MARKETING VERSUS DATABASE MARKETING

Having defined traditional and nontraditional direct marketing companies, we can begin to discuss in more detail how each of these types employs both classical direct marketing and database marketing methods. The principal difference between the two methods is that for all intents and purposes, classical direct marketing does not really deal with information about individuals; and database marketing, if it does nothing else, attempts to deal with information about individuals. Now that's a fairly broad generalization that requires some elaboration.

When we say that classical direct marketing does not really deal with individuals, what we mean is that the classical direct marketing methods used in traditional direct marketing companies focus attention on the behavior of groups of individuals. Traditional direct marketing companies include:

- Mail-order companies selling individual products or services.
- Negative option book or record clubs.
- Continuity programs.
- Catalog companies.
- Magazines.
- Newsletters.
- Electronic subscription services.

Anyone who has ever worked in a traditional direct marketing company knows that nearly all of the analysis work is directed at groups of customers: all of the customers recruited from a particular list, or a segment of a list, or from a particular print ad, or from a particular TV spot. Even in firms using techniques generally associated with database marketing, such as *Prizm Clusters,* the emphasis is on how well did all of the customers or the average customer from a particular cluster perform.

The way this is done, for those readers not familiar with the mechanics of the direct marketing business, is that each promotion vehicle, be it a rented list or an ad in a magazine, is assigned a source code or key code (terminology changes from company to company) and all new customers acquired from that list or print ad are forever associated with that original source code.

The analysis task is then reduced to evaluating the cost of the promotion compared to the profit generated from all of the new customers acquired from the promotion. If the profit is sufficiently greater than the costs, then, all other things being equal, the direct marketer will probably decide to use that promotion vehicle, that is, that list or magazine, again in the future. We'll spend a lot of time on the mechanics of this decision-making process, but the basic point we want to stress is this focus on average or group behavior and how this information is used for decision-making purposes.

Later on we'll see that even within traditional direct marketing companies, more and more analysis work is being done at the individual level, thus affecting the way marketing decisions are made. In other words, classical direct marketers, too, are becoming database marketers.

So, classical direct marketing deals with groups or averages, and database marketing, in ways yet to be discussed, deals with individuals. That's only the beginning. Classical direct marketing tends to search for the perfect average solution to a variety of direct marketing business problems; database marketing searches for the perfect individual solution to the same set of problems. Both methods do a lot of compromising.

THE SEARCH FOR THE PERFECT CONTROL

A good example of the difference between classical direct marketing and database marketing is the way in which each method searches for the perfect new-customer acquisition strategy. Emotionally, the classical direct marketer would like to find one direct mail package that could be mailed to all prospects on all rented lists, regardless of the mix of lists that make up the total mailing and the composition of individuals within each list. The reasons for this are obvious and are perfectly valid. It's cheaper to create, produce, and mail one package to everybody than it is to create, develop, and mail multiple packages to different groups of individuals.

The database marketer, on the other hand, while understanding the economic impossibility of mailing a different package to each individual, would intuitively prefer to move in this direction. Emotionally, the database marketer understands that there must be more than one market segment in a mailing going to a few million individuals. So, the database marketer reasons, doesn't it make economic sense to attempt to segment individuals on a mailing list or on a combination of mailing lists into at least a handful of different market segments and create unique mailing packages that address the individual needs of the individual segments? Maybe, maybe not. Later, we'll see that the answer depends on one's ability to implement a cost-effective segmentation strategy.

ONCE THE CUSTOMER IS ON THE FILE

New-customer acquisition is not the only area in which classical direct marketing differs from database marketing. In fact, new-customer acquisition is probably the one area in which classical direct marketers have moved closest to database marketing, without the aid of a marketing database. Once the direct marketing process moves beyond the new-customer acquisition phase, that is, after the new customer is acquired and is included on the customer file, there are even stronger reasons for treating all new customers in the same way.

Think about a book club or a continuity program or even a catalog operation for a moment. All of these traditional direct marketing businesses are supported by computer systems (fulfillment systems, inventory systems, accounts receivable systems) that are infinitely easier to operate if all customers are treated in exactly the same way after they become part of the file. Remember, most computer support systems were originally designed to operate in only one way, and they have been fine-tuned over the years to handle larger and larger volumes with increasing efficiency.

Let's concentrate our attention again on the negative option book club, a business most readers will be familiar with as users or at least as readers of the *New York Times* Book Review section. It's obviously easier, and therefore, from a data processing perspective, more cost-efficient, to treat all new members the same way:

- Send the new member the four books they chose within 48 hours.
- Place the new member on the member file and send every member the same advance announcement every four weeks.
- Give every member 10 days to return or not return the same negative option refusal form.

- Send every member who does not return the form within 10 days the same "Featured Selection."
- Provide every member with the same credit limits, and so on.

Compare this procedure with a process that attempts to place members into even as few as three or four segments based on information about the individual member:

- The books they selected when they joined.
- The books they purchased as members.
- Their buying and paying patterns.
- Individual household level demographics.
- Lifestyle data obtained from internal research or overlays, and so on.

Obviously, even if the data processing department could do it, implementation of a customized fulfillment system would cost considerably more, take more time, and so forth. Is it worth it? The answer depends on how much better individual members would respond to a more customized service.

The same argument, albeit to a lesser degree, applies to catalog marketers. One could argue that it's easier and therefore less expensive to send the same catalog to every catalog customer, with equal frequency, than it is to design special catalogs for individual market segments and to design customized mailing programs for customers based on individual performance data. And that's true — it is easier and less expensive. But catalog mailers, given their implied and therefore discretionary relationships with their customers, realized long before database marketing became fashionable that they could increase their profits by segmenting their file on three simple measures: recency of purchase, frequency of purchase, and some measure of the dollar volume of purchase. The shorthand for this methodology is *RFM,* which stands for recency, frequency, and monetary value. Based on relatively simple treatments of these three measures, catalogers determined whom to mail to and how often to mail. However, as we'll see shortly, one contribution of database marketing to this name selection process has been the introduction of more sophisticated analytical tools that allow the introduction of a broader set of predictive variables and make even better use of RFM data.

CHAPTER 15

BACK TO BASICS: THE ECONOMICS OF CLASSICAL DIRECT MARKETING

This chapter will deal entirely with the economics of traditional direct marketing.[1] We will begin with a review of the major business issues associated with:

- Solo promotions.
- Multistep promotions.
- Catalogs.
- Continuities.
- Clubs.
- Newsletters.
- Magazines.

This review will initially focus attention on the economic trade-offs that direct marketers deal with on a day-to-day basis. After a general discussion of each business form, we will return to analyze each business in terms of the relationship between acquiring new customers, which direct marketers refer to as *front-end analysis,* and the profitability that results from transactions that occur after the customer is acquired, called *back-end analysis.*

Long before databases were fashionable, direct marketers understood that long-term growth and profitability depended primarily on the direct marketer's ability to manage the equation that balances expenditures on new-customer acquisition with the flow of sales and profits that come back

---

[1] Portions of the following section first appeared in the *Direct Marketing Handbook* (New York: McGraw-Hill, 1984).

over the economic life of the acquired customer. Of course, it's a lot simpler to measure the immediate costs of acquiring a new customer than it is to measure the value of an acquired customer, particularly when that value may take years to fully materialize. And, as we'll see shortly, in an increasing number of direct marketing situations, the long-term value of an acquired customer is not simply a value waiting to be discovered; the long-term value of a customer is directly related to the way in which the customer is served by the direct marketing company. So we have a kind of a chicken-and-egg problem that we'll try to solve after we've established some of the basic economic ground rules.

SOLO PROMOTIONS

The simplest form of direct marketing is the solo, or single-shot, promotion. Assume for the moment that the marketer has no other use for the name of the customer acquired. The only economic reason for the promotion is to make an immediate profit on this one mailing. In this situation, the marketer must design, produce, and mail promotion pieces to enough potential buyers to generate a response that will cover the cost of the promotion and yield an acceptable level of profit.

Single-shot promotions are relatively simple but the seller must still answer many questions in the course of the promotion process. Should the promotion piece be a classical, direct response, full-mailing package, including an outer envelope, letter, brochure, business reply card, and return envelope? Or should the seller use a less expensive mailing piece? If the classical full-mailing package is used, should the letter be two pages or four pages, and should the flier be black and white or in full color? Should the seller offer credit or require cash with the order? Should credit cards be used? Should the seller offer an inexpensive premium to hype sales or as a reward for cash with order? Should the mailing use third-class postage or would the extra costs of first-class postage somehow result in extra sales and thereby pay for itself? Should an 800 number be used? How strong should the guarantee be? Should the outer envelope contain copy and an illustration of the product, or just inviting copy, or no copy at all?

The list of legitimate questions that can be raised about even the simplest form of direct marketing is extensive, and answers to these questions will affect the economics of the promotion. Many of these questions have to do with economic trade-offs. Does it pay to spend more on the promotion piece, to offer a premium, to offer credit, to mail first class, and so on? These questions raised with regard to a solo promotion apply to all types of direct response businesses and will be raised again and again throughout this chapter.

MULTISTEP PROMOTIONS LEADING TO
A DIRECT SALE

Frequently, it is possible to identify the potential market for a product in terms of the circulation of one or more magazines while at the same time it is not profitable or legally possible to sell the product "off the page" in those magazines regardless of the unit of space employed. In some situations, the price of the product is exceptionally high, and closing the sale requires the power of a more expensive direct mail package with full-color illustrations and sufficient copy to define all the features and benefits of the product. Or, in the case of financial services, it may be neither economically feasible nor legally possible to attempt to directly consummate a sale. In these instances, magazine space often is used to generate leads or inquiries, which are followed up by one or a series of direct mail pieces. In some cases, the initial leads are followed up by a combination of mail and phone. Products sold in this fashion include, in addition to financial services, encyclopedias, expensive exercise equipment, office equipment, and many business-to-business services. The "bingo cards" found in trade magazines and airline magazines are prime examples of this kind of direct response marketing.

The economics of multistep marketing differs from the economics of single-shot promotions in that the total costs of both the initial effort and the costs of all of the follow-up efforts must be tracked carefully and balanced against the sales and gross margin resulting from the total effort.

CATALOG SALES

A catalog may be thought of as a very expensive solo mailing, selling anywhere from a few dozen to hundreds or even thousands of products. It is also possible, as in the case of the solo mailing, to compare the total gross margin resulting from a catalog mailing with the total costs of the mailing, but the analogy between a catalog business and a business based on solo mailings cannot be taken much further.

The success of a catalog business is related directly to a catalog manager's ability to efficiently develop and manage a company's database of past buyers, or its *house list,* as it is still referred to by many in the industry. In very general terms, the response of an outside rented list to a catalog mailing may range anywhere from .5 percent to 2 or 3 percent, depending on the quality of the rented names and their predisposition to the products being offered in the catalog. By way of comparison, the response of past buyers to another catalog offering may range from 5 to 20 percent or even higher.

Naturally, a new catalog company cannot open its doors with a list of past buyers. However, catalog operators have developed a number of techniques for developing house lists. One technique is to develop a relatively inexpensive "prospecting" catalog that can be mailed to names that have been rented from outside list owners. Respondents to these prospect mailings then are entered on the catalog company's prospect list. Of course, it is possible to mail a company's complete catalog to an outside rented list, and the limiting or deciding factor in this decision often is the catalog company's willingness and ability to sustain a large negative cash position while building its house file. Large companies wishing to enter the direct marketing business often are in a position to finance this development period, provided that they are convinced the eventual returns will justify the initial cash investment.

Smaller entrepreneurs generally attempt to exhaust all the other more conservative ways of building prospecting lists that can be converted eventually into buyers lists. Other techniques for building house lists include advertising the catalog free or for a token price in targeted-space media, using the same space to sell the most popular items in the catalog, and sending out solo mailings of individual popular products to names on rented lists. In general, regardless of the techniques used, it is common for a catalog operation to be in a net loss position with regard to new names added to the house list. As the mix between new names that result from cold prospect mailings, space advertising, and catalog buyer names changes in favor of the buyers, the profitability of the catalog operation will increase.

However, even after the initial start-up period is behind the cataloger, this issue of allocating the amount spent on new-customer acquisition versus the amount spent on mailing catalogs to customers will remain. In fact, this decision is one of the most crucial decisions a cataloger must make.

Ironically, advances in database marketing techniques have made this decision even more difficult. In predatabase days, most catalogers had a limited number of catalogs, which were mailed to all of the customers on their buyers file. In many cases, the entire customer mailing strategy could be summed up in a sentence: "We mail four general catalogs a year to all customers on our file who have made a purchase within the last two years."

Now, given the ability to segment a file not only in terms of how frequently different customer segments should be mailed, but also in terms of which customers might respond better to specialized as opposed to general catalogs, the decision-making process has become infinitely more complex. Because of the importance of this subject, not only to catalogers but to all direct marketers that have implied as opposed to contractual relationships with their customers, let's spend some more time on the issue.

To the extent that a cataloger spends promotion dollars on acquiring new customers, the potential size of the business will grow. However, as we have seen, the response rate on new-customer acquisition mailings is significantly less than the response rate to mailings to the customer file. So in any one year, a dollar spent on new-customer acquisition, as opposed to customer mailings, will reduce both sales and profits. On the other hand, if year after year, decreasing amounts are spent on new-customer acquisition, the potential of the business will diminish and eventually the actual size of the business will shrink as the customer file fatigues. Therefore, there has to be a strategy for managing both potential growth and annual profits.

In the simpler times referred to above, a cataloger could estimate the sales and profits expected from mailing a single catalog to the house file, say, three or four times a year. After allowing for overheads and desired profits, the cataloger could calculate the amount available for new-customer acquisition, and that would be that. The first complication was the discovery that not all customers need be or should be mailed the same number of catalogs each year. Relatively simple RFM models were developed by catalogers that allowed them to segment a file into dozens of segments or cells based on recency of purchase, frequency of purchase, and the various measures of the dollar value of past purchases. The basic conclusion drawn from RFM cell segmentation was that individuals within the highest performing cells should be mailed more frequently than individuals within the poorest performing cells. So even if a cataloger still only produced four general catalogs a year, the best performing customers might receive those four catalogs 8 to 12 times a year (perhaps with a cover change), the poorest performing customers might receive only one catalog a year, and some customers would in fact be dropped from the file of active buyers.

The introduction of more sophisticated forms of predictive modeling (regression, logistic, discriminant analyses) did nothing to change the basic finding that some customers should be mailed more frequently than others. However, the introduction of these techniques and the introduction of models that predict falloff from mailing to mailing have improved the efficiency of the modeling process.

What did make a fundamental difference for some catalogers was the not surprising discovery that not all buyers bought the same mix of products, and that segmentation techniques could be extended to include the kinds of products purchased as well as the quantity of products purchased. Now the decision-making process also had to be extended to include consideration of the creation and distribution of specialty catalogs. It is obviously a more difficult problem to decide who shall get what mix of catalogs with what frequency than it is to simply decide how many general catalogs any one individual should receive.

Unfortunately, while predictive models are good at scoring customers in terms of their probability of responding to a promotion similar to one received in the past, the complications discussed above do not lend themselves easily to statistical modeling solutions of the regression variety. To answer these kinds of economic trade-off questions we must rely on computer models that simulate an entire business structure and that are capable of answering "what if" questions. The good news is that such models are relatively easy to build using spreadsheet programs such as Lotus 1-2-3; the bad news is that the output of the models is only as good as the input assumptions. The model will tell you, for example, what the fiscal impact will be if you create a specialty catalog that will increase response for 30 percent of the file by 20 percent, but only old-fashioned direct marketing testing will tell you if the 20 percent number is correct.

Finally, no discussion of the catalog business would be complete without mention of the extraordinary problems of inventory control and fulfillment that are inherent in the catalog business. Success in mail order requires almost immediate fulfillment of orders as they are received and, with high interest rates, the costs of carrying excess inventory can be as disastrous as the cost of being out of stock. Again, the ability of the catalog manager to perform advanced statistical analyses comes into play. Not only must catalog managers be able to forecast the expected level of overall response to a catalog mailing, they must be able to forecast the mix of products purchased so as to be in a position to manage inventories correctly.

CONTINUITY PROGRAMS

Continuity programs represent an important segment of the traditional direct marketing business. The continuity formula involves the periodic delivery of a product or service against periodic payments from the customer. The Time-Life Books series, the various Cooking Card programs, and the books and collectibles sold by the Franklin Mint are prime examples of products that are marketed this way. Because of the contractual nature of continuity programs, the management of a continuity operation is in many ways much less complicated than the management of a catalog operation. Given the product, such as a series of books, cards, or coins, the marketing problem is relatively straightforward. Options are severely limited relative to our catalog example.

New members or subscribers are acquired through the classical direct marketing channels: direct mail, magazine advertisements, newspaper preprints, broadcast (generally spot TV), and package inserts. In most cases, the first item in the continuity program is offered free or at a substantial discount. The subscriber then receives periodic shipments of the remaining items in the program until all the items have been shipped or until the subscriber notifies the seller to stop shipping the product.

From the subscriber's point of view, continuity programs are simple and easy to understand. From the seller's viewpoint, a number of key questions must be answered before the program can become operational. How should the items in the series be priced? Should the items be priced relatively high and therefore targeted against the upper end of the potential market, or should a lower-price/higher-volume strategy be attempted? How generous should the initial offer be? Should the first item in the series be given away free, or for $1, or at no discount at all? Should the interval between shipments be four weeks, six weeks, or eight weeks? How much open credit should be granted? Does it make sense to ship the third item in a series if payment has not been received for the first item? How does the credit decision depend on the interval between shipments? Should the program be open ended with no limit on the number of items in the series, or should the series be limited to a fixed number of items, and if so, what is that number?

Clearly, the answers to these questions will have an important impact on the economics of the continuity program. Again, we are faced with a question of trade-offs. The more generous the offer and credit policy, the larger the program in terms of subscribers and sales volume. But what will be the effect on returns, bad debts, and profits?

Finally, let us briefly discuss the concept of a continuity load-up. The continuity programs we have described rely on periodic shipment of a product until cancellation or completion of the program. In continuity load-ups, the subscriber is informed that after he or she receives three or four single shipments, the balance of the items in the program will be shipped in a single load-up shipment. The load-up plan is an effective device for increasing the total number of items shipped to the average subscriber but again, there are economic trade-offs to consider. Federal trade regulations require that the load-up provision be defined clearly in all promotional messages, and this can reduce the total number of respondents to any given promotion. Second, most load-up programs follow a policy of reminding subscribers that the load-up shipment is about to be mailed unless the subscriber notifies the company not to proceed with the shipment and to cancel membership in the program. This reminder will cause some subscribers to cancel their membership faster than they might have done in an open-ended continuity program. Finally, there is the problem of credit collections. A load-up program is based on the assumption that after the subscriber receives the full load-up shipment, he or she will pay for the shipment on a monthly or bimonthly basis. Of course, some percentage of the load-up shipment will not be paid for and eventually will have to be written off as a bad debt.

On balance, only testing the load-up concept against the open-ended, or "till forbid," continuity plan will determine which plan is best for any given product.

NEGATIVE OPTION CLUBS

We have discussed negative option clubs before and they are indeed efficient vehicles for the distribution of books and records. The Book of the Month Club and the Columbia Record Club are well-known examples of this type of direct marketing business. There are some similarities between continuity operations and negative option clubs. Most importantly, both employ contractual relationships with their members, thereby limiting service options. Both vehicles often are used as a means of distributing books, and both use the same media and direct marketing techniques for acquiring new members. But after the new member is acquired, the similarity from an operations or fulfillment point of view ends.

Negative option clubs constantly must ask their subscribers whether they wish to receive the coming selection, receive an alternative selection, or receive no product at all from the current catalog offering. If the member fails to respond, the shipment of the month is sent automatically. The fulfillment systems needed to handle a negative option club are much more complicated than those needed for a continuity program. In addition, the Federal Trade Commission has placed stringent restrictions on negative option clubs to ensure that members have sufficient time to return the negative option card should they not wish to receive the automatic shipment of the month.

Despite the differences in operating characteristics between negative option clubs and continuity programs, the economics of both types of businesses are remarkably similar. In both operations, new members are always acquired at a loss. The $1.00 or even the $4.95 that is often charged for the introductory shipment (the first book in a continuity series or the four books chosen from a book club's lead list) is never enough to cover the costs of promotion plus the cost of the introductory shipment. Therefore, continuity programs and negative option clubs are always in an investment position. The return on investment stems from future sales to the continuity subscriber or club member. In the case of continuity programs, future sales are simply a function of the price of the items in the program and the number of periods a subscriber chooses to stay in the program. In a negative option club, the member need not buy from every catalog offering, and therefore sales are more dependent on the perceived quality of the merchandise offered and the effectiveness of the ongoing marketing effort. In both continuity and negative option, the final measure of profitability is the relationship between the cost of acquiring new members and the sales and payments those members yield over their economic life in the club or program. Later in this chapter, we will develop the techniques used to measure and forecast these statistics.

As mentioned previously, up until quite recently, nearly all negative option clubs operated on the principle that all members would receive the same set of promotional materials. The notable exception was the record clubs, which have always asked their members to place themselves within listening preference segments. But within the book clubs, equality of treatment among all members was the general rule. Recently, the larger clubs have begun experimenting with customizing the negative option book selection to individuals based on the demonstrated reading preferences of the individuals. And, clearly in a major book club that offers both a wide range of fiction and nonfiction, it makes sense to do so. This is particularly true in data processing environments in which this kind of decision making can be handled efficiently. Of course, there are production costs to pay for not treating all members the same but these costs are offset by higher acceptance and lower returns of the negative option selection, increased purchase of alternate selections, and a longer member life as club members receive more and more selections that match their reading preferences.

NEWSLETTERS

Newsletters can be very profitable vehicles for distributing information to highly targeted markets. The most profitable newsletters often are aimed at small professional or business markets. Newsletters that are editorially able to provide critically needed information to a business audience that has both the need to know and the ability to pay (often referred to as "company money") have the greatest chance for success. This does not mean that more broadly based, lower-priced, mass-market newsletters can't be profitable, as witnessed by the continued success of the *Kiplinger Washington Newsletter* and the popularity of a number of relatively new consumer health newsletters such as the *Harvard Medical Letter* and the *Mayo Clinic Letter,* to name just two.

The economics of newsletters centers on four key variables: pricing, new-order acquisition, conversion or pay rates, and renewal rates. Pricing is the most controllable of all the variables and perhaps the most important. Newsletters targeted at business markets can be priced anywhere from $9.95 to $495. Generally, it is not difficult to determine whether the value of the information is worth closer to $10 than to $500, but it is often next to impossible to tell without testing whether a given newsletter should be priced at $37, $49, or even $97.

Clearly, pricing can make an enormous difference in profitability. Price testing is therefore almost always a necessity when one starts out in the newsletter business, particularly if the newsletter has little or no perceived competition.

Newsletters are almost always marketed solely by direct mail; therefore, it is critical that, before starting out in the newsletter business, the publisher be assured of continued access to the target market. If access to the market depends on the cooperation of a trade association, provisions should be made with the association to guarantee a continuous supply of names.

Properly priced newsletters can be successful with a relatively small response to initial new-subscriber promotions. Profits can be achieved with initial response rates as low as 5 to 10 orders per thousand names mailed because renewal rates are usually high.

However, before a newsletter can be considered a proven success, it must demonstrate the merits of the editorial material. The first test of the quality of the editorial material is the pay rate or conversion rate on new orders. Most newsletter promotions allow for payment (and cancellation) after one or more issues have been sampled by the reader. A high pay rate (over 70 percent) will be indicative of a high future renewal rate. Products that demonstrate a high cancellation rate should not count on a high renewal rate to ensure the profits of the newsletter venture.

MAGAZINES

Magazines are, of course, much like newsletters in that they depend on direct mail for much of their new-subscriber marketing and are highly sensitive to fluctuations in pay rates and renewal rates. The obvious differences between newsletters and magazines are that magazines are much more costly to produce and have two additional revenue streams: newsstand sales and advertising revenues. But even in the subscription circulation area, where one finds the greatest similarity to newsletters, there are important differences.

Magazine subscriptions are sold in many more ways than newsletter subscriptions. There are door-to-door sales, telephone sales, and sweepstakes-sold subscriptions from companies such as Publishers Clearing House. In addition, a magazine company's direct mail efforts may be dependent on preview or premium offers to an extent not often found in newsletter circulation. Each of these promotional channels and devices runs the risk of producing subscriptions with relatively low pay and renewal rates. Therefore, the evaluation and management of a magazine's circulation list is considerably more complicated and subject to greater risk than the evaluation and management of a newsletter.

PERFORMANCE MEASUREMENT

Front-End versus Back-End Performance

Front-end performance and *front-end analysis* are terms used by direct marketers to describe the process of measuring the initial costs of and response to a direct marketing promotion. The economic analysis of the process that takes place after an initial response is received is referred to as back-end analysis or back-end performance.

FRONT–END PERFORMANCE

Measuring Promotion Expense

The first step in the process of measuring front-end performance is the measurement of the total expense attributable to a promotion. The only difficulty associated with this task is deciding which expenses will be included in the analysis and which expenses, if any, will be excluded.

   Later we shall see how direct marketers generally approach this problem, but for now, let's assume we agree that it costs exactly $19,000 to mail 50,000 pieces of direct mail. The first statistic to be calculated is cost per thousand pieces mailed, more simply referred to as cost per thousand (CPM).

$$\text{CPM} = \frac{\text{Total promotion expense}}{\text{Number of pieces mailed}} \times 1{,}000$$

In our example:

$$\text{CPM} = \frac{\$19{,}000}{50{,}000} \times 1{,}000$$
$$\text{CPM} = \$380$$

   The CPM concept applies to space advertising as well as to direct mail. In space advertising, CPM is calculated by dividing total media costs plus the costs of printing any special insert material by the circulation of the magazine.

$$\text{Space CPM} = \frac{\text{Media costs} + \text{Insert costs}}{\text{Circulation}} \times 1{,}000$$

For example, consider a magazine with a circulation of 1 million and ad or media costs of $40,000 running an insert card that cost $20 per thousand to print.

$$\text{Space CPM} = \frac{\$40,000 + (20 \times 1,000)}{1,000,000} \times 1,000$$

$$\text{Space CPM} = \$60.00$$

In both direct mail and space advertising, the question always arises whether the fixed creative fees paid to an agency or a free-lancer and the fixed mechanical preparation and art expenses should be included in the calculation of CPM. Opinion is divided on this subject. Some direct response marketers insist on including all costs in the calculation of CPM to ensure that their profitability analyses will include consideration of all costs associated with the promotion. Other direct marketers argue that creative material and mechanicals are intended for use in multiple promotions. These marketers either allocate a portion of the fixed creative expenses to each use of the material or maintain separate budgets and controls for creative expenses. They do not include consideration of fixed nonrecurring costs in the analysis of promotion results. This latter approach, which is more oriented to decision making, is favored by most large mailers who are concerned more with the decision to remail a promotion or repeat a space insertion than with the recording of historical costs. For decision-making purposes, the direct marketer wants to know the incremental costs of repeating a promotion that has been used in the past, regardless of such costs.

Calculating CPM for Different Direct Response Media

Direct Mail
There are three major types of direct mail promotion pieces, excluding catalogs, that are used by direct marketers to generate new orders or new leads: the full-package solo mailing, the less expensive self-mailer, and the insert piece.

Full-Package Solo Mailings. Table 15–1 shows the components of a standard direct mail package, including a four-page letter and color brochure. The CPM of the full package is shown at two mailing quantities: 50,000 and 250,000. Printing costs per thousand are shown to vary with the quantity printed as the fixed printing preparation expenses (which must be incurred at each print run) are amortized over the number of pieces to be

TABLE 15–1
Calculating CPM for a Typical Direct Mail Promotion at Two Mailing Quantities

	Quantity	
Package Element	50,000	250,000
Outer envelope	$ 30	$ 22
Four-page letter	38	28
Four-color brochure	90	65
Reply card	23	15
Return envelope	22	17
Total printing cost	$203	$147
Outside list rental	75	75
Letter shop	23	20
Merge/purge	6	6
Postage	132	132
Total CPM	$439	$380

mailed. These fixed printing preparation expenses should not be confused with creative fees and mechanical costs, which are truly one-time costs and do not vary with the quantity mailed or the number of print runs.

The example shown in Table 15–1 is typical of a consumer mailing of the kind used by book and record clubs, continuity programs, and magazines. In these situations, a color brochure generally is required to display the product fully, and third-class postage almost always is employed.

On the other end of the direct-response spectrum, a high-priced newsletter aimed at top corporate management may not use a full-color brochure but may be mailed first class to create a more businesslike impression in order to get past the secretary. In this case, the cost of the promotion will be reduced because the flier has been removed but increased because of the use of first-class postage.

Therefore, there is no hard and fast rule to determine the correct cost of direct mail promotion. Costs are a function of the components of the mailing package. Direct mail package costs can vary from $300 to $1,000 per thousand. The real question is what mailing package will be most profitable for the product or service being offered.

Self-Mailers.   One sure way to reduce mailing costs is to use a self-mailer, which is a promotion piece that does not contain multiple loose components. The most common format is the two- or three-panel 8½ by

11-inch card stock format. A self-mailer eliminates the need for an outer envelope, reduces letter shop expense, and combines the selling message of the letter and the brochure in one format. There is also no need for a separate business reply card and business reply envelope. The self-mailer is a perforated form, one portion of which is a business reply card, and the respondent is instructed to tear off this card and return it to the mailer. With the use of a self-mailer, promotion costs can be reduced significantly, but again the question arises as to what will happen to response. Will the self-mailer turn out to be more or less profitable than a full-mailing package? As usual in direct response, only testing can provide the answer.

Inserts or Enclosures.   Another very inexpensive but cost-effective mailing format is the insert piece or enclosure promotion. An insert or enclosure is any promotion piece that is mailed at no additional postage expense inside an invoice, statement, merchandise shipment, or other primary mailing piece. Insert pieces that are mailed along with first-class mailings such as bills or statements must be small so that they do not increase postage expenses. Enclosures in third-class mailings and merchandise shipments are not weight-restricted.

In general, insert pieces pull a much lower response than direct mail packages or self-mailers. However, because of the lower cost, which can be as low as $20 per thousand, response does not have to be very great in order to generate a profit.

Space Advertising

The cost per thousand for space advertising is considerably lower than the CPM for direct mail. A typical magazine page may cost from $5 to $75 per thousand circulation, as compared with direct mail, which ranges between $300 and $1,000 per thousand pieces mailed. Of course, the response to a space advertisement will be less than the response to a direct mail promotion. In direct mail, a 3 percent response (30 orders per thousand) to a promotion costing $600 per thousand will result in a cost per response of $20, and is not atypical. In space advertising, a $20 cost per response is likely to be the result of a response rate of $\frac{1}{10}$ of 1 percent in a medium with a CPM of $20.

As small as these numbers seem, they nevertheless result in very significant absolute numbers. For example, consider a mass-market magazine with a circulation of 3 million. The cost of a single black-and-white page is likely to be around $24,000 for a CPM of $8. If an ad in that magazine pulls at a rate of just .05 percent, or a rate of .5 orders per

TABLE 15–2
Calculating Front-End Space Results

Total circulation	3,000,000
Cost per single black-and-white page	$24,000
Total response	1,500
CPM	$8
Percent Response: (1,500/3 million) × 100	.05%
Orders per thousand circulation (OPM): (1,500/3,000)	.50
Cost per response (CPR): CPM/OPM = $8.00/.50	$16.00

thousand circulation, the ad will generate 1,500 responses at an average cost of $16 per response. (See Table 15–2.)

The actual CPM for an ad in any magazine will vary greatly, depending on a number of factors. For example, cover positions cost more than inside-the-book positions, color costs more than black and white, advertising in the direct mail section frequently costs less than advertising in the general editorial section, and discounts are available for multiple usage. Regional editions may be purchased, generally increasing the CPM but lowering the total dollar expenditure, and so on. The point is that buying space advertising is not simply a matter of placing an ad in a magazine. As always, the key decision is whether the more expensive ad format will result in a significantly greater response and increased profitability or, conversely, whether the less expensive format will result in fewer responses and lower profits.

Broadcast

Broadcast is an increasingly important direct response vehicle, and the emergence of cable TV with its highly targeted audiences has increased the significance of this medium.

TV broadcast advertising generally is purchased in one of two ways. In the first instance, an advertiser will purchase a certain amount of time from a local station or national network at an agreed-on price. The exact times the commercial is to be aired and the number of spots or showings are agreed to in advance. This procedure is similar to placing an ad in a magazine. Before the running of the ad or the showing of the commercial, the total investment in the medium is known. The cost per response will depend on the number of responses in the form of telephone calls to the local station or to an 800 number or on the number of responses received in the mail.

The second method of purchase is per inquiry (PI). Very often, a broadcast station will agree with an advertiser to run a given commercial at times chosen by the station. In exchange for this airtime, the advertiser will pay the station an amount based on the number of responses received. This method of payment also is referred to as PO (per order). In these situations, the initial response usually is directed to the local station and sent from there to the advertiser. PI or PO arrangements also are frequently available in space advertising.

When broadcast is used either to consummate a final sale or to generate leads, the key economic considerations are the length and frequency of the spot. Traditionally, direct response spots ran for 90 or 120 seconds, the argument for this length being the 20 seconds or so necessary for the tag line and the time it takes to establish the product and the offer in the viewer's mind. From the very outset, buying a two-minute spot on network TV was expensive and very often not available. Thus, direct marketers turned to local spot TV with its larger inventory of late night or non–prime time spots. The advent of cable TV opened up a whole new inventory of available times and the cable networks were more than happy to sell 90-second and two-minute spots to direct response advertisers. However, as cable's popularity grew, the inventory of two-minute spots decreased and direct marketers are once again trying to make 30- and 60-second spots pay for themselves. Closely aligned with the issue of the length of a direct response ad is the issue of frequency. How frequently should the spot appear in any one station? In any one market? Conceptually, there is a buildup period, a time in which response may be low but building, and then there is the falloff period after response has peaked. Obviously, the profits of a successful flight can be erased if airtime is purchased in significant quantity after the spot has peaked.

Thus, the economics of broadcast TV depend heavily on one's ability to forecast response patterns and to tightly control spending decisions.

A second important use of broadcast is in support of a major direct mail, newspaper insert, or magazine promotion. It is intuitive that broadcast spots urging the viewer to look in the paper, mailbox, or TV guide will increase response, but the economic question is how much airtime is enough and how much is too much? Up to a certain point or media weight, the broadcast advertising will not be able to make a significant impact and the support money will be wasted; on the other hand, too many spots can be equally unproductive. The answer, of course, is testing to determine the appropriate mix of broadcast support.

Finally, on the subject of broadcast, TV is not the only broadcast medium; we shouldn't forget radio. Radio, particularly drive-time radio with its upscale commuting audience, has always been a great captive market. But until the advent of the cellular car phone it has not been a great direct response medium. Of course, all that is changing rapidly as car phones move from luxury to necessity status among the most desirable market segments. So we see a great future for direct response radio, and when that happens, the same issues of time and frequency that affect broadcast TV will have to be addressed for radio.

Telemarketing
Outbound telemarketing is apparently here to stay, certainly for magazine renewals as well as for cold solicitations offering a one-issue trial examination offer. The phone also is used with great success in business-to-business direct response, in which the goal is to generate a lead or qualify a lead generated from a space ad or a direct mail offer.

Independent telephone operations currently sell their services at rates of approximately $30 to $40 per hour. Within this time period, a qualified phone operator can make between 6 and 20 contacts. The contact rate will vary depending on the time of day, the day of the week, and whether the call is to a consumer at home or to a business executive or professional at the place of work. Because of its ability to generate low-cost trial subscriptions or leads, the telephone must be used with care. A low conversion rate can transform a very low cost per lead into a very high cost per order, as we'll see a little later on in this chapter.

MEASURING RESPONSE

One-Step Promotions

The response to a direct mail promotion is expressed as a percentage of the quantity mailed or stated in terms of the number of responses per thousand pieces mailed (RPM). If the response is an order, the term *orders per thousand* (OPM) is used.

$$\text{Percentage response} = \frac{\text{Total response}}{\text{Quantity mailed}} \times 100$$

$$\text{RPM} = \frac{\text{Total response}}{\text{Quantity mailed}/1,000}$$

$$\text{OPM} = \frac{\text{Total orders}}{\text{Quantity mailed}/1,000}$$

Because the response to a direct mail promotion often is less than 1 percent, many direct marketers prefer to use the RPM or OPM terminology rather than express results in terms of a fraction of a percent. This is particularly true with regard to space advertising, in which a response of one order per thousand or even less is not uncommon.

Two-Step Promotions

As discussed above, not all direct response promotions are one-step promotions. Often, the initial response to a direct response promotion is only the first step in a two-step or even a multistep promotion process. A magazine promoted by direct mail, using an offer that allows the potential subscriber to cancel after previewing one issue, is an example of a two-step promotion.

Consider a direct mail promotion of a magazine through a preview offer. Assume that 500,000 pieces are mailed and that 10,000 responses are received. The initial RPM is equal to:

$$\text{RPM} = \frac{10,000}{500,000/1,000}$$
$$\text{RPM} = 20$$

If only 40 percent of the respondents to the preview offer convert to paid subscriptions, the final paid orders per thousand pieces mailed will be equal to:

$$\text{OPM} = 20 \text{ RPM} \times 40\%$$
$$\text{OPM} = 8$$

CALCULATING COST PER RESPONSE

One-Step Promotions

In a one-step promotion, the cost per response can be calculated by dividing the total number of responses into the total cost of the promotion. A quicker way that is preferred by many direct marketers is to divide the cost per thousand of the promotion by the number of responses per thousand to arrive at the cost per response (CPR):

$$CPR = \frac{CPM}{RPM}$$

Referring back to our magazine example, assume that the cost of the mailing was $350 per thousand. The initial cost per response would be:

$$CPR = \frac{\$350}{20} = \$17.50$$

Two-Step Promotions

In two-step promotions, the promotion portion of the total cost per order is equal to the promotion cost per response divided by the conversion rate. In our magazine example, the cost per response is $17.50 and the conversion rate was 40 percent. Therefore, the promotion cost per order is equal to:

$$\text{Promotion CPO} = \frac{\text{Initial CPR}}{\text{Conversion rate}}$$

$$\text{Promotion CPO} = \frac{\$17.50}{.40} = \$43.75$$

However, dividing the promotion cost per response by the conversion rate understates the cost of acquiring a new magazine subscriber.

Assume that in the process of converting preview subscribers into paid subscribers, those potential subscribers who eventually will cancel will receive three issues of the magazine and five invoices. Let's also assume that those who decide to subscribe will receive an average of three invoices before paying. The costs of this conversion process can be added legitimately to the cost of acquiring the average paid subscription.

The calculations would be as follows. If the cost of one issue of the magazine on an incremental basis is $.75, and the cost of one invoice, including first-class postage, computer expense, and printing, is $.55, the amount spent on each eventual nonsubscriber or "cancel" is equal to:

$$
\begin{array}{ll}
\text{3 issues} \times \text{\$.75 per issue} & = \$2.25 \\
+\ \text{5 invoices} \times \text{\$.55 per invoice} & = \$2.75 \\
\text{Total cost per cancel} & = \$5.00
\end{array}
$$

Since only 40 percent of the initial respondents will subscribe, the cost of attempting to convert the eventual cancels or nonsubscribers must be allocated over those who do subscribe. The equation for this calculation is as follows:

$$
\begin{array}{l}
\text{Conversion expense per} \\
\text{subscriber because of} \\
\text{cancellations}
\end{array}
= \frac{\text{Cost per cancel} \times (1 - \text{Pay rate})}{\text{Pay rate}}
$$

$$
\text{Conversion expense per subscriber} = \frac{\$5.00 \times (1 - .40)}{.40}
$$

$$
\text{Conversion expense per subscriber} = \$7.50
$$

In addition, the cost of billing the respondents who eventually will pay will be equal to $3 \times \$.55$, or $1.65. Therefore, the total conversion expense is equal to $7.50 plus $1.65, or $9.15 per paid order.

The total cost per new subscriber, including both promotion expense and conversion expense, is equal to the total new-subscriber acquisition expense:

$$
\begin{array}{ccccc}
\text{Promotion expense} & + & \text{Conversion expense} & = & \text{Total acquisition expense} \\
\$43.75 & + & \$9.15 & = & \$52.90
\end{array}
$$

The lesson to be remembered from this example is that the initial CPR may be only a small part of the total cost per final order in a multistep promotion. The costs of converting initial responses or leads can be particularly expensive when the conversion process requires expensive sales literature or requires a sales call.

TRACKING BACK–END PERFORMANCE

In the section on front-end performance, we discussed the techniques used to measure the costs of acquiring leads, buyers, or subscribers. In each case, costs were expressed not in terms of the total dollars spent but rather in terms of the amount spent to acquire the average customer from a particular media investment. By defining costs in terms of the average cost per customer, it is possible for us to compare alternative media without regard to their size.

This same approach will be followed in the discussion of back-end performance. In general, back-end performance refers to the purchase behavior of a group of respondents from the time their names are entered on the customer file. More specifically, we shall define back-end performance as the sales, contribution, and profits resulting from a group of respondents acquired from a particular advertising medium.

In order to measure, or track, back-end performance, it is necessary to maintain a system in which each individual customer is identified as coming from a specific advertising medium: a list, a space insertion, or a broadcast spot. When this is done, it is possible to accumulate the behavior of all customers from the same initial source medium and calculate average sales, contribution, or profits.

For this reason, direct marketing advertisers include a key code on every coupon in every space ad and print a key code on the return card or label of every direct mail promotion. The key code identifies the advertising medium and becomes a permanent part of the responding customer's record, along with name, address, and purchase history.

Direct marketers have proved over and over that for a given order, back-end performance will vary significantly from one advertising medium to another. In general, direct marketers have discovered that buyers acquired from direct mail behave better than buyers acquired from space or magazine advertisements and that buyers acquired from direct mail or space will perform better than buyers acquired from broadcast promotions. However, there are wide variations in performance within the same media category. The best customers acquired from space media will perform better than the worst customers acquired from direct mail, and so on.

The critical concept to remember is that back-end performance will vary from medium to medium and that the only way to operate a profitable direct response business is to be able to track the performance of customers in terms of the original source group so that the decision to reinvest promotion dollars can be made on the basis of proven performance.

At this point, it will pay to remind the reader that what is being described is classical direct marketing theory. Concern is with the performance of the average customer, and what is being measured and about to be evaluated is the relationship between back-end performance and front-end or acquisition expense.

Back-end performance in this classical approach is assumed to be the same for every individual acquired from a given source code. In practice, when direct marketers set out to influence back-end performance, they do so using a natural extension of the source group concept. For example, if a classical direct marketer thought that it might be better in a continuity situation to ship books every six weeks instead of the usual four-week shipment cycle, the procedure most likely to be followed would be to run an A/B split in one or more important media sources disclosing the six-week shipment cycle to the A group and a four-week shipment cycle to the B group. The marketer could then measure if there was any immediate difference in up-front response and begin the process of waiting to see if back-end performance was better or worse for either group. More on influencing back-end response, through classical as well as database methods, later. First, let's finish the discussion of how back-end performance is measured.

Measuring Back-End Performance

Single-Shot Mailing

The measurement of back-end performance for a solo, or single-shot, mailing is simply the statement of profit or loss for the promotion. Table 15–3 lists the assumptions that would be typical of a solo mailing of a product with a sales price of $60. The profit and loss statement that follows (Table 15–4) is based on the assumptions defined in Table 15–3.

Clubs and Continuity Programs

In clubs and continuity programs, the statistic that measures back-end performance is the contribution to promotion, overhead, and profit. If this contribution for a group of new orders or starters is greater than the cost of acquiring the starting group, the investment in the starting group can be considered to be at least marginally profitable.

This contribution statistic sometimes is referred to as the *order margin,* the *allowable,* or the *breakeven.* Each term implies a comparison to the cost per order expended to bring the starters into the business.

The contribution statistic excludes consideration of all fixed costs and overhead. Contribution is calculated by subtracting all direct expenses from the net sales of a group of starters and then dividing the result by the number of starters in the group.

In a club or continuity program, sales accumulate over the economic life of the starting group, and that life often can extend over a number of

TABLE 15–3
Assumptions for a Single-Shot Promotion

Selling price	$65.00
Shipping and handling charge	$3.00
Return rate (percent of gross sales)	10.0%
Percentage of returns reusable	90.0%
Cost of product per unit	$15.00
Order processing:	
Reply postage per gross response	$.25
Order processing and setup per gross response	$2.00
Percentage of gross orders using:	
Credit cards	75.0%
Checks	25.0%
Credit card expense	3.0%
Percentage of charge orders with bad checks	5.0%
Shipping and handling per gross response	$3.00
Return processing:	
Return postage per return	$1.50
Handling per gross return	$.50
Refurbishing costs per usable return	$2.00
Premium expense per gross response	$6.00
Promotion CPM	$350.00
Quantity mailed	100,000
Percent response	2.0%
Overhead factor as a percent of net sales	10.0%

years. Therefore, in clubs or programs with an exceptionally long member life, the contribution from each monthly cycle should be discounted by some amount, generally the seller's cost of capital or opportunity cost, to take the time value of money into consideration.

The ability to forecast final sales and payments from individual starting groups on the basis of early performance data is critical in clubs and continuity programs. In these businesses, as in most direct response businesses, the key marketing decision is the decision to reinvest in media that have already been tested. Because of the long economic life of a club or continuity member, the decision to reinvest must be made on the basis of forecasted behavior. For example, if a new list is mailed in the winter and pulls as well as most other lists used by the club, the marketer may wish to remail the same names or test a larger segment of the list universe in the summer or fall campaign. However, by that time only a few cycles of actual data will be available for analysis. The decision, therefore, must be made on the basis of expected final contribution per starter. The forecast itself is based on the actual data accumulated to date.

TABLE 15–4
Profit and Loss Statement for a Single-Shot Promotion

	Units	Amount	Percent
Gross sales	2,000	$130,000	
Shipping and handling	2,000	6,000	
Total revenue	2,000	136,000	111.1%
Returns	200	13,600	11.1
Net sales	1,800	$122,400	100.0%
Cost of sales:			
Product:			
Net shipments	1,800	$ 27,000	22.1%
Nonreusable units	20	300	.2
Order processing:			
Reply postage	2,000	500	.4
Setup costs	2,000	4,000	3.3
Credit card costs	1,500	3,060	2.5
Bad check expense	25	1,700	1.4
Shipping and handling	2,000	6,000	4.9
Return processing:			
Postage	200	300	.2
Handling	200	100	.1
Refurbishing	180	360	.3
Premium	2,000	12,000	9.8
Total cost of sales		$ 55,320	45.2%
Operating gross margin		$ 67,080	54.8%
Promotion expense		35,000	28.6
Contribution to overhead and profit		$ 32,080	26.2%
Overhead allocation		12,240	10.0
Profit		$ 19,840	16.2%

In both clubs and continuity programs, one of the most important forecasting variables is the *attrition rate*. This is the term used to measure the rate at which members in a club or program either cancel their memberships or are canceled because of failure to pay for previously shipped items.

In negative option clubs, the attrition pattern measures the percentage of original starters eligible to receive the periodic advance announcements that advertise the negative option selection of the cycle and the alternative selections. In addition to being able to forecast the attrition pattern, it is also necessary to be able to forecast the acceptance rate of the featured negative option selection and the acceptance of the alternative selections as well as the average price of each category of sale.

Table 15–5 shows a simplified negative option club model that forecasts and accumulates average gross sales per starting member. As was mentioned before, in an actual club operation, the forecast would include separate estimates for the negative option selection and the alternative selections.

According to the model shown in Table 15–5, the average sale per starter will be $48.19. Assuming that direct costs, excluding all promotion and premium costs, are equal to 35 percent of gross sales, the contribution to promotion, overhead, and profit from this group of starters would be $31.32. It is this number minus premium costs that would be compared with promotion costs to determine the profitability of the starting group.

In continuity programs, there are two attrition patterns to be concerned with. The first pattern measures the percentage of starters who initially receive each shipment level at the earliest possible date. This attrition pattern reflects the payment behavior of starters who pay for each shipment on time and continue in the program. The second pattern represents the percentage of original starters who eventually receive each shipment level by the end of the economic life of the starting group. The difference in the two patterns is due to starters who fall behind in their payments and are suspended temporarily from receiving further shipments. As these starters eventually pay, the percentage of starters receiving each shipment level gradually increases.

In order to forecast sales properly, it is necessary to be able to forecast both attrition patterns. A forecast using only the first attrition pattern will understate eventual sales. A forecast using just the second pattern will forecast final sales correctly but will not be able to forecast when those sales will occur. Table 15–6 provides an example of continuity attrition and the growth of the average number of units shipped over time to a group of starters in a continuity program in which one item is shipped per month.

Newsletters and Magazines

The key economic variables that determine the profitability of a newsletter are (1) price, (2) the initial pay or conversion rate, (3) renewal rates, and (4) the response rate to direct mail promotions at different levels of promotion expense.

As was mentioned earlier in this chapter, many newsletters and magazines are successful in attracting trial subscribers through the use of preview offers that allow the potential subscriber to cancel without paying after examining one or a few sample issues. In these situations, the initial pay rate or conversion rate is the single most important variable affecting

TABLE 15–5
Average Sales Accumulated over Time in a Negative Option Club

	Percent			Sales per Starting Member	
Cycle	Still Active	Buying Product	Average Price	Incremental	Cumulative
			Actual Data		
1	97.0%	51%	$12	$5.94	$ 5.94
2	95.0	47	12	5.36	11.29
3	83.0	42	12	4.18	15.48
4	75.0	38	12	3.42	18.90
5	70.0	33	12	2.77	21.67
			Forecast Data		
6	65.1	32	12	2.50	24.17
7	60.5	31	12	2.25	26.42
8	56.3	31	12	2.09	28.52
9	52.4	30	12	1.89	30.40
10	48.7	30	12	1.75	32.15
11	45.3	30	12	1.63	33.78
12	42.1	30	12	1.52	35.30
13	39.2	30	12	1.41	36.71
14	36.4	30	12	1.31	38.02
15	33.9	30	12	1.22	39.24
16	31.5	30	12	1.13	40.38
17	29.3	30	12	1.05	41.43
18	27.3	30	12	.98	42.41
19	25.3	30	12	.91	43.32
20	23.6	30	12	.85	44.17
21	21.9	30	12	.79	44.96
22	20.4	30	12	.73	45.70
23	19.0	30	12	.68	46.38
24	17.6	30	12	.63	47.01
25	16.4	30	12	.59	47.60
26	15.2	30	12	.55	48.15
27	14.2	30	12	.51	48.66
28	13.2	30	12	.47	49.14
29	12.3	30	12	.44	49.58
30	11.4	30	12	.41	49.99
31	10.6	30	12	.38	50.37
32	9.9	30	12	.36	50.73
33	9.2	30	12	.33	51.06
34	8.5	30	12	.31	51.36
35	7.9	30	12	.29	51.65
36	7.4	30	12	.27	51.92
37	6.9	30	12	.25	52.16
38	6.4	30	12	.23	52.39
39	5.9	30	12	.21	52.61
40	5.5	30	12	.20	52.81

TABLE 15–6
Attrition Patterns in a Continuity Program

Shipment Number	Attrition Pattern Start	Attrition Pattern End	By End of Cycle	Average Units Shipped	By End of Week	Average Units Shipped
1	100%	100%	1	1.00	40	5.09
2	92	92	2	1.00	41	5.23
3	85	85	3	1.00	42	5.25
4	50	60	4	1.00	43	5.26
5	35	45	5	1.92	44	5.27
6	30	40	6	1.92	45	5.39
7	20	28	7	1.92	46	5.40
8	18	25	8	1.92	47	5.41
9	16	23	9	2.77	48	5.42
10	15	20	10	2.77	49	5.54
11	13	18	11	2.77	50	5.55
12	12	17	12	2.77	51	5.56
13	11	15	13	3.29	52	5.56
14	10	13	14	3.30	53	5.67
15	9	12	15	3.32	54	5.68
Total		5.94%	16	3.34	55	5.69
			17	3.70	56	5.69
			18	3.74	57	5.79
			19	3.75	58	5.80
			20	3.77	59	5.80
			21	4.10	60	5.81
			22	4.14	61	5.83
			23	4.17	62	5.83
			24	4.19	63	5.84
			25	4.40	64	5.85
			26	4.43	65	5.86
			27	4.45	66	5.86
			28	4.46	67	5.87
			29	4.65	68	5.88
			30	4.67	69	5.88
			31	4.69	70	5.89
			32	4.70	71	5.89
			33	4.88	72	5.90
			34	4.89	73	5.91
			35	4.90	74	5.91
			36	4.91	75	5.92
			37	5.00	76	5.92
			38	5.07	77	5.93
			39	5.08	78	5.94

TABLE 15–7
The Economics of Newsletter Direct Mail Marketing

		Initial Pay or Conversion Rate				
		30 Percent	*40 Percent*	*50 Percent*	*60 Percent*	*70 Percent*
First-Year Results						
Subscribers		60	80	100	120	140
Revenues		$2,820	$3,760	$4,700	$5,640	$6,580
Fulfillment and renewal costs		750	850	950	1,050	1,150
Promotion costs		3,000	3,000	3,000	3,000	3,000
First-year profits		$ (930)	$ (90)	$ 750	$1,590	$2,430
*Second-Year Profits**						
If renewal rates are:	40.00%	$ 864	$1,152	$1,440	$1,728	$2,016
	50.00	1,118	1,490	1,863	2,235	2,608
	60.00	1,371	1,828	2,285	2,742	3,199
	70.00	1,625	2,166	2,708	3,249	3,790
Cumulative Second-Year Profits						
If renewal rates are:	40.00%	$ (66)	$1,062	$2,190	$3,318	$4,446
	50.00	188	1,400	2,613	3,825	5,038
	60.00	441	1,738	3,035	4,332	5,629
	70.00	695	2,076	3,458	4,839	6,221

the ultimate success of the venture. However, even a relatively high initial pay rate can be offset by a poor renewal rate. Only after both conversion rates and renewal rates have been tested can one be sure of the potential profits of a newsletter. Table 15–7 shows the range of profits after two years from a direct mail investment of $3,000 that resulted in 200 responses. In this situation, the $3,000 investment is recovered in the first year if the conversion rate is 60 percent or greater. The investment is profitable within two years if the initial conversion rate is 40 percent or more and the first renewal rate is 50 percent or better.

The profits that can be generated from a newsletter are related directly to the price charged for the newsletter, since editorial costs and printing costs are not affected by the price of the service. Thus, it is very

TABLE 15–7
(continued)

Assumptions

The price of the newsletter	$ 47.00
The cost of fulfilling a paying subscriber	6.00
The cost of fulfilling a canceling subscriber	2.25
The cost of renewing a subscriber per starting subscriber	1.25
The cost of fulfilling a subscriber who fails to renew	2.50
Range of possible conversion rates from trial to paid subscriber	30% to 70%
Range of possible first renewal rates	40% to 70%
Mailing quantity	10,000
Mailing costs	$ 3,000
Percent response	2.00%

Results

Number of gross orders (.02 × 10,000)	200

*Second-year profits if renewal rate is 70 percent and conversion rate is 70 percent:
Subscribers: (10,000 × .02 × .7 × .7) = 98
Revenue = 98 subscribers × $35 = $3,430
Fulfillment and renewal costs: 98 subscribers × (6 + 1.25) = $710.50
Issues to nonrenewals: 42 × 2.50 = 105
Second-year profits: $3,430 − $710.50 − $105 = $2,614.50

important that price testing be employed at the outset to determine the best and most profitable price for the service. Tables 15–8 and 15–9 show the effect of a $10 increase or decrease in price on the newsletter described in Table 15–7.

The economics of magazines is similar to the economics of newsletters but with a number of critical differences. First, magazines rely heavily on newsstand sales and advertising to supplement the revenue stream provided by subscription income. Second, because of competition and because magazines are targeted to reach circulation levels measured in the hundreds of thousands rather than just thousands, as is the case with most newsletters, there is much less price-setting flexibility. However, just as in newsletters, the response rate to direct mail, the conversion rate, and the renewal rates are the key economic variables that eventually will determine the success or lack of success of the magazine venture.

Catalogs

The term *back-end analysis* in a catalog operation can have multiple meanings. We may use the term with regard to the analysis of past media

TABLE 15–8
Cumulative Second-Year Profits If Price Is Reduced to $27

Renewal Rates	Conversion Rate				
	30 Percent	40 Percent	50 Percent	60 Percent	70 Percent
40%	$(1,746)	$(1,178)	$(610)	$ (42)	$ 526
50	(1,613)	(1,000)	(388)	225	838
60	(1,479)	(822)	(165)	492	1,149
70	(1,346)	(644)	58	759	1,460

TABLE 15–9
Cumulative Second-Year Profits If Price Is Increased to $47

Renewal Rates	Conversion Rate				
	30 Percent	40 Percent	50 Percent	60 Percent	70 Percent
40%	$ (66)	$1,062	$2,190	$3,318	$4,446
50	188	1,400	2,613	3,825	5,038
60	441	1,738	3,035	4,332	5,629
70	695	2,076	3,458	4,839	6,221

selections in much the same way as we analyze media performance in a club or continuity situation. Or we may be concerned with the profitability of an individual catalog mailing, that is, did the catalog make a profit, which items sold well, which didn't, and so on. Or we may be referring to the decision-making process in which we attempt to decide which customers should be mailed which catalogs and with what frequency in the future.

The first decision deals with the evaluation of individual media sources, and we act as if all customers acquired behave in exactly the same way by looking at the average performance of all customers acquired from the media source. Again, this is the classical direct marketing approach, as opposed to the database approach, which focuses its attention on the performance of individual customers across media sources. The reason we need two approaches is that two different decisions are involved. When evaluating a media source, we are asking, "is this media source profitable?" and "should we invest in it again?" What counts is the total or the average performance of all customers expected to be acquired from a future investment when compared to the cost of the investment. And we use past performance as a guide to future performance.

In a noncontractual relationship, after a customer is acquired from any media source, the decision to promote that customer is an independent decision. This decision should be based on the expected future performance of the individual, regardless of the source from which he or she was acquired, even though the original media source may be, as we'll see later, an important variable in making a prediction of future performance.

The mechanics of media source evaluation in a catalog or in any noncontractual relationship requires computer systems that track performance by original source code. Again, as always, the key question is, "will the eventual contribution from the customers acquired be greater than the cost of acquiring those customers, and if so, by how much?"

In practice, the same media source will have been used many times in the past, and an evaluation of each use will reveal that profitability will vary from use to use. Not only will the prediction of eventual contribution vary but the cost of acquiring new customers, as measured by the cost per order, will vary from promotion to promotion. Therefore, the prediction of future performance, both front-end CPO and back-end contribution, must be based on a forecasting procedure that takes this variability into account. Time-series analysis, taking such factors as trend and seasonality into account, may be employed if the data is suitable, or the analyst may use simpler averaging techniques giving greater weight to more recent occurrences. In practice, this becomes much more of an art than a science, and to imply that there are highly reliable standard procedures for this process would be misleading.

Financial Services

The provider of financial services is, in theory, in a nearly identical position to the traditional catalog marketer with respect to the noncontractual nature of the relationship between the company and the customer. However, in practice, we've found financial service providers to be more concerned with individual level database marketing decisions than with the classical direct marketing issue of relating back-end performance to initial cost per acquired customer. There are a variety of reasons for this, none of which justify current practices but go a long way toward explaining why things are the way they are.

To begin with, many financial services providers using direct marketing methods are not traditional self-contained direct marketing companies whose only contact with the customer is through direct marketing media. Therefore, since it is difficult if not impossible to attribute response to a single ad or direct mail promotion, little attempt is made to do so. More significant, we suspect, is the fact that many direct marketing operations within financial services firms are developed in an ad hoc manner. Someone at a high level within the firm, perhaps because of exposure to competitive direct marketing offers, decided that direct mail or direct marketing should be done within the firm, and set out to do so using the existing computer support systems, which were not designed for direct marketing purposes but were, in all likelihood, designed to support a sales force network.

In an information or database environment, where decision making is based on knowledge about the individual customer, one might argue that knowledge about the average behavior of all customers acquired from the same media source is unimportant. This argument, while it seems reasonable, is wrong for two reasons. The first reason is that the original media source is an important piece of individual information. The second reason is that it confuses the need to make decisions about customers with the need to make decisions about where one shall prospect for customers. Again and again, direct marketers must make trade-off decisions about how much to spend on current-customer marketing and how much to spend on new-customer marketing. This is true for any company using direct marketing methods, be they a traditional direct marketing firm or one of the newer nontraditional users of direct marketing.

The Return of the Chicken-or-the-Egg Problem

By now, the reader who has been paying close attention should have realized that we're back to the chicken-or-the-egg problem raised earlier in this chapter. The argument goes as follows. We wish to compare the lifetime performance or behavior of customers acquired from a media source to the cost of acquiring those customers. However, their performance will be a function of what we send them and how often we promote them. If our promotion decisions are faulty, if we mail too often or too infrequently, or if we mail the wrong products, the contribution of the group of customers will be less than it would have been if our decisions had been better. Fortunately, the only practical way to treat this problem is to ignore it, and that's OK if all media source groups have been treated in the same way, however good or bad that way was, and if all we're trying to do is rank media sources in terms of relative performance in order to decide how to allocate future media acquisition dollars. On the other hand, we always have to guard against self-fulfilling prophecies. If, for example, customers from a particular media source are always mailed less frequently because their performance is expected to be less than average, then we shouldn't be surprised to find that indeed sales from these customers always turn out to be less than sales from customers acquired from other sources. The solution to this problem, if the problem is thought to exist, is to create and track test groups across all media sources that are always treated in the same fashion.

We'll come back to the subject of how individuals should be evaluated for inclusion in future mailings in Chapter 16, where we discuss modeling and the relationship between modeling and RFM analyses. For now, let's assume that we can agree on an acceptable way to estimate the lifetime performance of customers acquired from individual media sources, and that we can even agree on the expected CPO and the expected lifetime contribution of customers to be acquired in the future. How do we use this information in decision making?

MEASURING PROFITABILITY: COMBINING FRONT–END AND BACK–END STATISTICS

In the previous discussion, it was implied that if the contribution to promotion, overhead, and profit for a given media investment was greater than the cost per order, the investment could be considered to be at least marginally profitable. We shall now continue to develop the relationship between front-end and back-end statistics.

Many direct marketers, particularly those engaged in club and continuity programs, prefer to use the concept of return on promotion to measure the relationship between front-end and back-end performance. Return on promotion (ROP) is defined as the ratio of the contribution to promotion, overhead, and profit minus the cost per order divided by the cost per order.

$$\text{ROP} = \frac{[\text{Contribution} - \text{Cost per order}]}{\text{Cost per order}} \times 100$$

Conceptually, the ROP approach treats the decision to run a space ad or mail a list as an investment against which some financial return is expected. The return is measured by the difference between the contribution that results from all the purchases that occur after the order enters the house and the cost of acquiring the order.

For example, in the discussion on clubs and continuities, we showed how a group of starters with average sales of $52.81 might generate a

TABLE 15–10
Using Incremental ROP to Evaluate New Offers (from 20 to 25 OPM)

	Case 1	Case 2	Incremental Results
	Assumptions		
Quantity mailed	50,000	50,000	
Orders per thousand	20	25	
Average revenue per starter	$70.00	$70.00	
Direct costs excluding premium expense	$30.00	$30.00	
Contribution	$40.00	$40.00	
Advertising CPM	$350.00	$350.00	
Advertising expense	$17,500.00	$17,500.00	
Advertising CPO	$17.50	$14.00	
Premium expense	$6.00	$9.00	
	Results		
Orders	1,000	1,250	250
Sales	$70,000	$87,500	$17,500
Costs	$30,000	$37,500	$7,500
Contributions	$40,000	$50,000	$10,000
Advertising	$17,500	$17,500	$0
Premium	$6,000	$11,250	$5,250
Total contribution to overhead and profit	$16,500	$21,250	$4,750
Per starter	$16.50	$17.00	$.50
ROP	94.3 %	121.4 %	0

contribution per starter of $34.21. Let's assume that the cost of acquiring this group of starters was $20 per starter. In this case, the ROP would be:

$$\text{ROP} = \frac{[\$34.32 - \$20.00]}{\$20.00} \times 100 = 71.6\%$$

The ROP statistic can be used in a variety of ways by direct marketers. One important use of this statistic is to evaluate alternative offers. The decision rule to be followed is that if the media investment required to implement both offers is the same, the offer with the highest ROP is the best offer.

Consider the example described in Table 15–10. In this example, the decision concerns whether to use a premium costing $6 per starter or a premium costing $9 per starter. The assumption is made that the average sales resulting from the use of either premium offer will be the same and will be equal to $70 per starter.

Naturally, increasing premium expense will reduce profits unless the premium offer results in an increased response. Thus, the question is, "what increase in response is necessary to justify the use of a $9 premium?" One way to answer this question is to assume a response rate to the $6 premium offer and then search by trial and error for a response rate to the $9 offer that would result in the same profit and loss as the profit and loss resulting from the $6 offer.

Under the Results column for Case 1 in Table 15–10, we see the profit and loss resulting from the $6 premium if a response rate of 20 OPM is assumed. For Case 2, at a response rate of 25 OPM, which is assumed to result from the use of the $9 premium, contribution to overhead and profit would be increased by a total of $4,750. The ROP for each case is shown at the bottom of Table 15–10. The ROP for Case 2 is 121.4 percent, which is greater than the ROP of 94.3 percent for Case 1. As long as the media investment is the same—in this case, the $17,500 required to mail 50,000 pieces at a CPM of $350—the alternative with the higher ROP will be the most profitable.

Therefore, it is possible to use the ROP equation directly to determine the response rate that would cause the ROP on the $9 premium offer to equal the ROP on the $6 premium offer:

$$\text{ROP} = \frac{\text{Contribution} - \text{Premium} - \text{CPO}}{\text{CPO}}$$

$$\text{Old ROP} = .943 = \frac{\$40 - \$6 - \$17.50}{\$17.50}$$

$$\text{New ROP} = .943 = \frac{\$40 - \$9 - \text{New CPO}}{\text{New CPO}}$$

$$\text{New CPO} = \$15.95$$

$$\text{New OPM} = \frac{\text{CPM}}{\text{New CPO}} = \frac{\$350}{\$15.95} = 21.94$$

The required new response rate is 21.94 orders per thousand.

When the initial media investment is not the same, the ROP analysis must be applied to the incremental investment in order to result in the correct decision. In this situation, if the incremental ROP is greater than zero, there will be an increase in the contribution to overhead and profit.

TABLE 15–11
Using Incremental ROP to Evaluate New Offers (from 20 to 22 OPM)

	Case 1	Case 2	Incremental Results
	Assumptions		
Quantity mailed	50,000	50,000	
Orders per thousand	20	22	
Average revenue per starter	$70.00	$70.00	
Direct costs excluding premium expense	$30.00	$30.00	
Contribution	$40.00	$40.00	
Advertising CPM	$350.00	$400.00	
Advertising expense	$17,500.00	$20,000.00	
Advertising CPO	$17.50	$18.18	
Premium expense	$5.00	$5.00	
	Results		
Orders	1,000	1,100	100
Sales	$70,000	$77,000	$7,000
Costs	$30,000	$33,000	$3,000
Contributions	$40,000	$44,000	$4,000
Advertising	$17,500	$20,000	$2,500
Premium	$5,000	$5,500	$500
Total contribution to overhead and profit	$17,500	$18,500	$1,000
Per starter	$17.50	$16.82	$.68
ROP	100.0 %	92.5 %	0
Incremental ROP	100.0 %	92.5 %	40.0 %

Refer to Table 15–11. In this example, the decision is whether to increase the quality of the mailing package in order to increase response. Costs are expected to increase from $350 per thousand to $400 per thousand, and the response rate is expected to increase from 20 OPM to 22 OPM. In Table 15–11, we see that if the more expensive mailing package was chosen, the average ROP would decline from 100 to 92.5 percent, but the incremental ROP would be 40 percent and total dollar contribution would increase by $1,000.

However, if the response rate increased to only 21 OPM, as shown in Table 15–12, the incremental ROP would be negative, and contribution would decline.

TABLE 15–12
Using Incremental ROP to Evaluate New Offers (from 20 to 21 OPM)

	Case 1	Case 2	Incremental Results
Assumptions			
Quantity mailed	50,000	50,000	
Orders per thousand	20	21	
Average revenue per starter	$70.00	$70.00	
Direct costs excluding premium expense	$30.00	$30.00	
Contribution	$40.00	$40.00	
Advertising CPM	$350.00	$400.00	
Advertising expense	$17,500.00	$20,000.00	
Advertising CPO	$17.50	$19.05	
Premium expense	$5.00	$5.00	
Results			
Orders	1,000	1,050	50
Sales	$70,000	$73,500	$3,500
Costs	$30,000	$31,500	$1,500
Contributions	$40,000	$42,000	$2,000
Advertising	$17,500	$20,000	$2,500
Premium	$5,000	$5,250	$250
Total contribution to overhead and profit	$17,500	$16,750	$(750)
Per starter	$17.50	$15.95	$(1.55)
ROP	100.0 %	83.8 %	0
Incremental ROP			−30.0 %

The decision to invest funds up to the point at which the incremental ROP is zero is a management decision. Generally, the cutoff rate is substantially higher, around 30 percent, to reflect other factors such as risk, the company's cost of capital, and opportunity costs resulting from competing uses of funds from other investments.

Another important use of the return on promotion statistic is to rank alternative investment opportunities for budget allocations. We have already seen that if the size of the investment is held constant, the investment alternative with the highest ROP is the most profitable.

In planning annual media budgets, a good first step is to begin by calculating the expected ROP for each independent media opportunity and then to rank all such opportunities in terms of descending order of

ROP. Conceptually, as the size of the media budget increases, the average ROP generated by the budget decreases, but for any given budget total, a media budget constructed in such a fashion will always yield the highest possible ROP.

One caution in the use of ROP in budget planning: The ROP statistic is an economic measure and does not take fiscal year profit and loss considerations into account. An investment with a 50 percent ROP and a first-of-the-year expense date is considered to be the same in an ROP ranking scheme as an investment with a 50 percent ROP with an end-of-the-fiscal-year expense date. From a financial accounting point of view, the investment made on the first of the year will result in sales from new members in that same fiscal year. The investment made at the end of the fiscal year will result only in expense; the corresponding sales will come in the next fiscal year.

This problem is alleviated to some extent by accounting procedures that allow new-member acquisition expense to be amortized over the economic life of the acquired new members or subscribers. For example, assuming an economic life of 12 months, only one twelfth of the expense of a promotion that was released in the last fiscal month would be charged to the current fiscal year.

ROP AND THE INFAMOUS 2 PERCENT RESPONSE RATE

It is customary for direct marketers to be accused of settling for low response rates. The implicit assumption is that through better targeting, response rates will increase to a rate higher than 2 percent — 2 percent in this case being used as a kind of shorthand for a break-even level of response. Of course, adoption of the ROP principle suggests that direct marketers should, if funds are available and fiscal budget restraints are not an issue, always continue investing promotion dollars until the marginal rate of return on promotion approaches the cost of capital, and if that happens at a 2 percent response level, so be it. The goal of targeting should therefore not be to increase the marginal cutoff rate from 2 percent to some higher number; the goal of targeting should be to find more names that can be mailed with a response rate of 2 percent (that is, the break-even level) or better, and in this way to increase the size of one's business. Of course, if promotion funds are limited, then the effect of targeting will be to increase the average response rate over its current level, in turn increasing the average return on promotion.

CHAPTER 16

THE ROLE OF MODELING IN
THE NEW DIRECT MARKETING

In recent years, a great deal of attention has been given to the role of statistical modeling in direct marketing. The idea of a model of one's business that can measurably improve the decision-making process is obviously desirable. If such a model exists, or can be made to exist, it deserves considerable attention. Unfortunately, there is no such thing as a single model that will solve all of one's marketing problems. For some reason, within the industry there is still the notion that one can build a model and that this model will perform indefinitely as a reliable guide to all future promotion decision making. Nothing could be further from the truth.

RESPONSE MODELING: RFM VERSUS REGRESSION

To understand the proper role of modeling in direct marketing, a simple example may help. Let's assume that we are managing a catalog company with 2 million customers that have been acquired and marketed to continuously over a five-year period. Our customer file contains the following information about each of our customers:

- Date the customer first came on the file.
- Original source code — both at the detail and major media level (direct mail, print, broadcast, etc.).
- Dates of all customer purchases.
- Dollar value of each purchase — associated with each purchase date.
- Total number of purchases made.
- Total dollar value of purchases.
- Major product areas in which at least one purchase was made — assume there are a dozen possible product areas.

- Total dollars spent in each product area.
- Number of times the customer has been mailed.

Suppose we wished to mail the next catalog to only 1 million customers, rather than to the entire file of 2 million. Let's further assume that the last catalog mailing went to the entire file of 2 million and that we kept a copy of the file at the time of the mailing and have since updated that file with results from the mailing. What analysis could be done—with and without statistical modeling?

The experienced direct marketer, though perhaps not familiar with formal statistical modeling, will immedateily recognize all the necessary ingredients for a traditional RFM (recency, frequency, monetary value) analysis, plus the data needed to extend RFM to include product information. So for starters, we could do an RFM model. Suppose we decided to create five recency periods:

Period 1—Includes all customers whose last purchase was within 6 months of the mailing date.

Period 2—Includes all customers whose last purchase was within 7 to 12 months of the mailing date.

Period 3—Includes all customers whose last purchase was within 13 to 24 months of the mailing date.

Period 4—Includes all customers whose last purchase was within 24 to 36 months of the mailing date.

Period 5—Includes all customers whose last purchase was within 37 to 60 months of the mailing date.

Now our 2 million names would be divided into five groups and undoubtedly we would find that the response rate to the promotion being studied would be highest among those that purchased most recently.

The next step in the RFM process is to decide how to treat frequency of purchase. Within any of the five recency groups, the frequency of purchase may vary. For example, within the group whose last purchase was within the last six months, we will find individuals whose frequency of purchase, within any time period, will vary from 1 to some higher number, which raises the question of the time period in which we measure frequency. Just because one's recency group is within six months, it does not necessarily follow that the frequency in question is the frequency of purchase within that same period. It could be and often is the same, but we could also measure frequency of purchase over some longer period, or define frequency of purchase as the ratio of times purchased divided by times mailed, or as the ratio of times purchased divided by the number of months on the file.

For the sake of argument, let's assume that we agree that each recency group should be divided into five frequency groups and that frequency should be measured within the same time period as recency. We would now have 25 different cells, five recency cells times five frequency cells. What about monetary value? It's intuitive that someone who purchases three times within any time period and whose total purchases equaled $300 is a better prospect for our next mailing than someone who also purchased three times within the same time period but whose purchases totaled only $30.

Therefore, to complete this simple RFM model (yes, RFM can be called a model) we need to decide on rules for dividing each of the 25 cells by some measure of monetary value. Assume we can agree that each cell should be split three ways, depending on the amount spent during that same time period. We would arrive at a final model with 75 cells, each cell of different size but averaging 26,667 customers.

Even a cursory review of the above procedure makes clear the arbitrary nature of RFM analysis—why only five recency periods and why those five? What's more, it's clear, on further reflection, that a tremendous amount of data is lost in the RFM process. In our example, times mailed never had a chance to enter the picture, nor did purchase per times mailed, or even the dollar value of purchases made outside of the defined time frame, and on and on. We could, of course, have continued dividing cells by other variables, but doing so would quickly result in a very large number of very small and statistically unusable cells.

For all of these reasons, models other than RFM have been adopted by direct marketers. The most popular of these models is the linear regression model. Section 4 dealt with the mechanics of regression modeling, whereas this chapter will treat the subject in a more general fashion.

Regression modeling begins at the exact same place as RFM modeling—with the available data. In regression modeling, the first decision is the selection of the dependent variable—in English, what do we want to model or predict? Let's assume that we choose to predict response. We will be in a position to predict response if the things we know about our customers, more formally referred to as the independent variables, are themselves good predictors of response.

Again, in English, do we believe that knowing past performance data, the same kinds of data that go into an RFM model, can help us predict who will and will not be likely to respond to a future mailing? And of course, since we know that RFM works, the real question is whether using all the information available to use in combination with the regression tool will produce a better result than the same information used in an RFM environment.

Let's review the list at the beginning of this chapter — the data we have to work with for each customer. Each type of information can be used to create a set of independent variables that will go into a regression model. Generally, the data needs to be massaged before it can become useful for modeling. For example, the data types in the list could be turned into the following set of independent variables:

VAR 1 = Number of months on the file.

VAR 2 = Number of months since last purchase.

VAR 3 = Total dollars.

VAR 4 = Total dollars divided by months on file.

VAR 5 = Total dollars divided by number of times mailed.

VAR 6 = Total dollars divided by number of purchases.

VAR 7 = Number of times mailed.

VAR 8 = Number of responses.

VAR 9 . . . n = Number of purchases within last (3, 6, 9, 12 . . .) months.

VAR 10 = Number of purchases divided by times mailed.

VAR 11 = Number of purchases divided by months on file.

VAR 12 . . . n = Dollars per purchase within each product category.

VAR 13 = Number of product categories with purchases.

The list of independent variables that could be created from the data set is extensive and is indicative of the power of the modeling technique. It should be said immediately that the final model will contain only a few of the many possible variables. In fact, a sign of a good model is the presence of relatively few variables. The converse is also true; a model with a dozen or so variables is probably, despite its impressive appearance, a relatively poor model. (Much more about this subject is contained in Section 4 of this book.)

Now let's assume that a regression model is built based on the data from the recent mailing to the entire file. What will it look like, and what will it do for you?

First, what will it look like?

The modeling process will determine which of the many available variables are important in predicting response. Let's assume the following variables are important.

Variable Name	Variable Description
VAR 2	= Number of months since last purchase
VAR 10	= Number of purchases divided by times mailed
VAR 6	= Total dollars divided by number of purchases

In addition to identifying those variables that are significant predictors of response, the model will assign weights to each variable such that the final regression equation or model might look something like:

Expected response = $2.3 - .04 \times$ (VAR 2) $+ .08 \times$ (VAR 10) $+ .0012 \times$ (VAR 6)

Each customer on the file will be scored according to the above equation. For example, assume a customer with the following values for each of the performance variables:

VAR 2 $=$ 6   Six months have elapsed since last purchase

VAR 10 $=$ .10 Customer buys once out of every 10 times mailed

VAR 6 $=$ 55.33 Average purchase equals $55.33

The equation or the model (the model is simply the equation) makes intuitive sense. Each customer will start off with a score of 2.3 (the model provides this number, which could be positive or negative—in this case, it's positive). The weight of the variable VAR 2, number of months since last purchase, is negative and equal to $-.04$, so $-.24$ ($-.04 \times 6$) will be added to the score. Since adding a negative number decreases the score, the longer the time since the last purchase, the smaller the score, which makes sense. The higher the score, the greater the propensity to respond and we know from experience that the likelihood of responding is greater among persons who have purchased from us in the recent past.

The second variable, VAR 10, represents the average response to all prior in-house mailings; the larger this number, the higher the score. In this case, we will add .08 (.8 × .10) to the customer's score. The third variable, VAR 6, represents the average sale from all prior purchases, and again we would expect a person's score to increase as this number increases. The value of the variable, its coefficient, is .0012; therefore, the person's score is increased by .07 (.0012 × 55.33).

Adding up all of the above, we determine that this person's score is equal to .14 (2.3 − 2.4 + .08 + .07). This same procedure would be repeated for every customer on the file. Each customer would be scored and then all customers would be sorted or ranked, in descending sequence, in terms of their score. The last step in the procedure is to divide the entire file into at least 10 groups of equal size, called deciles. The persons in the top decile will have the highest scores and are expected to perform the best in an upcoming mailing.

TYPICAL RESPONSE MODEL RESULTS

The next question we have to ask ourselves is, "how will response rates vary among deciles?" It's very important for anyone working with models to have some rules of thumb in mind. Most good models built on performance data will show that the top two deciles behave much better than the bottom two deciles; that the six deciles in the middle will be kind of flat, though below the top two and above the bottom two deciles. For example, if our mailing to our house file of 2 million names pulled 8 percent on average, it would be reasonable, given the quality of the data discussed above, to expect the decile result shown in Table 16–1.

Each of the first four examples shown in Table 16–1 is based on a real case involving the modeling of response to mailing a house file. In each case, the independent variables were performance variables: when, what, and how much customers purchased in the past, how often were they promoted, and so on.

As the examples in the table show, models based on this kind of data allow users to divide a single house file into 10 distinct groups, each with its own expected response rate. We would describe Model 1 as a very powerful model. The best 10 percent of the file pulled 26.0 percent compared to the bottom decile, which pulled only 1.9 percent. Another way to look at the results is to compare the response rate of the top two deciles or the top eight deciles to the average. You might want to look at the top two deciles if you were considering a large mailing, whereas you would want to look at the top eight deciles if you were contemplating a small (20 percent) cut in mailing quantities. Again, referring to Model 1, the top two deciles (20 percent) did 2.3 times better than average (26 percent + 11.2 percent)/2 = 17.1 percent and 17.1 percent/8 percent = 2.3); the sum of the top eight deciles did 1.16 times better than average.

TABLE 16–1
Typical Regression Modeling Results

| | Modeling Internal Performance Data | | | | | | | | Modeling Census Data | | | | | |
| | Example 1 | | Example 2 | | Example 3 | | Example 4 | | Example 1 | | Example 2 | | Example 3 | |
Decile	Percent Response	Index	Percent Response	Index	Percent Response	Index	Percent Response	Index	Percent Response	Index	Percent Response	Index	Percent Response	Index
1	26.0%	326	23.8%	298	18.3%	229	19.3%	241	3.2%	162	2.7%	137	2.3%	113
2	11.2	140	13.3	167	12.9	161	11.4	142	2.8	138	2.5	125	2.2	109
3	8.4	105	9.5	119	10.7	134	8.6	108	2.5	125	2.3	113	2.1	106
4	7.4	93	7.1	89	9.4	118	8.0	100	2.2	110	2.2	110	2.1	106
5	7.0	87	6.7	83	7.7	96	7.4	92	2.2	108	2.0	98	2.0	102
6	5.6	70	5.5	69	6.5	81	6.3	78	1.8	92	1.8	90	2.0	102
7	4.7	58	4.1	51	5.0	62	5.6	70	1.7	85	1.8	92	1.9	96
8	4.2	52	3.8	48	3.9	49	5.3	66	1.5	77	1.7	86	1.8	92
9	3.7	47	3.3	42	3.2	40	4.2	53	1.2	62	1.6	82	1.7	87
10	1.9	23	2.9	36	2.4	30	3.9	49	.9	46	1.4	72	1.7	87
Average	8.0%	100	8.0%	100	8.0%	100	8.0%	100	2.0%	100	2.0%	100	2.0%	100
Best to worst	1400.0%		833.3%		767.1%		492.5%		350.0%		189.6%		130.4%	
Best 20 percent to average	232.6%		232.1%		195.0%		191.8%		150.0%		130.8%		111.3%	
Best 80 percent to average	116.3%		115.5%		116.3%		112.3%		112.1%		106.4%		103.3%	

Performance Models 2, 3, and 4 are not as powerful as Model 1, but they are still strong models, each capable of creating groups that perform significantly better or significantly worse than average.

It's important to understand just what you can expect from modeling for a variety of reasons, not the least of which is the fact that knowing what to expect can save you considerable time and money. For example, suppose you are a financial services company. The market has turned down drastically, and your house list, which used to pull 5 percent, now only pulls 2 percent, and you need to pull 3 percent to break even. Can modeling help? Let's apply the indexes from Table 16–1 to a 2 percent average response rate and see what conclusions we can draw. The results are shown in Table 16–2.

As you can see from Table 16–2, any of the four models will allow you to mail the first decile and achieve a response rate well above 3 percent. All of the models will also allow you to mail the second decile and receive a response rate close to 3 percent. But if your goal was to mail 50 percent of your file, modeling can't do that for you — at least the four models shown here can't.

Now let's assume for the moment that you didn't have a response model but the same conditions applied — you were pulling 2 percent and needed 3 percent to break even. Should you consider building a model to help solve your problem? The answer is yes if finding 20 percent of your file is useful. The answer is no if you think modeling will let you mail 50 to 75 percent of your file. What if you were pulling not 2 percent but only one half of 1 percent? Table 16–3 shows that modeling can't help you, and you should look elsewhere for relief.

ZIP CODE MODELS

The last section referred to models based on internal performance data. What about response models that are based on mailings to outside rented lists? In this situation, there is no "hard" performance data. Generally, all you have to work with is ZIP code–based census data. There are a number of issues to consider, but first let's take a look at some typical ZIP/census-based models. Referring back to Table 16–1, you'll see, not surprisingly, that the census models are not nearly as strong as the models built on internal performance data. In the best case shown, Model 1, the best decile does only 3.5 times better than the worst decile, and mailing to 80 percent of the universe of names corresponding to this model will only

TABLE 16–2
Regression Modeling against a 2 Percent Response Rate

Modeling Internal Performance Data

Decile	Example 1		Example 2		Example 3		Example 4	
	Percent Response	Index	Percent Response	Index	Percent Response	Index	Percent Response	Index
1	6.5%	326	6.0%	298	4.6%	229	4.8%	241
2	2.8	140	3.3	167	3.2	161	2.8	142
3	2.1	105	2.4	119	2.7	134	2.2	108
4	1.9	93	1.8	89	2.4	118	2.0	100
5	1.7	87	1.7	83	1.9	96	1.8	92
6	1.4	70	1.4	69	1.6	81	1.6	78
7	1.2	58	1.0	51	1.2	62	1.4	70
8	1.0	52	1.0	48	1.0	49	1.3	66
9	.9	47	.8	42	.8	40	1.1	53
10	.5	23	.7	36	.6	30	1.0	49
Average	2.0%	100	2.0%	100	2.0%	100	2.0%	100

TABLE 16–3
Regression Modeling against a .5 Percent Response Rate

Modeling Internal Performance Data

Decile	Example 1		Example 2		Example 3		Example 4	
	Percent Response	Index	Percent Response	Index	Percent Response	Index	Percent Response	Index
1	1.6%	326	1.5%	298	1.1%	229	1.2%	241
2	.7	140	.8	167	.8	161	.7	142
3	.5	105	.6	119	.7	134	.5	108
4	.5	93	.4	89	.6	118	.5	100
5	.4	87	.4	83	.5	96	.5	92
6	.3	70	.3	69	.4	81	.4	78
7	.3	58	.2	51	.3	62	.3	70
8	.3	52	.2	48	.2	49	.3	66
9	.2	47	.2	42	.2	40	.3	53
10	.1	23	.2	36	.1	30	.2	49
Average	.5%	100	.5%	100	.5%	100	.5%	100

lift response by 12 percent. The results are still less impressive for Models 2 and 3.

Despite the fact that census data–based response models are not as strong as internal performance models, they may still be worthwhile. For example, suppose you were doing a mailing to 3 million outside names and were expecting a 2 percent response or 60,000 orders. A 10 percent improvement would mean another 6,000 orders and if each order were worth $30, this would mean another $180,000 in contribution. Of course, the larger the universe, the larger the potential profits.

Response models based on census data are complicated and there are a number of issues of which both users and modelers should be aware. First of all, a model of a mailing to a million or more names means that we will be mailing to a large number of individual lists, and much fewer but still a significant number of list categories. One of the underlying assumptions of ZIP code modeling is that the impact of the demographic characteristics associated with each ZIP code will work across all list categories and across all lists within a category. The report that accompanies a good ZIP code model will show you exactly how well the model does across categories and by list within a category.

It is not unusual to find that the model performs better within some list categories than within others. See Table 16–4.

In Table 16–4, the general model is represented by the row labeled Total; we see that the response rate in the best decile is about 3.2 percent and the response rate in the poorest performing decile is about 1.1 percent. Further, response rates decline nicely from decile 1 through decile 10. However, on closer inspection of the model's performance, among the four major list categories that make up the total universe of names mailed, we see that the model works very well for list categories 1 and 4, but the model doesn't work well for list category 2, and that list category 3 behaves contrary to the model predictions. What should the user and the modeler do at this point?

One option is to eliminate list categories 2 and 3 from the analysis and build a new model just based on the results of lists within categories 1 and 4. This would be a perfectly good solution if the mailing were very large and enough names were mailed in each list category. Generally, we try to build models in situations where there are 2,000 or more responders. One thousand responders and a sampling of nonresponders are used to build the model, and the model is validated by applying the results of the model to the remaining 1,000 responders and a corresponding sample of nonresponders.

TABLE 16–4
ZIP Code Regression Modeling

					Decile					
Category	1	2	3	4	5	6	7	8	9	10
				Percent Response within Decile						
1	5.00%	3.90%	2.80%	2.60%	2.60%	1.60%	1.50%	1.10%	.40%	.01%
2	3.30	3.30	3.30	3.30	3.20	2.80	2.80	2.70	2.60	2.75
3	.50	.60	.70	.80	.90	1.10	1.20	1.30	1.40	1.50
4	3.80	3.20	3.00	• 2.20	2.20	1.70	1.50	1.00	.50	.00
Total	3.15%	2.75%	2.45%	2.23%	2.23%	1.80%	1.75%	1.53%	1.23%	1.07%
				Indexed Response						
1	232	181	130	121	121	74	70	51	19	0
2	110	110	110	110	106	93	93	90	87	92
3	50	60	70	80	90	110	120	130	140	150
4	199	168	157	115	115	89	79	52	26	0
Total	156	136	121	110	110	89	87	76	61	53

However, suppose the mailing in question went to only 100,000 names and had a 2 percent response rate producing just 2,000 orders. Assuming that each category was equally represented would mean that a model built on just two list categories would include a total of only 1,000 responders. That would leave only 500 responders on which to build the model and 500 responders on which to validate the model. One could attempt to build a model on only 500 responders, but the odds of achieving a significant response model decrease as the number of responders decreases. Of course, there's no harm in trying, and the statistics that accompany the output of the model will tell the analyst whether the model is or is not significant.

Let's assume that a model based on list categories 2 and 3 proves not to be statistically significant. What's the alternative, and how could one use the model shown in Table 16–4? The model could certainly be used when using lists in categories 1 and 4. We would not use the model against lists selected from category 3, and we would probably consider using the model to select ZIPs from lists selected from category 2.

Another consideration in ZIP code models is the selection of the independent variables. As discussed in Chapter 2, each ZIP code is associated with a string of census demographics. And while it is true that each ZIP code may therefore be described in terms of hundreds of census variables, it's also true that many of these variables are highly correlated with each other. Simply put, affluent people have high incomes, live in expensive homes, are better educated, have professional or managerial jobs, and so on. Therefore, a model that includes each, or many, of these variables is likely to suffer from the problems of multicollinearity. (See Section 4 for more details about multicollinearity.)

Analysts experienced with census data will be sure not to include variables that are highly correlated with each other, or will perform a factor analysis prior to beginning a regression analysis in order to avoid this problem. Using factor analysis in this case, the many variables that measure affluence would be combined into a single affluence factor that will be used as just one independent variable in a regression analysis. Another factor may measure the degree to which the ZIP code is an urban ZIP code, a third factor may be a measure ethnicity, and so on.

Adjusting for ZIP Code Size

A third issue in ZIP code modeling is the small mailing quantity and the correspondingly small number of responses achieved within any one ZIP code. For example, even a mailing of 1 million pieces and 20,000

TABLE 16–5
Weighting Schemes for ZIP Code Regression Analysis

Quantity Mailed	Response Rate	Orders	Square Root of Mailings	Response Rate × Square Root of Mailings	Index
10	2%	0	3	.06	3
20	2	0	4	.09	4
40	2	1	6	.13	5
80	2	2	9	.18	7
160	2	3	13	.25	10
320	2	6	18	.36	15
640	2	13	25	.51	21
1,280	2	26	36	.72	29
2,560	2	51	51	1.01	42
5,120	2	102	72	1.43	59
10,240	2	205	101	2.02	83
20,480	2	410	143	2.86	118
40,960	2	819	202	4.05	166
81,920	2	1,638	286	5.72	235
163,840	2	3,277	405	8.10	333
327,680	2	6,554	572	11.45	470
Average				2.43	100

responses will average only 36 pieces per ZIP code and less than 1 response per ZIP code. (Based on 28,000 residential ZIP codes.) To adjust for this condition, analysts experiment with different weighting schemes so that the response rates from ZIP codes that receive relatively large numbers of pieces count for more in the regression model than ZIP codes that receive only a few pieces and whose response rates would distort the model if the number of pieces mailed were not taken into consideration.

Table 16–5 presents an example in which a 2 percent response rate is achieved in mailings of different sizes into 20 ZIP codes. Intuitively, the ZIP code receiving 327,680 pieces and producing 6,554 orders should receive more consideration or weight than the ZIP code into which only 80 pieces were mailed and only 2 responses were generated, even though the response rate (2 percent) is the same. This adjustment is accomplished by assigning each ZIP code a weight equal to the response rate times the square root of the number of mailings. In our example, the ZIP code with the larger mailing would count 65.6 times (197/3 or 11.45/.18) more than the ZIP code with the smaller mailing.

MODELING VARIABLES OTHER THAN RESPONSE

Up to now we have focused our attention on modeling response. There's good reason for this. First of all, response is critically important to direct marketers and needs to be modeled. Second, in practice, much of the earlier modeling work focused on modeling response was based on ZIP code–related census data.

However, there's no reason to think of modeling as being limited to response modeling. It's often just as important, if not more important, to model back-end performance as it is to model up-front response. And while it's not a reason for doing so, it's a lot easier to model back-end performance than it is to model response. Response modeling suffers from the fact that only a small percentage of those mailed ever respond. This percentage can range from below 1 percent on outside mailings to rented lists to 10 to 15 percent on mailings to the house file. In general, and without getting into the technical details in this chapter, the lower the response rate, the more difficulty simple least squares regression techniques have in developing reliable models.

On the other hand, models of back-end performance do not suffer from this yes/no, buy/no buy condition. In a back-end model, all respondents generally, but not always, show some level of performance. For example, in a catalog model based on mailings to outside lists, perhaps 2 or 3 percent of the names mailed will respond, but all those that do respond will buy some amount of product. The back-end performance model will include only those that responded to the promotion, and the variable to be predicted, the dependent variable, will be the continuous variable SALES.

In a book club or a book or record continuity program, not all respondents will execute a repeat purchase. There will be some significant number that never buy another product. In a magazine performance model, not all respondents will convert and not all those that convert will renew. Nevertheless, the buy/no buy condition found in the extreme in response models is not as significant a factor in performance models.

Performance models are similar to response models in the sense that the independent variables, the things we know about the customer or prospect, may be the same as those used in a response model. This may be ZIP code–related data if we are modeling performance against outside lists, or internal behavior versus overlay data or other research data if we are modeling existing customers.

COMBINING MODELS—MODELING PROFIT

Before modeling was a factor in direct marketing, direct marketers knew that response could be increased by softening or increasing the value of the offer. The rule of thumb is simple: increase the value of the offer, increase response—and watch out for poorer back-end performance. The same effect could be accomplished by extending payment terms, adding a trial offer, and so on. Direct marketers are good at increasing response, but they have always understood there is no such thing as a free lunch, and payment would be in the form of poorer performance.

The earlier response modeling efforts sometimes missed this point, so models were built to identify those most likely to respond, rather than those most likely to respond and produce profits. Today, most experienced modelers understand that in situations in which the back-end is as important as the response itself—which is almost always the case, unless you are selling a fixed price product for cash with order—you must build two models, a response model and a performance model, and then combine the two models into a profit model.

In theory, the response model will provide you with an expected response rate or a probability of response, and the performance model will provide you with a measure of expected lifetime profits. The product of expected response times expected profits is equal to expected profits per name mailed.

For example, a person with an expected response rate of 5 percent and an expected back-end profit of $15 has an overall expected value of $.45 ($15 × .03 = $.45); a person with a lower expected response rate of 3 percent, but a higher expected back-end profit of $50 has an expected value of $1.50. Clearly, you would be better off mailing to the latter person with the lower expected response rate but the significantly higher expected back-end performance.

From a practical implementation perspective, it's sometime difficult to obtain an exact probability of response from a regression model, or even from a logistic regression model. In regression modeling of response, scores are frequently greater than 1 or less than 0 and all real probabilities range between 0 and 1. The procedure used is to:

- Divide the total mailing file into two parts, a calibration sample and a validation sample.
- From the calibration sample, select all responders and a sample of nonresponders and build a response model from this sample.

- Apply the response model, the regression equation, to the names on the validation sample.
- Sort the validation file and create a decile analysis.
- Empirically determine the *actual response rate* within each decile.
- Among just the responders from the calibration sample, build a back-end performance model.
- Test the performance model on the validation sample responders.
- For each record on the validation file, multiply the appropriate decile response rate by the expected back-end performance measure. The result is expected profit per name mailed.
- Sort the file in terms of expected profit per name mailed.
- Check to see if the actual profit per name mailed is consistent with the predictions of the model.

FALLOFF MODELS – LEAD CONVERSION PROGRAMS

One of the frequently used applications of response models is in lead generation and fulfillment situations. Many companies generate leads through print advertising or broadcast advertising and attempt to convert the leads into sales through a series of direct mailings.

If we consider the conversion rate as being similar to a response rate in a response model, it's clear that it's possible to model conversions. In fact, it's sometimes easier to model conversion than simple response, particularly if in the process of getting the lead one is able to capture additional information either on the coupon or in a telephone conversation.

In a conversion model, the objective is to divide all leads into deciles or some other scheme, and assign a probability of conversion to each decile. The deciles with the highest probability of conversion should justify more follow-up mailings than the deciles in which the response rate is lower.

Table 16–6 shows a typical conversion sequence resulting in an overall conversion rate of 9.24 percent. The example describes a situation in which all leads receive a four-part follow-up series. The response rate to the first effort is 3.68 percent, the response rate to the second effort is 2.52 percent, and so on.

Table 16–6 also shows the effect of a regression analysis that resulted in a model such that the response rate among those in the top decile to the first effort was 10 percent and the response rate among those in the last decile was 1.57 percent.

TABLE 16–6

Results of Traditional Four-Part Follow-Up Conversion Efforts

Falloff for deciles 1 to 5: 75 percent
Falloff for deciles 6 to 10: 50 percent

Decile	Percent Falloff	Effort 1	Effort 2	Effort 3	Effort 4
1		10.00%	7.50%	5.63%	4.22%
2	69.5%	6.95	5.21	3.91	2.93
3	43.8	4.38	3.28	2.46	1.85
4	34.6	3.46	2.60	1.95	1.46
5	24.9	2.49	1.86	1.40	1.05
6	21.0	2.10	1.05	.53	.26
7	19.8	1.98	.99	.50	.25
8	19.8	1.98	.99	.50	.25
9	18.6	1.86	.93	.47	.23
10	15.7	1.57	.78	.39	.20
Conversion rate		3.68%	2.52%	1.77%	1.27%
Cumulative rate			6.20%	7.97%	9.24%

Decile	Percent Falloff	Effort 1	Effort 2	Effort 3	Effort 4
1		5,000	3,750	2,813	2,109
2	69.5%	3,476	2,607	1,955	1,467
3	43.8	2,189	1,642	1,232	924
4	34.6	1,731	1,298	974	730
5	24.9	1,243	932	699	524
6	21.0	1,050	525	263	131
7	19.8	991	496	248	124
8	19.8	991	496	248	124
9	18.6	932	466	233	116
10	15.7	784	392	196	98
Conversions		18,388	12,604	8,859	6,348
Cumulative			30,991	39,850	46,198
Conversion rate		3.68%	2.52%	1.77%	1.27%
Cumulative rate			6.20%	7.97%	9.24%

The table is completed using the assumption of a 75 percent falloff rate among the bottom five deciles.

Continuing with these assumptions, the fourth effort to the top decile will result in a 4.22 percent response, while the fourth effort to the bottom decile will result in a conversion rate of only 0.20 percent. Clearly, it would appear that the money spent mailing the fourth effort to the bottom decile would have been better spent mailing a fifth effort to the persons in the top decile.

TABLE 16–7
Results of Six-Part Database Conversion Effort

Falloff for deciles 1 to 5: 75 percent
Falloff for deciles 6 to 10: 50 percent

Decile	Percent Falloff	Effort 1	Effort 2	Effort 3	Effort 4	Effort 5	Effort 6
1		12.00%	9.00%	6.75%	5.06%	3.80%	2.85%
2	69.5%	8.34	6.26	4.69	3.52	2.64	1.98
3	43.8	5.25	3.94	2.96	2.22	1.66	1.25
4	34.6	4.15	3.12	2.34	1.75	1.31	.99
5	24.9	2.98	2.24	1.68	1.26	.94	.71
6	21.0	2.52	1.26			.00	.00
7	19.8	2.38	1.19			.00	.00
8	19.8	2.38	1.19			.00	.00
9	18.6	2.24	1.12			.00	.00
10	15.7	1.88	.94			.00	.00
Average		4.41%	3.02%	2.30%	2.76%	2.35%	2.02%

Decile	Percent Falloff	Effort 1	Effort 2	Effort 3	Effort 4	Effort 5	Effort 6
1		6,000	4,500	3,375	2,531	1,898	1,424
2	69.5%	4,172	3,129	2,347	1,760	1,320	990
3	43.8	2,627	1,970	1,478	1,108	831	623
4	34.6	2,077	1,558	1,168	876	657	493
5	24.9	1,491	1,118	839	629	472	354
6	21.0	1,260	630	0	0	0	0
7	19.8	1,189	595	0	0	0	0
8	19.8	1,189	595	0	0	0	0
9	18.6	1,118	559	0	0	0	0
10	15.7	941	470	0	0	0	0
Conversions		22,065	15,124	9,206	6,905	5,179	3,884
Cumulative average			37,189	46,396	53,300	58,479	62,363
Conversion rate		4.41%	3.02%	2.30%	2.76%	2.59%	2.59%
Cumulative rate			7.44%	9.28%	10.66%	11.70%	12.47%

Table 16–7 completes this argument. Assuming that each person, regardless of decile assignment, must receive two efforts and further assuming that the total number of pieces mailed cannot be increased, Table 16–8 shows that it makes the most sense to send members of the top five deciles six efforts and members of the lower deciles only the two required mailings.

By following this strategy, the overall conversion rate is increased from 9.24 to 12.47 percent. The economic impact of this is shown in Table 16–8.

TABLE 16–8

	Traditional Marketing	Database Marketing	Difference
Annual number of leads	500,000	500,000	
Number of mailing efforts	4	4	
Total pieces mailed	2,000,000	2,000,000	
Overall response rate	9.24%	12.47%	
Number of conversions	46,198	62,363	16,165
Value of a customer	$200	$200	$0
Contribution to marketing and profits	$9,239,553	$12,472,598	$3,233,046
Mailing CPM	$450	$450	$0
Mailing costs	$900,000	$900,000	$0
Contribution to profits	$8,339,552	$11,572,598	$3,233,046
Decile	50,000		

From Table 16–8, we see that this company received 500,000 leads a year. Traditionally, each lead was mailed four efforts, or a total of 2 million pieces. (In practice, converters from early efforts would not be mailed again.) Using the database marketing approach, which in this case evaluates an individual customer on the basis of a regression model score, the same number of total pieces are mailed but more mailings are directed at higher potential prospects, increasing the overall response rate to 12.47 percent and increasing the total number of converted prospects by 16,165. In our example, each converted prospect is worth $200, so this exercise is worth an additional $3,233,046 per year. Of course, if the margin were less, the overall increase in profits would be correspondingly reduced.

The example above assumed that the falloff between mailings was a constant 75 percent for the top deciles and a constant 50 percent for the bottom five deciles. Fortunately, there is a better way to estimate falloff rates between mailings that are equally spaced. In the Summer 1988 edition of the *Journal of Direct Marketing,* Professors Bruce Buchanan and Donald G. Morrison presented a model for estimating the falloff rates for a third, fourth, fifth, or higher level mailing based on the response rates to the first and second mailings, assuming a constant period between mailings. This is nearly the perfect situation for a lead generation model. The author of this chapter was asked to critique the article, and in the process of doing so, wrote a simple Lotus 1-2-3 model that was published along with the article itself. The Lotus model is presented in Table 16–9

TABLE 16–9
A Method for Estimating Falloff

A1: [W31] 'DESCRIPTIONS   READY

	A	B	C	D
	DESCRIPTIONS			LOTUS 1-2-3 EQUATIONS
1	DESCRIPTIONS			
2	Input: response to 1st mailing	5.00%	b2	
3	Input: response to 2nd mailing	3.00%	b3	
4	Calculate: Fall Off Factor	0.4000	$1-(b3/b2)$	
5	Input: Unit Margin	$80.00		
6	Input: Cost Per M Pieces Mailed	$1,000		
7	Calculate: BE Response Rate	1.25%	b6/b5/1000	
8	General Equation		$1-((1+b4*(1-2))/(1+b4*(j-2)))$	
9	Fall off between 2nd & 3rd	28.57%	$1-((1+b4*(2-2))/(1+b4*(3-2)))$	
10	Fall off between 3rd & 4th	22.22%	$1-((1+b4*(3-2))/(1+b4*(4-2)))$	
11	Fall off between 4th & 5th	18.18%	$1-((1+b4*(4-2))/(1+b4*(5-2)))$	
12	Fall off between 5th & 6th	15.38%	$1-((1+b4*(5-2))/(1+b4*(6-2)))$	
13	3rd Response	2.14%	b3 *(1-b9)	
14	4th Response	1.67%	b13*(1-b10)	
15	5th Response	1.36%	b14*(1-b11)	
16	6th Response	1.15%	b15*(1-b12)	
17	Cost Per Order on 3rd mlg	$46.67	b$6/(b13*1000)	
18	Cost Per Order on 4th mlg	$60.00	b$6/(b14*1000)	
19	Cost Per Order on 5th mlg	$73.33	b$6/(b15*1000)	
20	Cost Per Order on 6th mlg	$86.67	b$6/(b16*1000)	

and can be easily recreated by any Lotus user. To understand the consumer behavior implications of the model and its mathematical underpinnings, the reader is directed to Bruce Buchanan and Donald G. Morrison, "A Stochastic Model of List Falloff with Implications for Repeat Mailings," in the *Journal of Direct Marketing,* Summer 1988 edition, which is published by John Wiley & Sons.

ADDING ENHANCEMENT DATA TO MODELS

In Section 2, a great deal of attention was paid to the sources and uses of enhancement data. In this chapter, we will focus on the economics of enhancement data. As before, we first have to define whether we are concerned with new-customer acquisition through the use of rented lists, or whether we are considering enhancing our customer database.

New-Customer Acquisition Models

Most new-customer acquisition models are built around ZIP code data. The basic steps are as follows:

- Execute a large mailing, the larger the better (for modeling purposes) but at least large enough to produce a minimum of 2,000 responses.
- Split the responders into two groups and the nonresponders into two groups (at random).
- Create a calibration sample using one half of the responders and a sample of the nonresponders. The nonresponder sample should be between 5,000 and 10,000 names.
- Prepare a validation sample that will include the balance of the responders and another sample of nonresponders.
- Enhance both files with ZIP code level data.
- Build a regression or logistic model of response using the calibration sample.
- Apply the model to the validation sample by scoring each name on the validation sample using the equation developed in the modeling process.
- See how well the model works by ranking each ZIP code in descending order of its predicted score. Create a decile analysis by

dividing the entire validation file into 10 parts and, finally, calculating the actual response rate in each decile.

- If the model is satisfactory, the response rates in the lower deciles will be below your minimum cutoff rates and the response rates in the higher deciles will be well above the cutoff rate. As discussed before, the actual response rate of the top decile will probably be between two to four times the response rate of the bottom decile.
- If the model is satisfactory, apply the model equation to each of the 28,000 residential ZIP codes. An outside vendor familiar with census data and scoring can easily do this for you.
- Each ZIP code, after it is scored, will then be assigned to a decile. This can be accomplished by sorting after the ZIP codes are scored, or by the use of a table that relates ZIP code scores to decile levels.
- The vendor will now return one or more ZIP code tapes that will contain the ZIP code number and the decile score.

The ZIP code tapes can now be used when ordering outside lists. The marketer may request only names from the best deciles, or may use the ZIP code tape as a suppression file and not accept names selected from the lower deciles.

The process just described is the standard ZIP code analysis process. There is an alternative. It's possible to build stronger demographic/psychographic models based on individual or household level data. The argument for considering this alternative is based on the fact that individual level data is more accurate than ZIP code level data (when measuring the same variable), and that there is data available at the individual level that is not available at the ZIP code level. Car ownership is one example.

There are two potential problems associated with this method.

1. In order to apply the method, a significantly larger number of names has to be ordered than mailed.
2. All names ordered have to be overlaid with data and scored so that only the better (to be defined) names are mailed.

Let's look at the first problem, that is, ordering more names than the number eventually mailed. How many more? Maybe 50 to 100 percent more, depending on the effectiveness of the model. Doing this is not the problem; the problem is getting the list owner's permission and paying for the right to screen the scored names and decide on just how many you wish to mail.

If a list owner insists on being paid full rate card for names not mailed, it will take an unusually good model to make the economics of this transaction pay for itself. If, on the other hand, the list owner is reasonable, understands what you are trying to accomplish, understands that this may be the only way you can use the lists, and finally is willing to accept some reduced rate on names ordered but not mailed, the first hurdle is overcome.

The second issue is that all names ordered will have to be overlaid with data and scored. If only half the names scored are mailed, then the effective cost of the data overlay in terms of the names mailed is doubled. This too may be acceptable provided the model is sufficiently strong. And again, the data owner, understanding what you are trying to accomplish, may very well provide you with a favorable rate for data.

So these are the two key issues — the need to rent names that will not be mailed, and the need to overlay all names with data so that scoring can take place. As you can see, both issues get down to a question of costs. Is it going to be worth it to go to all this trouble and expense? Shouldn't we just continue doing business as usual, or maybe just use a simple ZIP code level model? And again, it all depends, as we shall see, on the strength of the model.

However, before getting to the economics of the model, there are a couple of other difficulties associated with this method that should be addressed. The first is that this process obviously takes time and effort on the part of a number of persons and departments. The costs of starting the mailing analysis sooner (all of the work discussed must occur after the merge but before the actual mailing) and the cost of all of the data processing work involved may be hard to quantify, but they are nevertheless real and must be figured into the decision to go ahead with the process.

Another issue is the fact that not all names will match against the overlay source. Generally, you can count on somewhere between 45 and 65 percent of your names matching against a national database such as Infobase, Polk, Donnelley, or Metromail. The exact match rate will depend on the source and the quality of the names supplied to the outside party. Names that do not match will also have to be scored, usually on the basis of the block group or carrier route averages provided by the outside vendor. (Matching or not matching is often itself a variable in the model.)

Having said all this, let's get to the model itself and the decision making involved.

Table 16–10 presents the output of a model of a 1 million name mailing.

TABLE 16–10
The Economics of Predictive Modeling

CPM	$400
Profit per order	$30.00
Cost of data	$50.00
Cost of unused lists	$30.00
Extra lists	1,000,000
Pieces mailed	1,000,000
Average	3.21%

Ratio of Response by Decile

Decile	Individual Segmentation	ZIP
1	240	150
2	170	135
3	138	125
4	112	120
5	93	105
6	61	95
7	55	89
8	50	80
9	43	52
10	40	50
Top/bottom	9.6	3.0
Index	100	100
Average response	3.91%	3.48%

One Million Piece Mailing

Contribution with individual segmentation	$772,089
Cost of data enhancement	100,000
Extra list rental costs	30,000
Profit with individual segmentation	$642,089
Profit with ZIP code segmentation	$644,187
Difference	$ (2,098)
Profit without ZIP segmentation	$563,031
Difference	$ 81,156

The mailing is assumed to have a CPM of $400 and each order is worth $30.00. In the absence of modeling, the mailer is assumed to have selected the best lists such that the mailing is expected to pull 3.21 percent. The profit from this mailing would be $563,031.

$$(1,000,000 \times .0321 \times 30) - (1,000 \times 400) = \$563,300$$

Table 16–11 defines the mailer's list universe of 2 million names and shows all of the calculations leading to the $563,000 profit. For simplicity, we have grouped individual lists together in groups of 100,000. The best responding lists are shown to have an average response rate of 4.0 percent, the next best a response rate of 3.80 percent, and so on until you come to the poorest performing lists, whose average response rate is 1.51 percent. The traditional direct marketing procedure, if the objective were to mail 1 million names, would be to stop after the 10th list grouping. That group's response rate is estimated to be 2.52 percent and the average expected response rate from the top 10 groups is shown to be 3.2 percent.

Now let's assume that a ZIP code model is available to the mailer, based on a prior mailing of the same offer to the same lists.

The model is shown in Table 16–10 under the heading ZIP. As you can see, this model shows the top decile performing at 150 percent of average and the bottom decile performing at 50 percent of average. This is an example of a typical three to one ZIP code model.

How the mailer would apply the ZIP code model to the list universe of 2 million names is shown in Table 16–12. The first assumption is that the model would work equally well across all list segments. Thus, we would expect 10 percent of the best list segment, the segment that averages 4 percent, to pull at 150 percent of 4 percent or at 6 percent. Similarly, the bottom 10 percent of this list segment should pull 2 percent, 50 percent of average.

Table 16–12 therefore creates a 20 by 10 matrix. Each of the 20 list segments is broken up into 10 smaller segments based on the model. Using the traditional method for selecting lists, no list in the 11th segment (the segment that averages 2.4 percent) would have been mailed, and all names in the top 10 segments would have been mailed. However, it's obvious that the top decile of lists in the 11th segment (they pull 3.6 percent) perform better than the bottom decile of the 1st segment (they pull 2 percent). In fact, the top decile of the 11th segment is expected to pull better than almost any decile other than the top decile of the 10th segment.

In theory, what the mailer would like to do is obvious. The mailer would like to sort all of the 200 cells in descending order of expected

TABLE 16–11
Traditional List Selection Methods

List	Cumulative Quantity	Percent Response	Cumulative Percent Response	Orders	Profit	Cumulative Profit
100,000	100,000	4.00%	4.0%	4,000	$80,000	$80,000
100,000	200,000	3.80	3.9	3,800	74,000	154,000
100,000	300,000	3.61	3.8	3,610	68,300	222,300
100,000	400,000	3.43	3.7	3,430	62,885	285,185
100,000	500,000	3.26	3.6	3,258	57,741	342,926
100,000	600,000	3.10	3.5	3,095	52,854	395,779
100,000	700,000	2.94	3.4	2,940	48,211	443,990
100,000	800,000	2.79	3.4	2,793	43,800	487,791
100,000	900,000	2.65	3.3	2,654	39,610	527,401
100,000	1,000,000	2.52	3.2	2,521	35,630	563,031
100,000	1,100,000	2.39	3.1	2,395	31,848	594,880
100,000	1,200,000	2.28	3.1	2,275	28,256	623,136
100,000	1,300,000	2.16	3.0	2,161	24,843	647,979
100,000	1,400,000	2.05	2.9	2,053	21,601	669,580
100,000	1,500,000	1.95	2.9	1,951	18,521	688,101
100,000	1,600,000	1.85	2.8	1,853	15,595	703,696
100,000	1,700,000	1.76	2.7	1,761	12,815	716,511
100,000	1,800,000	1.67	2.7	1,672	10,174	726,686
100,000	1,900,000	1.59	2.6	1,589	7,666	734,351
100,000	2,000,000	1.51	2.6	1,509	5,282	739,634

response and mail only those segments that make up the top 1 million names. In practice, the mailer will not be able to perform with this degree of accuracy and what he or she will do will approximate this procedure. For example, the mailer may mail all ZIPs where the expected average rate is above 3.5 percent; suppress the ZIPs represented by the bottom two deciles among lists expected to pull between 3 and 3.5 percent; suppress ZIPs from the bottom four deciles among lists expected to pull between 2 and 3 percent; and finally, order only names from the top two deciles from among lists expected to pull between 1.5 and 1.99 percent.

Returning to Table 16–10, we see that use of the ZIP code model would result in the average response rate going from 3.21 to 3.48 percent and profits going from $563,031 to $644,187, an increase of $81,156.

Now let's consider the question of whether the mailer should attempt to build a more sophisticated model, built not on ZIP code census data but built instead on individual specific level data. The questions to ask are, "how good will this model be?" "what will it cost to overlay all of my 2

TABLE 16–12
The ZIP Code Model (List Segments Split on the Basis of the ZIP Code Model)

Quantity	List	D1	D2	D3	D4	D5	D6	D7	D8	D9	D10
100,000	4.0%	6.0%	5.4%	5.0%	4.8%	4.2%	3.8%	3.6%	3.2%	2.1%	2.0%
100,000	3.8	5.7	5.1	4.8	4.6	4.0	3.6	3.4	3.0	2.0	1.9
100,000	3.6	5.4	4.9	4.5	4.3	3.8	3.4	3.2	2.9	1.9	1.8
100,000	3.4	5.1	4.6	4.3	4.1	3.6	3.3	3.1	2.7	1.8	1.7
100,000	3.3	4.9	4.4	4.1	3.9	3.4	3.1	2.9	2.6	1.7	1.6
100,000	3.1	4.6	4.2	3.9	3.7	3.2	2.9	2.8	2.5	1.6	1.5
100,000	2.9	4.4	4.0	3.7	3.5	3.1	2.8	2.6	2.4	1.5	1.5
100,000	2.8	4.2	3.8	3.5	3.4	2.9	2.7	2.5	2.2	1.5	1.4
100,000	2.7	4.0	3.6	3.3	3.2	2.8	2.5	2.4	2.1	1.4	1.3
100,000	2.5	3.8	3.4	3.2	3.0	2.6	2.4	2.2	2.0	1.3	1.3
100,000	2.4	3.6	3.2	3.0	2.9	2.5	2.3	2.1	1.9	1.2	1.2
100,000	2.3	3.4	3.1	2.8	2.7	2.4	2.2	2.0	1.8	1.2	1.1
100,000	2.2	3.2	2.9	2.7	2.6	2.3	2.1	1.9	1.7	1.1	1.1
100,000	2.1	3.1	2.8	2.6	2.5	2.2	2.0	1.8	1.6	1.1	1.0
100,000	2.0	2.9	2.6	2.4	2.3	2.0	1.9	1.7	1.6	1.0	1.0
100,000	1.9	2.8	2.5	2.3	2.2	1.9	1.8	1.6	1.5	1.0	.9
100,000	1.8	2.6	2.4	2.2	2.1	1.8	1.7	1.6	1.4	.9	.9
100,000	1.7	2.5	2.3	2.1	2.0	1.8	1.6	1.5	1.3	.9	.8
100,000	1.6	2.4	2.1	2.0	1.9	1.7	1.5	1.4	1.3	.8	.8
100,000	1.5	2.3	2.0	1.9	1.8	1.6	1.4	1.3	1.2	.8	.8
2,000,000											

million names with data?" and "what will I have to pay for names that are examined but not mailed?"

The answer to the first question—how good will the model be—is shown in Table 16–10 under the heading Individual Segmentation, short for the individual level of segmentation. As you can see, the model is much stronger than the ZIP code model. In statistical shorthand, it's a six-to-one model, whereas the ZIP code model was a three-to-one model. Further, the model assumes that overlay data and model scoring will cost $50 per thousand, and list owners have agreed to accept $30 per million for names not mailed.

If everything were to work as planned and the model could be applied with great precision across all lists, in theory, response rates would increase to 3.91 percent, and profits would increase to $772,424 before data and extra list rental expense and would equal $642,424 after these expenses are taken into consideration. Table 16–13 shows how the decile segmentation would work in theory and Table 16–14 details how the individual cells would be sorted and how the 1 million piece mailing would be constructed.

TABLE 16–13
The Individual Data Prediction Model (List Segments Split on the Basis of Individual Level Data)

Quantity	List	D1	D2	D3	D4	D5	D6	D7	D8	D9	D10
100,000	4.0%	9.6%	6.8%	5.5%	4.5%	3.7%	2.4%	2.2%	2.0%	1.7%	1.6%
100,000	3.8	9.1	6.5	5.2	4.3	3.5	2.3	2.1	1.9	1.6	1.5
100,000	3.6	8.7	6.1	5.0	4.0	3.4	2.2	2.0	1.8	1.6	1.4
100,000	3.4	8.2	5.8	4.7	3.8	3.2	2.1	1.9	1.7	1.5	1.4
100,000	3.3	7.8	5.5	4.5	3.6	3.0	2.0	1.8	1.6	1.4	1.3
100,000	3.1	7.4	5.3	4.3	3.5	2.9	1.9	1.7	1.5	1.3	1.2
100,000	2.9	7.1	5.0	4.1	3.3	2.7	1.8	1.6	1.5	1.3	1.2
100,000	2.8	6.7	4.7	3.9	3.1	2.6	1.7	1.5	1.4	1.2	1.1
100,000	2.7	6.4	4.5	3.7	3.0	2.5	1.6	1.5	1.3	1.1	1.1
100,000	2.5	6.1	4.3	3.5	2.8	2.3	1.5	1.4	1.3	1.1	1.0
100,000	2.4	5.7	4.1	3.3	2.7	2.2	1.5	1.3	1.2	1.0	1.0
100,000	2.3	5.5	3.9	3.1	2.5	2.1	1.4	1.3	1.1	1.0	.9
100,000	2.2	5.2	3.7	3.0	2.4	2.0	1.3	1.2	1.1	.9	.9
100,000	2.1	4.9	3.5	2.8	2.3	1.9	1.3	1.1	1.0	.9	.8
100,000	2.0	4.7	3.3	2.7	2.2	1.8	1.2	1.1	1.0	.8	.8
100,000	1.9	4.4	3.2	2.6	2.1	1.7	1.1	1.0	.9	.8	.7
100,000	1.8	4.2	3.0	2.4	2.0	1.6	1.1	1.0	.9	.8	.7
100,000	1.7	4.0	2.8	2.3	1.9	1.6	1.0	.9	.8	.7	.7
100,000	1.6	3.8	2.7	2.2	1.8	1.5	1.0	.9	.8	.7	.6
100,000	1.5	3.6	2.6	2.1	1.7	1.4	.9	.8	.8	.6	.6
2,000,000											

This is a better statistical model but a less profitable model than the simpler and less expensive ZIP code model. Does this example mean that one should never try to use individual level data to build customer-acquisition models? Not at all; it just means that the models have to be significantly stronger to warrant their costs. Table 16–15 shows what would happen if the individual level model were not a 6-to-1 model but rather a 10-to-1 model. In this case, the additional profits after list and data expense exceed the results of the ZIP code model by $58,258.

Is $58,258 enough extra profit to cover the additional costs not explicitly defined in the model? That's a difficult question to answer and different companies will answer it differently. However, the purpose of this exercise is primarily to provide mailers with a framework for evaluating model proposals. The questions that have to be answered are: "how powerful will the model be?" and "what will it cost (in terms of time, data, scoring, and so on) to implement the model?" Armed with a framework in which to measure the likelihood of a model performing as promised, and

TABLE 16–14
Sorting List Segments

Decile Segment Quantity	Cumulative Quantity	List Segment Ranked	Average	Orders	Profit	Cumulative Profit
10,000	10,000	9.6%	9.6%	960	$24,800	$ 24,800
10,000	20,000	9.1	9.4	912	23,360	48,160
10,000	30,000	8.7	9.1	866	21,992	70,152
10,000	40,000	8.2	8.9	823	20,692	90,844
10,000	50,000	7.8	8.7	782	19,458	110,302
10,000	60,000	7.4	8.5	743	18,285	128,587
10,000	70,000	7.1	8.3	706	17,171	145,758
10,000	80,000	6.8	8.1	680	16,400	162,158
10,000	90,000	6.7	7.9	670	16,112	178,270
10,000	100,000	6.5	7.8	646	15,380	193,650
10,000	110,000	6.4	7.7	637	15,107	208,756
10,000	120,000	6.1	7.5	614	14,411	223,167
10,000	130,000	6.1	7.4	605	14,151	237,319
10,000	140,000	5.8	7.3	583	13,490	250,809
10,000	150,000	5.7	7.2	575	13,244	264,053
10,000	160,000	5.5	7.1	554	12,616	276,669
10,000	170,000	5.5	7.0	552	12,560	289,229
10,000	180,000	5.5	6.9	546	12,381	301,610
10,000	190,000	5.3	6.8	526	11,785	313,395
10,000	200,000	5.2	6.8	524	11,732	325,127
10,000	210,000	5.2	6.7	519	11,562	336,689
10,000	220,000	5.0	6.6	500	10,996	347,685
10,000	230,000	5.0	6.5	498	10,945	358,631
10,000	240,000	4.9	6.5	493	10,784	369,415
10,000	250,000	4.7	6.4	475	10,246	379,661
10,000	260,000	4.7	6.3	473	10,198	389,859
10,000	270,000	4.7	6.3	468	10,045	399,904
10,000	280,000	4.5	6.2	451	9,534	409,438
10,000	290,000	4.5	6.1	450	9,488	418,926
10,000	300,000	4.5	6.1	448	9,440	428,366
10,000	310,000	4.4	6.0	445	9,343	437,709
10,000	320,000	4.3	6.0	429	8,857	446,566
10,000	330,000	4.3	5.9	427	8,814	455,380
10,000	340,000	4.3	5.9	426	8,768	464,148
10,000	350,000	4.2	5.8	423	8,676	472,824
10,000	360,000	4.1	5.8	407	8,214	481,038
10,000	370,000	4.1	5.7	406	8,173	489,211
10,000	380,000	4.0	5.7	404	8,130	497,341
10,000	390,000	4.0	5.7	401	8,042	505,382
10,000	400,000	3.9	5.6	387	7,604	512,986
10,000	410,000	3.9	5.6	385	7,564	520,550
10,000	420,000	3.8	5.5	384	7,523	528,074
10,000	430,000	3.8	5.5	381	7,440	535,513
10,000	440,000	3.7	5.4	372	7,160	542,673

TABLE 16–14
(continued)

Decile Segment Quantity	Cumulative Quantity	List Segment Ranked	Average	Orders	Profit	Cumulative Profit
10,000	450,000	3.7	5.4	367	$7,023	$549,697
10,000	460,000	3.7	5.4	366	6,986	556,683
10,000	470,000	3.6	5.3	365	6,947	563,630
10,000	480,000	3.6	5.3	362	6,868	570,498
10,000	490,000	3.5	5.3	353	6,602	577,100
10,000	500,000	3.5	5.2	349	6,472	583,572
10,000	510,000	3.5	5.2	348	6,437	590,009
10,000	520,000	3.5	5.2	347	6,400	596,408
10,000	530,000	3.4	5.1	336	6,072	602,480
10,000	540,000	3.3	5.1	332	5,949	608,429
10,000	550,000	3.3	5.1	331	5,915	614,344
10,000	560,000	3.3	5.0	329	5,880	620,224
10,000	570,000	3.2	5.0	319	5,568	625,792
10,000	580,000	3.2	5.0	315	5,451	631,243
10,000	590,000	3.1	4.9	314	5,419	636,662
10,000	600,000	3.1	4.9	313	5,386	642,048
10,000	610,000	3.0	4.9	303	5,090	647,138
10,000	620,000	3.0	4.8	299	4,979	652,116
10,000	630,000	3.0	4.8	298	4,948	657,065
10,000	640,000	3.0	4.8	297	4,916	661,981
10,000	650,000	2.9	4.8	288	4,635	666,617
10,000	660,000	2.8	4.7	284	4,530	671,146
10,000	670,000	2.8	4.7	283	4,501	675,647
10,000	680,000	2.8	4.7	282	4,471	680,118
10,000	690,000	2.7	4.6	273	4,204	684,321
10,000	700,000	2.7	4.6	270	4,103	688,425
10,000	710,000	2.7	4.6	269	4,076	692,500
10,000	720,000	2.7	4.6	268	4,047	696,547
10,000	730,000	2.6	4.5	260	3,793	700,341
10,000	740,000	2.6	4.5	257	3,698	704,039
10,000	750,000	2.6	4.5	256	3,672	707,711
10,000	760,000	2.5	4.5	255	3,645	711,356
10,000	770,000	2.5	4.4	247	3,404	714,759
10,000	780,000	2.4	4.4	244	3,320	718,079
10,000	790,000	2.4	4.4	243	3,288	721,368
10,000	800,000	2.4	4.4	242	3,262	724,630
10,000	810,000	2.3	4.3	234	3,034	727,664
10,000	820,000	2.3	4.3	232	2,954	730,618
10,000	830,000	2.3	4.3	231	2,924	733,542
10,000	840,000	2.3	4.3	230	2,899	736,441
10,000	850,000	2.2	4.2	223	2,682	739,123
10,000	860,000	2.2	4.2	220	2,606	741,730
10,000	870,000	2.2	4.2	220	2,600	744,330

TABLE 16–14
(concluded)

Decile Segment Quantity	Cumulative Quantity	List Segment Ranked	Average	Orders	Profit	Cumulative Profit
10,000	880,000	2.2	4.2	219	$2,578	$746,907
10,000	890,000	2.2	4.1	218	2,554	749,462
10,000	900,000	2.1	4.1	212	2,348	751,810
10,000	910,000	2.1	4.1	209	2,276	754,086
10,000	920,000	2.1	4.1	209	2,270	756,356
10,000	930,000	2.1	4.1	208	2,249	758,605
10,000	940,000	2.1	4.0	208	2,227	760,831
10,000	950,000	2.0	4.0	201	2,030	762,862
10,000	960,000	2.0	4.0	199	1,962	764,824
10,000	970,000	2.0	4.0	199	1,957	766,780
10,000	980,000	2.0	3.9	197	1,915	768,696
10,000	990,000	1.9	3.9	191	1,729	770,424
10,000	1,000,000	1.9	3.9	189	1,664	772,089
10,000	1,010,000	1.9	3.9	189	1,659	773,747
10,000	1,020,000	1.9	3.9	187	1,620	775,367
10,000	1,030,000	1.8	3.8	181	1,442	776,809
10,000	1,040,000	1.8	3.8	180	1,400	778,209
10,000	1,050,000	1.8	3.8	179	1,381	779,590
10,000	1,060,000	1.8	3.8	179	1,376	780,966

knowing what cost questions to ask, mailers can make their own decisions about the value of new-customer acquisition modeling.

Adding Enhancement Data to Build Better Internal Customer Models

While new-customer acquisition models are totally dependent on ZIP code level data or individual level data appended from external sources, internal models of customer performance don't necessarily need to include enhancement data. In fact, the recommended procedure for building internal predictive models is to start with internal data and proceed to build the best model possible. Then, add external enhancement data to the set of independent data and see if the external data will allow you to build a more powerful model.

What are you likely to find? It depends on your business. If you are in the financial services business, selling expensive products or age-dependent products (and age and income are not normally captured

TABLE 16–15
The Economics of Predictive Modeling

CPM	$400
Profit per order	$30.00
Cost of data	$50.00
Cost of unused lists	$30.00
Extra lists	1,000,000
Pieces mailed	1,000,000
Average	3.21%

One Million Piece Mailing

Contribution with individual segmentation	$832,445
Cost of data enhancement	100,000
Extra list rental costs	30,000
Profit with individual segmentation	$702,445
Profit with ZIP code segmentation	$644,187
Difference	$ 58,258
Profit without segmentation	$563,031
Difference	$ 81,156

Ratio of Response by Decile

Decile	Individual Segmentation	ZIP
1	250	150
2	200	135
3	150	125
4	110	120
5	80	105
6	61	95
7	50	89
8	40	80
9	33	52
10	25	50
Top/bottom	10.0	3.0
Index	100	100
Average response	4.11%	3.48%

internal variables on your prospect file), then there is a good likelihood that adding this kind of information will result in more powerful models. On the other hand, if the kinds of external demographic and/or psychographic data available to you are not as critical to the sale of your product or service, then the chances are less likely that the addition of external data will make a difference in your ability to develop predictive models.

So the answer is that you have to experiment and see if external data makes a difference. There are really two questions that need to be answered. First, "will external data produce a better model, in a statistical sense?" That is, have the external variables entered the model and are they statistically significant? Second, "will the model account for more variation (have a higher R-squared)?" And, most importantly, "will the validation study assign more customers to the top deciles than was the case based on the models that excluded external data?"

If the answers to all of these questions are yes, the model is better from a statistical standpoint. The second issue is then one of costs. How much did it cost to overlay your entire file, and are the extra costs worth the added power they brought to your model? This kind of question can be answered quickly with a simple Lotus 1-2-3 model like the one shown in Table 16–16.

The example shown in Table 16–15 is that of a mailer with 2 million names on the customer database. Let's assume that the mailer has built a model based just on internal performance data, and that the model predicts that the response rate to the next mailing among the top half of the file will be 8 percent and will produce $1.6 million in profits.

Would this mailer have been better off if the entire file had been overlaid with external data and a model that included both internal and external variables had been built? Let's assume that to build and implement such a model, the mailer would have had to overlay the entire file with data and that data costs $50 per thousand names, or $100,000. Well, if a model built on this data could result in a 10 percent improvement in response (from 8 to 8.8 percent), profits before enhancement data from just this one mailing alone will increase by $160,000. Profits after enhancement data costs would be up by $60,000. So in this case, enhancing the file would have made sense. And it's important to point out that an enhanced file can support many mailings and many models and there is no need for enhanced data to pay for itself on the basis of just one mailing application.

Of course, if the mailer wished to mail less than 50 percent of the file,

TABLE 16–16
The Value of Enhancement Data to Predictive Customer Models

	ASSUMPTIONS	RESULTS
• TOTAL CUSTOMER DATABASE	2,000,000	
• PERCENT OF CUSTOMERS TO BE MAILED	50.00%	
• NUMBER OF NAMES TO BE MAILED		1,000,000
INTERNAL DATA MODEL		
• EXPECTED RESPONSE RATE USING INTERNAL DATA ONLY MODEL	8.00%	
• EXPECTED NUMBER OF RESPONSES		80,000
• VALUE OF AN ORDER	$20.00	
• VALUE OF ALL ORDERS		$1,600,000
INTERNAL PLUS ENHANCEMENT DATA MODEL		
• EXPECTED RESPONSE RATE USING ENHANCED DATA MODEL	8.80%	
• EXPECTED NUMBER OF RESPONSES		88,000
• VALUE OF AN ORDER	$20.00	
• VALUE OF ALL ORDERS		$1,760,000
INCREMENTAL RESULTS		
• INCREMENTAL RESPONSES		8,000
• INCREMENTAL VALUE FROM EN-HANCED MODEL BEFORE DATA COSTS		$160,000
• COST OF ENHANCEMENT DATA/M	$50.00	
• TOTAL COST OF ENHANCEMENT DATA		$100,000
• INCREMENTAL VALUE FROM EN-HANCED MODEL AFTER DATA COSTS		$60,000

or if the enhanced model were less powerful, or if data costs were more than $50 per thousand, the results would have been different. For example, Table 16–17 shows that if the mailing quantity were reduced to only 20 percent of the customer database, the result of this exercise would be $36,000 in reduced profits.

The point of this exercise is that each mailer will have to decide what are the likely benefits of enhancing the file. Of course, predictive modeling may not be the only reason to enhance a database with overlay information. It may not even be the best reason.

Let's assume for the moment that enhancement does not result in better, cost-effective predictive models, but that an examination of the customer file, based on enhanced data, shows that those customers in the

TABLE 16–17
The Value of Enhancement Data to Predictive Customer Models

	ASSUMPTIONS	RESULTS
• TOTAL CUSTOMER DATABASE	2,000,000	
• PERCENT OF CUSTOMERS TO BE MAILED	20.00%	
• NUMBER OF NAMES TO BE MAILED		400,000
INTERNAL DATA MODEL		
• EXPECTED RESPONSE RATE USING INTERNAL DATA ONLY MODEL	8.00%	
• EXPECTED NUMBER OF RESPONSES		32,000
• VALUE OF AN ORDER	$20.00	
• VALUE OF ALL ORDERS		$640,000
INTERNAL PLUS ENHANCEMENT DATA MODEL		
• EXPECTED RESPONSE RATE USING ENHANCED DATA MODEL	8.80%	
• EXPECTED NUMBER OF RESPONSES		35,200
• VALUE OF AN ORDER	$20.00	
• VALUE OF ALL ORDERS		$704,000
INCREMENTAL RESULTS		
• INCREMENTAL RESPONSES		3,200
• INCREMENTAL VALUE FROM EN- HANCED MODEL BEFORE DATA COSTS		$64,000
• COST OF ENHANCEMENT DATA/M	$50.00	
• TOTAL COST OF ENHANCEMENT DATA		$100,000
• INCREMENTAL VALUE FROM EN- HANCED MODEL AFTER DATA COSTS		$(36,000)

best performing deciles have a different demographic profile than those customers in the poorer performing deciles. Let's assume that age and sex are the demographic variables in question and that younger males are performing better than older males and that both male groups are performing worse than females of any age. Wouldn't it make sense to develop either different creative strategies for each market segment, or to attempt to develop different products for males? It's important to remember that predictive modeling will only forecast what is likely to happen if you repeat the same offer to the same population. Predictive modeling won't necessarily tell you anything about the characteristics of your buyers and your nonbuyers. Profiling will, and profiling generally requires overlay data.

ENHANCING YOUR DATABASE WITH INTERNAL SURVEY DATA

Up to now we have dealt with only two kinds of data—internal performance data and external demographic or psychographic overlay data. We expect that the next major source of data will be individual level research data based on internal customer surveys.

One of the interesting things about predictive models is that despite their ability to identify the best and poorest responding customers or prospects, even the best models, particularly response models, generally account for less than 5 or 10 percent of the variation we see in response. What's missing from our models is better, more relevant data. It's obvious that persons living within the same ZIP code, or even within the same block group, differ dramatically with regard to their product and service needs, and even individuals with identical demographic characteristics will differ significantly in their response to our promotions. So we need to know much more about the individual needs and wants of our customers and prospects and this can only happen by creating a dialogue with the customer.

For years, Lester Wunderman has talked about the three essential ingredients of a direct sale. A customer has to be (1) able, (2) willing, and (3) ready to buy before a direct sale can be consummated. Overlay data is helpful in determining if a prospect has the economic ability to buy from us, but overlay data provides little or no information about the prospect's willingness or readiness to buy. So we have to ask.

The alternative to asking is to continue as usual, sending mailing pieces to lists and geographic areas within lists that analysis has proven tend to work for our product or service. The problem with asking is that it is perceived to be difficult and expensive. Like everything else in this book, we eventually get back to the question of economic trade-offs.

Fortunately, we at least know how to ask questions if costs are of no concern. For years, market researchers have performed in-depth segmentation studies for traditional and nontraditional direct marketing companies. The process involves both survey design skills and statistical skills, and goes as follows:

- Select a random sample from 500 to a few thousand customers or prospects.
- Design an in-depth questionnaire. The total questionnaire may contain 100 or more questions. Frequently, the questionnaire is divided into three sections.

    a. Behavior information. Do you belong to a book club? Do you subscribe to magazines? Do you buy financial services through the mail? Do you have a stockbroker?

    b. Attitudes about the category. Do you read to relax or for information? Would you describe yourself as an intellectual? How important is it to you to be aware of best sellers? Would you describe yourself as a financial risk taker? Do you rely on others for financial advice? Do you think banks provide good investment advice?

    c. Demographic questions. The usual age, income, education, occupation, family size questions.

- Perform a factor and a cluster analysis on the results. (See Chapter 13). If you are successful, you will probably discover that there are three to six different market segments within your prospect or customer file.

Staying with our book club and financial services examples, the book club might discover that there is a segment of its market that looks on *books* as being absolutely critical to their existence – to these people, books are the key to knowledge and information and without books they could not perform. Conversely, they are likely to find that there is another segment that reads a lot but reads entirely for escape. A third segment may consist of infrequent readers who feel guilty about not reading more, and so on.

On the financial services side there may be a segment of independent risk takers. These people do their own research, make up their own minds, and aren't afraid to invest by mail. On the other end of the spectrum may be the very conservative, who need the comfort of a personal represen tative to close a transaction. Nevertheless, this segment responds to mailings that promise financial rewards – great leads but very difficult to convert into customers.

The information and insights that this kind of segmentation analysis provides is clearly invaluable to direct marketers. If we knew to which segment an individual belonged, we could tailor our creative strategy and offers accordingly. However, the problem for direct marketers has been an inability to translate research results into actionable marketing informa-tion. Obviously, you can't send a 100-question survey to all of your customers, much less to all of your prospects.

Two solutions are being experimented with by database marketers who are committed to making this process work.

The first solution involves building a model in which the dependent variable is segment membership, and the independent variables are all those performance and overlay variables we know about the customer or prospect. In this model, each customer is scored on his or her likelihood of belonging to any one segment according to values on the variables that were statistically determined to be linked with segment membership. In this case, each customer will have a probability of belonging to any of the market segments discovered by the survey.

If the model is successful, then every customer on the database can be scored and the database will maintain a record of each customer's probability of belonging to each market segment. The direct marketer will then be able to develop a targeted appeal to members of each segment, and mail only to members whose probability of belonging to the particular segment exceeds some chosen level. Of course, it's possible that modeling will not be able to reliably link segment membership with the known performance and demographic variables.

In that case, there is a second method that is being tested. This method starts by using statistical methods to identify the smallest number of questions that can reliably define segment membership. The hope is that the analysis will discover a handful of questions that can be asked of everyone and that this information can economically be added to the database. This method offers particular promise to those companies that maintain large prospect files consisting of leads that have failed to respond to prior efforts but who may respond to more targeted appeals.

Table 16–18 provides a framework for examining the economics of this methodology. Table 16–18 begins by assuming a prospect file of 100,000 names to which a cumulative 14.33 percent response would be achieved if each person received up to six mailings. However, as shown, the response rates to the fourth, fifth, and sixth mailings are below 2 percent. If we assume that 2 percent is the cutoff rate, then this company would make only three mailings to the entire file.

What if, instead of mailing everyone on the file three times, we began by mailing everyone on the file a short questionnaire designed to determine if the prospect wished to receive more offers from the company, and if so, would the respondent supply us with the answers to a few attitude and demographic questions so that we could better serve his or her needs. We'll use this information to place the respondent in the correct market segment and send members of each segment the most appropriate mailing packages.

Can this process possibly pay for itself? As usual, the answer depends on the validity of some set of assumptions. Let's assume that 30 percent of

336   The Economics of the New Direct Marketing

TABLE 16–18
The Economics of Questionnaire Research (Initial Quantity: 100,000)

Mailing Effort	Percent Response	Mailed	Cost	Orders	CPO	Cumulative Orders	Cumulative Costs	Cumulative Costs per Order
1	5.00%	100,000	$ 35,000	5,000	$ 7.00	5,000	$ 35,000	$ 7.00
2	3.00	95,000	33,250	2,850	11.67	7,850	68,250	8.69
3	2.14	92,000	32,200	1,971	16.33	9,821	100,450	10.23
4	1.67	89,857	31,450	1,498	21.00	11,319	131,900	11.65
5	1.36	88,190	30,867	1,203	25.67	12,522	162,767	13.00
6	1.15	86,827	30,389	1,002	30.33	13,523	193,156	14.28

Cumulative	14.33%		$193,156	13,523	$14.28			
Cost per piece	$ .35							
Cost per response				$ 14.28				

Assume that 30.00 percent answer and that percent includes 80.00 percent of all orders.

Number answering questionnaire	30,000
Percent wishing to be dropped from file	33.33%
Cost of mailing questionnaire to 100,000 names	$.35
Cost of processing completed questionnaires	$1.00
Cost of processing "takeoff file"	$.25
Average cost per questionnaire mailed	$.58
Number answering questionnaire	10,000
Cost of mailing questionnaire to 100,000 names	$35,000
Cost of processing completed questionnaires	$20,000
Cost of processing "takeoff file"	$2,500
Dollar cost of questionnaire	$57,500
Number of mailings to respondents	6
Number of mailings	120,000
	42,000
Total costs: questionnaire costs plus promotion costs	$99,500
Number of orders	10,818
Cost per order	$9.20
Number of incremental orders (10,818 − 9,821 = 997)	997
Incremental costs using survey method	$(922)
Number of "normal" efforts	3
Number of orders	9,821
Normal mailing costs	$100,450
Cost per order normal method	$10.23

the names receiving the questionnaire respond but that these 30 percent include 80 percent of the orders that would have resulted from a six-part mailing. Let's further assume that it costs $.35 to mail out the questionnaires to everyone, an additional $1.00 to process the respondents that complete the questionnaire and wish to receive more mailings, and $.25 to take a customer off the file, with one third of the respondents asking to be taken off the file.

This means that a total of $57,508 will be spent before the first promotional mailing is made. Then, all of the respondents who wish to receive more information will stay on the database and receive six mailings. The nonrespondents will not receive additional mailings.

The result of all this work will be an additional 997 orders and a cost savings of $922. This is not a terribly large cost savings, but if the additional orders are worth $100 each, an additional $99,700 will have been made. And if the database consisted of 1 million persons instead of just 100,000 persons, both the savings and the incremental earnings become very large.

How repeatable are these numbers? Again, it's very hard to say and the results will vary from company to company. Once more, our primary objective is not to produce a set of rules but rather to provide a framework for thinking about the economics of database marketing.

CHAPTER 17

FINANCIAL MODELS

In this last chapter, we will attempt to tie everything we've been talking about together with the aid of financial business planning models. At the start of this section, we examined traditional direct marketers and the classical direct marketing they practice — marketing that focuses on groups of people linked together because they come from the same list or the same print media ad. We said that the emphasis in classical direct marketing is on the new-customer acquisition decision. In order to decide whether to use a particular medium again, or with what frequency, it is necessary to know how customers recruited from that medium behave, thus the emphasis on measuring and evaluating group performance. Then we switched gears and discussed the movement toward measuring and improving the performance of the individual, and we associated this development with the development of database marketing. Now, the source from which an individual is recruited is only one of many pieces of data that will influence our decision to promote or not to promote, and what to promote to the individual.

In both models, the traditional group behavior model and the individual database marketing model, we acted as if financial time constraints didn't exist. Maximizing profits and return on promotion were the tools on which economic decision making was based. But the reality is that all direct marketing operations exist within companies that are required to report on their financial performance on at least an annual, if not a quarterly, basis. So our decision-making apparatus must include provisions for the realities of the financial world. Investments cannot be made just because they make economic sense in the long run. Investments have to be funded and their effect on current period profits has to be taken into account.

We also stated in the beginning of this section that one of the most critical decisions a direct marketing manager has to make is the decision regarding how much to invest in new-customer acquisition promotion and how much to invest in current-customer promotions. Spending more on current customers tends to increase short-term profits at the expense of long-term customer growth, and vice versa.

The decision-making tool that allows direct marketers to make this decision is the financial planning model. The financial planning model lets the marketer experiment with the option of investing more or less in new-customer promotions, and it allows the marketer to immediately see the effect of new-customer decisions on long-term fiscal profits. What's more, the financial planning model starts with a model of lifetime value.

We will present the inputs and outputs of two Lotus 1-2-3 models, and then show and discuss the effect on annual profits stemming from changing just a few critical assumptions.

A FINANCIAL MODEL OF A NEW BOOK CLUB BUSINESS

We'll begin with the inputs to a five-year book club model.

Lifetime Value

Table 17–1 deals with the lifetime value of the average customer. For simplicity, we will assume that all customers behave the same regardless of their source. In practice, we would create different models for each class of customer and then add all the models together to arrive at a model for the total club.

The key assumptions in a book club model regarding lifetime value are:

- **Attrition rate.** In this example, we assume that 3 percent of the starting group drops out or is canceled each cycle. (This model assumes 13 shipping cycles a year and runs for five years. Only the first three years are shown in detail, to save space.)
- **Negative option acceptance, return, and bad debt rates.** The rates shown are for the remaining members at each point in time, not the averages for the starting group. Here, we have assumed that the negative option rate will decline over time as members become accustomed to the negative option procedure. Returns are assumed to be a constant 20 percent and bad debts are shown to decline as

TABLE 17–1
Lifetime Value Assumptions

| CYCLE | ATTRITION | --NEGATIVE OPTION-- | | | OTHER ACCPT RATE | OTHER RTN RATE | OTHER BD DBT RATE | AVERAGE CLUB PRICE NEG OPT | AVERAGE CLUB PRICE ALT SEL |
		ACCEPT RATE	RTN RATE	BD DBT RATE					
01	100	29%	20.0%	20.0%	5.0%	15.0%	3.0%	$22.00	$16.50
02	97	28%	20.0%	15.0%	6.0%	15.0%	3.0%	$22.00	$16.50
03	94	27%	20.0%	12.0%	7.0%	15.0%	3.0%	$22.00	$16.50
04	91	26%	20.0%	10.0%	8.0%	15.0%	3.0%	$22.00	$16.50
05	89	25%	20.0%	6.0%	9.0%	15.0%	3.0%	$22.00	$16.50
06	86	24%	20.0%	6.0%	10.0%	15.0%	3.0%	$22.00	$16.50
07	83	23%	20.0%	6.0%	11.0%	15.0%	3.0%	$22.00	$16.50
08	81	22%	20.0%	6.0%	12.0%	15.0%	3.0%	$22.00	$16.50
09	78	21%	20.0%	6.0%	13.0%	15.0%	3.0%	$22.00	$16.50
10	76	20%	20.0%	6.0%	13.0%	15.0%	3.0%	$22.00	$16.50
11	74	19%	20.0%	6.0%	13.0%	15.0%	3.0%	$22.00	$16.50
12	72	18%	20.0%	6.0%	13.0%	15.0%	3.0%	$22.00	$16.50
13	69	17%	20.0%	6.0%	13.0%	15.0%	3.0%	$22.00	$16.50
YR.2	67	16%	20.0%	6.0%	13.0%	15.0%	3.0%	$22.00	$16.50
02	65	13%	20.0%	6.0%	13.0%	15.0%	3.0%	$22.00	$16.50
03	63	13%	20.0%	6.0%	13.0%	15.0%	3.0%	$22.00	$16.50
04	61	13%	20.0%	6.0%	13.0%	15.0%	3.0%	$22.00	$16.50
05	60	13%	20.0%	6.0%	13.0%	15.0%	3.0%	$22.00	$16.50
06	58	13%	20.0%	6.0%	13.0%	15.0%	3.0%	$22.00	$16.50
07	56	13%	20.0%	6.0%	13.0%	15.0%	3.0%	$22.00	$16.50
08	54	13%	20.0%	6.0%	13.0%	15.0%	3.0%	$22.00	$16.50
09	53	13%	20.0%	6.0%	13.0%	15.0%	3.0%	$22.00	$16.50
10	51	13%	20.0%	6.0%	13.0%	15.0%	3.0%	$22.00	$16.50
11	50	13%	20.0%	6.0%	13.0%	15.0%	3.0%	$22.00	$16.50
12	48	13%	20.0%	6.0%	13.0%	15.0%	3.0%	$22.00	$16.50
13	47	13%	20.0%	6.0%	13.0%	15.0%	3.0%	$22.00	$16.50
YR.3+	45	13%	20.0%	6.0%	13.0%	15.0%	3.0%	$22.00	$16.50

TABLE 17-2

-------------------- KEY ASSUMPTIONS DIRECT MAIL ADVERTISING --------------------

BASE RESPONSE RATE IN OPM'S:				35.0

RESPONSE RATE IN FOLLOWING YEARS			YEAR TWO	100.00%
INDEXED TO YEAR ONE			YEAR THREE	100.00%
			YEAR FOUR	100.00%
			YEAR FIVE	100.00%
			YEAR SIX	100.00%

QUANTITY MAILED		QUANTITY MAILED		YEAR 2 - 5 STANDARD DISTRIBUTION	
YEAR ONE		YEAR 2	2,000	CYCLE 1	50.00%
CYCLE 1	0	YEAR 3	6,000	CYCLE 2	0.00%
CYCLE 2	0	YEAR 4	8,000	CYCLE 3	0.00%
CYCLE 3	0	YEAR 5	10,000	CYCLE 4	0.00%
CYCLE 4	0	YEAR 6	0	CYCLE 5	0.00%
CYCLE 5	0			CYCLE 6	0.00%
CYCLE 6	0			CYCLE 7	0.00%
CYCLE 7	0			CYCLE 8	0.00%
CYCLE 8	0			CYCLE 9	50.00%
CYCLE 9	200			CYCLE 10	0.00%
CYCLE 10	0			CYCLE 11	0.00%
CYCLE 11	0			CYCLE 12	0.00%
CYCLE 12	0			CYCLE 13	0.00%
CYCLE 13	0			TOTAL	100.00%

the remaining members become more sophisticated about the negative option.

- **Similar acceptance, return, and bad debt assumptions regarding alternate selections.** All alternates are treated as a group.
- **Average price of the negative option and alternate selections.** Adjustments for inflation are handled separately by an inflation multiplier so that the analyst can think in terms of constant dollars.

Combining all of these assumptions together with other assumptions regarding product and fulfillment costs results in a lifetime value of $43.67. (See Year 5 in Table 17-7.)

Tables 17-2, 17-3, and 17-4 provide all of the other assumptions to the model. Table 17-2 provides the input assumptions regarding direct mail advertising. The key assumption, which we will change shortly, is a response rate of 35 OPM (3.5 percent), which in this first pass of the model is not shown to change even though the quantity mailed increases from 200,000 in the test year to 10 million pieces in Year 5. Table 17-3 provides the details of our print or space advertising plan. According to this first pass of the model, print orders will cost $20 per customer and will stay at that

TABLE 17–3

-----------------KEY ASSUMPTIONS PRINT OR SPACE ADVERTISING-----------------

BASE RESPONSE IN COST PER ORDER $20.00

COST PER ORDER IN FOLLOWING YEARS	YEAR TWO	100.00%
INDEXED TO YEAR ONE	YEAR THREE	100.00%
	YEAR FOUR	100.00%
	YEAR FIVE	100.00%
	YEAR SIX	100.00%

PRINT MEDIA BUDGET YEAR ONE		PRINT MEDIA BUDGET		YEAR 2 - 5 STANDARD DISTRIBUTION	
CYCLE 1	$0	YEAR 2	$65,000	CYCLE 1	7.69%
CYCLE 2	$0	YEAR 3	$1,000,000	CYCLE 2	7.69%
CYCLE 3	$0	YEAR 4	$1,250,000	CYCLE 3	7.69%
CYCLE 4	$0	YEAR 5	$2,000,000	CYCLE 4	7.69%
CYCLE 5	$0	YEAR 6	$3,000,000	CYCLE 5	7.69%
CYCLE 6	$0			CYCLE 6	7.69%
CYCLE 7	$0	OTHER		CYCLE 7	7.69%
CYCLE 8	$0	ORDERS/CYCLE	50	CYCLE 8	7.69%
CYCLE 9	$5,000			CYCLE 9	7.69%
CYCLE 10	$5,000			CYCLE 10	7.69%
CYCLE 11	$5,000			CYCLE 11	7.69%
CYCLE 12	$5,000			CYCLE 12	7.69%
CYCLE 13	$5,000			CYCLE 13	7.69%
				TOTAL	100.00%

rate over five years as print media budgets go from $25,000 in the first year to $3 million in the fifth year.

Table 17–4 provides the balance of the assumptions needed to complete the model:

- Direct mail cost per thousand.
- New-member premium expense.
- Provision for package insert orders.
- Product costs and revenue associated with new orders.
- Cost of the periodic catalog (advance announcement, or AA) that announces the featured negative option selection and all of the alternate selections.
- Provision for preparation expense defined as a percent of the total promotion budget.
- Product cost of sales rates.
- Bad debt and return rates for new customers.
- Fulfillment, warehousing, and customer service costs measured as a percentage of net sales.

- Summary provision for fixed overheads (which would be supported by detailed schedules and budgets).
- A vehicle for adjusting the model for inflation.

"What If"

The five-year P&L resulting from the combination of all of the assumptions is shown in Table 17–5. As you can see from an inspection of the last two lines in Table 17–5, the assumptions provided have resulted in a very profitable business. Profit as a percentage of sales in Year 5 is 15.2 percent, the business breaks even on an annual basis in Year 3, and breaks even on a cumulative basis in Year 4. Additional diagnostics are presented in Tables 17–6, 17–7, and 17–8.

Some skeptics might refer to this as a typically rosy consultant's projection. So let's change it; that's what models are for.

Let's review our assumptions and see what effect a less optimistic set of assumptions would have on projected profits.

We can begin with a key assumption regarding lifetime value. While the initial model assumed that customers would leave the club at the rate of 3 percent per cycle, let's make that 4 percent per cycle.

The results of this change can be seen in Table 17–9. This seemingly small change has the effect of reducing profits over five years from $8,094,000 to $5,147,000. Not such a small change. However, it is not surprising when you stop to consider that a change from 3 to 4 percent is a 33 percent change, and in fact profits dropped by exactly 36 percent.

Now let's examine the assumption that direct mail and print response rates will not change over time and in the face of rising expenditures. We agree that this set of assumptions is not realistic, so let's decrease direct mail OPMs and print CPOs by 5 percent per year. The result is that the direct mail change reduced five-year profits by $1.8 million, and the print changes reduced five-year profits by another $441,000.

Now let's look at what would happen if we reduced the sales rate from 26 to 24 percent per cycle for all members that stayed past three years. The effect on five-year profits would be a decrease of less than $17,000 because, first, the change itself was small, and second, not many members stay for more than three years so the effect on total sales is therefore relatively small.

The point of the above "sensitivity" exercise is to demonstrate the usefulness (really the necessity) of a financial model in measuring the effect on profits based on changes in key variables.

TABLE 17-4

KEY INPUT ASSUMPTIONS FOR P&L PROJECTIONS
NEW MEMBER PROMOTION ASSUMPTIONS - NOT ADJUSTED FOR INFLATION

	DIRECT MAIL AVERAGE CPM	PREMIUM EXPENSE	INSERT CPO	NEW ORDR PRODUCT COSTS INCLUDING SHIPPING		NEW ORDER REVENUE	
				SPACE	DM/INSRTS	SPACE	DM/INSRTS
YEAR 1	$375.00	$3.00	$5.00	$9.00	$9.00	$3.98	$3.98
YEAR 2	$375.00	$3.00	$5.00	$9.00	$9.00	$3.98	$3.98
YEAR 3	$375.00	$3.00	$5.00	$9.00	$9.00	$3.98	$3.98
YEAR 4	$375.00	$3.00	$5.00	$9.00	$9.00	$3.98	$3.98
YEAR 5	$375.00	$3.00	$5.00	$9.00	$9.00	$3.98	$3.98

OTHER NEW MEMBER EXPENSES, CURRENT MEMBER AND PRODUCT COST ASSUMPTIONS

	PREP EXP AS A % OF VAR PROMO	ANNOUNCEMENT EXPENSE PER MEMBER	COSTS AS A PERCENT OF NET SALES			
			PRODUCT NEG OPT	PRODUCT ALT SEL	INV W/O PERCENT	BD RATE NEW ORD
YEAR 1	5.00%	$0.35	71%	71%	3.00%	5.00%
YEAR 2	5.00%	$0.35	40%	40%	3.00%	5.00%
YEAR 3	5.00%	$0.35	28%	28%	3.00%	5.00%
YEAR 4	5.00%	$0.35	28%	28%	3.00%	5.00%
YEAR 5	5.00%	$0.35	28%	28%	3.00%	5.00%

OPERATING COSTS AS A PERCENTAGE OF NET SALES - OVERHEADS

	FULFILL-MENT	WARE-HOUSING	CUSTOMER SERVICE	OVERHEAD EXPENSE	INFLATION FACTORS REVENUE/PRODUCT COSTS	EXPENSES
YEAR 1	15.00%	4.00%	6.00%	150,000	100.0%	100.0%
YEAR 2	14.00%	3.00%	5.00%	300,000	100.0%	100.0%
YEAR 3	12.00%	2.00%	4.00%	450,000	100.0%	100.0%
YEAR 4	9.00%	2.00%	4.00%	600,000	100.0%	100.0%
YEAR 5	9.00%	2.00%	4.00%	750,000	100.0%	100.0%

OTHER COST ASSUMPTIONS

	% RETURNS REUSABLE	COST OF RETURNS	RETURN % GROSS NEW ORDS	NET DELIVERY EXPENSE/ GROSS BOOKS SHIPPED
YEAR 1	20.00%	$1.00	5.00%	$0.00
YEAR 2	20.00%	$1.00	5.00%	$0.00
YEAR 3	20.00%	$1.00	5.00%	$0.00
YEAR 4	20.00%	$1.00	5.00%	$0.00
YEAR 5	20.00%	$1.00	5.00%	$0.00

TABLE 17–5

FIVE YEAR P&L STATEMENT

	YEAR 1	YEAR 2	YEAR 3	YEAR 4	YEAR 5	TOTAL
GROSS SALES:						
NEGATIVE OPTION	$213	$3,251	$12,440	$22,853	$33,381	$72,138
ALTERNATE SALES	40	947	4,074	9,112	14,541	28,714
TOTAL GROSS SALES	$253	$4,198	$16,514	$31,965	$47,922	$100,852
RETURNS:						
NEGATIVE OPTION	43	650	2,488	4,571	6,676	$14,428
ALTERNATE SALES	6	142	611	1,367	2,181	$4,307
TOTAL RETURNS	$49	$792	$3,099	$5,937	$8,857	$18,735
NET SALES:	$205	$3,406	$13,415	$26,027	$39,065	$82,117
COST OF SALES:						
PRODUCT COSTS	$145	$1,362	$3,756	$7,288	$10,938	$23,489
INVENTORY W/O	6	102	402	781	1,172	$2,464
PRODUCT DEVELOPMENT	0	0	0	0	0	$0
DELIVERY	0	0	0	0	0	$0
RETURN PROCESSING	0	8	30	58	87	$183
TOTAL COST OF SALES	$152	$1,472	$4,189	$8,127	$12,197	$26,136
GROSS MARGIN	$53	$1,934	$9,226	$17,901	$26,868	$55,981

CUSTOMER SERVICE	12	170	537	1,041	1,563	$3,323
FULFILLMENT/EDP	31	477	1,610	2,342	3,516	$7,976
WAREHOUSING	8	102	268	521	781	$1,680
OPERATIONS-BAD DBT	30	368	1,370	2,318	3,320	$7,407
NEW ORDER-BAD DEBT	2	15	52	68	89	$226
TOTAL OPER COSTS	$83	$1,132	$3,837	$6,290	$9,269	$20,611
OPERATING MARGIN	($31)	$801	$5,390	$11,610	$17,599	$35,370
AMORTIZED PROMO/ACQUISITION	$49	$799	$2,999	$4,872	$6,448	$15,167
NEW ORDER REVENUE	35	294	1,030	1,364	1,788	$4,511
NEW ORDER RETURNS	$2	$15	$52	$68	$89	$226
NW ORDR CST OF SLS	79	665	2,330	3,084	4,043	$10,201
CURR MEMBER EXPENSE	$12	$215	$878	$1,788	$2,766	$5,661
FIXED AA EXPENSE	7	7	7	7	7	$33
TOTAL MARKETING	$114	$1,407	$5,235	$8,455	$11,565	$26,776
CONTRIBUTION TO OVERHEAD & PROFIT	($144)	($605)	$155	$3,155	$6,033	$8,594
OVERHEAD	$100	$100	$100	$100	$100	$500
CONTRIBUTION TO PROFIT	($244)	($705)	$55	$3,055	$5,933	$8,094
% NET SALES	-119.4%	-20.7%	0.4%	11.7%	15.2%	15.2%
CUMULATIVE	($244)	($949)	($895)	$2,160	$8,094	$8,094

TABLE 17-6

	YEAR 1	YEAR 2	YEAR 3	YEAR 4	YEAR 5
BOOKS SHIPPED					
NEGATIVE OPTION	10	148	565	1,039	1,517
ALTERNATES	2	57	247	552	881
TOTAL BOOKS SHIPPED	12	205	812	1,591	2,399
BOOKS RETURNED					
NEGATIVE OPTION	2	30	113	208	303
ALTERNATE SALES	0	9	37	83	132
TOTAL BOOKS RETURN	2	38	150	291	436
AA'S MAILED TO MEMBERS	36	616	2510	5110	7904
YEAR END MEMBERS	7,943	65,093	254,706	449,940	668,584
AVERAGE MEMBERSHIP	2,744	47,346	193,070	393,041	608,010
NET BKS/MBR SERVICED	0.28	0.27	0.26	0.25	0.25
NET BKS/YEAR	3.6	3.5	3.4	3.3	3.0

Another use of the financial model, as discussed above, is to measure the effect on annual profits of major changes in new-customer spending. Let's start with the last set of assumptions, which produced a five-year cumulative profit of $2,950,000. (Please refer again to Table 17–9.)

Let's now increase print advertising expenditures in Year 4 from $1,250,000 to $5 million, and let's increase expenditures in Year 5 from $2 million to $9 million. Even if we assume no reduction in response rates (increases in print CPOs) or in the quality of the member acquired (both bad assumptions), annual profits will be reduced significantly. And it should be remembered that this model does not treat new-member acquisition expenditures as an expense taken in the month incurred. New-customer expenditures are written off over a 12-month period. However, if new-member expenses were written off over the full life of the member, the effect on profits would be reduced. On the other hand, if the company followed a practice of immediately writing off acquisition expenditures, the effect on annual profits would be significantly worse. The point is that accounting practices and the effect of new-member expenditures on reported profits must be carefully watched; direct marketing decisions cannot be made solely on the basis of long-term lifetime value and ROP considerations.

TABLE 17-7

	YEAR 1	YEAR 2	YEAR 3	YEAR 4	YEAR 5
TOTAL NEW ORDERS	9	74	261	343	451
TOTAL CPO	$11.60	$11.07	$12.48	$12.39	$12.77
PIECES MAILED	200	2,000	6,000	8,000	10,000
DM ORDERS (000'S)	7	70	210	280	350
OPM	35.0	35.0	35.0	35.0	35.0
PROMOTION EXPENSE	103,250	818,250	3,253,250	4,253,250	5,753,250
DIRECT MAIL	75,000	750,000	2,250,000	3,000,000	3,750,000
SPACE	25,000	65,000	1,000,000	1,250,000	2,000,000
INSERTS	3,250	3,250	3,250	3,250	3,250
TOTAL PROMOTION	103,250	818,250	3,253,250	4,253,250	5,753,250
COST PER ORDER					
DIRECT MAIL	$10.71	$10.71	$10.71	$10.71	$10.71
SPACE	$20.00	$20.00	$20.00	$20.00	$20.00
INSERTS	$5.00	$5.00	$5.00	$5.00	$5.00
TOTAL PROMOTION	$11.60	$11.07	$12.48	$12.39	$12.77
SUBSCRIBER STATS					
START OF YEAR	50	7,943	65,093	254,706	449,940
ADDED	8,775	73,900	258,852	342,669	449,208
END OF YEAR	7,943	65,093	254,706	449,940	668,584
LOST	882	16,751	69,239	147,435	230,564
% AVE LOST	5.52%	11.47%	10.83%	10.46%	10.31%

TABLE 17-7 (continued)

GROSS SALES/STARTER	$164.12	$164.12	$164.12	$164.12	$164.12
RETURNS/STARTER	$30.02	$30.02	$30.02	$30.02	$30.02
NET SALES/STARTER	$134.10	$134.10	$134.10	$134.10	$134.10
PROD COSTS/STARTER	$95.21	$53.64	$37.55	$37.55	$37.55
VAR COSTS/STARTER	$33.83	$29.80	$24.44	$20.41	$20.41
BAD DEBTS/STARTER	$10.14	$10.14	$10.14	$10.14	$10.14
MARGIN/STARTER	($5.08)	$40.52	$61.97	$66.00	$66.00
GIFT REVENUE	$3.58	$3.58	$3.58	$3.58	$3.58
NEW ORDER EXPENSE	$9.00	$9.00	$9.00	$9.00	$9.00
PREMIUM EXPENSE	$3.00	$3.00	$3.00	$3.00	$3.00
NET GIFT EXPENSE	$8.42	$8.42	$8.42	$8.42	$8.42
CONTRIBUTION TO:					
OH, PROMO & PROFIT	($13.50)	$32.10	$53.56	$57.58	$57.58
OH & PROFIT	($25.10)	$21.03	$41.08	$45.19	$44.81
ROP	-71.2%	342.0%	464.0%	500.4%	482.9%
AVERAGE MEMBER LIFE.........		28.73			
# NO. OF AA'S /YR	13	13	13	13	13
PERCENT RESPONSE					

TABLE 17-8

	PERCENT OF NET SALES:				
	YEAR 1	YEAR 2	YEAR 3	YEAR 4	YEAR 5
GROSS SALES:					
NEGATIVE OPTION	84.1%	77.4%	75.3%	71.5%	69.7%
ALTERNATIVE SALES	15.9%	22.6%	24.7%	28.5%	30.3%
TOTAL GROSS SALES	100.0%	100.0%	100.0%	100.0%	100.0%
RETURNS:					
NEGATIVE OPTION	20.0%	20.0%	20.0%	20.0%	20.0%
ALTERNATE SALES	15.0%	15.0%	15.0%	15.0%	15.0%
TOTAL RETURNS	19.2%	18.9%	18.8%	18.6%	18.5%
NET SALES:	100.0%	100.0%	100.0%	100.0%	100.0%
COST OF SALES:					
PRODUCT COSTS	71.0%	40.0%	28.0%	28.0%	28.0%
INVENTORY W/O	3.0%	3.0%	3.0%	3.0%	3.0%
PROD DEVELOPMENT	0.0%	0.0%	0.0%	0.0%	0.0%
OPER DELIVERY	0.0%	0.0%	0.0%	0.0%	0.0%
RETURN PROCESSING	0.2%	0.2%	0.2%	0.2%	0.2%
TOTAL COST OF SALES	74.2%	43.2%	31.2%	31.2%	31.2%
GROSS MARGIN	25.8%	56.8%	68.8%	68.8%	68.8%

TABLE 17–8 (continued)

CUSTOMER SERVICE	6.0%	5.0%	4.0%	4.0%	4.0%
FULFILLMENT/EDP	15.0%	14.0%	12.0%	9.0%	9.0%
WAREHOUSING	4.0%	3.0%	2.0%	2.0%	2.0%
OPERATIONS-BAD DBT	14.9%	10.8%	10.2%	8.9%	8.5%
NEW ORDER-BAD DEBT	0.9%	0.4%	0.4%	0.3%	0.2%
TOTAL OPER COSTS	40.7%	33.2%	28.6%	24.2%	23.7%
OPERATING MARGIN	−15.0%	23.5%	40.2%	44.6%	45.1%
AMORTIZED					
PROMO/ACQUISITION	23.9%	23.5%	22.4%	18.7%	16.5%
NEW ORDER REVENUE	17.1%	8.6%	7.7%	5.2%	4.6%
NEW ORDER RETURNS	0.9%	0.4%	0.4%	0.3%	0.2%
NEW ORDR CST OF SLS	38.6%	19.5%	17.4%	11.8%	10.3%
CURR MEM EXPENSE	6.1%	6.3%	6.5%	6.9%	7.1%
FIXED AA EXPENSE	3.2%	0.2%	0.0%	0.0%	0.0%
TOTAL MARKETING	55.5%	41.3%	39.0%	32.5%	29.6%
OH EXPENSE	48.9%	2.9%	0.7%	0.4%	0.3%
CONTRIBUTN OH/PFT	−119.37%	−20.71%	0.41%	11.74%	15.19%

TABLE 17–9

BASE EXAMPLE						
TOTAL GROSS SALES	$253	$4,198	$16,514	$31,965	$47,922	$100,852
CNTRBTN TO PRFT	($244)	($705)	$55	$3,055	$5,933	$8,094
% NET SALES	-119.4%	-20.7%	0.4%	11.7%	15.2%	
CUMULATIVE	($244)	($949)	($895)	$2,160	$8,094	
THE EFFECT OF INCREASING ATTRITION FROM 3% TO 4% PER CYCLE						
TOTAL GROSS SALES	$249	$4,000	$15,507	$29,183	$42,707	$91,646
CNTRBTN TO PRFT	($244)	($739)	($249)	$2,147	$4,233	$5,147
% NET SALES	-121.3%	-22.8%	-2.0%	9.0%	12.2%	
CUMULATIVE	($244)	($983)	($1,232)	$914	$5,147	
THE EFFECT OF DECREASING DIRECT MAIL RESPONSE RATES 5% PER YEAR						
TOTAL GROSS SALES	$249	$3,831	$14,372	$26,305	$37,371	$82,128
CNTRBTN TO PRFT	($244)	($736)	($402)	$1,589	$3,118	$3,324
% NET SALES	-121.3%	-23.7%	-3.4%	7.4%	10.2%	
CUMULATIVE	($244)	($980)	($1,382)	$207	$3,324	

TABLE 17-9 (continued)

THE EFFECT OF INCREASING PRINT CPO'S BY 5% PER YEAR

TOTAL GROSS SALES	$249	$3,825	$14,183	$25,744	$36,156	$80,158
CNTRBTN TO PRFT	($244)	($736)	($420)	$1,484	$2,883	$2,968
% NET SALES	-121.3%	-23.7%	-3.6%	7.1%	9.8%	
CUMULATIVE	($244)	($980)	($1,400)	$85	$2,968	$2,968

THE EFFECT OF REDUCING BOOK ACCEPTANCE RATES FROM 26 PERCENT TO 24 PERCENT IN YEARS 4-5

TOTAL GROSS SALES	$249	$3,825	$14,183	$25,742	$36,112	$80,111
CNTRBTN TO PRFT	($244)	($736)	($420)	$1,483	$2,866	$2,950
% NET SALES	-121.3%	-23.7%	-3.6%	7.1%	9.7%	
CUMULATIVE	($244)	($980)	($1,400)	$83	$2,950	$2,950

THE EFFECT OF INCREASING PRINT PROMOTION IN YEAR 4 TO $5,000,000 AND TO $9,000,000 IN YEAR FIVE

TOTAL GROSS SALES	$249	$3,825	$14,183	$32,085	$55,170	$105,512
CNTRBTN TO PRFT	($244)	($736)	($420)	$34	$794	($572)
% NET SALES	-121.3%	-23.7%	-3.6%	0.1%	1.8%	
CUMULATIVE	($244)	($980)	($1,400)	($1,366)	($572)	($572)

A CATALOG EXAMPLE

At the beginning of this section, we discussed the differences between traditional direct marketing companies that had contractual relationships and those that had implied relationships and said that book clubs were good examples of the former and catalogs were good examples of the latter.

In the five-year planning model discussed above, you will notice that the book club had relatively little discretion in terms of trading dollars between new-member acquisition and current-member marketing. More or less could be spent on new-customer acquisition but the money for new-customer marketing did not come at the expense of current-customer marketing.

In a catalog operation, the choices are more interesting since no contractual amount need be spent on current-customer marketing. As we said before, it's up to the cataloger to decide how much will be spent on each.

Since catalog models are much more complicated than book club models, we won't attempt to reproduce all of the assumptions that go into even a relatively simple model but rather we'll focus on one use of the model—the economic trade-off between new-customer acquisition and current-customer marketing.

Our base case scenario starts with a new catalog operation. The initial business plan is developed on the assumption that the company will develop two catalogs a year. The catalogs will be mailed to the customer file a total of six times. Each catalog will be repeated with minimal changes three times. A summary P&L taken from the budget model is shown in Table 17–10.

Lifetime Value

A key question to ask when reviewing this budget, and there are literally hundreds of assumptions to question, is, "what is the assumed lifetime value of the average catalog acquired customer and what assumptions are behind this estimate?" The answer is provided in Table 17–11.

Table 17–11 leads the marketing manager through a series of questions whose answers will result in an estimate of lifetime value. The questions are relatively simple. (The answers that appear in Table 17–11 are repeated in parentheses below.)

TABLE 17–10

SUMMARY STATEMENT OF PROFIT AND LOSS ($000'S)

	YEAR 1	YEAR 2	YEAR 3	YEAR 4	YEAR 5
GROSS SALES ($000'S)					
REPEAT BUSINESS	$20	$476	$1,902	$4,104	$6,465
NEW CUSTOMERS	$310	$2,050	$4,850	$6,250	$7,650
TOTAL GROSS SALES	$331	$2,527	$6,752	$10,354	$14,116
RETURNS:					
REPEAT BUSINESS	$3	$73	$289	$621	$976
NEW CUSTOMERS	$62	$410	$970	$1,250	$1,530
TOTAL RETURNS	$65	$483	$1,259	$1,871	$2,506
NET SALES					
REPEAT BUSINESS	$17	$403	$1,613	$3,483	$5,489
NEW CUSTOMERS	$248	$1,640	$3,880	$5,000	$4
TOTAL NET SALES	$265	$2,043	$5,493	$8,483	$11,609
COST OF SALES	$126	$623	$1,677	$2,594	$3,552
% OF NET SALES	47.4%	30.5%	30.5%	30.6%	30.6%
GROSS MARGIN	$140	$1,420	$3,816	$5,889	$8,057
% OF NET SALES	52.6%	69.5%	69.5%	69.4%	69.4%
OPERATING COSTS	$77	$388	$1,097	$1,817	$2,588
% OF NET SALES	29.0%	19.0%	20.0%	21.4%	22.3%
OPERATING MARGIN	$62	$1,032	$2,719	$4,073	$5,470
% OF NET SALES	23.5%	50.5%	49.5%	48.0%	47.1%

MARKETING COSTS					
NEW CUSTOMERS	$133	$945	$2,659	$3,515	$4,371
REPEAT BUSINESS	$57	$138	$328	$609	$922
TOTAL MARKETING	$190	$1,083	$2,987	$4,124	$5,294
% OF NET SALES	71.4%	53.0%	54.4%	48.6%	45.6%
CONTRIBUTION	($127)	($51)	($268)	($51)	$176
% OF NET SALES	-48%	-2%	-5%	-1%	2%
OVERHEAD AND BUSINESS DEVELPMNT	$103	$195	$250	$300	$350
LIST RENTAL INC	$7	$318	$767	$1,310	$1,997
PROFIT OR (LOSS)	($222)	$72	$249	$959	$1,823
% OF NET SALES	-83.7%	3.5%	4.5%	11.3%	15.7%
CUM P & (L)	($222)	($150)	$99	$1,058	$2,881

TABLE 17–11
Lifetime Value Assumptions

CATALOG SOLD CUSTOMERS: REPEAT PURCHASE RATE ASSUMPTIONS

% NEW CUSTOMERS BUYING IN FIRST 12 MONTHS	40.00%	INPUT
% NOT BUYING IN FIRST 12 MONTHS	60.00%	
% YR. 1 BUYERS BUYING IN YEAR 2	60.00%	INPUT
% YR. 1 BUYERS NOT BUYING IN YEAR 2	40.00%	
% YR. 1 NON-BUYERS BUYING IN YEAR 2	25.00%	INPUT
% YR. 1 NON-BUYERS NOT BUYING IN YR. 2	75.00%	
THE YEAR TWO BUY RATE IS THEREFORE:	39.00%	

COMPOSITION OF FILE AT END OF 24 MONTHS - ANY START GROUP

PERCENT YEAR 1 ONLY BUYERS ON FILE	16.00%	GROUP 1
PERCENT YEAR 2 ONLY BUYERS ON FILE	15.00%	GROUP 2
PERCENT YEARS 1&2 BUYERS ON FILE	24.00%	GROUP 3
PERCENT OF NON-BUYERS ON FILE	45.00%	GROUP 4
TOTAL	100.00%	
YEAR 3 BUY RATE FOR GROUP 1	20.00%	INPUT
YEAR 3 BUY RATE FOR GROUP 2	44.00%	INPUT
YEAR 3 BUY RATE FOR GROUP 3	75.00%	INPUT
YEAR 3 BUY RATE FOR GROUP 4	10.00%	INPUT
THE YEAR 3 BUY RATE IS THEREFORE:	32.30%	
FALL-OFF RATE IN YEAR 4 AND 5	80.00%	
YEAR 4 BUY RATE	25.84%	
YEAR 5/6 BUY RATE	20.67%	

	# OF CATALOGS PRODUCED	% ACTIVE BUYERS	# OF MAILING PERIODS	AVERAGE CAT RES RATE	AVE ANNUAL RESPONSE RATE
YEAR 1	2	40.00%	6	6.67%	40.00%
YEAR 2	2	39.00%	6	6.50%	39.00%
YEAR 3	2	32.30%	6	5.38%	32.30%
YEAR 4	2	25.84%	6	4.31%	25.84%
YEAR 5	2	20.67%	6	3.45%	20.67%
YEAR 6	2	20.67%	6	3.45%	20.67%

AVG LIFETIME SALES	$41.92
AVERAGE COST PER ORDER	$14.29
AVERAGE PROFIT ON SALES BEFORE PROMOTION COSTS	40.00%
CONTRIBUTION TO PROMOTION, OVERHEAD AND PROFIT	$16.77
RETURN ON PROMOTION/ BEFORE LIST RENTAL	17.37%
NUMBER OF TIMES LIST RENTED	100
NET LIST RENTAL INCOME	$0.07
LIST RENTAL INCOME	$7.00
ADJUSTED RETURN ON PROMOTION AFTER LIST RENTAL	66.37%

- What percent of new customers will make at least one purchase within the next 12 months? (Assume an estimate of 40 percent, therefore 60 percent don't buy.)
- Among those that purchase in the first 12 months, what percent will purchase in the following 12 months? (Assume 60 percent, therefore 40 percent will not become repeat purchasers.)
- Among those that *failed to purchase* in the first 12 months, what percent, if mailed, will purchase within the following 12 months? (Assume that 25 percent buy and 75 percent continue to not buy.)

The answers to these questions will provide enough information to estimate Year 2 buy rates for the entire starting group. In addition, at the end of two years, all customers will be divided into four parts:

- The best customers, those that purchased in both years. They will represent 24 percent of the original group. (40% × 60% = 24%.)
- Customers who purchased in the most recent year but not in the first year, 15 percent of the file. (60% × 25% = 15%.)
- Those that purchased in the first year but not in the second, 16 percent of the file. (40% × 40% = 16%.)
- Those that never purchased, your worst customers, 45 percent of the file. (60% × 75% = 45%.)

It's relatively easy from this point on to estimate the purchase rate for each of the four groups in Year 3, and to apply a falloff rate to estimate purchase rates for subsequent years.

Needless to say, it's easy enough to complicate this argument even further by asking for estimates of multiple purchases as opposed to single purchases. But then you must ask, who is smart enough to answer more complicated questions more or less correctly?

When these assumptions are combined with other assumptions regarding attrition rates, prices, costs, and expenses, the model will produce an estimate of the lifetime value of a catalog customer.

At the bottom of Table 17–11 we see that the lifetime sales corresponding to the above set of purchase assumptions is equal to $41.92. From other sections of the model (not shown) we see that the average profit on sales before promotion expenses is 40 percent of sales, or $16.77. The average cost per new customer is shown to be $14.29, so that the difference (the contribution to overhead and profit) is only

$2.48 and the return on promotion is only 17.37 percent ($2.48/ 14.20 = 17.37%).

Interestingly, the profit from this model comes from list rentals and the assumption that a single name will be rented 100 times over a five-year period, adding $7 to the value of a customer and increasing the after–list rental return on promotion rate to 66 percent.

"What If"

Now, assuming that we have satisfied ourselves with the assumptions of the basic model (a job we hardly began), let's play "what if." What if the business were built on the assumption of three catalogs a year, not two? Obviously, expenses would increase, but what if repeat purchase rates also increased by 20 percent each year? The results of this set of assumptions are shown (in summary form) in Table 17–12, under the heading Option One. Both sales and marketing costs increased, but unfortunately costs increased faster than sales, and the net effect is a reduction in profits over five years from $2,881,000 to $2,450,000. A good idea, but one not supported by the model. Of course, if we had assumed that sales would have increased by 50 percent or by 33 percent, we might have come to a different conclusion, which is a dangerous thing about "what if" models. You can make them support almost any answer you are trying to justify, so learn to live with your best estimates, and resist the urge to change them when they don't support your objectives.

But let's not give up on making this model better. What if we took the extra dollars that would have gone into a third catalog and put them into customer acquisition? Option Two shows what would happen if we increased the acquisition budgets in each year by roughly the amount we would have spent on a third catalog. As you can see, cumulative profits are up from $2.89 million to $3.26 million, and the number of year-end customers has gone from 646,841 to 717,284.

CONCLUSION

We hope this last chapter on financial modeling has provided the reader with a better understanding of how all of the elements of the economics of traditional direct marketing fit together. Front-end, back-end, lifetime

TABLE 17–12

BASE CASE TWO CATALOGS PER YEAR MAILED AN AVERAGE OF SIX TIMES					
TOTAL GROSS SALES	$331	$2,527	$6,752	$10,354	$14,116
MARKETING COSTS					
NEW CUSTOMERS	$133	$945	$2,659	$3,515	$4,371
REPEAT BUSINESS	$57	$138	$328	$609	$922
TOTAL MARKETING	$190	$1,083	$2,987	$4,124	$5,294
CUSTOMERS	45,300	170,317	249,609	438,857	646,841
PROFIT OR (LOSS)	($222)	$72	$249	$959	$1,823
% OF NET SALES	−83.7%	3.5%	4.5%	11.3%	15.7%
CUM P & (L)	($222)	($150)	$99	$1,058	$2,881

OPTION ONE: THREE CATALOGS MAILED NINE TIMES SALES UP 20%					
TOTAL GROSS SALES	$326	$2,623	$7,177	$11,318	$15,690
MARKETING COSTS					
NEW CUSTOMERS	$133	$945	$2,659	$3,515	$4,371
REPEAT BUSINESS	$78	$198	$486	$910	$1,383
TOTAL MARKETING	$211	$1,143	$3,145	$4,425	$5,755
CUSTOMERS	45,300	170,317	249,609	438,857	646,841
PROFIT OR (LOSS)	($244)	$20	$158	$840	$1,676
% OF NET SALES	−93.3%	1.0%	2.7%	9.0%	12.9%
CUM P & (L)	($244)	($224)	($66)	$774	$2,450

OPTION TWO: PUT ADDITIONAL PROMOTION MONEY IN NEW CUSTOMER ACQUISITION					
TOTAL GROSS SALES	$382	$2,712	$7,262	$11,457	$15,844
MARKETING COSTS					
NEW CUSTOMERS	$165	$1,024	$2,868	$3,943	$4,971
REPEAT BUSINESS	$58	$144	$347	$655	$1,010
TOTAL MARKETING	$224	$1,168	$3,215	$4,599	$5,981
CUSTOMERS	49,538	182,951	267,581	479,870	717,284
PROFIT OR (LOSS)	($246)	$94	$297	$1,062	$2,055
% OF NET SALES	−80.0%	4.3%	5.0%	11.3%	15.8%
CUM P & (L)	($246)	($151)	$146	$1,207	$3,263

value, and return on promotion all come together in the financial model. When this type of financial planning and analysis is combined with the database marketing methods discussed in the prior chapters of this book, the result is what we have called *The New Direct Marketing*.

APPENDIX I

VENDORS OF DATA AND COMPUTER SERVICES

The six vendors included in Appendix I are representative of the data and computer services that are available commercially.

Vendors are divided into two major groups—Original Data Providers and Service Bureaus. Original Data Providers consists of two categories—Consumer Data and Business Data. The Consumer Data section contains information about Claritas, Donnelley, and R. L. Polk, while the Business Data section describes the data and services available from Dun & Bradstreet's D-U-N-S Numbers.

The Service Bureau section contains data about Infobase and May & Speh. Each of these companies offers data that was originally developed by a number of other suppliers including R. L. Polk, Donnelley, Equifax, SmartNames, etc.

The list is not meant to be exhaustive, but is intended to provide readers with an idea of the range of data selections and computer services that are available in the direct marketing marketplace. For a more complete listing of services available, readers are advised to contact the Direct Marketing Association, which maintains a list of services, by category, offered by member organizations.

TABLE OF CONTENTS FOR DATA VENDOR EXHIBIT

Business Data
    Dun & Bradstreet Information Resources
        D-U-N-S Numbers
Service Bureaus
    Infobase Services
        Infobase Premier
        National Demographics & Lifestyles
        R. L. Polk and Company Data
        SmartNames, Inc.
        Donnelly Marketing Data
    May & Speh Direct Data Enhancement Services
        National Demographics & Lifestyles
        Equifax Power Overlay Data
        R. L. Polk X-1 Enhancement Data
        PRIZM Cluster Code
        GEOPLUS
        National Decision Systems' VISION Summary Descriptions
        Equifax Marketing Services' Equis Targeting System Descriptions

ORIGINAL DATA PROVIDERS

CONSUMER DATA

Why PRIZM Is the Recognized Leader in Cluster Segmentation Systems

THE PRIZM CONTRIBUTION TO MARKETING SCIENCE

Originally conceived and pioneered by CLARITAS in 1974, PRIZM is a market segmentation system that . . .

- Classifies every American neighborhood into forty basic lifestyle segments, or *Clusters.*
- Needs *only* home addresses to assign consumers into these forty Clusters, and . . .
- Is designed to explain, predict and target consumer behavior.

Compared to all other segmentation methods, the PRIZM System offers three unique advantages:

1. Customer File Enhancement

Needing *only* street addresses, PRIZM can Cluster-encode your own in-house customer files, and convert these previously dormant files into the driving engines of your marketing action plans.

2. Integrated Market Analysis

Once coded, your customer files can then be integrated with all other marketing databases, including:

- Consumer market surveys & purchase records
- Broadcast audiences & cable TV subscribers
- Print media circulations & reader surveys
- Compiled & direct-response mailing lists
- Retail stores & trading areas by type/SIC
- Media, metro & custom market definitions

Thus PRIZM links every key marketing resource into *one* predictive framework for the selection of consumer targets.

3. Pinpoint Market Targeting

And once consumer targets are defined by PRIZM Clusters, then the system becomes a pinpoint targeting tool. Because every PRIZM target is locatable by address, you can *hit* these targets, right where they live, using local print, TV, radio, and outdoor media, direct-mail promotions, selective retail merchandising and site analyses.

No other segmentation method ever combined such analytic and targeting power in a single marketer's tool.

WHY LEADING MARKETERS CHOOSE THE PRIZM SYSTEM

During the past three years alone, some 2,000 marketers in every business sector have chosen PRIZM for market segmentation & strategic planning; for media & promotion targeting; for retail-site and direct-response analysis; and for target-market sales tracking. Their reasons include:

A Superior Cluster System

Only the PRIZM System was created by nationally recognized experts using:

- The smallest levels of neighborhood geography (Census Block Groups, Tracts, and MCDs) consistent with statistical reliability.
- The most significant demographic variables discovered through factor analysis.
- A definitive battery of consumer data to fine-tune the PRIZM Clusters for behavioral discrimination.

The centerfold of this brochure explains why the PRIZM System is the considered choice of the nation's leading marketers.

The PRIZM Interlock

Clusters alone do not comprise a marketing system. They must be fully encoded on *all* of the primary syndications of market and media data used by the industry. The PRIZM Interlock includes Nielsen, Arbitron, Birch Radio, Media-Mark Research, Simmons Market Research Bureau, National Family Opinion, Market Facts, MRCA, NPD Research, and many others. Only PRIZM is fully integrated.

The PRIZM•WARE System

PRIZM•WARE is a powerful, menu-driven microcomputer software system, which goes far beyond typical demographic retrieval systems to *integrate client customer files* with the PRIZM Interlock and neighborhood demographics for definitive target analyses.

Experience in Depth

PRIZM has a proven twelve-year track record. CLARITAS marketers have the training and expertise to produce measurable bottom-line results on every PRIZM project.

If you believe the PRIZM System may be the right answer for you, simply phone your nearest CLARITAS representative.

New York	Washington, D.C.	Chicago	Los Angeles
(212) 532-8200	(703) 683-8300	(312) 693-4200	(213) 394-6897

PREPARING THE CENSUS DATA FOR ANALYSIS

Cluster analysis began with the 1980 U.S. Census, a vast database containing hundreds of thousands of pieces of neighborhood geography, each measured by thousands of demographic variables.

Thus, our first critical task was to determine *which neighborhood geographies* and *which Census demographic variables* were capable of producing a statistically-valid, behavioral model of American neighborhood lifestyles.

CLARITAS effectively solved these problems.

The PRIZM Solution

We first created an optimal neighborhood database covering the entire nation. This database included the smallest neighborhood geographies (Census Block Groups, Tracts & MCD's) offering statistically reliable Census counts and sample-data projections.

The Smallest Neighborhood Geographies Consistent with Statistical Reliability

URBAN ➤ **SUBURBAN** ➤ **NON-METRO**

| Block Groups | Census Tracts & Block Groups | Minor Civil Divisions |

These optimal neighborhood geographies were then subjected to a rigorous *demographic factor analysis*. This analysis disclosed the *key factors* (from six broad domains of lifestyle data) which delivered the full explanatory power of the 1980 Census.

Primary Demographic Factor Analysis
Key Factors...In Six Domains

Social Rank

Housing

HH Composition

EXPLAIN ALL DEMOGRAPHIC VARIANCE IN THE CENSUS DATABASE

MOVING

Urbanization

Mobility

Ethnicity

How the PRIZM System Was Designed & Built to Target Consumer Behavior

DEFINING THE FORTY LIFESTYLE CLUSTERS

This unique PRIZM combination of optimal geographies and key factors was then introduced into Cluster analysis, which produced forty basic *demographic* classifications of neighborhoods.

Had this been our first effort (as in 1974) the process would have ended here. But this was 1983. We had nine years of PRIZM applications experience, our tape library was full of national customer files, and we had a unique opportunity to go beyond demographics and enhance the power of our system.

Behavioral Optimization

With client authorization, sixty of our most powerful customer files were organized into a multi-dimensional, behavioral test screen. Our demographic Cluster model was then modified by a systematic adjustment of factor weightings, in over thirty feed-back test iterations, to produce a clear winner, a PRIZM Cluster model with maximal discriminating power across *every* dimension of consumer behavior.

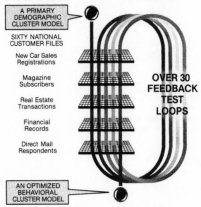

A PRIMARY DEMOGRAPHIC CLUSTER MODEL

SIXTY NATIONAL CUSTOMER FILES

New Car Sales Registrations

Magazine Subscribers

Real Estate Transactions

Financial Records

Direct Mail Respondents

OVER 30 FEEDBACK TEST LOOPS

AN OPTIMIZED BEHAVIORAL CLUSTER MODEL

Only CLARITAS had this capability; only the PRIZM System was fine-tuned for differentiation of consumer behavior.

ASSIGNING EVERY NEIGHBORHOOD TO ITS CORRECT PRIZM CLUSTER

Final Cluster Assignments

We now had forty optimal Cluster definitions, which might be likened to statistical 'cookie cutters'. Using *these* definitions, we then proceeded to assign each piece of neighborhood geography (in all, some 540,000 neighborhood units) to one of the forty PRIZM Clusters.

Each neighborhood unit, be it a Block-Group, Enumeration District, Census Tract, Minor Civil Division, ZIP Code or Postal Carrier Route, was *individually assigned* according to its own unique demographic characteristics, without reference to *any* other neighborhood unit. PRIZM Block-Group Cluster assignments were not governed by PRIZM ZIP Cluster assignments, or vice versa.

PRIZM Block Group Assignments

To illustrate the depth of the PRIZM System, seen below is a map and profile of the Block-Group Cluster composition of a single Manhattan ZIP Code (10019, Radio City). Viewing the colorful extremes across *eight* Block-Group Clusters in this one ZIP Code, it is easy to appreciate both the accuracy and utility of the PRIZM Cluster system.

Manhattan ZIP Code 10019

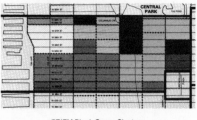

PRIZM Block-Group Clusters

Bohemian Mix	Downtown Dixie-Style
Gray Power	Hispanic Mix
Single City Blues	Public Assistance
Urban Gold Coast	New Melting Pot

SELECTING THE RIGHT NEIGHBORHOOD TARGETS

Because the forty PRIZM Clusters were statistically replicated at every neighborhood level from Block Groups to ZIP Codes, marketers can freely shift up and down across the PRIZM System for any analytic or targeting need.

There has been much debate about which of these levels is "best". This is as pointless as arguing over which golf club is best. For all are valid, useful tools, and each offers unique targeting advantages.

Block-Group Clusters are ideal for PRIZM profile analyses of geo-coded customer files, for list segmentation, and for analyzing/targeting local retail trading areas and sites. Tract Clusters are also well suited for trading-area analyses, especially over time, and are ideal for local-market mapping of sales data and client-defined PRIZM targets. And where geo-coding is not feasible, ZIP Clusters suit most analytic needs.

Where applications and data availability permit, targeting efficiencies improve at the smaller neighborhood levels.

Relative Targeting Efficiencies at Three Neighborhood Levels

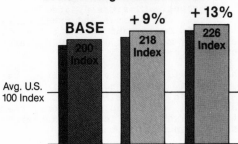

As measured across many PRIZM profiles of client customer records, the variance in behavioral discrimination for the top 20% of ranked Cluster profiles shows average gains of 9% and 13% for Tract and Block-Group Clusters vs. ZIP Clusters, respectively. These gains reflect the underlying variance inherent in the Census data as we shift down across neighborhood levels from ZIP Codes to Block Groups.

Only PRIZM combines the right Cluster system with twelve years of experience. We have been there, through thousands of client case histories. We *know* how to make it work for you.

Claritas Direct Marketing Services

Claritas Corporation has been assisting direct marketers in targeting their products since 1974. Claritas direct marketing services include:

o PRIZM Neighborhood Targeting system

o Direct Response Analyses

o Custom Name Scoring Models

In 1974, Claritas launched PRIZM, the first neighborhood lifestyle ("geo-demographic") segmentation system in the U.S. PRIZM is based on the principle that "Birds of a feather flock together..."

People choose to live in neighborhoods in which they find compatible lifestyles. Thus communities with common circumstances and similar consumer behavior patterns are created. Once established, the character of a community tends to persist over time, even though individual residents may come and go.

The Claritas Clusters are the end result of complex statistical techniques which employ U.S. Census Data plus many additional types of actual consumer data to uncover the latent structure of these natural social groups. Claritas updates the PRIZM assignments using census data updates and fresh consumer data. This method enables us to define and locate all similar communities wherever they may occur in the U.S., and to assign them to homogeneous Clusters.

These Cluster exhibit vivid, predictable behavior patterns toward products, services, media, and promotions. Moreover, because all these data can be correlated by Cluster, then projected back into local market configurations, the marketer can now target at the neighborhood level, and thereby increase his leverage, his efficiency, or both.

The following pages describe the 40 homogeneous Clusters of U.S. residential neighborhoods. Every neighborhood in the nation has been computer assigned to one of these 40 Clusters at the ZIP, Tract, and Block Group level, and the Clusters have, in turn, been assigned to 12 more general Cluster Groups.

The system is introduced as follows:

o Description of the 12 Cluster Groups
o Description of the 40 Clusters.

Taken together, these descriptions provide a dimensional view of each Cluster and its assigned neighborhoods.

THE PRIZM CLUSTER MODEL

THE TWELVE SOCIAL GROUPS			THE FORTY CLUSTERS	
Codes	Descriptive Titles	Numbers		Nicknames
S1	Educated, Affluent Executives and Professionals in Elite Metro Suburbs	28 8 5		Blue Blood Estates Money & Brains Furs & Station Wagons
S2	Pre- and Post-Child Families and Singles in Upscale, White-Collar Suburbs	7 25 20		Pools & Patios Two More Rungs Young Influentials
S3	Upper-Middle, Child-Raising Families in Outlying, Owner-Occupied Suburbs	24 30		Young Suburbia Blue-Chip Blues
U1	Educated, White-Collar Singles and Ethnics in Upscale, Urban Areas	21 37 31 23		Urban Gold Coast Bohemian Mix Black Enterprise New Beginnings
T1	Educated, Young, Mobile Families in Exurban Satellites and Boom Towns	1 17 12		God's Country New Homesteaders Towns & Gowns
S4	Middle-Class, Post-Child Families in Aging Suburbs and Retirement Areas	27 39 2		Levittown, U.S.A. Gray Power Rank & File
T2	Mid-Scale, Child-Raising Blue-Collar Families in Remote Suburbs and Towns	40 16 29		Blue-Collar Nursery Middle America Coalburg & Corntown
U2	Mid-Scale Families, Singles and Elders in Dense, Urban Row and High-Rise Areas	3 36 14 26		New Melting Pot Old Yankee Rows Emergent Minorities Single City Blues
R1	Rural Towns and Villages Amidst Farms and Ranches Across Agrarian Mid-America	19 34 35		Shotguns & Pickups Agri-Business Grain Belt
T3	Mixed Gentry and Blue-Collar Labor in Low-Mid Rustic, Mill, and Factory Towns	33 22 13 18		Golden Ponds Mines & Mills Norma Rae-Ville Smalltown Downtown
R2	Landowners, Migrants and Rustics in Poor Rural Towns, Farms, and Uplands	10 38 15 6		Back-Country Folks Share Croppers Tobacco Roads Hard Scrabble
U3	Mixed, Unskilled Service and Labor in Aging, Urban Rows and High-Rise Areas	4 11 9 32		Heavy Industry Downtown Dixie-Style Hispanic Mix Public Assistance

THE TWELVE PRIZM SOCIAL GROUPS

S1

Educated, Affluent Executives and Professionals in Elite Metro Suburbs
(Includes **Blue Blood Estates, Money & Brains,** and **Furs & Station Wagons**)

The three Clusters in Group S1 are characterized by top socio-economic status,
college-plus educations, executive and professional occupations, expensive
owner-occupied housing, and   conspicuous consumption levels for many products,
goods, and services. Representing 5 percent of U.S. households, Group S1 contains
about 32 percent of the nation's $75K+ household incomes, and an estimated third of its
personal net worth.

Clusters in S1

Blue Blood Estates (28)

These are America's wealthiest socio-economic neighborhoods, populated by
super-upper established managers, professionals, and heirs to "old money," accustomed
to privilege and living in luxurious surroundings. One in ten millionaires can be found
in **Blue Blood Estates,** and there is a considerable drop from these heights to the next
level of affluence.

Money & Brains (8)

Money & Brains enjoys the nation's second highest socio-economic rank. These
neighborhoods are typified by swank, shipshape townhouses, apartments and condos.
Money & Brains has relatively few children and is dominated by childless couples and
a mix of upscale singles. They are sophisticated consumers of adult luxuries -- apparel,
restaurants, travel, and the like.

Furs & Station Wagons (5)

Third in socio-economic rank, **Furs & Station Wagons** is typified by "new money,"
living in expensive new neighborhoods in the greenbelt suburbs of the nation's major
metros, coast to coast. These are well-educated, mobile professionals and managers
with the nation's highest incidence of teenage children. They are winners - - big
producers, and big spenders.

S2

Pre & Post-Child Families and Singles in Upscale, White-Collar Suburbs
(Includes **Pools & Patios, Two More Rungs,** and **Young Influentials**)

The three Clusters of Group S2 typify a major U.S. trend toward pre- and post-child communities, with predominantly one- and two-person households surrounding closed and half-filled schools. While significantly below S1 in socio-economic levels, S2s display all of the characteristics of success, including high-end educations, incomes, white-collar occupations, and home values, with consumption levels to match.

Clusters in S2

Pools & Patios (7)

Pools & Patios once resembled **Furs & Station Wagons,** being upscale greenbelt suburbs in a late child-rearing mode. But today, most of these children have grown and departed, leaving aging couples in empty nests too costly for young homemakers. Good educations, high white-collar employment levels, and double incomes assure "the good life" in these neighborhoods.

Young Influentials (20)

Young Influentials could be imagined as tomorrow's **Money & Brains.** These are young, metropolitan sophisticates, with exceptional high-tech, white-collar employment levels. Double incomes afford high spending, and lifestyles are open, with singles, childless couples, and unrelated adults predominating in expensive one- and two-person homes, apartments, and condos. They are skewed to the new West.

Two More Rungs (25)

Just behind **Pools & Patios** in affluence, **Two More Rungs** has a high concentration of foreign-born European ethnics and is somewhat older, with even fewer children. It is also more dense, with a higher incidence of renters in multiple-unit, high-rise housing, and has a northeastern geo-center. **Two More Rungs** neighborhoods show a high index for professionals, and somewhat conservative spending patterns.

4

S3

Upper-Middle, Child-Raising Families in Outlying, Owner-Occupied Suburbs
(Includes **Young Suburbia** and **Blue-Chip Blues**)

The two Clusters of Group S3 represent our newest minority - - the traditional family - - Mom, Dad, and the kids. In this case, the families are upscale. Both Clusters show high indices for married couples, school-age children, double incomes, two or more cars, and single-unit, owner-occupied, suburban housing. In short, S3 is the essence of the traditional American Dream.

Clusters in S3

Young Suburbia (24)

Young Suburbia is one of our largest Clusters, found coast to coast in most major markets. It runs to large, young families, and ranks second in incidence of married couples with children. These neighborhoods are distinguished by their relative affluence and high white-collar employment levels. As a result, they are strong consumers of most family products.

Blue-Chip Blues (30)

Blue-Chip Blues, ranked fourth in married couples with children, is similar to **Young Suburbia** on most dimensions save social rank, its predominant high school educations and blue-collar occupations being reflected in fewer high-end incomes and lower home values. However, high employment and double incomes yield similar discretionary spending patterns, and make this Cluster an outstanding market.

5

U1

Educated, White-Collar Singles and Couples in Upscale, Urban Areas
(Includes **Urban Gold Coast, Bohemian Mix, Black Enterprise, and New Beginnings**)

With minor exceptions for **Black Enterprise**, Group U1 is characterized by millions of young, white-collar couples and singles (many divorced and separated), dense mid- and high-rise housing, upscale socio-economic status, cosmopolitan lifestyles, big-city universities and students, high concentrations of foreign born, and an undeniable panache and notoriety. In mega-city America, this is where the action is.

Clusters in U1

Urban Gold Coast (21)

Urban Gold Coast is altogether unique. It is the most densely populated per square mile, with the highest concentration of one-person households in multi-unit, high-rise buildings, and the lowest incidence of auto ownership. Other mosts: most white-collar, most childless, and most New York. **Urban Gold Coast** is the top in Urbania, a fit address for the 21 Club.

Bohemian Mix (37)

It's only a five-dollar cab ride from "the East Side" to "the Village." The drop in income and shift in perspective are far more dramatic. **Bohemian Mix** is America's Bohemia, a largely integrated, singles-dominated, high-rise hodge-podge of white-collars, students, divorced persons, actors, writers, artists, aging hippies, and races.

Black Enterprise (31)

Black Enterprise neighborhoods are nearly 70 percent black, with median black household incomes well above average and with consumption behavior to match. It is the most family-oriented of the U1 Clusters. A few downscale pockets can be found, but the majority of blacks in Cluster 31 are educated, employed, and solidly set in the upper middle class.

New Beginnings (23)

New Beginnings is represented in nearly all markets, but shows its strongest concentrations in the West. It provides new homes to many victims of the divorce boom in search of new job opportunities and lifestyles. The predominant age is 18-34, and the mode is pre-child with employment concentrated in lower-level white-collar and clerical occupations.

6

T1

Educated, Young, Mobile Families in Exurban Satellites and Boom Towns
(Includes **God's Country, New Homesteaders,** and **Towns & Gowns**)

The three Clusters of Group T1 share a lot of American geography, most of it around our younger boom towns or in the satellite towns and exurbs far beyond the beltways of major metros. Other shared characteristics are young, native-born, white-collar adults, extremely high mobility rates, and new, low-density single-unit housing. Most evident is growth. T1s have been the chief recipients of a major urban exodus, and are among the nation's fastest growing areas.

Clusters in T1

God's Country (1)

God's Country contains the highest socio-economic, white-collar neighborhoods primarily located outside major metros. These are well-educated frontier types, who have opted to live away from the big metros in some of our most beautiful mountain and coastal areas. They are highly mobile, and are among the nation's fastest growing neighborhoods. **God's Country** is an outstanding consumer of both products and media.

New Homesteaders (17)

New Homesteaders is much like **God's Country** in its mobility, housing, and family characteristics. The big difference is that these neighborhoods are nine rungs down on the socio-economic scale, with all measures of education and affluence being significantly lower. It shows peak concentrations of military personnel, and has a strong Western skew. It is one of our largest and fastest-growing Clusters.

Towns & Gowns (12)

Towns & Gowns contains hundreds of mid-scale college and university towns in non-metropolitan America. The population ratio is three-quarters locals ("towns") to one-quarter students ("gowns"), giving this Cluster its name and unique profile. It shows extreme concentrations of age 18-24 singles and students in group quarters, very high educational, professional, and technical levels in contrast with modest incomes and home values, and a taste for prestige products.

7

S4

Middle-Class, Post-Child Families in Aging Suburbs & Retirement Areas
(Includes **Levittown, U.S.A., Gray Power,** and **Rank & File**)

The three Clusters of Group S4, while each distinct, all represent a continuing U.S. trend towards post-child communities. As a group, S4s include many aging married couples, widows, and retirees on pensions and Social Security incomes. Except **Gray Power,** they are tightly geo-centered in the Northeast.

Cluster in S4

Levittown, U.S.A. (27)

The post-WWII baby boom caused an explosion of tract housing in the late 40s and 50s -- brand new suburbs for young white-collar and well-paid blue-collar families. As with **Pools & Patios,** the children are now largely grown and gone. Aging couples remain in comfortable, middle-class, suburban homes. Employment levels are still high, including double incomes, and living is comfortable in **Levittown, U.S.A.**

Gray Power (39)

Gray Power represents nearly two million senior citizens who have chosen to pull up their roots and retire amongst their peers. Primarily concentrated in sunbelt communities of the South Atlantic and Pacific regions, these are the nation's most affluent elderly, retired, and widowed neighborhoods, with the highest concentration of childless married couples, living in mixed multi-units, condos, and mobile homes on nonsalaried incomes.

Rank & File (2)

Rank & File is a blue-collar version of **Levittown, U.S.A.,** five rungs down on the socio-economic scale. This Cluster contains many traditional, blue-collar family neighborhoods whose children have grown and departed, leaving an aging population. This Cluster shows high concentrations of protective-service and blue-collar workers living in aged duplex rows and multi-unit "railroad" flats. It leads the nation in durable manufacturing.

8

T2

Mid-Class, Child-Raising, Blue-Collar Families in Remote Suburbs and Towns
(Includes **Blue-Collar Nursery, Middle America,** and **Coalburg & Corntown**)

The three Clusters in Group T2 might be characterized as America's blue-collar baby factories (equivalent to white-collar **Furs & Station Wagons** and **Young Suburbia**). These neighborhoods are very middle class and married. They show high indices for large families, household incomes close to the U.S. mean, and owner-occupied single-unit houses in factory towns and remote suburbs of industrial metros. While anchored in the Midwest, T2s are broadly distributed across the nation.

Clusters in T2

Blue-Collar Nursery (40)

Blue-Collar Nursery leads the nation in craftsmen, the elite of the blue-collar world. It is also No. 1 in married couples with children and households of three or more. These are low-density satellite towns and suburbs of smaller industrial cities. They are well paid and very stable.

Middle America (16)

Middle America is well-named on several counts. It is composed of mid-sized, middle-class satellite suburbs and towns. It is at center on the socio-economic scale, and is close to the U.S. average on most measures of age, ethnicity, household composition and life cycle. It is also centered in the Great Lakes industrial region, near the population geo-center of the United States.

Coalburg & Corntown (29)

Coalburg & Corntown fits a popular image of the Midwest, being concentrated in small peaceful cities with names like Terre Haute, Indiana, and Lima, Ohio, surrounded by rich farmland, and populated by solid, blue-collar citizens raising sturdy, Tom Sawyer-ish children in decent, front-porch houses. Well, that's pretty much it . . . July 4th parades are still boffo in these neighborhoods.

U2

Mid-Scale Families, Singles and Elders in Dense, Urban Row and High-Rise Areas
(Includes **New Melting Pot, Old Yankee Rows, Emergent Minorities,** and **Single City Blues**)

The four Clusters in Group U2 encompass densely, urban, middle-class neighborhoods, mainly composed of duplex rows and multi-unit rented flats built more than thirty years ago in second-city centers and major-market fringes. As a group, U2s show high concentrations of foreign born, working women, clerical and service occupations, singles and widows in one-person households, continuing deterioration, and increasing minority presence. The differences between U2 Clusters are as significant as the similarities.

Clusters in U2

New Melting Pot (3)

The original European stock of many old urban neighborhoods has given way to new immigrant populations, often with Hispanic, Asian, and Middle-Eastern origins. These trends have formed a "New" Melting Pot, which includes many traditional Melting Pot areas along with new immigrant neighborhoods. As a result, **New Melting Pot** neighborhoods are situated in the major ports of entry on both East and West Coasts.

Old Yankee Rows (36)

Old Yankee Rows is well matched to **New Melting Pot** in age, housing mix, family composition, and income. However, it is dominated by high-school educated Catholics of European origin and has comparatively few minorities. These are well-paid, mixed blue/white-collar areas, firmly geo-centered in the older industrial cities of the Northeast.

Emergent Minorities (14)

Emergent Minorities is almost 80 percent black, the remainder largely composed of Hispanics and other foreign-born minorities. Unlike other U2s, **Emergent Minorities** shows above-average concentrations for children of all ages, almost half of them in homes with single parents. It also shows below-average levels of education and white-collar employment. The struggle for emergence from poverty is still evident in these neighborhoods.

Single City Blues (26)

This Cluster represents the nation's densely urban, downscale singles areas, found in most major markets, including those of the new West. Many are located near city colleges, and the Cluster displays a bi-modal education profile. With very few children and its odd mixture of races, classes, transients, and night trades, **Single City Blues** could be aptly described as the poor man's Bohemia.

10

R1

Rural Towns and Villages Amidst Farms and Ranches Across Agrarian Mid-America
(Includes Shotguns & Pickups, Agri-Business, and Grain Belt)

The three Clusters of Group R1 are geo-centered in a broad swath across the Corn Belt, through the wheat fields of the Great Plains states, and on into ranch and mining country. R1 Clusters share large numbers of sparsely populated communites, lower-middle to downscale socio-economic levels, extreme concentrations of German and Scandinavian ancestries, negligible black presence, high incidence of large families headed by married parents, low incidence of college educations, and maximum stability. These people are well described as "rugged conservatives."

Clusters in R1

Shotguns & Pickups (19)

Shotguns & Pickups aggregates hundreds of small, outlying townships and crossroad villages which serve the nation's breadbasket and other rural areas. It has a more easterly distribution than other R1s, and shows peak indices for large families with school-age children, headed by blue-collar craftsmen, equipment operators, and transport workers with high school educations. These areas are home to many dedicated outdoorsmen.

Agri-Business (34)

Agri-Business is geo-centered in the Great Plains and mountain states. These are, in good part, prosperous ranching, farming, lumbering, and mining areas. However, the picture is marred by rural poverty -- from the Dakotas to the Colorados -- where weather-worn old men and a continuing youth exodus testify to hard living.

Grain Belt (35)

Grain Belt is a close match to **Agri-Business** on most demographic measures. However, these areas show a far higher concentration of working farm owners and less affluent tenant farmers. Tightly geo-centered in the Great Plains and mountain states, these are the nation's most stable and sparsely populated rural communities, with one in five of the nation's farmers.

11

T3

Mixed Gentry and Blue-Collar Labor in Low-Mid Rustic, Mill and Factory Towns
(Includes **Golden Ponds, Mines & Mills, Norma Rae-Ville,** and **Smalltown Downtown**)

The four Clusters in Group T3 cover a host of predominantly blue-collar neighborhoods in the nation's smaller industrial cities, factory, mining and mill towns, and rustic coastal villages. The T3 Clusters share a few broad characteristics such as lower-middle incomes, limited educations, and (except **Smalltown Downtown**) single units and mobile homes in medium- to low-density areas. However, it is the differences between Clusters which make Group T3 interesting.

Clusters in T3

Golden Ponds (33)

Golden Ponds includes hundreds of small, rustic towns and villages in coastal resort, mountain, lake and valley areas, where seniors in cottages choose to retire amongst country neighbors. While neither as affluent nor as elderly as **Gray Power, Golden Ponds** ranks high on all measures of independence in retirement.

Mines & Mills (22)

Industry is king in **Mines & Mills**, including both light and heavy industry. This Cluster gathers hundreds of mining and mill towns scattered throughout the Appalachian mountains, from New England to the Pennsylvania-Ohio industrial complex and points south. It ranks first in total manufacturing and blue-collar occupations.

Norma Rae-Ville (13)

Norma Rae-Ville is concentrated in the South, with its geo-center in the Appalachian and Piedmont regions. These neighborhoods include hundreds of industrial suburbs and mill towns, a great many in textiles and other light industries. They are country folk with minimal educations, unique amongst the T3s in having a high index for blacks, and lead the nation in non-durable manufacturing.

Smalltown Downtown (18)

A hundred-odd years ago, our nation was laced with railroads and booming with heavy industry. All along these tracks, factory towns sprang up to be filled with laborers, in working-class row-house neighborhoods. Many can be seen today in **Smalltown Downtown**, mixed with the aging, downtown portions of other minor cities and towns. It is unique among the T3s in its relatively high population densities.

12

R2

Landowners, Migrants and Rustics in Poor Rural Towns, Farms and Uplands
(Includes **Back Country Folks, Share Croppers, Tobacco Roads,** and **Hard Scrabble**)

The four Clusters in group R2 pepper rural America and blanket the rural South with thousands of small agrarian communities, towns, villages, and hamlets. As a group, R2s have long shared such characteristics as very low population densities, low socio-economic rankings, minimal educations, large, highly stable households with widowed elders, predominantly blue-collar/farm labor, and peak concentrations of mobile homes. Since 1970, they have also shared rapid short-term growth and economic gains.

Clusters in R2

Back-Country Folks (10)

You can't get much farther out than Guntersville, Alabama; Elkins, Arkansas; Saltville, Virginia; or Caribou, Maine. **Back-Country Folks** abounds in such remote rural towns, geo-centered in the Ozark and Appalachian uplands. It is predominantly white, strongly blue-collar, and leads all Clusters in concentration of mobile homes and trailers.

Share Croppers (38)

Share Croppers is represented in forty-eight states but is deeply rooted in the heart of Dixie. Traditionally, these areas were devoted to such industries as tenant farming, chicken breeding, pulpwood and paper milling, etc. But sunbelt migration and a ready labor pool have continued to attract light industry and some population growth.

Tobacco Roads (15)

Tobacco Roads is found throughout the South from Virginia to Texas. However, its greatest concentrations are seen in the river basins and coastal, scrub-pine flatlands of the Carolinas, Georgia, and the Gulf states. These areas are above average for children of all ages, nearly a third in single-parent households. There is some light industry, but poor, unskilled labor predominates. Dependent upon agriculture, **Tobacco Roads** ranks at the bottom in white-collar occupations.

Hard Scrabble (6)

The term "hard scrabble" is an old phrase meaning to scratch a hard living from hard soil. **Hard Scrabble** neighborhoods represent our poorest rural areas, from Appalachia to the Ozarks, Mexican border country, and the Dakota Bad Lands. **Hard Scrabble** leads all other Clusters in concentration of adults with less than eight years of education, and trails all other Clusters in concentration of working women.

U3

Mixed,Unskilled Service & Labor in Aging, Urban Row and High-Rise Areas
(Includes Heavy Industry, Downtown Dixie-Style, Hispanic Mix, and Public Assistance)

The four Clusters of Group U3 represent the least advantaged neighborhoods of urban America. As a group, they show peak indices for minorities, high indices for equipment operators, service workers and laborers, very low income and education levels, large families headed by solo parents, high concentrations of singles (widowed, divorced, separated, and never married), peak concentrations of renters in multi-unit housing, and chronic unemployment.

Clusters in U3

Heavy Industry (4)

Heavy Industry is much like **Rank & File**, nine rungs down on the socio-economic scale and hard-hit by unemployment. It is chiefly concentrated in the older industrial markets of the northeastern U.S. quadrant and is very Catholic, with an above-average incidence of Hispanics. These neighborhoods have aged and deteriorated rapidly during the past decade. There are fewer children, and many broken homes.

Downtown Dixie-Style (11)

Downtown Dixie-Style has a southern geo-center, with high concentrations in three-dozen southern metros. These middle-density urban neighborhoods are nearly 70 percent black and fall between **Emergent Minorities** and **Public Assistance** in relative affluence. Unemployment is high, with service occupations dominating amongst the employed portion of the labor force.

Hispanic Mix (9)

Hispanic Mix represents the nation's Hispanic barrios and is, therefore, chiefly concentrated in the major markets of the Mid-Atlantic and West. These neighborhoods feature dense, row-house areas containing large families with small children, many headed by solo parents. They rank second in percent foreign born, first in short-term immigration, and are essentially bilingual neighborhoods.

Public Assistance (32)

With 70 percent of its households black, **Public Assistance** represents the Harlems of America. These are the nation's poorest neighborhoods, with twice its unemployment level, and nine times its share of public assistance incomes. These areas have been urban-renewal targets for three decades and show large, solo-parent families in rented or public high-rise buildings interspersed with aging tenement rows.

What Makes A List More
"On-Target" and "In-Demand"?

DONNELLEY MARKETING

L I S T   •   E N H A N C E M E N T

L I S T   •   E N H A N C E M E N T

L I S T   •   E N H A N C E M E N T

L I S T   •   E N H A N C E M E N T

L I S T   •   E N H A N C E M E N T

L I S T   •   E N H A N C E M E N T

L I S T   •   E N H A N C E M E N T

L I S T   •   E N H A N C E M E N T

Improve List Responsiveness and Efficiency.

Response with successful conversion is the true measure of list performance, and improved responsiveness is a direct result of better segmentation. List enhancement is the key to better segmentation.

Increase List Value and Revenues.

If you're a list owner or list manager, enhancement makes your list properties more valuable to you by making them more valuable to your prospective clients. It's the way to make any list more productive... for everyone.

Use Donnelley and Get the Best Results.

Accuracy for mailing purposes, for telemarketing, for targeting...that's what enhancement brings to a list. To guarantee this accuracy, the enhancement data you use has to be of the highest quality. It has to be verified, current information...The only type of data Donnelley Marketing provides. From sophisticated lifestyle segmentation to more basic enhancements such as telephone number appending, list cleaning, geocoding and the appending of demographic data, nobody provides more accurate, up-to-date consumer marketing information. That's why so many direct marketers consider Donnelley Marketing the "source."

Hundreds of Enhancement Elements Available

With Donnelley Marketing you can choose from an extraordinary array of enhancements—over 400 in all, many of which are proprietary and not available anywhere else.

For list cleaning: With continued increases in mailing costs, cleaning a house file or mailing list becomes increasingly important. Donnelley Marketing offers three list cleaning options designed to improve deliverability, increase response rates and lower these mailing costs. You can match your list to the U.S. Postal Service National Change of Address (NCOA)* file. You can eliminate NIXIES identified by Donnelley over the past four years or perform a positive match against Donnelley's DQI[2]

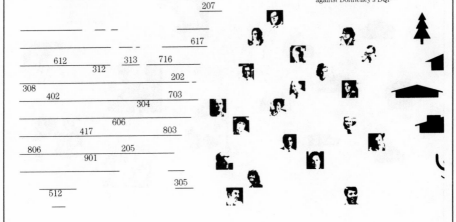

207

617

612   313   716

312   202

308   703

402   304

606

417   803

806   205

901

305

512

Masterfile. To insure maximum deliverability you may combine all three options.

For telemarketing, when you go with Donnelley Marketing, you assure yourself greater telephone number coverage. You're not only getting more telephone numbers, you're getting the most accurate, current telephone numbers available—accumulated from Donnelley Marketing's direct access to more than 4,700 telephone directories nationwide.

For precise targeting, you'll get the finest market segmentation data available from Donnelley Marketing's database resources, including:

- **Census Demographics** —Nearly 100 Key Census Demographics, Proprietary Neighborhood Statistics, 47 CLUSTERPLUS™ lifestyle Classifications and SESI (Socio-Economic Status Indicator)

- **DQI² Masterfile**—considered by direct marketers to be the most comprehensive, accurate, up-to-date consumer database; it provides you with access to information on more than 80 million unduplicated U.S. households—90% of all U.S. households. Constantly updated with data from over 4,700 telephone directories, auto registration files and millions of additional records, DQI² Masterfile represents quality you can rely on...always. Offering such enhancements as family income and purchasing power indicators, age (Head of Household), 23 age and gender related marketing targets, household size, dwelling unit size, length of residence, mail responsiveness, credit card ownership and donors —DQI² is the perfect enhancement resource for household level targeting of product and service offerings with broad appeal.

- **PeopleBank**—exact name, middle initial, gender and birth date information on over 115 million family members. It represents data collected from voter registrations and drivers licenses, as well as other external files. With it identify exactly "who" lives in a household by first name, middle initial, gender and age. PeopleBank lets you target a specific family member within a household—with personalized 'first name" impact that sells via "personally" addressed direct mail, or a "personalized" telemarketing script.

- **Donnelley's Lifestyle Lists**—the ultimate in lifestyle segmentation data. It contains highly specific lifestyle information from more than 16 million mail-responsive homes. With over 125 lifestyle characteristics in all, you can use it to build highly discriminating Lifestyle segmentation models. If specific lifestyle segmentation is the key to your market, Donnelley's Lifestyle File is the enhancement resource for you.

Whatever your application, Donnelley Marketing has the resources to meet your enhancement needs, with the "quality" that's essential to the success of your marketing efforts.

Donnelley
Direct▶▶▶▶

Donnelley Marketing

a company of
The Dun & Bradstreet Corporation

Regional Offices

EASTERN	CENTRAL	WESTERN
70 Seaview Avenue	1901 S. Meyers Road	2401 E. Katella Avenue
P.O. Box 10250	Oakbrook Terrace, IL 60181-5299	Anaheim, CA 92806-5941
Stamford, CT 06904-2250	(312) 495-1211	(714) 978-1122
(203) 353-7000		

ClusterPlus Descriptions

Cluster Code	Demographic Characteristics
S 01	Highest SESI, Highest Income, Prime Real Estate Areas, Highly Educated, Professionally Employed, Low Mobility, Homeowners, Children in Private Schools
S 02	Very High Income, New Homes and Condominiums, Prime Real Estate Areas, Highly Mobile, Well Educated, Professionally Employed, Homeowners, Families with Children
S 03	High Income, High Home Values, New Homes, Highly Mobile, Younger, Well Educated, Professionally Employed, Homeowners, Married Couples, High Incidence of Children, Larger Families
S 04	High Income, High Home Values, Well Educated, Professionally Employed, Married Couples, Larger Families, Highest Incidence of Teenagers, Homeowners, Homes Built in 60's
S 05	High Income, High Home Values, Well Educated, Professionally Employed, Low Mobility, Homeowners, Homes Built in 50's and 60's
S 06	Highest Incidence of Children, Large Families, New Homes, Highly Mobile, Younger, Married Couples, Above Average Income and Education, Homeowners
S 07	Apartments and Condominiums, High Rent, Above Average Income, Well Educated, Professionally Employed, Mobile, Singles, Few Children, Urban Areas
S 08	Above Average Income, Above Average Education, Older, Fewer Children, White Collar Workers
S 09	Above Average Income, Average Education, Households with Two or More Workers, Homes Built in 60's and 70's
S 10	Well Educated, Average Income, Professionally Employed, Younger, Mobile, Apartment Dwellers, Above Average Rents
S 11	Above Average Income, Average Education, Families with Children, High Incidence of Teenagers, Homeowners, Homes Built in 60's, Small Towns
S 12	Highly Mobile, Young, Working Couples, Young Children, New Homes, Above Average Income and Education, White Collar Workers
S 13	Older, Fewer Children, Above Average Income, Average Education, White Collar Workers, Homeowners, Homes Built in 50's, Very Low Mobility, Small Towns
S 14	Retirees, Condominiums and Apartments, Few Children, Above Average Income and Education, Professionally Employed, High Home Values and Rents, Urban Areas
S 15	Older, Very Low Mobility, Fewer Children, Above Average Income and Education, White Collar Workers, Old Housing, Urban Areas
S 16	Working Couples, Very Low Mobility, Above Average Income, Average Education, Homeowners, Homes Built in 50's, Urban Areas
S 17	Very Young, Below Average Income, Well Educated, Professionally Employed, Highly Mobile, Singles, Few Children, Apartment Dwellers, High Rent Areas
S 18	High Incidence of Children, Larger Families, Above Average Income, Average Education, Working Couples, Homeowners

Donnelley
Marketing Information Services   1351 Washington Blvd., Stamford, CT 06902 203-965-5454
CP385

ClusterPlus Descriptions

Cluster Code	Demographic Characteristics
S 19	High Incidence of Children, Larger Families, Above Average Income, Average Education, Younger, Married Couples, Homeowners, Homes Built in 60's and 70's, Primarily Rural Areas
S 20	Areas with High Proportion of Group Quarters Population, Sub-divisions available including College Dormitories, Homes for the Aged, Mental Hospitals and Prisons
S 21	Average Income and Education, Blue Collar Workers, Families with Children, Homeowners, Lower Home Values, Rural Areas
S 22	Below Average Income and Education, Older, Fewer Children, Single Family Homes, Primarily in the South
S 23	Below Average Income, Average Education, Low Mobility, Married Couples, Old Homes, Farm Areas, North Central Region
S 24	Highly Mobile, Young, Few Children, Low Income, Average Education, Ethnic Mix, Singles, Apartments, Urban Areas
S 25	Younger, Mobile, Fewer Children, Below Average Income, Average Education, Apartment Dwellers
S 26	Older, Mobile, Fewer Children, Below Average Income, Average Education, Mobile Homes, Retirees, Higher Vacancy Rates, Primarily Rural Areas
S 27	Average Income and Education, Single Family Homes, Lower Home Values, Homes Built in 50's and 60's
S 28	Below Average Income, Less Educated, Younger, Mobile, High Incidence of Children, Mobile Homes, Primarily Rural Areas
S 29	Older, Low Mobility, High Proportion of Foreign Languages, Average Income, Below Average Education, Old Homes and Apartments, Urban Areas, Northeast Region
S 30	Low Income, Poorly Educated, Higher Vacancy Rates, Families with One Worker, Farms, Rural Areas
S 31	Older, Fewer Children, Low Income, Less Educated, Low Mobility, Retirees, Old Single Family Homes
S 32	Old, Few Children, Low Income, Below Average Education, One-Person Households, Retirees
S 33	Below Average Income, Less Educated, Blue Collar Workers, Manufacturing Plants, Homes Built in 50's and 60's, Very Low Mobility, Low Home Values
S 34	Older, Below Average Income, Average Education, Blue Collar Workers, Low Mobility, Rural Areas
S 35	Old Housing, Low Income, Average Education, Younger, Mobile, Fewer Children, Apartment Dwellers, Small Towns
S 36	Average Income, Less Educated, Blue Collar Workers, Hispanic, Families with Children
S 37	Average Income, Below Average Education, Blue Collar Workers, Manufacturing Areas, High Unemployment, Primarily in the North Central
S 38	Old, Lowest Incidence of Children, Very Low Income, Less Educated, Apartment Dwellers, One-Person Households, Retirees, Urban Areas

Donnelley
Marketing Information Services   1351 Washington Blvd., Stamford, CT 06902 203-965-5454
CP385

ClusterPlus Descriptions

Cluster Code	Demographic Characteristics
S 39	Older, Very Low Mobility, Very Old Housing, Below Average Income and Education, Blue Collar Workers, Manufacturing Areas
S 40	Older, Very Low Income, Less Educated, One-Person Households, Retirees, Few Children, Old Homes and Apartments
S 41	Below Average Income, Less Educated, Blue Collar Workers, Manufacturing Plants, High Unemployment, Rural Areas
S 42	Low Income, Poorly Educated, Low Mobility, Blue Collar Workers, Manufacturing Plants, Rural South
S 43	Southern Blacks, Families with Children, Single Family Homes, Low Mobility, Low Income, Less Educated, Unskilled, High Unemployment
S 44	Urban Blacks, Very Low Income, Less Educated, High Unemployment, Singles, Mobile, Apartment Dwellers, Large Metro Areas
S 45	Urban Blacks, Very Low Income, Less Educated, Unskilled, High Unemployment, Old Housing
S 46	Poorly Educated, Very Low Income, Hispanic, Families with Children, Apartment Dwellers, Unskilled, High Unemployment
S 47	Lowest SESI, Urban Blacks, Very Low Income, Less Educated, Unskilled, Very High Unemployment, High Incidence of Female Householders with Children, Old Housing

Donnelley Marketing Information Services   1351 Washington Blvd., Stamford, CT 06902 203-965-5454
CP385

DONNELLEY MARKETING'S MASTER FILE

DQI^2

DQI^2, the Donnelley Quality Index raised to a higher power, is the largest consumer database available in the private sector.

The DQI^2 database contains information on over 84 million individual households across the country, which accounts for approximately 90% of all U.S. households.

Information for DQI^2 is compiled from two sources:

1. The first is telephone directories. The "Telephone List" is compiled by Don-nelley Marketing from over 4,700 directories. This list, which yields national coverage, is updated daily.

2. The second source of information is official records of state Motor Vehicle Registration departments. This "Auto List" data is currently available in 37 states plus the District of Columbia. Where avaiable, the Auto List is updated annually (twice a year for certain states).

The DQI^2 Master File is actually a merge of all records from the Auto and Telephone lists. Each household record within DQI^2 is identified according to its source or list type.

One such list type is AT, auto and telephone households. These are households that have both a registered car and a listed telephone. They therefore show up on both the Auto List and Telephone List. The match of these two records not only provides more information about the household, but gives double address verification as well.

DQI^2 is set apart from any other residential database by the use of external files to verify the age and sex of household members. Sources of this enrichment data include birth records, lists of children's book buyers, student lists, driver's licenses and voter registration lists. One of the largest sources of such data is Shareforce. Shareforce, a Donnelley Marketing product, is a questionnaire sent out twice a year to approximately 30 to 45 million households. Through this questionnaire, Donnelley obtains information on the respondent's age as well as usage of certain products and interest in various activities.

External files are validated in order to determine the quality of the data before such information is included in DQI^2. It is important to note that these lists are not used to add households to the database; they are simply used to enhance existing data.

The DQI^2 database can serve as a resource for you in two ways:

1. As a means of collecting information on your customers through a household level match.

2. As a source for new prospects that can be identified based on criteria established in the analysis (each record in the DQI^2 file is cluster coded).

DONNELLEY MARKETING RESIDENTIAL DATABASE

Individual Household Characteristics

Telephone Number

Donnelley Household Types

Donnelley households in City Delivery Postal Service (CDS) and non-CDS areas include those with both registered autos and listed phones (Auto and Telephone),
those with only automobiles (Auto Only) and those with only telephones (Telephone
Only).

Estimated Age Score

A statistical estimate of the probable age category for the Head of Household.

Estimated FIND Score

A statistical estimate of the probable income category for each household.

Length of Residence

The length of time that Donnelley Telephone Households have been at their present
address.

Purchasing Power Indicator

A statistical estimate of the probable spending power of each household (based on
household income).

Size of Dwelling

The number of households which reside at a single dwelling unit address ranging from 1 (Single Family) to 100+ (Multi-Family).

Title/Gender of Addressee

The household's sex is determined from the titles found in the Auto Registration and Telephone Directory Lists when available. Otherwise, an analysis of the given name is performed. Categories are Male, Female, and Not Designated.

AUTO DATA

Number of Cars owned
The list of cars registered to each household on the Auto Registration List.

Number of Cylinders
The number of cylinders (4, 5, 6, 8) present in each car owned.

Body Style
The style of each car owned (two-door, four-door, hardtop, convertible, sedan, hatchback, station wagon, jeep).

Model Year
The model year (1987, 1986, etc.) of the newest car among auto owning households.

Price Class
The Detroit price class of the newest car among auto owning households (economy through luxury).

Mean Value of Highest Priced Vehicle
An estimate of the current market value of the most expensive car.

Aggregate Value of the Two Newest Vehicles
An estimate of the current market value of the two newest vehicles.

Pimy-Purchase in Model Year
An indicator that the vehicle was purchased in the model year.

DONNELLEY MARKETING DQI² RESIDENTIAL FILE

AUTO LIST STATES (4/87)

01	ALABAMA	AL
04	ARIZONA	AZ
05	ARKANSAS	AR
06	CALIFORNIA	CA
08	COLORADO	CO
10	DELAWARE	DE
11	DISTRICT OF COLUMBIA	DC
12	FLORIDA	FL
13	GEORGIA	GA
16	IDAHO	ID
17	ILLINOIS	IL
19	IOWA	IA
21	KENTUCKY	KY
22	LOUISIANA	LA
23	MAINE	ME
24	MARYLAND	MD
25	MASSACHUSETTS	MA
26	MICHIGAN	MI
27	MINNESOTA	MN
28	MISSISSIPPI	MS
29	MISSOURI	MO
30	MONTANA	MT
31	NEBRASKA	NE
32	NEVADA	NV
33	NEW HAMPSHIRE	NH
36	NEW YORK	NY
37	NORTH CAROLINA	NC
38	NORTH DAKOTA	ND
39	OHIO	OH
41	OREGON	OR
44	RHODE ISLAND	RI*
45	SOUTH CAROLINA	SC
47	TENNESSEE	TN
48	TEXAS	TX
49	UTAH	UT
50	VERMONT	VT
54	WEST VIRGINIA	WV*
55	WISCONSIN	WI

* Restrictions apply to the data from these states

DONNELLEY MARKETING RESIDENTIAL DATA BASE

AGGREGATE LIST STATISTICS

AGE

AGE MIDPOINT

The midpoint of head of household age scores for Donnelley telephone households.

AUTO

% MULTI-CAR

The percent of Donnelley auto households which own two or more cars.

% LUXURY CARS

The percent of Donnelley auto households which own luxury model cars made during the last four model years.

% LATE MODEL CARS

The percent of Donnelley auto households which own cars made during the last five model years.

% STATION WAGONS

The percent of Donnelley auto households which own station wagons.

% TRUCKS

The percent of Donnelley auto households which own one or more light trucks.

MEAN VALUE OF HIGHEST PRICED VEHICLE

The average value of the highest priced vehicle of the Donnelley auto households.

MEAN VALUE OF THE TWO NEWEST VEHICLES

The average value of the two newest vehicles of the Donnelley auto households.

HOUSING

% SINGLE FAMILY DWELLINGS

The percent of Donnelley telephone households which live in single family dwellings.

% 10+ HOUSING UNITS

The percent of Donnelley telephone households which live in dwellings containing 10 or more units.

INCOME

FIND MIDPOINT

The midpoint of FIND scores for Donnelley auto owning households.

% FIND $35,000+

The percent of Donnelley households which have FIND scores of $35,000 or more.

% FIND $25,000+

The percent of Donnelley households which have FIND scores of $25,000 or more.

MOBILITY

% NEWCOMERS

The percent of Donnelley telephone households which moved to their present address within the last year.

% STABLE HOUSEHOLDS

The percent of Donnelley telephone households which have lived at their present address for more than one year.

% MOVE-INS LAST 5 YEARS

The percent of Donnelley telephone households which moved to their present address within the last five years.

% LENGTH OF RESIDENCE 15+ YEARS

The percent of Donnelley telephone households which have been at their present address for 15 years or more.

LOR MIDPOINT

The midpoint of the length of residence distribution for all Donnelley telephone households.

DONNELLEY MARKETING RESIDENTIAL DATA BASE

SELECTED CENSUS DEMOGRAPHICS

AGE

MEDIAN AGE OF POPULATION

The median age of the total population.

MEDIAN AGE OF POPULATION 18+

The median age of the adult population.

CHILDREN UNDER 6

The number of children under age 6 per 100 households.

CHILDREN 6 - 11

The number of children 6 - 11 per 100 households.

POPULATION 12 - 17

The number of persons age 12 - 17 per 100 households.

FEMALES 12 - 17

The number of females age 12 - 17 per 100 households.

MALES 12 - 17

The number of males age 12 - 17 per 100 households.

FEMALES 18 - 24

The number of females age 18 - 24 per 100 households.

MALES 18 - 24

The number of males age 18 - 24 per 100 households.

FEMALES 25 - 34

The number of females age 25 - 34 per 100 households.

MALES 25 - 34

The number of males age 25 - 34 per 100 households.

FEMALES 35 - 44

The number of females age 35 - 44 per 100 households.

MALES 35 - 44

The number of males age 35 - 44 per 100 households.

FEMALES 45 - 54

The number of females age 45 - 54 per 100 households.

MALES 45 - 54

The number of males age 45 - 54 per 100 households.

POPULATION 55 - 64

The number of persons age 55 - 64 per 100 households.

FEMALES 55 - 64

The number of females age 55 - 64 per 100 households.

MALES 55 - 64

The number of males age 55 - 64 per 100 households.

POPULATION 65+

The number of persons age 65 or older per 100 households.

FEMALES 65+

The number of females age 65 or older per 100 households.

MALES 65+

The number of males age 65 or older per 100 households.

% HOUSEHOLDERS 65+

The percent of householders age 65 or older among all households.

AUTO

% 1980 HOUSEHOLDS WITH 3+ AUTOS

The percent of all households in 1980 that had three or more autos.

% 1980 HOUSEHOLDS WITH 2 AUTOS

The percent of all households in 1980 that had two autos.

% 1980 HOUSEHOLDS WITH 1 AUTO

The percent of all households in 1980 that had one auto.

EDUCATION

MEDIAN SCHOOL YEARS COMPLETED

The median number of years of school completed by all persons age 25 or older.

% COLLEGE EDUCATED

The percent of persons age 25 or older who have completed 4 or more years of college.

% SOME COLLEGE

The percent of persons age 25 or older who have completed one to three years of college.

% HIGH SCHOOL GRADUATES

The percent of persons age 25 or older who have completed high school.

% SOME HIGH SCHOOL EDUCATED

The percent of persons age 25 or older who have completed one to three years of high school.

% ENROLLED IN PRIVATE SCHOOLS

The percent of the population enrolled in school who attend a private or parochial school.

HOUSEHOLD COMPOSITION

MEDIAN HOUSEHOLD SIZE

The median number of persons per household.

MEAN FAMILY SIZE

The average number of persons per family.

% FAMILIES

The percent of families among all households.

% 1 PERSON HOUSEHOLDS

The percent of all households having one member.

% 2 PERSON HOUSEHOLDS

The percent of all households having two members.

% 3+ PERSON HOUSEHOLDS

The percent of all households having three or more members.

% 4+ PERSON HOUSEHOLDS

The percent of all households having four or more members.

% HOUSEHOLDS WITH CHILDREN UNDER 18

The percent of all households which have members under the age of 18.

% MARRIED COUPLES

The percent of all households which have married couples.

% MARRIED COUPLES WITH CHILDREN

The percent of all households having married couples with children under age 18.

% FEMALE HOUSEHOLDERS

The percent of female heads of household among all households.

HOUSING

MEDIAN HOUSING VALUE

The median dollar value of all owner occupied housing units excluding condominiums.

MEDIAN RENT

The median contract rent for all renter occupied dwelling units.

% OWNER OCCUPIED

The percent of all housing units which are owner occupied.

% OWNER OCCUPIED HOUSING VALUED AT $100,000+

The percent of owner occupied housing units (excluding condominiums) valued at $100,000 or more.

% OWNER OCCUPIED HOUSING VALUED UNDER $20,000

The percent of owner occupied housing units (excluding condominiums) valued at less than $20,000.

% HOUSING IN URBAN AREAS

The percent of housing that is in urban areas.

% HOUSING WITH AIR CONDITIONING

The percent of year-round housing units which have air conditioning.

% HOUSING WITH 2+ BATHS

The percent of occupied housing units which have 2 or more baths.

% HOUSING WITH 6+ ROOMS

The percent of all year-round housing units that have six or more rooms.

% HOUSING WITH 1.01+ PERSONS PER ROOM

The percent of all occupied housing units that have 1.01 or more persons per room.

% TOTAL OCCUPIED BUILT 1970-80

The percent of all occupied housing units which were built between 1970 and March 1980.

% TOTAL OCCUPIED BUILT PRE-1940

The percent of all occupied housing units which were built before 1940.

% OWNER OCCUPIED BUILT 1975-80

The percent of occupied housing units which were built between 1975 and 1980 and which are owner occupied.

% OWNER OCCUPIED BUILT 1960-74

The percent of owner occupied housing units which were built between 1960 and 1974.

% OWNER OCCUPIED BUILT 1940-59

The percent of owner occupied housing units which were built between 1940 and 1959.

% OWNER OCCUPIED BUILT PRE-1940

The percent of occupied housing units which were built before 1940 and which are owner occupied.

% MOBILE HOME/TRAILER

The percent of all year-round housing units that are mobile homes or trailers.

% VACANT HOUSING

The percent of all year-round housing units that are vacant.

% 1980 HOUSING WITH 1 UNIT

The percent of 1980 year-round housing units that are single family dwellings.

% 1980 HOUSING WITH 10+ UNITS

The percent of 1980 year-round housing units that are 10 or more units.

INCOME

MEDIAN HOUSEHOLD INCOME

The median income of all households in 1979.

MEDIAN FAMILY INCOME

The median income of all families in 1979.

% HOUSEHOLDS WITH INCOMES OF $50,000+

The percent of all households which had 1979 incomes of $50,000 or more.

% HOUSEHOLDS WITH INCOMES OF $40,000+

The percent of all households which had 1979 incomes of $40,000 or more.

% HOUSEHOLDS WITH INCOMES OF $25,000+

The percent of all households which had 1979 incomes of $25,000 or more.

% HOUSEHOLDS WITH INCOMES UNDER $10,000

The percent of all households which had 1979 incomes of $9,999 or less.

% HOUSEHOLDS WITH INCOMES UNDER $7,500

The percent of all households which had 1979 incomes of $7,499 or less.

% HOUSEHOLDS WITH PUBLIC ASSISTANCE INCOME

The percent of all households with Public Assistance income in 1979.

% PERSONS WITH POVERTY STATUS

The percent of all persons at or below poverty status.

MOBILITY

% MOVE-INS 1975-1980

The percent of occupied housing units which were moved into between 1975 and 1980.

R·L·POLK & CO.

January, 1989

II. **X-1**

A. General

From the beginning, X-1 was designed to be a growing, highly dynamic
list which would be in a constant state of improvement.

Our objectives for maximum coverage, accuracy, deliverability, and
selectivity could only be met through a crossing of many sources of:
- names and addresses;
- demographic and behavioral information about individuals and
  households;
- and demographic information about small geographical areas.

Introduced in 1973 with these objectives, X-1 started as a merger of
only three lists. Today, it is the product of crossing 22 sources of
important information six times a year!

B. Sources

As of January, 1989, X-1 contained 79,278,000 households addressable
by name--87.1% of the 91,066,000 total households in the United
States.[1]

It also contained an additional 7,821,000 households addressable
RESIDENT for a total of 87,099,000 deliverable addresses--95.6% of
total U.S. households.

---

(1) U.S. household count is as of March, 1988. Source is Households,
     Families, Marital Status, And Living Arrangements, U.S. Department of
     Commerce, Bureau of the Census, Current Population Reports, Series
     P-20 No. 432, September, 1988.

This list is the result of merging over one billion records annually from the following 22 sources.

Polk's List X-1
Sources & Counts

| | | Number Of HH In X-1 (000) With: | |
	Annual Record Input (M)	Names/Addresses And Selection Data From:	Selection Data Coding Only From:
1. Current Automobile	103,358	45,978	
2. Current Truck	17,010	11,330	
3. Current Recreational Vehicle	7,645	5,287	
4. Current Motorcycle	3,002	2,281	
5. Current Monthly New Car Buyers	6,000/Yr.	5,400/Yr.	
6. Current Monthly New Truck Buyers	2,600/Yr.	2,340/Yr.	
7. Household Census List (HCL)	23,000	19,533	
8. Telephone List	65,583	49,001	
9. Last Available Automobile	3,545		3,545
10. Last Available Truck	657		657
11. Last Available Rec. Vehicle	185		185
12. Last Available Motorcycle	136		136
13. New Car Buyers (Back to '64)	21,640		21,640
14. New Truck Buyers (Back to '68)	8,365		8,365
15. Birth, High School, College Info.	53,400		14,992
16. Mail Response Coding 1/	63,823		35,318
17. Mail Responder/Buyer/Donor Coding 1/	40,000		30,380
18. Adult Birthdate Information	240,000		43,059
19. Questionnaire Data	27,725		15,403
20. Credit Card Users	140,000		35,202
21. Homeowners	52,400		24,046
22. NDL Demographic	149,400		12,984
	1,029,474	141,150	245,912

X-1 non-duplicating households addressable by name
as of January, 1989 79,278,000

Additional households addressable RESIDENT 7,821,000

Total non-duplicating, mailable addresses 87,099,000

Percent of total U.S. households (91,066,000) 95.6

1/ The use of the Mail Response data in Item 16 is restricted to the contributing suppliers. The Mail Responder/Buyer/Donor data in Item 17 may be used by anyone.

- 3 -

Note that sources 1 through 8 supply both names/addresses and
selection data while the other sources provide selection data only
and confirmation of continued residence at the last known address.
For example, in a state which no longer permits the use of the
automobile list for mail, selection data for a particular household
from the last available automobile list is kept only if the household
to which it applies is still at the same address as demonstrated by
its presence on a current list.

The sources are merged in six updates per year. Households input
in one update may be eliminated in the next one due to more recent
information. Of course, most of the name input in each update
duplicate with ones already there--merely adding new or additional
selection data and reconfirming from later sources the fact the
households are still at the address shown.

Each of the list sources has its own strengths and weaknesses.
X-1 goes further in combining their strengths and minimizing their
weaknesses than any other list compilation ever undertaken.

C. Accuracy

The most important of our objectives in maintaining X-1 is to make it
the most accurate mass list compiled.

Accuracy refers to all of the elements of the name and address, the
selection factors available, and especially the deliverability of the
list.

For each element in the X-1 record, such as title, first name, middle
initial, last name, house number, apartment number, street spelling,
and street directionals, among many others, a list source priority has
been established.

- 4 -

That is, each list is rated in terms of its reliability on each element. X-1 chooses those elements from each list which will make the record more complete and more accurate. Thus, if Telephone List input to X-1 shows R. S. Far<u>mer</u> at 132 Brookside and input from the Household Census List (which is compiled from Polk's City Directories) shows <u>Robert</u> S. Far<u>men</u> at 132 Brookside <u>Dr.</u>, <u>Apt. C</u>, X-1 will select "<u>Robert</u>" from the HCL for the first name and "<u>Dr.</u>" and "<u>Apt. C</u>" from the address, but will retain the last name spelling (Far<u>mer</u>) from the Telephone List since that source is more likely to be accurate on that element.

This improvement, in turn, permits us to infer from the first name that Farmer is a male householder rather than of unknown sex as was the case when only first initial was known. It also permits a more complete address by adding the suffix "Dr." and by adding "Apt. C".

In both the Auto List and Telephone List compilations, if only one surname appears at an address without an apartment number, we infer that it is a single dwelling unit. The HCL does not depend simply on inference. It supplies apartment numbers in far more cases than any other list.

In addition to accuracy and completeness, the inclusion of other list input permits the development of a <u>more deliverable</u> list since each input record is dated according to the month the data was known to be accurate. Thus, in single dwelling units, the <u>latest</u> information is substituted when there is a conflict.

Example:

J. P. Eck 125 Main St.	is a 1/88 telephone listing in a single dwelling
Raymond A. Donald 125 Main St.	is a 4/88 HCL listing input to X-1. HCL confirms the address is a single dwelling unit. Eck is deleted and Donald added to X-1. This updating would not have occurred on the Telephone List until 1989--nearly a whole year later!

- 5 -

In multiple dwelling units, the update process requires further rules, other than freshness, to avoid allowing the apartment building to grow inordinately with input from each input source.

When a later source for an individual record validates an earlier one, the new validation date is substituted. This feature makes it possible to specify, on a name-by-name basis, a date beyond which no names are to be selected.

This is an extremely important point. No longer must otherwise qualified names be passed over for selection simply because the date of the source list as a whole is too old. Now all such names can be selected which have an acceptable validation date furnished by another source.

For example, one might want to select certain households from the Telephone List provided the issue date of the directory was not over twelve months old. This precludes selections from many directories. With List X-1 you may specify those households for selection which have an individual validation date of twelve months or less. Why not select a name from a 14-month old directory if, within the past two months, the Monthly New Car Buyers List confirms that name is still at the same address?

Another extremely important point with respect to deliverability is the number of lists on which a name appears. Here are five case histories bearing on that subject:

| | Cards To USPS For Correction | | "Address Correction Requested" | Response Rates To Mailings | | Overall Average |
	1	2	3	4	5	
Total List	100	100	100	100	100	100
1 Source	78	82	90	77	70	79
2 Sources	104	102	102	103	99	102
3 Sources	112	113	107	123	129	117
4 Sources	124	119	109	117	135	121

X-1

Column 1 is read as follows: 1-source names were only 78% as correct as the total list; 2-source names were 4% better; 3-source names, 12% better; and 4-source names, 24% better than the total list.

Column 5 is read as follows: 1-source names pulled only 70% as many orders as the total list; 2-source names pulled 99% as many; 3-source names, 29% more orders; and 4-source names, 35% more orders than the total list.

- 6 -

In considering why the 1-source names were relatively so poor, one must understand that, by the very nature of the compilation process, the unique names and addresses from each source list survive in X-1.

Thus, a name from a 20-month old directory unconfirmed by another list will be found in X-1 with a 20-month validation date. However, all names not validated within 24 months of updating are automatically deleted from X-1.

The way to improve the deliverability of 1-source names is to specify a validation date beyond which a name is not to be selected or to address those households on a "Resident" basis (possible mainly for CDS addresses). This date can vary based on the mobility of the class selected.

For example:

> Because the mobility rate of retired people is quite low and that of laborers is quite high, one might specify that all retired persons be selected with a validation date of 24 months or less and all laborers be selected with a validation date of 9 months or less.

Deliverability of X-1 is further improved by applying to it the NCOA (National Change of Address) system. Being an NCOA licensee, Polk receives all the moves and address changes reported to the U.S. Postal Service. That file, enhanced twice a month by new moves and address changes, now has over 68 million records. Each month the entire file is passed against X-1 and where the new address for a moved household is known, the X-1 record is updated accordingly. In cases where a move has been reported but the new address is not known, the household record is removed from the list. At this time over 30 characteristics (date and distance of last move are two examples) of households involved in a move are placed in the record.

These are but a few examples of the way X-1 operates to make a more complete, accurate, and deliverable list.

D. Selectivity

There are three types of selectivity in X-1:

    1. Inherent
    2. Geographic
    3. Individual

1. Inherent

    This refers to the selectivity inherent by virtue of merely being
    on a certain list. If you are selling automobile insurance, the
    Automobile List inherently "selects" your market. The Phone or
    Household Census Lists do not because they both include non-car
    owners.

    The Phone, New Car Buyer, and Auto Lists have important inherent
    selectivity. For all practical purposes, the HCL has none since
    it covers everyone in the directory canvass area.

2. Geographical

    X-1 is subject to selection by:

        a. state;
        b. postal sectional center;
        c. county;
        d. zip code (basic + Zip + 4);
        e. 1980 Census tracts (where they exist);
        f. 1980 Census block groups (where they exist);
        g. 1980 Census enumeration districts (in many places);
        h. USPS carrier routes.

For those various units, a wealth of demographic data is
available. For example, for Census units, twelve demographic
factors are actually coded in the list, such as median income,
median school years completed, percent owner-occupied dwellings,
percent white population, etc. Besides those coded in the list
itself, 291 additional factors are available for use if it
appears they might be useful.

3. Individual

X-1 combines the individual selection factors available on each
source list.

Although X-1 is, by far, the most selective mass list ever
compiled, the full range of selectivity is not present for each
name. This is so because not all names are present on all input
lists. The principal factors and their sources are listed on
the next page.

23 OF THE MOST IMPORTANT INDIVIDUAL HOUSEHOLD SELECTION FACTORS IN X-1

	DERIVED FROM THESE LISTS:				
	HCL	Vehicle	Phone	New Vehicle	Other
1. Household income estimate	X	X		X	X
2. Sex of head of household	X	X	X	X	X
3. Type of dwelling unit (single or multiple)	X	X	X		
4. Month/Year of birth					X
5. Marital status	X				X
6. Home owner	X				X
7. Number of children under 18	X				X
8. Number of persons employed	X				
9. Number of persons in household	X				X
10. Occupation of head of household	X				X
11. Spouse's name	X	X			X
12. Birth, high school, college information					X
13. Mail responsive household					X
14. Length of residence	X	X	X		
15. Possession of telephone; telephone number.	X		X		
16. Credit card user					X
17. Year model, make, body style of up to 3 cars owned, plus number of cars owned up to 6		X			
18. Year model, make, body style of up to 2 trucks or RV's and motorcycles owned, plus number of motorcycles owned up to 4		X			
19. Current market value of vehicles owned (CMVI)		X		X	
20. Number of cars purchased new since 1964 with detail on most recent 4				X	
21. Number of new trucks or RV's purchased since 1968 with detail on most recent 4				X	
22. Move data					X
23. Ethnic and religious coding					X

- 10 -

E. Updating

X-1 is updated on a state-by-state basis six times a year. It is,
therefore, a highly dynamic list.

Bear in mind that there are 22 lists which are regularly input to
X-1. The compilation procedure has been designed to capitalize on the
strengths of each list and minimize its weaknesses.

F. Coverage

X-1 is the largest name/address list available because of the number
and size of the sources used to compile it. The Telephone List, for
example, is one of the larger lists put into X-1. Yet the Automobile
List, another X-1 input list, is 19% larger than the Telephone List in
states where it can be used for direct mail advertising. Polk's
Household Census List, a third input list, provides virtually 100%
coverage in areas where it is compiled.

To illustrate how this extended coverage is achieved, here are the
household counts for the Telephone List, Automobile List, and
Household Census List <u>before</u> being input into X-1 and the resulting
counts in X-1 <u>after</u> the merger in six markets[1] where all three
lists are used to compile X-1:

HOUSEHOLDS IN THE TELEPHONE, AUTOMOBILE, HOUSEHOLD CENSUS, AND X-1 LISTS

	MFDU'S				
List	Apt. # Avail.	No Apt. \#	Total MFDU's	SFDU's	Total HH
Telephone	12,941	465,270	478,211	1,346,652	1,824,863
Automobile	229,843	430,360	660,203	1,435,932	2,096,135
Household Census	343,617	128,964	472,581	1,016,086	1,488,667
X-1	367,979	304,001	671,980	1,754,097	2,426,077

1/ Atlanta (Georgia), Peoria (Illinois), Providence-Pawtucket-Woonsocket
(Rhode Island), Salt Lake City-Ogden (Utah), Santa Barbara-Santa
Maria-Lompoc (California), and Tampa-St. Petersburg-Clearwater (Florida).

- 11 -

<u>X-1 has more total households than any of the three contributing lists</u>. This holds true in both multiple family dwelling units and single family dwelling units and in all areas of the country.

Note also the enormous difference between X-1 and the Telephone List in the availability of apartment numbers in multi-family dwelling units. The presence of so many more apartment numbers is another plus in the superior deliverability power of X-1.

However, we do not play a simple "numbers" game in producing X-1. Our goal is not only to produce the <u>largest</u> list, but also to produce the <u>cleanest</u> list. On that account extensive procedures are used to identify and remove duplicating households and undeliverable addresses--the latest procedure instituted being the application of the NCOA system.

In addition to the household head addressable by name, X-1 has the given names of millions of other household members. It has more spouses' names by far than any other list because we have more sources for that information.

    The next page shows:

- the latest state counts of <u>households</u> addressable by name;

- which states do and do not permit the use of the Motor Vehicle List for non-auto related purposes.

- 12 -

X-1 TOTAL HOUSEHOLDS AS OF JANUARY, 1989

State	Motor Vehicle List Usable For Non-Auto Related Purposes		X-1 Household Count
	Yes	No	
Alabama	X		1,413,000
Alaska		X	97,000
Arizona	X		1,132,000
Arkansas		X	626,000
California	X		8,376,000
Colorado	X		1,209,000
Connecticut		X	941,000
Delaware	X		241,000
D.C.	X		179,000
Florida	X		4,799,000
Georgia		X	1,615,000
Hawaii		X	227,000
Idaho	X		353,000
Illinois	X		3,893,000
Indiana		X	1,543,000
Iowa	X		1,090,000
Kansas		X	801,000
Kentucky	X		1,235,000
Louisiana	X		1,355,000
Maine	X		470,000
Maryland	X		1,579,000
Massachusetts	X		2,218,000
Michigan	X		3,178,000
Minnesota	X		1,654,000
Mississippi	X		813,000
Missouri	X		1,867,000
Montana	X		293,000
Nebraska	X		565,000
Nevada	X		332,000
New Hampshire	X		429,000
New Jersey		X	1,759,000
New Mexico		X	355,000
New York	X		5,685,000
North Carolina	X		2,321,000
North Dakota	X		235,000
Ohio	X		3,934,000
Oklahoma		X	885,000
Oregon	X		1,022,000
Pennsylvania		X	3,283,000
Rhode Island		X	323,000
South Carolina	X		1,151,000
South Dakota	X		195,000
Tennessee	X		1,763,000
Texas	X		5,557,000
Utah	X		512,000
Vermont	X		195,000
Virginia		X	1,622,000
Washington		X	1,381,000
West Virginia	X		637,000
Wisconsin	X		1,794,000
Wyoming		X	146,000
U. S. Total--name addressable			79,278,000
Additional households addressable RESIDENT			7,821,000
X-1 TOTAL			87,099,000

- 13 -

BUSINESS DATA

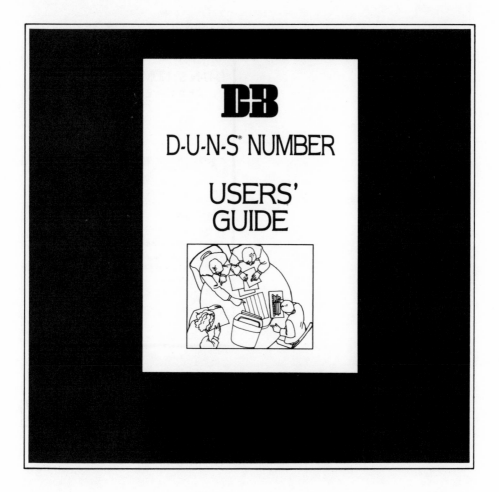

D·U·N·S® NUMBER
. . . At a Glance

- Uniquely Identifies Business Establishments
- Assigned And Maintained By Dun & Bradstreet
- Provides Common Identification Standards For Data Communication And Interchange
- International In Scope
- Non-indicative Nine-Digit Number
- Modulus Ten Check Digit
- Unique D-U-N-S Number Affixed to Different Units and Locations
- Linkage Maintained Between Related Companies Of An Organizational "Family"
- ANSI x .12 Identification Code Qualifier

1

DATA UNIVERSAL NUMBERING SYSTEM (D-U-N-S˚)

(Example: 00-194-7308)

HISTORY

In 1841 Dun & Bradstreet was founded—and with it, the business information industry. Almost 150 years later, D & B is still the preeminent marketer of business information.

For the first 120 years, D & B traditionally collected and manually stored business information on paper. As the need for business information grew, the increase of paper files became explosive.

DEVELOPMENT OF D-U-N-S

The establishment of the Data Universal Numbering System (D-U-N-S) in 1962 signified D & B's move into the computer era. This method enabled D & B to easily identify each business within our data base by assigning a specific and unique number to each case. Today, the D-U-N-S Number is recognized worldwide as a business identification standard.

WHAT IS A D-U-N-S NUMBER?

A **D-U-N-S Number** is a randomly generated nine-digit number assigned by Dun & Bradstreet to identify unique business establishments. Digits 1 through 8 are machine-generated and assigned. The 9th digit is a *check digit.*

WHY USE A CHECK DIGIT?

This distinguishing feature is built into the D-U-N-S Number to catch input errors. The ninth digit of the D-U-N-S Number is a *Modulus Ten Check Digit.* The check digit prevents nearly 98% of all single transposition errors.

MOD 10 Calculation
00-194-7308

This is a D-U-N-S Number assigned by Dun & Bradstreet. The ninth digit (the ''8'' in the example) is the check digit. The combination of digits used to check the number is:

$$1\ 2\ 1\ 2\ 1\ 2\ 1\ 2$$

In order to calculate the ninth digit, place the D-U-N-S Number—**without** check digit—directly above the checking combination as shown below. Then multiply each upper digit by the digit below it.

0	0	1	9	4	7	3	0
x1	x2	x1	x2	x1	x2	x1	x2

$$0+\ \ 0+\ \ 1+1+8+\ \ 4+1+4+\ \ 3+\ \ 0\ = 22$$

Add the digits, treating each one as a separate number (i.e., 18 becomes 1 and 8). In this example, the total is 22. Subtract this total—22—from the next highest multiple of 10 (i.e., 30 in this case).

$$30 - 22 = 8$$
$$8 = \text{check digit}$$

This matches the ninth digit in the given D-U-N-S Number 00-194-7308; therefore, the number is valid.

WHAT DOES THE D-U-N-S NUMBER TELL ME?

The D-U-N-S Number is the key to identifying information concerning a specific business establishment, enabling you to access data within the D & B file. It does **not** indicate information or signal changes of name, address, line of business, size, linkage, etc.

2

WHO IS ELIGIBLE FOR A D-U-N-S NUMBER?

Any business location with a unique, separate and distinct operation. Each D-U-N-S Number differs from any other related or non-related business which may or may not be at the same location.

For example: When a branch operates from the same location as its headquarters, each distinct operation may be assigned a separate D-U-N-S Number.

Headquarters	Branch
XYZ Inc.	XYZ Inc.
10 Main St.	10 Main St.
Anytown, US	Anytown, US
D-U-N-S Number:	D-U-N-S Number:
12-345-6782	01-234-5674
Line of Business:	Line of Business:
Corporate Headquarters	Manufacturing Division

A D-U-N-S Number will not be assigned to departments at the same location (i.e., XYZ accounting department or XYZ personnel department).

WHO ASSIGNS A D-U-N-S NUMBER?

The Data Universal Number System (D-U-N-S) is assigned and maintained by Dun & Bradstreet Information Resources, a division of the Dun & Bradstreet Corporation. The United States D-U-N-S Number File contains over 11 million D-U-N-S Number assignments. Dun & Bradstreet maintains marketing and credit information which can be purchased by our customers on most of the D-U-N-S Numbers assigned.

Dun & Bradstreet also maintains and assigns D-U-N-S Numbers outside the United States. Total international D-U-N-S Numbers exceed 6 million.

WHEN IS A D-U-N-S NUMBER ASSIGNED?

A D-U-N-S Number is assigned to identify data on a specific business, upon entry into the Dun & Bradstreet Business Information File. Unique D-U-N-S Numbers are assigned to different units and locations of businesses such as branches, headquarters, manufacturing plants, etc.

WHAT DOES A D-U-N-S NUMBER COST?

There is no charge for a D-U-N-S Number assignment for your establishment. However, many D & B customers do purchase services to look up the D-U-N-S Number to maintain their customer files, or to obtain additional information on a company (such as Family Tree Linkage — see p.7).

GUIDELINES FOR ASSIGNMENT AND MAINTENANCE

D-U-N-S Numbers are assigned to all business establishments which have data entered into Dun & Bradstreet's Business Information File. This list also includes individuals who are self-employed such as doctors, lawyers, contractors, etc. D-U-N-S Numbers are only assigned to individuals who are engaged in a specific business activity.

Each company location in our file (i.e., proprietorship, corporation, partnership, government body, etc.) is assigned a unique D-U-N-S Number. Unique D-U-N-S Numbers are also assigned to secondary locations (i.e., branches, divisions). By "linking" D-U-N-S Numbers of related companies, "families" of D-U-N-S Numbers can be identified within the data base. This type of linked data is obtained through various D & B products and services.

3

D-U-N-S NUMBER STATISTICS– UNITED STATES

D-U-N-S NUMBERS IN FILE	11,300,000+
FAMILY TREE MEMBERS	1,200,000+
BRANCHES/DIVISIONS	658,000+
SUBSIDIARIES	118,000+
TOTAL FAMILY TREES	215,000+
(ULTIMATE D-U-N-S NUMBERS)	

RELOCATIONS

If a business relocates, the D-U-N-S Number remains the same. If a move is the result of a merger or consolidation of locations — thus eliminating one or more separate business entities — only one D-U-N-S Number survives. The surviving D-U-N-S Number will, in most cases, be the oldest D-U-N-S (first assigned), or in the event of a merger, the D-U-N-S Number of the dominant company in that merger. If the headquarters moves to an existing branch location and operational functions of the branch cease to be separate and unique, the D-U-N-S Number of the headquarters is retained and the D-U-N-S Number of the former branch is eliminated.

CONTROL CHANGES

If a business is sold — or the controlling interest of a business changes while maintaining the same line of business — the original D-U-N-S Number is retained.

DISCONTINUANCES

If a business discontinues operations without a successor, the D-U-N-S Number is discontinued and will not be reissued or reassigned unless the business reopens.

4

THE D-U-N-S NUMBER AND ITS VALUE TO YOU
...Within Dun and Bradstreet

Dun and Bradstreet's various divisions offer many different products and services based on the data obtained through the D-U-N-S Number. This information will assist you in building your data base and maintaining your credit, marketing or vendor files:

Business Name	Business History
Street Address	Operations
Mailing Address	Antecedents *(see box)*
Telephone Number	Payment Experiences *(see box)*
Number of Employees	Public Filings *(see box)*
Line of Business	Bank Experiences
Financial Data	Branch Information
Parent/Headquarters	

antecedent — a description of the experience and background of the business owners, officers, partners or managers. Generally, details are from the age of 21 to present.

payment experiences — a record indicating the paying habits of a given business.

public filings — suits, liens and/or judgments which have been publicly filed within the city, state or local courthouse.

roll-up — the ability to aggregate data on members within one family tree through existing linkage.

...Internally/Within Your Organization

The D-U-N-S Number can be used to "link" your customer or vendor files together to identify duplicates within your data base or to "roll-up" *(see box)* or aggregate data on various divisions within a large corporation. Linkage (see p.7) and D-U-N-S Investigation (see p.6) are services which most directly relate to the Data Universal Numbering System.

...Your Customers

By reviewing Family Tree Linkage and identifying additional branch or subsidiary locations, you may be able to expand your marketing share within a specific corporation.

The D-U-N-S Number will also assist you in adopting applications such as EDI (Electronic Data Interchange, see p.12).

5

D·U·N·S INVESTIGATION

Some companies desire the D·U·N·S Number, Family Tree Linkage and limited business data on every account in their file. D·U·N·S Investigation is a service designed to fulfill this need.

A feature within D·U·N·S Investigation is the ability for a customer to have a D·U·N·S Number assigned immediately over the telephone by Dun and Bradstreet on all accounts eligible for D·U·N·S Number assignment.

With D·U·N·S Investigation, D & B conducts a limited telephone and/or mail investigation on requested customer accounts which are not already listed in the D & B file. A D·U·N·S Number is then assigned and the case is entered into the file with any additional information obtained.

6

LINKAGE

Since each unit or location of a business may have its own unique D-U-N-S Number, a large organization or company may have many different D-U-N-S Numbers within its corporate "family".

Dun & Bradstreet maintains linkage through the use of the D-U-N-S Number to easily identify "intra-family" relationships.

To better understand the possible relationships between companies, the following definitions will be useful.

SINGLE LOCATION

A business entity which has no other unique D-U-N-S Number or location relating to it.

HEADQUARTERS

A business entity which has at least one branch reporting to it. When a business has multiple branch locations, the designated headquarters' location is determined by the controlling management of the business.

BRANCH

A secondary location for which the headquarters has legal responsibility. Typically, a branch is at a separate location. However, a branch can be located together with its headquarters or sister branch, provided they have unique, separate, and distinct operations. Branches often have secondary names or trade styles under which they operate their business. Yet, the primary branch name must always be the same as the primary name of the headquarters. For example:

Headquarters' Name: ABC Company, INC.
Branch Name: ABC Company, INC.
Branch Trade Name: ABC Wholesale

DIVISION

A separate and unique operating unit of a business entity with a divisional name, performing a specific activity. The legal status of the division determines whether it is treated as a trade style, separate branch or subsidiary.

LOCK BOX

A lock box is a specific post office box designated for remittances--not to be confused with post office boxes used only for general mailing purposes. A lock box is eligible for unique D-U-N-S Number assignment and will relate back to its headquarters. A post office box used only for mailing purposes usually does not warrant separate assignment of a unique D-U-N-S Number.

PARENT

A business entity with controlling interest in another company through ownership of a majority (more than 50%) of its voting stock.

SUBSIDIARY

A corporation with more than 50% of its voting stock owned by another business.

TRADE STYLE

Not to be confused with a branch, a trade style is an additional name used by a business for advertising and/or buying purposes. A trade style alone does not warrant a unique D-U-N-S Number assignment.

7

HOW LINKAGE WORKS

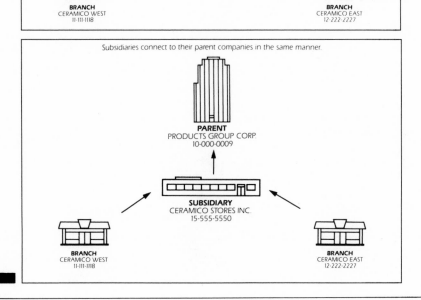

Branches, divisions and lock boxes are linked to their respective headquarters by carrying both their own D-U-N-S Numbers and that of the upward (next higher) related case within their families.

HEADQUARTERS
CERAMICO STORES INC.
15-555-5550

BRANCH
CERAMICO WEST
11-111-1118

BRANCH
CERAMICO EAST
12-222-2227

Subsidiaries connect to their parent companies in the same manner.

PARENT
PRODUCTS GROUP CORP.
10-000-0009

SUBSIDIARY
CERAMICO STORES INC.
15-555-5550

BRANCH
CERAMICO WEST
11-111-1118

BRANCH
CERAMICO EAST
12-222-2227

8

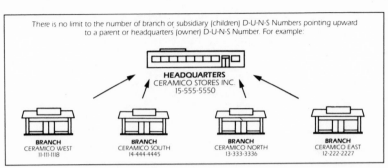

There is no limit to the number of branch or subsidiary (children) D-U-N-S Numbers pointing upward to a parent or headquarters (owner) D-U-N-S Number. For example:

HEADQUARTERS
CERAMICO STORES INC.
15-555-5550

BRANCH
CERAMICO WEST
11-111-1118

BRANCH
CERAMICO SOUTH
14-444-4445

BRANCH
CERAMICO NORTH
13-333-3336

BRANCH
CERAMICO EAST
12-222-2227

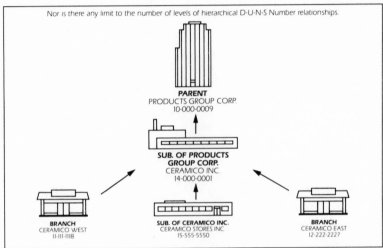

Nor is there any limit to the number of levels of hierarchical D-U-N-S Number relationships.

PARENT
PRODUCTS GROUP CORP.
10-000-0009

SUB. OF PRODUCTS GROUP CORP.
CERAMICO INC.
14-000-0001

BRANCH
CERAMICO WEST
11-111-1118

SUB. OF CERAMICO INC.
CERAMICO STORES INC.
15-555-5550

BRANCH
CERAMICO EAST
12-222-2227

9

The topmost company of a hierarchical relationship of D-U-N-S
Numbers is referred to as the ULTIMATE D-U-N-S Number.

ULTIMATE D-U-N-S

**The uppermost headquarters or parent D-U-N-S Number which
encompasses all directly related branches, subsidiaries or parents
of a specific business.**

This chaining technique and the Ultimate D-U-N-S Number allow
a user to identify and group entities within an organization.

	UNIQUE D-U-N-S NUMBER	HDQTRS D-U-N-S NUMBER	ULTIMATE D-U-N-S NUMBER
PRODUCTS GROUP CORP.	10-000-0009	10-000-0009	10-000-0009
CLAYCO INC.	12-000-0005	10-000-0009	10-000-0009
CLAYCO STORAGE DIV.	17-000-0004	12-000-0005	10-000-0009
CLAYCO REFINERY DIV.	18-000-0002	12-000-0005	10-000-0009
GLAZECO INC.	13-000-0003	10-000-0009	10-000-0009
GLAZECO STORAGE DIV.	19-000-0000	13-000-0003	10-000-0009
GLAZECO REFINERY DIV.	11-100-0007	13-000-0003	10-000-0009
CERAMICO INC.	14-000-0001	10-000-0009	10-000-0009
INDUSTERAMICO DIV.	15-000-0008	14-000-0001	10-000-0009
BUILDERAMICO DIV.	16-000-0006	14-000-0001	10-000-0009
CERAMICO STORES INC.	15-555-5550	14-000-0001	10-000-0009
CERAMICS EAST	12-222-2227	15-555-5550	10-000-0009
CERAMICS WEST	11-111-1118	15-555-5550	10-000-0009
CERAMICS NORTH	13-333-3336	15-555-5550	10-000-0009
CERAMICS SOUTH	14-444-4445	15-555-5550	10-000-0009

10

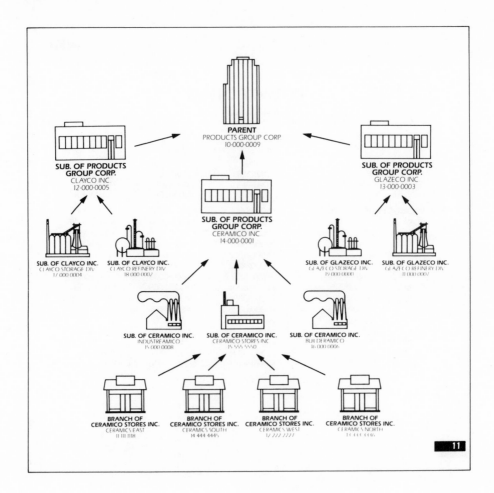

DMI DIRECT

DMI Direct is the core of the Dun's Direct interactive database information system, designed specifically for the business-to-business direct marketer.

Built on the proven Dun's Market Identifiers® (DMI) database, DMI Direct gives you access to essential marketing facts and figures on more than 8 million businesses and professionals.

DMI Direct is your most direct route to the CEO's and key decision-makers who are the most vital targets for your promotions and sales calls. You select the business criteria that best define your marketplace, according to *your* objectives, *your* marketing strategies.

Each of these more than 20 vital direct marketing selections is compiled by more than 2,000 business analysts, who call or visit thousands of locations every day.

The result? A highly targetable 3- or 4-line compiled list that sets the standards for accuracy and deliverability.

Target your high-quality prospects by your criteria.

DMI Direct gives you the utmost flexibility in pinpointing your best targets according to the criteria you select. Here are some of the criteria at your disposal:

- DUNS Number
- Geographic Codes
- Line of Business
- Year Started
- Sales Volume
- Parent and Headquarters
- Employee Size
- 5th-Digit SIC Code
- Population Code
- Status Indicators
- Names of Chief Executives
- And more. Much more.

With criteria as these, you can identify the people and businesses most likely to respond to your mail.

The data contained in DMI Direct is available in a variety of formats. You can order pressure-sensitive and cheshire labels; magnetic tape from which your lettershop can create personalized mail; or floppy disk—the perfect tool for in-house evaluation of your market, prospects, and for limited, controlled mailings.

For more information, call your Dun's Marketing Account Executive.

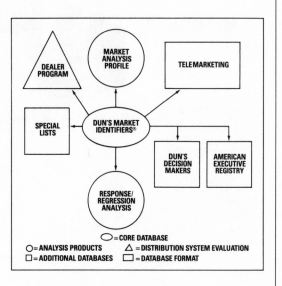

Dun's Marketing Services

a company of
The Dun & Bradstreet Corporation

DMID0488
10M

Dun's® File of Executive Women

What has a population greater than 31 of the 157 countries in the United Nations or 15 of the 50 states in the USA?

Dun's File of Executive Women— population 1,830,286!

Who is this woman executive?

She's dynamic. She's here now. She's in all lines and sizes of business. AND she makes *buying decisions* on all types of products—*your* products.

In fact, 549,557 of the executive women included in this extraordinary Dun's file have the title of Chairperson, President, Partner or Owner. These women are key decision-makers throughout the whole wide world of business.

Several of the 29 available titles are outlined below to give you a flavor of this thoroughly contemporary file.

Title	Number of Executive Women
Owner	167,034
Partner	236,949
Chairperson	5,727
President	139,847
Vice President	177,279
Secretary	574,953
Treasurer	417,254

Industry	Percentage of File of Executive Women
Agriculture	1.7%
Mining	.7%
Construction	10.5%
Manufacturing	11.0%
Transportation, Communications and Public Utilities	3.6%
Wholesale	12.1%
Retail	35.0%
Finance, Insurance and Real Estate	6.8%
Business Services	13.2%
Health, Social Services and Public Administration	5.2%

Statistics that translate into opportunity.

If your product or service is targeted specifically for the executive woman, then this matchless Dun's File is— without question—for *you*. It can put you in touch with 1.8 million prospective buyers with a business perspective—as well as the interests of the female consumer who also manages her own home and, quite possibly, her own family.

On the other hand, if your product or service has been marketed—up to now —to both male and female executives, you can now segment the "executive woman" for special offers. Or design a more personalized campaign to create product awareness among this dynamic audience that often controls the company purse strings.

An information need, answered.

The business needs of the executive woman have never been fully explored, due in large part to the lack of a single source that offered the quality, consistency and coverage needed to plan an effective ongoing campaign.

You now have that database. In the *Dun's File of Executive Women.*

Use any of Dun's selectivity yardsticks to target your market. No matter which industries you do business with, the executive woman is represented in ever-growing numbers.

Call your local Dun's Marketing office for more information regarding this important marketing resource.

Dun's Marketing Services

DB a company of The Dun & Bradstreet Corporation

EW0486

Dun's® Executive Age Indicator

You're not likely to sell IRAs to executives past retirement age. By the same token, magazines about retirement have limited appeal to youthful managers on the business scene.

It's another case of selective marketing —one in which, once again, Dun's Marketing is prepared to serve as a guide for opportunity-minded sales and marketing managers.

You can select your best executive prospects by name, title and *age*. With the Dun's Decision Makers File in hand, you can identify over 5 million executives within certain age ranges.

At last, selling by age comes of age.

If your product or service is best targeted to executives in a specific age range (the 40's, for instance) rather than executives of all ages, this selection option opens new opportunities for you.

Executive Age Brackets	Number of Executives	Percentage of Executives
20-24	49,000	.9
25-29	237,000	4.6
30-34	566,000	10.9
35-39	690,000	13.3
40-44	755,000	14.6
45-49	679,000	13.1
50-54	676,000	13.0
55-59	617,000	12.0
60-64	459,000	8.9
65-69	239,000	4.6
70-74	120,000	2.3
75+	92,000	1.8

We believe this is the largest file of age-selectable executives available today— and represents one of the most exciting developments in target marketing in many years.

The age factor applies to the marketing of everything from luxury aircraft to Sun Belt property.

Still, there are certain industries which are prime candidates for the enlightening data to be found in *Dun's Executive Age Indicator*. Among them: Insurance, Publishing, Banking and Financial Services, Merger and Acquisition Counseling, Real Estate, Securities Brokerage, Advertising,

Luxury Product Marketing, Executive Recruitment and Upscale Catalog Merchandising.

Now when you want to pinpoint your direct marketing campaign to executives by age (and lifestyle), you don't have to rely on bits of data from scattered sources. All you have to do is call your local Dun's Marketing office and ask for details on *Dun's Executive Age Indicator*.

Dun's Marketing Services

a company of
The Dun & Bradstreet Corporation

EA0486

Dun's ° Personalization Service

Are word processor or computer letters part of your sales plan?

If so, the tape *Personalization Service* of Dun's Marketing should be part and parcel of your plan.

This service consists of four programs and provides an important benefit in communicating with prospects. The first three programs convert the data configuration on your tapes to make it more immediately usable, giving you additional flexibility in tailoring your sales letters or documents. The fourth program provides an alternative delivery option in tune with today's increased usage of word processors and personal computers.

1. Name Inversion

This program of the *Dun's Personalization Service* modifies the *business* name from "alpha or filing style" to "reading or typing style."

FROM:

```
QUICK ROBERT L CO THE
1428 WILCREST AVE
NAPERVILLE IL 60540
```

TO:

```
THE ROBERT L QUICK CO
1428 WILCREST AVE
NAPERVILLE IL 60540
```

2. Upper Case Lower Case Print

This program converts the print from all upper case (or capital letters) to regular typing style of upper lower case.

FROM:

```
THE ROBERT L QUICK CO
1428 WILCREST AVE
NAPERVILLE IL 60540
```

TO:

```
The Robert L Quick Co
1428 Wilcrest Ave
Naperville IL 60540
```

Before ordering this conversion, check that your service bureau or in-house EDP department is able to read and program a tape which is in the upper lower case format.

3. Genderization of Personal Name

Now you can avoid the embarrassment of addressing recipients of your mailing in the wrong gender—or you can quickly cull names for a male-only or female-only mailing.

In this program, male first names are designated **M**...female first names by **F** ...names that can be either (Leslie, Gale, Lee, etc.) by **B**. Cases where only the initial of the first name is present are designated by a dash.

```
M    John J Cummings
F    Vanessa M Grimes
B    Jesse T Finn
—    F S Reynolds
```

4. Floppy Disk Deliverability

Working with a personal computer and want your list delivered on floppy disks?

No problem!

Dun's Marketing can supply data on either dual or single density 5¼″ disks ready for immediate use.

When you buy a file, you want to use the information—not spend your time trying to convert from tape to disk. At Dun's Marketing, we eliminate delays, because we can supply your data on a floppy disk for immediate use with your personal computer.

Call your local Dun's Marketing office for full details on how you can personalize your next direct mail program and get your list delivered the way you want it.

NOTE: If you are using a computer or pre-printed letter, we can provide your tape in print image format *at no extra charge*.

Dun's Marketing Services

a company of
The Dun & Bradstreet Corporation

PS0486

DUN'S DECISION MAKERS

Dun's Decision Makers (DDM) identifies more than 9 million key senior management decision-makers by name and functional responsibility.

These are the upper-echelon men and women with the power to buy or to influence the purchase of your product or service.

These are the top executives you must reach. And Dun's Decision Makers helps you reach them through a variety of selection criteria.

- Executive names and titles include:
  - —Chairman
  - —President
  - —Owner
  - —Partner
  - —Treasurer
  - —Secretary
  - —Senior V.P.
  - —Executive V.P.
  - —V.P., Finance
  - —V.P., Sales
  - —V.P., Marketing
  - —V.P., Manufacturing
  - —V.P., Purchasing
  - —V.P.
  - —And many more.

- Key business selectors are:
  - —SIC Code
  - —Employee Size
  - —Sales Volume
  - —Telephone
  - —Other DMI Direct data

DDM gives you Executive Clout.

To ensure accuracy, all information in DDM is updated by interviews by more than 2,000 business analysts.

With DDM, you're assured of the most accurate, most current listing of corporate executives.

You have broad coverage at all levels of top management—which helps you maximize your marketing efforts by identifying multiple contacts within prospect companies.

Dun's Decision Makers. An extension and enhancement of the Dun's Market Identifiers® database of more than 8 million businesses and professionals.

For more information, contact your Dun's Marketing Account Executive.

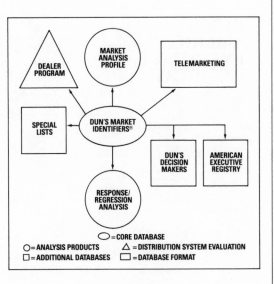

○ = CORE DATABASE
○ = ANALYSIS PRODUCTS   △ = DISTRIBUTION SYSTEM EVALUATION
□ = ADDITIONAL DATABASES   ▭ = DATABASE FORMAT

Dun's Marketing Services

DUN'S AMERICAN EXECUTIVE REGISTRY

Dun's American Executive Registry (AER) gives you access to the names and titles of more than 17 million top and middle management executives—executives who have proven themselves to be responsive direct mail buyers.

This is the most comprehensive executive database ever offered to direct marketers—a significant breakthrough in sophisticated direct response information gathering.

Gathered from more than 220 list sources, merged with top management executives from Dun's Decision Makers file, Dun's AER combines the deliverability of a top-quality compiled file with the responsiveness of a buyer's file.

Yet, AER costs less than a typical response file alone.

What's more, AER has now been enhanced with company characteristics from our Dun's Market Identifiers® file.

Now, with AER, you have a powerful business-to-business list that works extra hard for you. You can target your selections using such diverse criteria as:

- Prospect's Name (linked with his or her title)
- Job Title/Function (over 200 titles to choose from)
- Multi-Buyer
- Source (Seminar attendee, book buyer, controlled circulation, etc.)
- Age

- Gender
- Computer Site/Make Locations
- Field of Interest (You can even pinpoint by their interests, from accounting to art to self-employment, etc.)

Because the AER is response-based, use it to increase sales for your consumer solicitations as well.

All AER data is available on pressure-sensitive or cheshire labels, magnetic tape, and tele-marketing formats.

Dun's American Executive Registry. The most powerful business medium in America.

Use Dun's AER and you can reach four times the circulation of *Business Week, Forbes, Fortune* and *The Wall Street Journal!* Reach millions of top and middle management executives, who have proven by their responsiveness to be receptive to your direct response message.

Here's just a partial list of the many titles available to you:

- Chairman of the Board
- Owner
- President
- Chief Executive Officer
- Corporate Secretary
- Senior V.P.
- Treasurer
- General Manager
- V.P., Sales
- V.P., Marketing
- V.P., Purchasing
- V.P., Information Systems
- Controller
- Personnel Director
- Facilities Manager
- Office Manager
- Data Processing Operations Manager

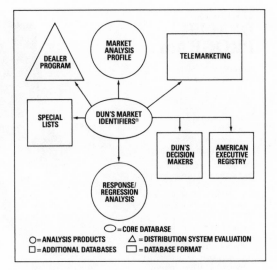

- Programming Manager
- Telecommunications Manager
- Sales Manager
- Marketing Services Manager
- Design Engineer
- Traffic Manager
- Production Manager
- Quality Control Manager
- And dozens more!

The Dun's American Executive Registry is among the nation's most popular tried-and-tested lists of top-quality business executives available. And is one of the most trusted sources of information for companies who wish to broaden the scope of their direct response programs.

For more information, call your Dun's Marketing Account Executive.

Dun's Marketing Services

DB a company of
The Dun & Bradstreet Corporation

DAER0488
10M

DUN'S DEALER PROGRAM

Dun's Dealer Program will help you support your dealer networks with more quality data for more bottom-line results in a number of important areas:

- Cooperative Direct-Response Programs
- Telemarketing Programs
- Lead Generation Programs

The data available to you and your dealer networks is derived from the Dun's Market Identifiers® file, which is loaded with vital information on more than 8 million businesses and professionals.

Information such as sales volume, employee size, 5th-digit SIC code, executive names and functional titles and much, much more. Updated monthly to ensure accuracy and deliverability.

With the Dun's Dealer Program, you'll be able to:

- Project sales quotes realistically.
- Design more effective market research studies.
- Increase accuracy of test market studies.
- Fine-tune criteria for site selection for new offices and franchises.
- Redefine sales territories to take full advantage of rapidly changing business patterns.
- And more!

This is the perfect tool for manufacturers and suppliers of business products and services who rely on dealer networks as part of their distribution channel.

Dun's Dealer Program puts *you* in control of the process.

And helps optimize your company's long-term goals while maximizing short-term strategies.

Dun's Dealer Program. For more quality, flexibility and profit-potential.

The Dun's Dealer Program includes some of the following reports:

Dealer Assignment Report:
Verifies dealer territory definition provided by the client at the appropriate geographic level—state, metro, county, zip code or a combination of these.

Market Assignment Report:
Divides each dealer territory into markets defined by sales volume, employee size (at location), or lines of business (SIC). The MAR displays these markets and their definitions.

Prospect Availability Report:
This report displays each dealer, the total available markets for each dealer, and the prospects within each market. Seeing a dealer-segmented profile prior to ordering output allows you to modify specifications according to profiled results.

Once the territories and markets are defined, you can generate mailing lists or telemarketing cards for any of your local dealers.

The system is flexible, so you can change territory or market defini-tions easily. And monthly updates by our more than 2,000 business analysts ensure the data is up-to-the-minute.

For complete details on this powerful computer-accessed data system, call your Dun's Marketing Account Executive.

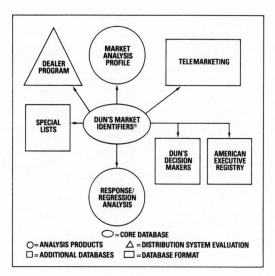

○ = CORE DATABASE
O = ANALYSIS PRODUCTS   △ = DISTRIBUTION SYSTEM EVALUATION
□ = ADDITIONAL DATABASES   ▭ = DATABASE FORMAT

Dun's Marketing Services

DB a company of
The Dun & Bradstreet Corporation

DDP0488
10M

DUN'S SPECIAL LISTS

In business-to-business direct marketing, strategic targeting is growing even more complex.

One of the most powerful tools you can use to help you pinpoint the cream of the direct marketing universe is Dun's Special Lists.

This is an array of specially selected lists culled from the Dun's Market Identifiers® database of more than 8 million businesses and professionals. With Dun's Special Lists, you have available a selection of specialized files and market-tested selections, which you can segment by related business characteristics.

The data is verified continually for accuracy.

With Dun's Special Lists, you can focus your strategies with high accuracy. You'll be able to make more well-informed, profit-increasing decisions—even with the most fragmented geographic mix, the most perplexing market profiles, the most exacting company criteria.

Whether you use the mail or tele-marketing programs or a combi-nation of the two...whether you use in-house services for pros-pecting or outside services... Dun's Special Lists is a mandatory direct marketing tool for the business-to-business marketer.

Dun's Special Lists. For direct response packages that give you the cream of your target universe.

Here are just a few examples of the pre-selected lists available:

- Truck/Fleet Owners (TRINC)
- Dun's Business Executives at Home
- Companies by Major Sales Growth Within Recent Years
- Mainframe & Minicomputer file
- Personal/Microcomputer file
- Office Products
- Captive Audience
- ERISA file
- Educational Establishments & Professionals file
- Hot List file
- Entrepreneurs, Sole Ownerships and Partnerships
- Multi-Location Companies
- Dun's Top 500 Companies and Subsidiaries
- Dun's Top 1300 Companies and Subsidiaries
- Importers/Exporters
- Hotels/Motels
- High-Tech Companies' Executives
- Female Executives
- And much, much more!

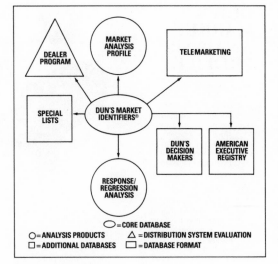

For example, here's where you'll find 108,000 companies related to the construction industry. And 5.6 million business owners, professionals and executives at their home addresses.

For more information on this powerful information source, call your Dun's Marketing Account Executive.

DUN'S MARKET ANALYSIS PROFILE

Before you make your final list selection, before you commit your budget and your people to any direct marketing program—especially if your prospecting and sales efforts have reached a plateau—how would you like to have a sharp, clear analytical portrait of your target market?

Dun's Market Analysis Profile (MAP) will give it to you.

MAP lays out the statistical information you need to help you profile and analyze the demographic makeup and business activity within a market. This is the kind of vital information you need to make well-informed, more effective bottom-line decisions. Use your budget and human resources to maximum advantage. Increase market penetration. Reach and sell prospects with more power. Give your marketing plans more focused direction.

MAP. It's the analytical tool you need. Now!

Dun's Market Analysis Profile. It shows you your market from many different angles.

Dun's MAP provides you with a comprehensive overview of your market drawn from the Dun's Market Identifiers® database of over 8 million businesses and professionals. You can see your market from these angles:

Geographic. Plot your target market by state, county, city or other standard geographic units. You select the one most meaningful for your program.

Industry. See how your prospects cluster in any broad-based or specific industry, using the Standard Industrial Classification system. This detailed 2-, 3-, 4- or 5-digit code pinpoints the exact industries you need to reach, and tells you where they are.

Business Size. Study and qualify your markets according to customized size range. Select prospects by:

• Employment level of individual business location or of the total company.

• Annual sales volume.

Dun's Market Analysis Profile. Available in bound-copy format or on print-image tape.

For more information about MAP and how it can benefit your bottom line, call your Dun's Marketing Account Executive.

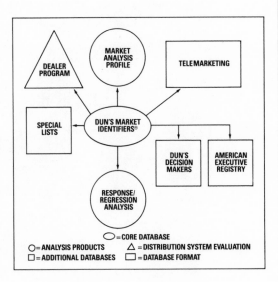

Dun's Marketing Services

D-B a company of
The Dun & Bradstreet Corporation

DMAP0488
10M

SERVICE BUREAUS

Consumer Infobase™

Data Element Catalog

Order Form

Infobase Services™

Infobase Premier™

Selected Consumer Infobase Data . . . accuracy, coverage and value.

Infobase Premier includes most R.L. Polk demographic data (except for vehicle model year and specific mail order information), plus demographic data from all of our other Infobase contributors, to guarantee that the most recent, most specific and most accurate data is provided for each Premier data element per individual record. In short, this sophisticated system architecture assures you the highest quality, maximum coverage on each element, and it is the easiest to use. You simply specify the data elements desired or use the bundled pricing to get all the available demographic data on every matched record. The system does the rest.

Sample Infobase Premier™ Record

Data Element	Source A	Source B	Source C	Source D
Children	Yes	1 @ 5 to 10 1 @ under 5	Yes	X
Income	25K to 30K	25K to 30K	X	X
Homeowner	X	No	Yes	X
Occupation	X	Blue Collar	Blue Collar	X
Age	28-29	27	X	28-29
Mail Order Buyer	Yes	X	X	Yes
Length of Residence	3 years	X	< 1 years	X
Dwelling Type	SFDU	X	X	X
Telephone	213-473-9876	X	213-473-1234	X

Source A Mass compiled source, address verified 6 months ago
Source B Verified 12 months ago, source from questionnaires
Source C Phone Survey, verified 4 months ago
Source D Multi-source compilation, data verification date varies by data element

A typical Infobase Premier Data record — describing this individual as blue collar, age 28-29 with an income of $25,000-$30,000, a single family home in which he has lived for less than a year, two children (one at 5-10 years and one under five years) and a history of having bought by mail.

Data Element No.	Description	Price per/M	Quantity (in millions)
611	Date of birth of head of household	$20.00	82.1
618	Date of birth - spouse (2nd individual)	$20.00	23.7
623	Date of birth of input individual	$20.00	105.8
624	Date of birth of input individual with default to head of household	$20.00	105.8
616	Age range in two year increments - head of household	$14.00	91.1
	Calculated from the exact date of birth, this element is delivered in the form of a 2-yr. age range. For example, 38-39, 70-71, 44-45. Provided for the individual whose first name is submitted for matching. Categories extend from under 18 to 100 plus.		
617	Age range in two year increments - spouse (2nd individual)	$14.00	26.2
626	Age range in two year increments of input individual	$14.00	117.3
627	Age range in two year increments of input individual with default to head of household	$14.00	117.3
600	Adult Age Ranges	$10.00	135.1

An inexpensive alternative to reporting age in 2-yr. increments, this segment categorizes ages in the following groups, including an indication of male, female or unknown gender.
- 16-25 male
- 16-25 female
- 16-25 ungendered
- 26-35 male
- 26-35 female
- 26-35 ungendered
- 36-45 male
- 36-45 female
- 36-45 ungendered
- 46-55 male
- 46-55 female
- 46-55 ungendered
- 56-64 male
- 56-64 female
- 56-64 ungendered
- Age 65 + male
- Age 65 + female
- Age 65 + ungendered

601	Children's Age Range	$6.00	16.3

Children's age, reported as:
- 0-6
- 7-12
- 13-18

602	Number of Children	$3.00	11.5

Counts the number of children in the household up to eight or more

603	Estimated Income	$10.00	87.6

An estimate of household income based on a variety of factors, including age, occupation, home ownership, median income for the local area, and more. Reported as one of the following:
- Under $15,000
- $15,000 - $19,999
- $20,000 - $24,999
- $25,000 - $34,999
- $35,000 - $49,999
- $50,000 - $74,999
- $75,000 plus

604	Occupation of head of household expressed as:	$10.00	33.5

- Professional/Technical
- Administrative/Managerial
- Sales/Service
- Clerical/White collar
- Craftsman/Blue collar
- Student
- Housewife
- Retired
- Farmer
- Military
- Religious

4

Data Element No.	Description	Price per/M	Quantity (in millions)
605	**Occupation of the spouse (2nd individual) expressed as:** • Professional/Technical • Administrative/Managerial • Sales/Service • Clerical/White collar • Craftsman/Blue collar • Student • Housewife • Retired • Farmer • Military • Religious	$10.00	11.7
606	**Homeowner/Renter** Gain a better understanding of your customer's status as a: • Non-owner • Owner	$5.00	52.8
607	**Length of residence expressed in one year increments from less than one to 15+ years.** Length of residence is a leading factor in credit reliability. Listings established prior to 1962 are included in the '62 range.	$3.00	88.7
608	**Dwelling size (single or multi-family)** An indicator is provided specifying single homes or structures with up to ten units each. Apartment buildings with more than 10 units are identified as well. Private homes or apartment residences will indicate an area's stable or transient nature.	$5.00	90.0
609	**Marital Status** • Married • Widowed • Single	$3.00	42.0
610	**Head of household name, gender and relationship**	$3.00	93.0
612	**Second individual - name, gender and relationship**	$3.00	33.7
613	**Area code, telephone, time zone** The continuous compilation of telephone directories offers marketers an inexpensive alternative to directory assistance service and manual look-up charges. Each listing has been made market-ready with time zones and area codes. • Under 1,000M input $20.00 • 1,000M-1,999M input 18.00 • 2,000M-3,999M input 16.00 • 4,000M-4,999M input 14.00 • 5,000M and over 12.00	$20.00	61.5
614	**Verification date** (year and quarter of data verification) • Under 500M input $5.00 • 500M-1,999M input 4.00 • 2,000M-4,999M input 3.00 • 5,000M and over 2.00		118.0
615	**Mail order buyer** Useful for identifying those individuals more likely to buy through direct mail.	$10.00	16.3
619	**Working woman** Working woman present in the household	$5.00	11.0
620	**Mail responders**	$5.00	29.8
621	**Credit card indicator** Indication of possession of the following types of credit cards, alone or in combination. • Retail/Other • Both • Bank Card • Credit Card Buyer	$12.00	42.0
622	**Presence of children** Indicates the known presence or absence of children in the household.	$3.00	17.0

Data Element No.	Description	Price per/M	Quantity (in millions)
160	**Apartment number** Missing apartment numbers can have a negative impact on deliverability of mail, disguise a household's status as renters, and lead to misdirected marketing efforts (such as mailing a home improvement offer to an apartment dweller). Application of apartment number adds value and deliverability to your file.	$2.00	6.9
164	**Registered cars/ aggregate value** The aggregate current retail value of all cars owned or leased in a household. This data, captures in one place the essential vehicle information most commonly sought by marketers. Learn as much as you can about the affluence of your customer.	$12.00	42.9
165	**Truck/motorcycle/ RV owners** Many of these specialty vehicle owners display a greater-than-average interest in outdoors and do-it-yourself activities.	$10.00	18.7
166	**Dominant vehicle lifestyle indicator** This indicator distinguishes the classification of the primary vehicle registered to the household: • Personal luxury car, e.g. Porsche, Audi 5000, Mazda 929, Eldorado • Truck or passenger utility vehicle • Station wagon • Import (standard or economy car), e.g. Honda Accord, Audi 4000, Mazda 626 • Regular (mid-size or small car), e.g. Cutlass Ciera, Ford Escort • Specialty (mid-size or luxury), e.g. Grand Prix, Firebird, Skyhawk • Full size (standard or luxury) e.g. LTD, New Yorker, DeVille	$8.00	43.7
625	**Positive match indicator** Help regenerate the lapsed, expired or inactive portion of your file; confirm addresses on outside lists. A match to Infobase Premier represents a strong likelihood that name and address records are valid and deliverable. • Under 500M input $5.00 • 500M-1,999M input 4.00 • 2,000M-4,999M input 3.00 • 5,000M and over 2.00		133.8
630	**Special rate for all Infobase Premier Data Elements appended except date of birth (but including phone numbers)** • Under 1,000M $45.00 • 1,000M-1,999M 40.00 • 2,000M-3,999M 35.00 • 4,000M-4,999M 30.00 • More than 5,000M 26.00		
635	**All Infobase Premier data elements appended, excluding date of birth and phone numbers** • Under 1,000M $35.00 • 1,000M-1,999M 30.00 • 2,000M-3,999M 25.00 • 4,000M-4,999M 20.00 • More than 5,000M 16.00		

You may also order demographic data from a specific Infobase data owner or a number of data owners, specifying which data you would like first. Your Infobase Customer Service Representative will be happy to provide you with complete details.

Note: All Premier Data, exclusive of that supplied by NDL, is available for list rental enhancement provided the list(s) remains at CCX Network.

5

National Demographics and Lifestyles

The National Demographics and Lifestyles data is provided by consumers who have filled out a questionnaire packaged with a consumer product and mailed it to NDL.

The NDL data is available for enhancement of customer files for a one year time period. The NDL data may not be used to enhance a customer file for list rental purposes; enhancing compiled/credit files; or any lists of names generated from warranty cards, product registration cards or questionnaires.

The NDL data is available at the individual level and the neighborhood level. You may order just individual level data or use the option of ordering individual household level data with an automatic default to neighborhood level data when individual household data is unavailable.

Demographic Data

Data Element No.	Description	Price per/M	Quantity (in millions)
201	**Income Range**	$12.00	16.0
	• Less than $15,000		
	• $15,000 - $19,999		
	• $20,000 - $24,999		
	• $25,000 - $29,999		
	• $30,000 - $34,999		
	• $35,000 - $39,999		
	• $40,000 - $44,999		
	• $45,000 - $49,999		
	• $50,000 plus		
202	**Occupation**	$12.00	20.9
	• Professional/Technical		
	• Management		
	• Sales/Marketing		
	• Clerical		
	• Blue collar		
	• Student		
	• Homemaker		
	• Retired		
	• Other		
203	**Self-reported credit card holder**	$12.00	15.2
	Indication of possession of the following types of credit cards, alone or in combination.		
	• Travel & Entertainment		
	• Bank Card		
	• Other (oil company, department store or specialty store)		
204	**Homeowner or renter**	$12.00	20.7
	Self-reported status as renter or owner of the home.		
280	**Age of spouse**	$12.00	2.0
281	**Head of household Adult age ranges**	$12.00	20.8
	Group Range		
	1 18-24		
	2 25-34		
	3 35-44		
	4 45-54		
	5 55-64		
	6 65 +		
282	**Date of birth, head of household**	$20.00	20.7
283	**Date of birth of spouse**	$20.00	2.0
284	**Spouse occupation**	$12.00	11.1
286	**Marital status**	$12.00	20.6
287	**Children's age range**	$12.00	11.3
288	**Verification date** (by quarter and year)	$12.00	22.6

Note: Much of the demographic data listed above can also be purchased as Infobase Premier data. Please see pages 4-5 for more details.

Infobase
Data Sources

Lifestyle Data

Consumers fill out questionnaires indicating the hobbies, interests and activities they or their spouse participate in on a regular basis. Lifestyle data is available at both the individual and neighborhood level*.

Data Element No.	Description	Indiv. Level	CRRT Level	Quantity (in millions)
205	Art/Antiques	$12.00	$7.50	2.2
206	Astrology	12.00	7.50	0.1
207	Automotive Work	12.00	7.50	3.1
208	Avid Book Reading	12.00	7.50	7.1
209	Bible/Devotional Reading	12.00	7.50	3.0
210	Bicycling	$12.00	$7.50	3.1
211	Boating/Sailing	12.00	7.50	3.4
212	Bowling	12.00	7.50	1.4
213	Cable TV Viewing	12.00	7.50	7.1
214	Camping/Hiking	12.00	7.50	5.3
215	CB Radio	$12.00	$7.50	0.8
216	Collectibles	12.00	7.50	2.3
217	Community/Civic Activities	12.00	7.50	2.5
218	Crafts	12.00	7.50	5.1
219	Crossword Puzzles	12.00	7.50	1.0
220	Cultural/Arts Events	$12.00	$7.50	3.2
221	Current Affairs/Politics	12.00	7.50	0.7
222	Electronics	12.00	7.50	1.6
223	Fashion Clothing	12.00	7.50	2.6
224	Fishing	12.00	7.50	5.6
225	Foreign Travel	$12.00	$7.50	2.8
226	Gardening	12.00	7.50	7.7
227	Grandchildren	12.00	7.50	2.9
228	Golf	12.00	7.50	3.9
229	Gourmet Cooking/ Foods, Cooking	12.00	7.50	3.6
230	Health Foods	$12.00	$7.50	2.9
231	Home Furnishings/ Decorating	12.00	7.50	1.1
232	Home Workshop	12.00	7.50	5.0
233	Household Pets	12.00	7.50	6.2
234	House Plants	12.00	7.50	1.5
235	Hunting/Shooting	$12.00	$7.50	3.6
236	Money Making Opportunities	12.00	7.50	1.7
237	Motorcycling	12.00	7.50	1.8
238	Needlework/Knitting	12.00	7.50	4.7
239	Our Nation's Heritage	12.00	7.50	0.9

Data Element No.	Description	Indiv. Level	CRRT Level	Quantity (in millions)
240	Personal and Home Computers	$12.00	$7.50	2.7
241	Photography	12.00	7.50	4.9
242	Physical Fitness/ Exercise	12.00	7.50	6.6
243	Racquetball	12.00	7.50	0.5
244	Real Estate Investments	12.00	7.50	1.8
245	Recreational Vehicle/ 4-Wheel Drive	$12.00	$7.50	2.0
246	Running/Jogging	12.00	7.50	2.7
247	Science fiction	12.00	7.50	0.9
248	Science/Technology	12.00	7.50	1.3
249	Self-Improvement	12.00	7.50	1.9
250	Sewing	$12.00	$7.50	4.6
251	Snow Skiing	12.00	7.50	2.2
252	Stamp/Coin Collecting	12.00	7.50	1.8
253	Stereo/Records/Tapes	12.00	7.50	8.6
254	Stocks & Bonds	12.00	7.50	2.9
255	Sweepstakes	$12.00	$7.50	3.7
256	Tennis	12.00	7.50	1.8
257	Watching TV Sports	12.00	7.50	7.7
258	Video Games	12.00	7.50	2.2
259	VCR Recording/ Home Video	12.00	7.50	7.4
260	Walking for Health	$12.00	$7.50	1.8
261	Wildlife/Environmental	12.00	7.50	2.9
262	Wines	12.00	7.50	2.7

Price Structure for "Lifestyle Coding" Customer Files

Prices per thousand **input** records for household and neighborhood level data.

Input File In 1000's	All Lifestyles	20 Selected Lifestyles	10 Selected Lifestyles
<1,000	$30.00M	$18.00M	$10.00M
1,000 - 4,999	20.00M	14.00M	8.00M
5,000 - 9,999	14.00M	10.00M	6.00M
10,000 - 14,999	12.00M	8.00M	4.00M

Minimum order $2,500

Additional $1.00/M input processing charge. See F5 on page 2 of the order form.

*An additional processing cost of $1.00/M input records is charged for adding neighborhood level data.

NDL *(continued)*

Lifestyle Dimensions

A lifestyle dimension is more tightly defined than a comparable Lifestyle Composite (see page 9). It consists of respondents who checked off more than one of the interests from a logical group of interests (depending on the particular dimension).

Data Element No.	Description	Price per/M	Quantity (in millions)
271	**Domestics** (Checked off three or more) • Crafts • Needlework/Knitting • Sewing • Gourmet Cooking/Foods, Cooking • Home Workshop • Gardening	$8.00	4.8
272	**Do-it-yourself** (Checked off two or more with at least one being *) • Automotive Work* • CB Radio • Electronics* • Home Workshop* • Motorcycling • Recreational Vehicle/4-wheel Drive	$8.00	3.4
273	**Fitness** (Checked off two or more with at least one being *) • Bicycling • Health Foods • Physical Fitness/Exercise* • Running/Jogging • Self-Improvement	$8.00	4.0
274	**Athletic** (Checked off two or more) • Bicycling • Golf • Racquetball • Running/Jogging • Snow Skiing • Tennis	$8.00	3.4

Data Element No.	Description	Price per/M	Quantity (in millions)
275	**Outdoors** (Checked off three or more) • Boating/Sailing • Camping/Hiking • CB Radio • Fishing • Hunting/Shooting • Motorcycling • Recreational Vehicle/4-wheel Drive	$8.00	3.2
276	**Good life** (Checked off three or more) • Cultural/Arts Events • Fashion Clothing • Gourmet Cooking/Foods, Cooking • Health Foods • Home Furnishings/Decorating • Wines	$8.00	2.4
277	**Culture** (Checked off two or more with at least one being *) • Collectibles • Crafts • Cultural/Arts Events* • Art/Antiques* • Foreign Travel	$8.00	3.0
278	**Blue chip** (Checked off two or more with at least one being *) • Community/Civic Activities • Real Estate Investment* • Self-Improvement • Stocks & Bonds*	$8.00	1.7
279	**Technology** (Checked off three or more) • Electronics • Photography • Science/Technology • Stereo/Records/Tapes • VCR Recording • Video Games	$8.00	3.5

8

Infobase
Data Sources

NDL *(continued)*

Lifestyle Composites

A lifestyle composite consists of the indication that at least one of the interests within the composite was checked as a positive response.

Data Element No.	Description	Price per/M	Quantity (in millions)
263	**Collecting** • Art/Antiques • Collectibles • Stamp/Coin Collecting	$8.00	4.7
264	**Crafts** • Crafts • Needlework/Knitting • Sewing	$8.00	8.2
265	**Do-it-yourself** • Automotive Work • Electronics • Home Workshop	$8.00	7.2
266	**Health and Fitness** • Bicycling • Health Foods • Physical Fitness/Exercise • Running/Jogging • Self-Improvement	$8.00	10.3
267	**Sports** • Golf • Motorcycling • Racquetball • Running/Jogging • Snow Skiing • Tennis	$8.00	8.8

Data Element No.	Description	Price per/M	Quantity (in millions)
268	**Outdoors** • Boating/Sailing • Camping/Hiking • CB Radio • Fishing • Hunting/Shooting • Recreational Vehicle/4-wheel Drive • Snow Skiing	$8.00	11.2
269	**Arts and culture** • Cultural/Art Events • Fashion Clothing • Art/Antiques • Foreign Travel • Gourmet Cooking/Foods, Cooking • Home Furnishing/Decorating • Wines	$8.00	9.4
270	**Technology** • Electronics • Personal/Home Computer • Photography • Science/Technology • Stereo/Records/Tapes • VCR Recording/Home Video • Video Games	$8.00	13.5

9

R.L. Polk and Company

The R.L. Polk data is derived from multiple sources. Information from motor vehicle registrations, Polk city directories and telephone directories is supplemented by numerous other sources.

Most of the Polk data is included in Infobase Premier. The exceptions are registered vehicle model year and the specific mail order data (#178-190).

Age and household composition

Data Element No.	Description	Price per/M	Quantity (in millions)
151	**Additional name/gender/ relationship**	$3.00	24.5

When the individual listed on the customer file matches a name and address on Consumer Infobase, up to five additional names of householders can be overlaid. Included with each name are the gender and the position in the household (head of household, spouse or other). Price per each set of name, gender and relationship overlaid.

| 152 | **Individual age in 2-year increments** | $12.00 | 41.4 |

Calculated from the exact date of birth, this element is delivered in the form of a 2-yr. age range. For example 38-39, 70-71, 44-45. Provided for the individual whose first name is submitted for matching. Categories extend from under 18 to 100 plus.

| 153 | **Household member age in 2-year increments** | $12.00 | 24.3 |

Similar to the preceding element, but a household (rather than individual) level match is performed, thereby allowing you to acquire valuable age information for additional household members.

| 154 | **Adult age ranges** | $8.00 | 114.5 |

An inexpensive alternative to reporting age in 2-yr. increments, this segment categorizes ages in the following groups, including an indication of male, female or unknown gender.
- 16-25
- 26-35
- 36-45
- 46-55
- 56-64
- Age 65 and over

| 155 | **Children's age ranges** | $5.00 | 6.8 |

Children's age, reported with gender (when known) as:
- 0-6
- 7-12
- 13-18

| 156 | **Number of adults in household** | $3.00 | 67.6 |

This element reports the presence of up to nine and more adults as members of the household.

| 168 | **Presence of children** | $3.00 | 24.2 |

Indicates the presence or absence of children in the household.

| 157 | **Number of children in household.** | $3.00 | 11.1 |

Counts the number of children in the household up to eight or more.

10

Data Element No.	Description	Price per/M	Quantity (in millions)
158	**Estimated income range**	$8.00	81.3

An estimate of household income based on a variety of factors, including age, occupation, home ownership, median income for the local area, and more. Reported as one of the following:
- Less than $ 8,000
- $ 8,000 - $ 9,999
- $10,000 - $14,999
- $15,000 - $19,999
- $20,000 - $24,999
- $25,000 - $34,999
- $35,000 - $49,999
- $50,000 - $74,000
- $75,000 and more

159	**Occupation**	$10.00	14.8

Coded for the following classifications:
- Professional/Technical
- Doctors
- Lawyers
- Teachers/Librarians
- Administrative/Managerial
- Management
- Proprietors
- Supervisors
- Sales/Service
- Clerical/White Collar
- Foreman
- Operatives
- Farm
- Unskilled
- Service Workers
- Military
- Student
- Retired
- Homemaker

169	**Marital Status**	$3.00	29.5

Housing

160	**Apartment number**	$2.00	6.9

Missing apartment numbers can have a negative impact on deliverability of mail, disguise a household's status as renters, and lead to misdirected marketing efforts (such as mailing a home improvement offer to an apartment dweller). Application of apartment number adds value and deliverability to your file.

161	**Home ownership**	$5.00	35.8

Gain a better understanding of your customer's status as a:
- Non-owner
- Owner
- Probable owner
- Probable renter of a home

162	**Dwelling unit size**	$5.00	80.5

Counts the number of known households at an address:

1	4	7	10-19	40-49
2	5	8	20-29	50-99
3	6	9	30-39	100 +

163	**Length of residence**	$3.00	81.3

Approximated by the year that the household first appeared on List X-1

172	**Mail order buyer**	$10.00	16.0

Useful for identifying those individuals more likely to buy through direct mail.

173	**Mail responder**	$5.00	23.8

Data Element No.	Description	Price per/M	Quantity (in millions)
174	**Credit card indicator**	$10.00	34.3

Indication of possession of the following types of credit cards, alone or in combination.
- Travel & Entertainment
- Bank Card
- Other (oil company, department store, etc.)

177	**Direct mail donors**	$10.00	4.5
178	**Mail order buyer by dollar amount**	$20.00	8.6

- Low (less than $15)
- Medium ($15 - $50)
- High (greater than $50)

179	**Mail order responder by dollar amount**	$20.00	9.5

- Low (less than $15)
- Medium ($15 - $50)
- High (greater than $50)

180	**Mail order donor by dollar amount**	$20.00	4.5

- Low (less than $50)
- Medium ($50 - $100)
- High (greater than $100)

182	**Mail order responder by type**	$20.00	7.3

- Catalog General Merchandise
- General Merchandise
- Health/Fitness/Exercise
- Books/Music
- Magazines
- Investments
- Bargain Seekers
- Health Donor

183	**Low dollar mail order buyer by type** (less than $15)	$20.00	6.3
184	**Medium dollar mail order buyer by type** ($15 - $50)	$20.00	3.8
185	**High dollar mail order buyer by type** (greater than $50)	$20.00	3.8
186	**Low dollar mail order donor by type** (less than $50)	$20.00	2.0

- Religious
- Environmental, Humanitarian, Educational
- Health Causes
- Political

187	**Medium dollar mail order donor by type** ($50 - $100)	$20.00	1.9
188	**High dollar mail order donor by type** (greater than $100)	$20.00	1.6
189	**Miscellaneous household data by type**	$20.00	4.6

- Electronic Users
- Smokers
- Veterans
- Farmer (non-owner)
- Farmer (owner)
- Resident Farmer/Owner

R.L. Polk and Co. *(continued)*

Data Element No.	Description	Price per/M	Quantity (in millions)
190	**Customer profile analysis data**	$10.00	81.3

Estimated household usage of various products and services expressed as quintiles based on formulas derived from analysis of survey data.
- Paint Spending
- Auto Products Use
- Monthly Coupon Use
- Total Mail Order Spending
- Auto Products/Self Installed
- Mail Order Spending/Clothing
- Mail Order Spending/Non-clothing
- Financial Services
- Auto Products/Dealer/Service Station Installed

Motor vehicle information

Data Element No.	Description	Price per/M	Quantity (in millions)
164	**Registered cars/ aggregate value**	$12.00	42.9

The aggregate current retail value of all cars owned or leased in a household. This data, captures in one place the essential vehicle information most commonly sought by marketers. Learn as much as you can about the affluence of your customer.

165	**Truck/motorcycle/ RV owners**	$10.00	18.7

Many of these specialty vehicle owners display a greater-than-average interest in outdoors and do-it-yourself activities

166	**Dominant vehicle lifestyle indicator**	$8.00	43.6

This indicator distinguishes the classification of the primary vehicle registered to the household:
- Personal luxury car, e.g. Porsche, Audi 5000, Mazda 929, Eldorado
- Truck or passenger utility vehicle
- Station wagon
- Import (standard or economy car), e.g. Honda Accord, Audi 4000, Mazda 626
- Regular (mid-size or small car), e.g. Cutlass Ciera, Ford Escort
- Specialty (mid-size or luxury), e.g. Grand Prix, Firebird, Skyhawk
- Full size (standard or luxury), e.g. LTD, New Yorker, DeVille

175	**Registered vehicle model years**	Call for Quote	42.8

Up to three registered vehicles' model years.

Address confirmation

Data Element No.	Description	Price per/M	Quantity (in millions)
167	**Positive match indicator**		135.9

Help regenerate the lapsed, expired or inactive portion of your file by identifying matches against any List X-1 record. Regularly recompiled and address-corrected, List X-1 matches represent a strong likelihood that name and address records are still valid and deliverable.

- Under 500M input — $5.00
- 500M - 1,999M input — 4.00
- 2,000M - 4,999M input — 3.00
- 5,000M and over — 2.00

171	**Telephone number**		53.1

The continuous compilation of telephone directories offers marketers an inexpensive alternative to directory assistance service and manual look-up charges. Each listing has been made market-ready with time zones and area codes.

- Under 1,000M input — $20.00
- 1,000M - 1,999M input — 18.00
- 2,000M - 3,999M input — 16.00
- 4,000M - 4,999M input — 14.00
- 5,000M and over — 12.00

176	**Special rate for all R.L. Polk & Co. data elements except telephone numbers**		

- Under 1,000M input — $30.00
- 1,000M - 1,999M input — 26.00
- 2,000M - 3,999M input — 21.00
- 4,000M - 4,999M input — 17.00
- 5,000M and over — 14.00

181	**Special rate for all R.L. Polk & Co. data elements including telephone numbers**		

- Under 1,000M input — $40.00
- 1,000M - 1,999M input — 36.00
- 2,000M - 3,999M input — 31.00
- 4,000M - 4,999M input — 27.00
- 5,000M and over — 24.00

Note: Most of the Polk data listed above can also be purchased in the Infobase Premier data. Please see pages 4-5 for more details.

Data Sources

SmartNames, Inc.

The SmartNames data is primarily derived from drivers' licenses, voter registration records and city and county real estate records. Selected SmartNames HOMES™ data is available for enhancement of files for list rental purposes.

HOMES™ Data

Dwelling Unit Size

Data Element No.	Description	Price per/M	Quantity (in millions)
561	Condominium	$10.00	1.6
562	Single/multi-family	$5.00	21.3

Purchase date

556	Month and year purchased	$25.00	14.2
560	Year purchased	$5.00	14.2
559	Month purchased	$25.00	13.5
557	Market value	$35.00	23.5

This element expresses the value of homes from $1,000 to $299,999 in $25,000 increments, from $300,000-$500,000 in $50,000 increments, and from $500,000-$1,000,000 in $275,000 increments.

558	Homeowner	$10.00	23.6

Indicates that the resident is a homeowner.

563	All HOMES™ Data	$55.00	23.6

13

Donnelley Marketing

Data Element No.	Description	Price per/M	Quantity (in millions)
001	**Telephone number, area code & time zone code**	$20.00	61.1

Income information

006	**Household income**	$10.00	75.0

Buying habits, vehicle ownership, and survey responses provide more specific data on household income level than can be gained from census reports alone. Income is among the strongest indicators of lifestyle, credit worthiness and purchasing power.

018	**Purchasing power indicator**	$10.00	75.0

Household income adjusted according to a cost-of-living index by city or county. This element identifies the relative purchasing power of the household income.

Housing information

009	**Year listed in phone directory**	$1.00	61.1

First year listed in phone directory is a strong indicator of length of residence, a leading factor in credit reliability. Listings established prior to 1962 are included in the '62 range.

010	**Dwelling unit size**	$1.00	79.0

An indicator is provided specifying single homes or structures with up to ten units each. Apartment buildings with more than 10 units are identified as well. Private homes or apartment residences will indicate an area's stable or transient nature.

14

Infobase
Data Sources

Age Indicators

Data Element No.	Description	Price per/M	Quantity (in millions)
011	**Presence of age indicators**	$15.00	60.5

This element provides indicators that reflect the probability of household members in specific age groups (see group listings below). Sex of individual is indicated when known. Age of household members is key to understanding the total family structure, a primary marketing tool. (See Table 1)

Data Element No.	Description	Price per/M	Quantity (in millions)
012	**Presence of children indicators**	$5.00	16.6

This element provides indicators that reflect the probability of household members from 0-17 years of age. Sex of child is indicated when known. This data, a specialty subset of Presence of Age, has strong applications in youth-related markets. (See Table 1)

TABLE 1

Presence of Age elements will be distinguished by a confidence level indicator (9, 8 or 7) to reflect the probability of a household member in the age ranges. An indicator of 9 reflects the strongest measure of confidence, while indicators of 8 and then 7 reflect lower probability in the specific age ranges. The list below depicts the 22 age groups.

Group No.	Range
1	Ungendered Age 0-5
2	Ungendered Age 0-11
3	Ungendered Age 0-17
4	Ungendered Age 6-11
5	Female 12-17
6	Male 12-17
7	Ungendered Age 12-17
8	Female 18-24
9	Male 18-24
10	Female 18-34
11	Male 18-34
12	Female 18-44
13	Female 35-44
14	Male 35-44
15	Female 35-54
16	Male 35-54
17	Female 45-54
18	Male 45-54
19	Ungendered Age 50 +
20	Female 55-64
21	Male 55-64
22	Ungendered Age 65 +

Additional List Enhancement Services

Infobase offers a variety of other options which you can purchase in conjunction with our data elements to add increased value and performance to your list.

Data Element No.	Description	Price Minimum	Price per/M
P1	**Equifax Deceased File Supression**	$250.00	$.50/M input $25.00/M matches
	Names of those deceased within the past 18 months with date reported.		
P2	**Elim-I-Nix Multi-Source Nixie Identification**	$250.00	$.50/M input $50.00/M matches
	R.L. Polk's multi-source nixie file of 45,000,000 address changes. It will tag your file with bad debt information, as well as correcting your address. Elim-I-Nix is updated quarterly.		
P3	**NCOA Address Standardization and Forwarding Address**	$750.00	$2.95/M input $25.00/M matches
	NCOA is the U.S. Postal Service's National Change of Address service. It represents a timely and cost-efficient way to increase the accuracy of a file and reduce undeliverables. NCOA contains records for all the permanent change of address records filed with the U.S. Postal Service in the last 36 months - giving you access to the most current consumer and business addresses available. Besides providing a forwarding address, the NCOA process also corrects five-digit ZIP Codes, standardizes addresses and applies ZIP + 4 Codes. The file is updated twice monthly.		
P4	**Address Standardization**	$300.00	$3.00/M input
	ORACLE will verify, correct and/or standardize street address - to provide users with a cost-effective means of increasing the accuracy of a file and reducing undeliverables.		
P5	**Geo Coding including census data - GeoPlus**	$500.00	$2.50/M input
	GeoPlus is a software system developed by R.L. Polk and Co. which will attach the following census geo data elements to a name and address record: • FIPS State Code • FIPS County Code • Census Tract Number • Block Group Number • Enumeration District Number • Small Area Characteristics (SMACS) **The GeoPlus system** contains information for all of the U.S. but not its territories or possessions. The primary difference between GeoPlus and ORACLE is that ORACLE does address verification and correction and GeoPlus does not.		

Data Element No.	Description	Price Minimum	Price per/M
P6	**Address Standardization, Geo Coding and Census Data**	$500.00	$4.50/M input

The R.L. Polk ORACLE system verifies and corrects addresses by standardizing and comparing each address record to a comprehensive database of all deliverable addresses recognized by the USPS. ORACLE also applies census demographic characteristics at the neighborhood level of block groups, census tract, enumeration district or zip code. One process option is to apply the Claritas PRIZM cluster codes. This is available with prior approval from Claritas.

Data Element No.	Description	Price Minimum	Price per/M
P7	**Carrier Route Marketing Information (CRMI)**	$250.00	$2.50/M input

Polk builds the CRMI file from over a billion data records each year. The X-1 file sources plus Ethnic and Religious lists are cross referenced with the U.S. Census information to create this dynamic source.

Data Element No.	Description	Price Minimum	Price per/M
P8	**Phone Confirmation**		
	Infobase format	$500.00	$1.50/M input
	Customer format	$600.00	$2.50/M input
	PLUS		
	Phones confirmed		$5.00/M matches
	or		
	New phones applied		$20.00/M matches

This service will update your file with new phone numbers and keep the phone already on your file if they are the same as ours. Call Customer Service for details.

Data Element No.	Description
P9	**PhoneLink™**

Identify those customers for whom you only have a phone number. For instance, a retailer may capture phones from point of sale registers and have their names and addresses applied. *(All orders must be pre-approved. Please call customer service for assistance and scheduling).

$1.50/M input ($250 min.) Standard Output
$2.50/M input ($350 min.) Customer Format
$250 minimum for Data
- Under $1,000M input — $20.00
- 1,000M-1,999M input — 18.00
- 2,000M-2,999M input — 16.00
- 4,000M-4,999M input — 14.00
- 5,000M and over — 12.00

17

MAY & SPEH DIRECT

DATA ENHANCEMENT SERVICES

MAY & SPEH DIRECT
1501 Opus Place
Downers Grove Il. 60515
(708) 964-1501

Data Resources:

May & Speh Direct has data covering the following lifestyle categories:

Demographics
Leisure Interests
Financial Indicators
Product Purchase Indicators

May & Speh Direct has the most comprehensive collection of information and the broadest coverage of any database enhancement resource.

III. NATIONAL DEMOGRAPHICS AND LIFESTYLES ENHANCEMENT OVERLAY DATA

National Demographics & Lifestyles database contains demographic and lifestyle interest information on over 20 million consumers. The database has been developed through the distribution of questionnaires packaged with a wide array of consumer products. NDL data is self-reported consumer information.

The NDL data is available by name at the individual level and summarized by data element at the carrier route geographic level. Data may be selected for overlay at the individual level, carrier route level or in combination by defaulting to carrier route level data if individual level data is not available.

Use of the data for overlay purposes requires prior approval from NDL. The data is restricted from use on files intended for list rental purposes or any list compiled from questionnaires, warranty cards or product registrations. The NDL data may be overlaid for enhancement purposes on customer files for use for one year.

May & Speh Direct

DEMOGRAPHIC DATA ELEMENTS

Gender of Respondent - 22.4MM

Marital Status - 21.2MM

Age of Respondent
Adult by Age Range - 21.3MM
18-24 Yrs. - 1.8MM
25-34 Yrs. - 5.0MM
35-44 Yrs. - 4.6MM
45-54 Yrs. - 3.2MM
55-64 Yrs. - 3.2MM
65 + Yrs. - 3.5MM

Income By Range - 15.9MM:
Under $15,000 - 2.7MM
$15,000 - $19,999 - 1.6MM
$20,000 - $24,999 - 1.8MM
$25,000 - $29,999 - 1.6MM
$30,000 - $34,999 - 1.6MM
$35,000 - $39,999 - 1.3MM
$40,000 - $44,999 - 1.2MM
$45,000 - $49,999 - 0.8MM
$50,000 - $74,999 - 2.8MM
$75,000 + 0.5MM

Respondent
Date of Birth - 22.1MM

Respondent Occupation - 21.3MM
Professional/Technical - 5.5MM
Management - 2.7MM
Sales/Marketing - 1.4MM
Clerical - 1.3MM
Blue Collar - 2.5MM
Student - 1.0MM
Homemaker - 3.3MM
Retired - 3.5MM
Other - 0.1MM

Spouse's Occupation - 13.0MM
Professional/Technical 2.7MM
Management - 1.4MM
Sales/Marketing - 0.6MM
Clerical - 0.9MM
Blue Collar - 1.4MM
Student - 0.1MM
Homemaker - 2.4MM
Retired - 3.5MM
Other (-)

Spouse's Age
Adult by Age Ranges - 2.1MM
18-24 Yrs. - 0.2MM
25-34 Yrs. - 0.4MM
35-44 Yrs. - 0.4MM
45-54 Yrs. - 0.4MM
55-64 Yrs. - 0.4MM
65 + Yrs. - 0.3MM

Spouse's Date of Birth - 2.1MM

Spouse's Gender - 2.2MM

Children's Age - 11.5MM
0 - 4 Yrs. - 2.7MM
5 - 10 Yrs. - 3.2MM
11 - 15 Yrs. - 2.7MM
16 - 18 Yrs. - 2.2MM
19 + Yrs. - 0.7MM

Presence of Credit Cards - 23.6MM
Travel/Entertainment - 3.7MM
Bank Card - 13.1MM
Other
(Oil/Gas,Dept./
Specialty,etc.) - 6.8MM

Home Owner or Renter - 21.0MM

LIFESTYLE INTEREST DATA ELEMENTS

Art/Antiques - 2.2MM
Astrology - 0.07MM
Automotive Work - 3.2MM
Avid Book Reading - 7.4MM
Bible/Devotional Reading - 3.2MM
Bicycling - 3.0MM
Boating/Sailing - 3.4MM
Bowling - 1.7MM
Cable TV Viewing - 7.7MM
Camping/Hiking - 5.2MM
CB Radio - 0.7MM
Collectibles - 2.4MM
Community/Civic Activities - 2.5MM
Crafts - 5.4MM
Crossword Puzzles - 1.5MM
Cultural/Arts Events - 3.2MM
Current Affairs/Politics - 1.1MM
Electronics - 1.7MM
Fashion Clothing - 2.7MM
Fishing - 5.6MM
Foreign Travel - 2.8MM
Gardening - 7.6MM
Grandchildren - 3.2MM
Golf - 3.9MM
Gourmet Cooking/Foods - 3.7MM
Health Foods - 3.0MM
Home Furnishing/
 Decorating - 0.8MM
Home Workshop - 5.5MM
Household Pets - 2.2MM
House Plants - 2.2MM
Hunting/Shooting - 3.6MM
Money Making
 Opportunities - 1.9MM
Motorcycling - 1.7MM
Needlework/Knitting - 4.6MM
Our Nations Heritage - 0.9MM
Personal/Home Computer - 3.0MM
Photography - 4.9MM
Physical Fitness/Exercise - 6.8MM
Racquetball - 0.35MM
Real Estate Investments - 1.8MM

Recreational Vehicle/
 4-Wheel Drive - 2.0MM
Running/Jogging - 2.8MM
Science Fiction - 1.0MM
Science/Technology - 1.4MM
Self Improvement - 2.2MM
Sewing - 4.5MM
Snow Skiing - 2.1MM
Stamp/Coin Collecting - 1.8MM
Stereo/Records/Tapes - 8.8MM
Stocks/Bonds - 2.9MM
Sweepstakes - 3.7MM
Tennis - 1.8MM
Watching TV Sports - 8.1MM
Video Games - 2.2MM
VCR Recording - 8.0MM
Walking for Health - 2.7MM
Wildlife/Environmental - 3.0MM
Wines - 2.7MM

May & Speh Direct

MULTI-BUYER INDICATOR

This indicates that the consumer responded to 2 or more manufacturer's warranty cards.

LIFESTYLE INTEREST COMPOSITES

A lifestyle composite consists of the indication that at least one of the lifestyle interest elements within the composite was checked as a positive response

Collecting - 4.8MM
Art/Antiques
Collectibles
Stamp/Coin

Crafts - 8.4MM
Needlework/Knitting
Other Crafts

Do It Yourself - 7.4MM
Automotive Work
Electronics
Home Workshop

Health and Fitness - 10.7MM
Bicycling
Physical Fitness/Exercise
Running/Jogging
Self-Improvement
Health/Natural Foods

Sports - 8.8MM
Motorcycling
Golf
Tennis
Racquetball
Snow Skiing
Running

Outdoors - 11.2MM
Boating/Sailing
Camping/Hiking
Hunting/Shooting
Fishing
Recreational Vehicle/
  4-Wheel Drive/
Skiing
CB Radio

Arts & Cultural - 9.5MM
Art/Antiques
Foreign Travel
Arts/Cultural Events
Wines
Fashion Clothing
Gourmet Cooking/Foods
Home Furnishing

Technology - 14.0MM
Stereo/Records/Tapes
VCR Recording
Video Games
Electronics
Photography
Science/New Technology
Personal/Home Computers

LIFESTYLE INTEREST DIMENSIONS

A lifestyle dimension is more tightly defined than a comparable lifestyle composite. It consists of respondents who checked off more than one of the lifestyle interest elements (depending on the dimension) from a logical group of interests.

Domestics - 4.8MM
(Indicated 3 or more)
  Crafts
  Needlework/Knitting
  Sewing/Needlework
  Gourmet Cooking/Food
  Home Workshop
  Gardening

Do It Yourself - 3.4MM
(Indicated 2 or more
with at least 1 *)
  Automotive Work*
  Electronics*
  Home Workshop*
  Motorcycling
  CB Radio
  Recreational Vehicle/
   4-Wheel Drive

Fitness - 4.1MM
(Indicated 2 or more
with at least 1 *)
  Bicycling
  Physical Fitness/Exercise*
  Running/Jogging
  Self-Improvement
  Health/Natural Foods

Athletic - 3.3MM
(Indicated 2 or more)
  Bicycling
  Golf
  Tennis
  Racquetball
  Snow Skiing
  Running

Outdoors - 3.1MM
(Indicated 3 or more)
  Boating/Sailing
  Camping/Hiking
  Hunting/Shooting
  Fishing
  Recreational Vehicle/
   4-Wheel Drive
  Motorbiking
  CB Radio

Good Life - 2.3MM
(Indicated 3 or more)
  Health/Natural Foods
  Foreign Travel
  Arts/Cultural Events
  Wines
  Fashion Clothing
  Gourmet Cooking/Foods
  Home Furnishing

Cultural - 3.1MM
(Indicated 2 or more,
with at least 1 *)
  Fine Arts/Antiques*
  Foreign Travel
  Crafts
  Arts/Cultural Events*
  Collectibles

Blue Chip - 1.8MM
(Indicated 2 or more,
with at least 1 *)
  Stocks and Bonds*
  Real Estate*
  Community/Civic Activities
  Self-Improvement

Technology - 3.7MM
(Indicated 3 or more)
    Stereo/Records/Tapes
    VCR Recording
    Video Games
    Electronics
    Photography
    Science/New Technology

IV. EQUIFAX POWER OVERLAY DATA

The Equifax Power Overlay Data provides financial-lifestyle indicators and demographic information on over 200 million individuals. The data overlays have been developed through modeling techniques based upon specific financial data compiled on each consumer.

The Power Overlay and Demographic Data Elements can be selected at the individual level. Vision codes are selectable at the carrier route level.

Use of the data for overlay purposes requires prior approval from Equifax. The data is restricted from use on files intended for list rental purposes. The Power Overlay and Demographic Data Elements may be overlaid for enhancement purposes on customer files for use for one year.

POWER OVERLAY DATA ELEMENTS

Shopping Psychographic Overlays - 59.1MM
(Based upon shopping preferences of individuals. Equifax has applied modeling techniques to reported consumer shopping activity and other measures to create nine distinct shopping/behavior segments described below.)

Flexible Shoppers - These shoppers play field with no specific buying loyalties. Middle income families with children who reside in suburban areas of small towns. Many of these shoppers reside in Western and Southern regions of the United States and have white collar or upper blue collar occupations. These shoppers' profiles greatly parallel those identified in the Lower Middle shopping group.

Prestige Shoppers - Shops for high fashion, prestige upscale products. High income families with school aged children, residing in affluent neighborhoods.

Upper Middle America - Shoppers Shop in multi-line and traditional department stores exclusively. Suburban families with middle to high incomes residing in moderately affluent neighborhoods. This shopping group also contains white collar families living in older housing and the upper end of the blue collar work force.

Middle America Shopper - Quality important, but price is a definite consideration. Middle income families with a blue collar/white collar occupational mix. These shoppers reside in neighborhoods which possess a gentle blend of single family dwellings and rental units.

Lower Middle America Shoppers - Price is a significant consideration; however, these individuals occasionally shop for higher quality products. Middle to older aged, middle income families residing in smaller towns or suburbs. Occupations are mixed, but have a definite blue collar flavor.

Value Shoppers - Price and value are major considerations. Families with children, people embarking on careers, and young Hispanic households constitute this group. Household incomes are varied, but tend to be in the middle to low range.

Price Shoppers - Price conscious, these shoppers look for the best deal and have more options to buy where they find the best prices. Residents of older blue collar neighborhoods. Dwelling units vary from row houses, to apartments, to owner occupied single family dwellings. Incomes are average and there is a definite presence of children.

Coupon Clippers - Shopping for these consumers means bargain hunting. Younger households with mixed incomes and a variety of occupation.

Cash Shoppers - These individuals have not yet established distinct shopping patterns. Residents of small towns and rural areas with middle to low income. Many of these shoppers are older aged and possess a wide range of occupations.

Credit Use Psychographics
The method of payment open to the consumer are many and complex. Just because a consumer has credit cards does not mean he or she will purchase more goods and services. The type of payment a consumer chooses to use provides targeting insight to marketers.

Activity Index - 60.6MM
Identifies how actively consumers use their revolving credit accounts. High, above average, average, below average and low indexed to a national mean.

Fixed Payment Index - 26.3MM
Identifies consumers by their willingness to accept fixed payments. Targets consumers who are willing to accept higher leverage to acquire products rather than wait.

Active Bank Card Index - 34.8MM
Identifies consumers based on a national indexed measure of the total number of active bank cards an individual possesses - low, average, high.

Active Retail Card Index - 46.4MM
Identifies consumers based on a national indexed measure of the total number of active retail cards an individual possesses - low, average, high.

Active Travel Card Index - 1.1MM
Indicates whether or not a consumer possesses a travel card.

Active Oil/Auto Card Index - 1.1MM
Indicates whether or not a consumer possesses an oil company card.

Presence of a Bank Card - 200.4MM
Indicates whether or not a consumer possesses an open bank card.

Credit Card Activity Index - 60.6MM
Identifies how actively credit accounts are used as indexed to a national average. Four segments include: High, above average, average and below average.

Buyability - 62.9MM
Identifies four relative levels of available spending power as a measure of available dollars indexed to a national mean. High, above average, average and below average.

Total Accounts Held Index - 71.0MM
Identifies consumers by relative use of revolving credit. Four levels: High, above average, average, average and below average.

Vision^R - 200.4MM
Provides geodemographic targeting information through 48 cluster codes to help you identify and locate your best customers. (See Appendix for descriptions.)

Equis (ETS Codes) - 200.4MM
Based upon each individual's unique data and geo-demographic data, Equis identifies 64 unique market segments that delineate a distinct consumer profile of demographic, financial and buying activity. (See Appendix for descriptions.)

DEMOGRAPHIC DATA ELEMENTS

Exact Date of Birth - 64.0MM
Individual specific age information derived from public records, mortgage
loan reports and other Equifax sources. (month and year; month, day, year
when available)

Gender - 165.3MM
Inferred from gender table based upon first name.

Marital Status - 200.4MM
Inferred from type of account status (single, joint, authorized user, etc.)

Dwelling Unit - 174.7MM
A classification derived from an address standardization process which
identifies the type of dwelling in which the consumer resides. (Single,
Multiple Family, or Business)

Estimated Household Income - 192.7MM
(Based on individual level and geodemographic census data)

V. X-1 ENHANCEMENT DATA

MAY & SPEH HOUSEHOLD LEVEL DEMOGRAPHIC OVERLAY DATA

May & Speh's Household File, derived from R.L.Polk's X-1 file, is a result of merging more than 456 million records annually from 21 different sources including:

Current Motor Vehicle Registration

Polk's Household Census List

Telephone Directories

Birthdate Information

Questionnaire Data

New Motor Vehicle Purchases and many other sources

The procedures used for compiling the Household File capitalize on the strength of each source and minimize the weaknesses. The result is important demographic information, which you can overlay (add) onto your files. The May & Speh Household File is updated three times per year.

One of the Household File's major strengths is apartment numbers. The file has 20 times more apartment numbers than any telephone list. Apartment numbers are particularly important for 3rd class delivery in major urban areas.

RESTRICTIONS

Certain data items have restricted usage. These restrictions are noted under the appropriate data items below.

May & Speh's data source, notably R.L.Polk and Company, reserves the right to refuse certain uses of overlay data due to competitive conflicts, inappropriate offers, etc., which they feel may be harmful to their clients interests.

HOUSEHOLD FILE DATA ELEMENTS

AGE, INCOME AND FAMILY INFORMATION.

Individual Name/Gender/Age - 77.0MM
Individual matching rules, gender and age in two year increments can be returned on up to five different household members per household. Ages are from date of birth information and are delivered in two year ranges; e.g., 18-19, 20-21, 30-31, etc. Ages range from 18 years to 100 years.

Adult Age Ranges - 73.8MM
A household level alternative to individual two year age increments. This element indicates the presence of adults and the gender mix of the age group.

16-25	46-55
26-35	56-64
36-45	65+

Children's Age Ranges - 14.4MM
Indicates presence of children and the gender mix of children in the age groups.

0- 6
7-12
13-18

Number of Adults in Household - 68.5MM
This element indicates the number of adults from 1-9 + in the household.

Number of Children in Household - 25.9MM
This element indicates the number of children in the household from 0-8 +.

Presence of Children - 11.2MM
Indicates the presence or absence of children in the household and their gender mix.

Number of Persons in Household - 68.7MM
Indicates number of household members from 1-9 +.

Estimated Income Range - 86.9MM
Estimated annual household income calculated from factors such as age, occupation, home ownership, median neighborhood income, etc. The following ranges are indicated:

Less than $ 8,000	$25,000 - $34,999
$ 8,000 - $ 9,999	$35,000 - $49,999
$10,000 - $14,999	$50,000 - $74,999
$15,000 - $19,999	$75,000 - and up
$20,000 - $24,999	

Occupation - 86.9MM
Coded data returned for the following categories:

Professional/Technical	Operatives
Doctors	Farm
Lawyers/Judges	Service Workers
Teachers/Librarians	Military
Administrative/Managerial	Student
Management	Retired
Proprietors	Housewife
Supervisors	Inferred Blue Collar
Sales/Service	Inferred Prof/
	Tech/Managerial
Clerical/White Collar	Inferred Retired
Foreman	Inferred 14 + year
	education

Gender of Household Head - 87.5MM

Gender and Marital Status - 76.3MM
Both martial status and gender of Head of Household is indicated. Following groups are available:

Unknown Gender and Status
Single Male
Married Male
Male - Unknown Marital Status
Single Female
Female (Widow, Divorced, Separated)
Female - Unknown Marital Status
Two Names - Unknown Gender and
   Marital Status
Male - Two Names
Male and Female - Status Unknown
Male and Unknown Gender
Female - Two Names
Female and Unknown Gender

HOUSING INFORMATION

Home Ownership - 40.6MM
Indicates whether the consumer is an owner or renter/probable owner or renter.

Dwelling Unit Size - 53.4MM
Provides number of records at an address. Values are 00 (unknown) through 99 (99 or more). Non CDS records always carry value 00.

Length of Residence - 77.0MM
A two digit number that indicates the number of years since this household appeared on the Household File. Values 00 (household just appeared) through 15 (15 or more years since household first appeared).

Apartment Number - 7.5MM
The May & Speh Household File can provide you more apartment numbers to vastly improve the deliverability of all mail, but especially 3rd class mail.

MOTOR VEHICLE INFORMATION

Current Market Value of all Registered Motor Vehicles
Provides the current total retail value of all cars and trucks in a household. Value provided in hundreds of dollars.

Number of Cars in Household - 46.3MM

Car Price Class - 21.0MM
Only cars bought new are included here. Price class is for last new car purchased. The following price classes are indicated:

Domestic Compact	Domestic Luxury
Domestic Low Price	Low Priced Foreign
Domestic Medium Price	Sporty and/or High Price Foreign
Domestic Low Luxury	

New Car Purchaser - 21.0MM
Indicates whether a household has ever purchased a new car (NCB) or truck (NTB). The values indicated are:

New Car Buyer (NCB) or New Truck Buyer (NTB)
Non-Purchaser
Not Coded

Truck/Motorcycle, RV Owner - 25.0MM
Indicates if household owns any of these three speciality vehicles.

Motor Vehicle Lifestyle Indicator - 49.9MM
Indicates classification of household's primary vehicle. The following classifications are identified:

Personal Luxury Car (e.g., Porsche, Eldorado, etc.)
Truck or Passenger Utility Vehicle (e.g., Jeep, Ford Ranger, etc.)
Station Wagon
Import (Standard or Economy)
Regular (Mid Size or Small)
Specialty (Mid Size or Luxury)
Full Size (Standard or Luxury)

ADDRESS CONFIRMATION DATA

Positive Match Indicator
Indicates a match between client file record and May & Speh Household File. Because the Household File is regularly verified and updated, a match is strong evidence of a value, deliverable record.

Telephone Number - 53.2MM
For telemarketers or anyone who requires phone numbers with their lists. Two services are available, adding phone numbers and verifying existing numbers. Area codes and numbers are available and can be separated.

Male Present (Y or N) - 80.1MM

Female Present (Y or N) - 56.5MM

CDS/Non CDS Code
Indicates whether record is part of city delivery service area or not.

New Mover/Move Date
From NCOA files, year and month move became effective. Current within last four months.

Zip Mobility Code - 9.3MM
A code derived by comparing a mover's old and new zip code.

Within Same Zip Code
Within Same Sectional Center
Within Same State
Moved to a New State

Move Distance
A code based on distance moved. - 6.4MM

Under 20 Miles	500 - 699 Miles
20 - 49 Miles	700 - 999 Miles
50 - 99 Miles	1,000 - 1,299 Miles
100 - 249 Miles	1,300 + Miles
250 - 499 Miles	

MAIL ORDER DATA

MAIL ORDER BUYERS/RESPONDERS/DONORS BY PRODUCT CATEGORY

Eight levels of Buyer/Responders/Donors are available by dollar amount of the offer or purchase. They are:

Low Dollar	High and Low Dollar
Medium Dollar	High and Medium Dollar
Low and Medium Dollar	High, Medium and Low Dollar
High Dollar	Amount Not Available

CURRENT HOUSEHOLD FILE COVERAGE

CATEGORY	CATEGORY
Catalog Merchandise	Magazines
General Merchandise	Investment-Financial
Women's Apparel	Opportunity
Crafts & Sewing	Bargain Seekers
Stamps, Coins	Other Mail Offers
& Collectibles	Religious
Children's Reading	Environmental,
Health, Fitness	Humanitarian and
& Exercise	Educational,
Entertainment	Health Causes
Books & Music	Political

CONSUMER DATA

CREDIT CARD USERS

Households where either a Bankcard (i.e., Visa, Mastercard) and/or Retail Card (i.e., J.C. Penney, Sears, etc.) is present and has been used recently. This source will be made available to us every four (4) months and will consist of those individuals that have made a payment on some form of retail or bankcard. The following classifications are available:

Bankcard Only	11.5MM
Retail Card Only	13.7MM
Both Bankcard and Retail	8.2MM
Unknown Type	.5MM

RESTRICTIONS

We cannot select credit card data as a stand alone demographic. It must be used in combination with at least one other demographic factor (i.e., estimated income over $8,000).

LIFESTYLE DATA

As a result of recent data acquisitions, we have information to indicate households which are:

Sweepstake Responders	6.9MM
Electronics Users	1.4MM
Smokers	1.7MM
Veterans	1.3MM
Farmers/Farm Owners	.5MM

SURVEY DATA COUNTS BY QUINTILE

PRODUCT CATEGORY	LOW	LOW/MED	MED	MED/HIGH	HIGH
Paint Spending	11,370,982	17,306,278	10,402,666	23,797,119	14,962,470
	14.6%	22.2%	13.4%	30.6%	19.2%
Auto Products Use	13,942,181	15,515,464	8,737,464	19,288,130	20,356,276
	17.9%	19.9%	11.2%	24.8%	26.2%
Monthly Coupon Use	20,141,638	5,929,749	19,553,489	17,118,231	15,096,408
	25.9%	7.6%	25.1%	22.0%	19.4%
Mail Order Spending	10,223,553	11,057,200	15,458,509	19,887,321	21,212,932
	13.1%	14.2%	19.9%	25.5%	27.3%
M.O.Spending Clothes	10,555,527	13,164,866	13,028,624	16,208,052	24,882,446
	13.6%	16.9%	16.7%	20.8%	32.0%
M.O.Spending Non-Cl	17,042,798	6,316,903	21,248,693	13,183,291	20,047,830
	21.9%	8.1%	27.3%	16.9%	25.8%
Financial Services	13,044,889	16,360,657	13,916,652	18,422,748	16,094,569
	16.8%	21.0%	17.9%	23.7%	20.7%

TRI-CELL CODE MATRIX

INCOME AND AGE

Income($)	50,000	35,000 to 49,999	25,000 to 34,999	20,000 to 24,999	15,000 to 19,000	10,000 to 14,999	8,000 to 9,999	Under 8,000
Age								
Under 25	00	01	02	03	04	05	06	07
25-34	10	11	12	13	14	15	16	17
35-44	20	21	22	23	24	25	26	27
Inferred younger	30	31	32	33	34	35	36	37
45-54	40	41	42	43	44	45	46	47
55-64	50	51	52	53	54	55	56	57
65+	60	61	62	63	64	65	66	67
Inferred older	70	71	72	73	74	75	76	77

HOUSING AND HOUSEHOLD COMPOSITION

Tenure	Owners		Other SFDU		Multi.Family		Rural	
Household Composition	-4 Yrs	4+ Yrs	-4 Yrs	4+Yrs	-4 Yrs	4+Yrs	-4Yrs	4+yrs
Male headed, child(ren) Present	00	01	02	03	04	05	06	07
Male headed, 2+ persons w/ no known children	10	11	12	13	14	15	16	17
Male headed, 1 person	20	21	22	23	24	25	26	27
Male headed, unknown	30	31	32	33	34	35	36	37
Female headed, child(ren) present	40	41	42	43	44	45	46	47
Female headed, 2+ persons w/no known children	50	51	52	53	54	55	56	57
Female headed, 1 person	60	61	62	63	64	65	66	67
Female headed, unknown	70	71	72	73	74	75	76	77

May & Speh Direct

OCCUPATION AND LIFE STYLE

Occupation	While Collar		Blue Shirt		Other		Unknown	
New Vehicle Purchased	NCB and/or NTB	NON and/or NTB	NCB and/or NTB	NON and/or NTB	NCB and/or NTB	NON and/or NTB	NCB and/or NTB	NCB NCB or NTB
Life Style Indicator								
Personal luxury car owner	00	01	02	03	04	05	06	07
Truck or passenger utility vehicle owner	10	11	12	13	14	15	16	17
Station wagon owner	20	21	22	23	24	25	26	27
Specialty (midsize or small) owner	30	31	32	33	34	35	36	37
Fullsize (standard or luxury) owner	40	41	42	43	44	45	46	47
Import (standard or economy) owner	50	51	52	53	54	55	56	57
Regular (midsize or small) owner	60	61	62	63	64	65	66	67
Unknown	70	71	72	73	74	75	76	77

VI. OTHER HOUSEHOLD LEVEL DATA

NCOA*
The NCOA process standardizes addresses, corrects zip codes, assigns ZIP + 4 codes, identifies movers within the last 36 months and returns the new address. It also flags records that have moved and left no forwarding address.

The NCOA master file contains over 55 million records and is updated every two weeks. NCOA represents one of the most cost efficient methods of increasing a file's deliverability.

Elim-i-Nix - Nixie Identification
Elim-i-Nix is R.L.Polk's file of address changes compiled from multiple sources. Over 40,000,000 records are on the Elim-i-Nix file. Your file can be tagged with moved records so that you can eliminate them from your mailing.

EXACT DATE OF BIRTH - 66.0MM
Unique single sourced file of exact age data not available from traditional compiled enhancement data resources. Since records on this file are unique, a low duplication rate will occur when matched against other age files.

DMA Pander File
A list of individuals who have indicated to DMA that they do not wish to receive direct mail.

NDL Nixie File
A file of approximately 2.3 million individuals who have indicated they do not wish to receive direct mail.

EQUIFAX Deceased File
A Suppress File of persons who are deceased over the last 18 months with dates. Can be used only for suppression.

---

* National Change of Address (NCOA) is a service of USPS operated by May & Speh under license from USPS.

VII. OTHER NEIGHBORHOOD LEVEL DATA

PRIZM Cluster Code

Originally conceived and pioneered by Claritas in 1974, PRIZM is a market segmentation system based on the principle that people with similar backgrounds, means and consumer behavior cluster in neighborhoods suited to their lifestyles.

Through analysis of its demographic characteristics and actual consumer behavior, every one of the 540,000 U.S. neighborhoods is assigned to one of 40 PRIZM Clusters.

Each neighborhood unit, be it a Block-Group, Enumeration District, Census Tract, Minor Civil Division, Zip Code or Postal Carrier Route, is individually assigned. It is assigned due to its own unique demographic characteristics without reference to any other neighborhood unit.

The 40 PRIZM Clusters are further organized into twelve broad social groups.

Uses of the PRIZM System include:

Strategic Planning:	Build a market plan focused on your best consumer prospects. Target the markets offering the highest concentration of your best prospects.
Retail Targeting	Locate stores where your best prospects live or work. See your product in the stores where your best prospects shop.
Direct Mail Promotion	Target direct mail promotions to your best prospects. Tailor ad messages to your best prospects' needs and lifestyles.

All that is required is a name and address file. You then choose any three or more PRIZM clusters to overlay onto the file. Your chosen PRIZM names are selected and the resulting targeted file contains only people who reside in the chosen PRIZM neighborhoods.

GEOPLUS

GEOPLUS is a sophisticated computer software system designed to append Census geographic codes and demographics to a file that contains valid 5-digit zip codes and accurate street address elements.

GEOPLUS, through the application of Census Tract, Enumeration District and Block Group Number, can provide more than 290 different demographic characteristics derived from 1980 census information. Optionally, through the use of the SMACS Data File, GEOPLUS can provide any combination of 1980 census demographics and PRIZM codes.

The GEOPLUS software system is designed to integrate smoothly with existing systems. Being a callable sub-routine, GEOPLUS can be utilized without having to reformat and reprocess address files.

Data provided through GEOPLUS:

FIPS (Federal Information processing Standard) State and County Codes

Census Tract

Block Group

Enumeration District

1980 Census Small Area Characteristics (SMACS)

Claritas PRIZM Cluster Codes

In conjunction with census geocoding, GEOPLUS produces a series of counts that will quantify the coding percentages and measure the quality of the input data.

On clean lists, coding is in the upper 90 percentile.

Carrier Route Marketing Information (CRMI)

R.L. Polk and Company has compiled various census and commercial data by carrier route and by zip code making demographic data available at these two levels.

There are approximately 37,000 active zips and 450,000 active carrier routes.

Data items fall into two major categories:

A. **Census Variables** - These data are based on 1980 U.S. Census information
    published as STF-1 and STF-3. In order to determine the appropriate values
    for households in a carrier route (which is not a geographical unit available
    from the Census Bureau), Polk uses Polk's List X-1, which is a compilation
    of nearly 75 million consumer households. It was thus possible to calculate
    weighted averages based on the actual distribution of families in a carrier
    route among the various census block groups and enumeration districts that
    the carrier route intersected.

B. **Polk Variables** - In the course of compiling List   X-1, Polk uses many
    commercial data sources. The data items in this category are derived by
    actual tabulation of these items as they appear on X-1, carrier route by
    carrier route. These data items will be dynamic, since the families that make
    up each carrier route will change from update to updated due to the current
    17% mobility rate. Sources include Polk's Household Census List (derived
    from city directories published for 26 million households in 6,000
    communities), Drivers License Files, Birth, High School and College Lists,
    Warranty Records, Ethnic and Religious Lists, New Car, New Truck and
    New Motorcycle Sales Records and several other sources. Altogether, over a
    billion data records containing many billions of data items enter the update
    procedure each year.

DATA ITEM DESCRIPTIONS

CENSUS VARIABLES - (All derived from U.S. Bureau of the Census, 1980)

Median Household Income (MED INC) - The total income of all members of the household that falls at the middle of all households when they are rank ordered by total income. Expressed in whole dollars.

Percent of Income Dollars from Dividends, Interest and Rent (INV INC) - Self-described.

Median Home Value (HOM VAL) - The 1980 market value of home that falls in the middle when all homes are ranked by market value. Due to census file STF-36 limits, this is a mean value at the zip level.

Percent of Homes Valued $50,000 or More (HOM 50+) - Self-described.

Median Age of Adults 18 or Over (AGE 18+) - The age of the adult 18 or over who falls in the middle when all adults 18 or over are ranked by age.

Median Age of Adults 25 or Over (AGE 25+) - The age of the adult 25 or over who falls in the middle when all adults 25 or over are ranked by age.

Percent of Households with Children (%HH CHI) - Self-described.

Percent Professional, Technical or Managerial (%HH PTM) - The percentage of all employed persons employed in a job classified as professional, technical or managerial.

Median School Years Completed by Persons Age 25 or Older (SCH YRS) - The number of school years completed by that person 25 or older who fall in the middle when all persons 25 or older are ranked by number of school years completed.

Percent of Housing Units with One Unit at an Address (%-1 ADD) - Based on housing units that have their own address (not considering apartment numbers) even if construction is garden style.

Percent of Housing Units in One Unit Structures   (%1 BLD) - The percentage of units in unattached single family unit buildings.

Percent Owner Occupied Housing Units (%-0 OCC) - Self-described.

Percent of Dwelling Units Built Since 1970 (%-U 70+) - Self-described.

Percent Moved in Since 1975 - (%-M 75+) - Percent of households who moved into the dwelling units they occupied on 4-1-80 between 1-1-76 and 4-1-80.

Percent Foreign Born (%-P FOR) - The percentage of the total population that was not born in the U.S.

Percent Black - (%-P BLK) - The percentage of the population that was black.

Percent Spanish - (%-P SPN) - The percentage of the population that was of Hispanic origin.

Dominant Ethnic Group (DOM ETH) - The ethnic group for which the largest percentage was found.

Percent Motor Vehicle Ownership (%HH M-V) - The percentage of households where ownership of a motor vehicle was indicated.

Place Description (PLA DES) - A code indicating the type of area.

Percent Urbanization (%-Z URB) - The percentage of the zip considered urban.

POLK VARIABLES

Percent Households with Adult Male (%HH MAL) - The percentage of households where Polk can identify an adult male by given name or possible male when only initials are given.

Percent Households with only Female Adult(s) Present (%HH FEM) - The percentage of households where only adult given names(s) is female.

Percent Single Family Dwellings or Unknown (%HH SFD) - The percentage of units either known or presumed to be occupied by only one family.

Percent Multiple Family Dwellings (%HH MFD) - The percentage of units known or inferred to be in multi-family structures.

Percent Length of Residence 0-2 Years (%HH 0-2) - The percentage of households who have appeared at their current address for two years or less.

Percent Length of Residence 10 + Years (%HH 10+) - The percentage of households who have appeared at their current address for ten years or longer.

Average Length of Residence (AVE LOR) - The mean of the length of residence, in years, for all households in the carrier route.

Length of Residence Flag (LOR FLG) - A code indicating that history on length of residence is limited in this carrier route.

Zip Quality Quartile (ZIP Q-Q) - Each zip is ranked according to the relative new car purchase frequency in that zip compared to all other zips.

Average Estimated Household Income (Ray Rating) (INC RAY) - The mean of incomes for all households in the carrier route as estimated by the Ray system, a proprietary Polk algorithm.

Latitude of Carrier Route Centroid - In degrees, minutes and tenths of minutes.

Longitude of Carrier Route Centroid - In degrees, minutes and tenths of minutes.

APPENDIX

to Equifax Descriptions and Definitions Section

Vision^R Summary Descriptions

Vision Code	Nickname	Description
1	Suburban Gentry	Super High Income, Education & Property Value, Families
2	Nouveau Riche	Younger Families, New Subs, Very High Income
3	Tuition & Braces	Older Families, Old Subs, Very High Income
4	Urban Gentry	Urban, Very Affluent Hi Rise, Rentals, Few Children
5	Young Urban Professionals	Younger Urban Singles & Couples, Multi-Unit Rentals
6	Condos & Palms	Older Urban Population, Condos, Hi-Rise, Singles, Retirees
7	Suburban Up & Comers	Young High Income Professionals, School Age Families
8	High Tech Frontiers	Young Families, High Income, New Subs, Many in West & SW
9	The Good Life	Established Empty Nesters, High Income & Property Value
10	Comfortable Suburbanites	Suburban Families, Teens, High Income & Property Value
11	Leave It To Beaver	Newer Housing, Mid High Prop Value, Some Renters
12	A Good Start	Young Families, 50% Renters, 2 Workers, New Housing

Vision Code	Nickname	Description
13	Little League & Barbecues	Upper Mid Income, New Sub, School Age Families, Owner Occ
14	Baby Boom Again	Mid Income, Some Blue Collar, Many Children, Subs
15	Industrial Upper Deck	Mid Income, Blue Collar, Fifties Housing
16	Porch Swings & Apple Pie	Older Housing, Mid/Hi Income, White Collar Families
17	Carports & Kids	Newer Housing, 50% Renters, Children, Mid Income
18	Declining Suburbia	Old Housing, Mixed Occupations, Mixed Income, Older Population
19	Ethnic Industrial	Blue Collar, East European, Old Housing, Duplex
20	Brownstones & Whitesteps	Urban Row Housing, Blue Collar, Some Low Income
21	Black Middle Class	Black, Mid Income, Single Family Housing, Some Renter
22	High Rise Blues	Mid & Hi Rise, Mid & Low Income, Singles & Couples, Retirees
23	Mainstreet, USA	Mid Income Towns, Children, Mixed Occupations, Mixed Housing
24	Town & Country	Older Families, Towns, Mid Income, White Collar
25	Hamlets & Hardhats	Blue Collar Towns, Older Housing, Mid Income
26	Tom Sawyerville	Small Towns, Mid Income, Many in Southern US
27	Mobile Homeville	Rural, Mobile Homes, Mid Income, Blue Collar

Vision Code	Nickname	Description
28	Ranches & Farmlands	Larger Farms, Mid Income, Old Housing, Some Mobile
29	Country Pleasure	Rural Retirees, Some Mobile Homes, Seasonal Housing
30	Young Beginners	Low to Mid Income, Subs, Renters, Singles & Couples
31	Young Hispanics	Hispanic, Low Income, Young Families with Children
32	Just Making It	Low Income Subs, Young & Old, Low Value Property, Blue Collar
33	Single Starters	Urban Singles, Low Income, Renters, Mixed Housing
34	Metro Hispanic Mix	Urban White & Hispanic, Low Income, Children
35	Urban Melting Pot	Inner City High Rise, Very Low Income, Blacks & Hispanics
36	Black Urban Fringe	Urban Black, Older Low Value, Housing, Very Low Income
37	Fixed Income Blues	Urban Older Population, Very Low Income, High Rise
38	Teening Tenenents	Urban Young Blacks, Overcrowded, High Rise, Poverty
39	Sun City	Retirees, Many in Sunbelt, Mid-High Value Property
40	Appalachian Trail	Low Income Towns, Blue Collar & Farm
41	Collegetown, USA	Small College Towns, Ages 18-29, Renters, Dorms
42	Tractors & Pickups	Small Farms, Low Income, Older Housing

Vision Code	Nickname	Description
43	Golden Years	Older Population, Very low-Low Income, Mobile Homes
44	Prairies People	Older Rural Population, Old Housing, Mixed Occupations
45	Tough Times	Rural Black & White Young Families, Very Low Income
46	Books & Beer	College Students, Dorms, Age 18-21, Renting
47	GI Joe	Military Areas, Mixed Income, Mobile Population
48	Institutions & Unclassified	Institutions, Some Military & Unclassified Population

Equis Targeting System Descriptions

Equis Code	Description
1	High income, metropolitan individuals in older households, very high leverage, very high consumer activity, mixed gender.
2	High income, metropolitan individuals in formative households, very high leverage and consumer activity, mixed gender.
3	Middle aged females, middle income, high leverage, very high consumer activity, metropolitan.
4	Middle income individuals in formative households with very high leverage and consumer activity.
5	High income individuals in older formative households with very high leverage and consumer activity.
6	Very low income individuals in formative households, metropolitan, very high leverage and consumer activity.
7	Low income males in formative households, rural location, high leverage and very high consumer activity.
8	Middle income males in formative households, metropolitan, high leverage, and very high consumer activity.
9	Middle income females, formative households, metropolitan, high leverage and very high consumer activity.
10	Middle income individuals, metropolitan in older households, with high leverage and very high consumer activity.
11	Middle income males, older households, high leverage and very high consumer activity.
12	Middle income males, formative households, high leverage, and very high consumer activity.
13	Middle income females in formative households, high leverage, and high consumer activity.

May & Speh Direct

Equis Code	Description
14	Very high income males, established households, low leverage, high consumer activity.
15	Middle income males in established households, low leverage, high consumer activity.
16	Low income males, rural formative households, average leverage, high consumer activity.
17	Low income females in formative households, high leverage, and high consumer activity.
18	Low income females in young, rural households, average leverage, high consumer activity.
19	Low income individuals, young households, average leverage, high consumer activity.
20	High income females, established households, low leverage, high consumer activity.
21	High income males, formative households, average leverage, high consumer activity.
22	Retired females, middle income, very low leverage, high consumer activity.
23	Females in middle income, established households, low leverage, high consumer activity.
24	High income males in older households, average leverage, high consumer activity.
25	Low income males, rural formative households, low leverage, high consumer activity.
26	High income females, young households, very low leverage, high consumer activity.
27	Low income formative households, very high leverage, medium consumer activity.
28	Very low income formative households, average leverage, and high consumer activity.

**Equis
Code**   Description

29   Very low income, formative households, average leverage, and high consumer activity.

30   Low income formative households, high leverage, medium consumer activity.

31   Very low income males in older households, very low leverage, medium consumer activity.

32   Low income males in young households, average leverage, medium consumer activity.

33   Middle income females in young households, average leverage, medium consumer activity.

34   Middle income males, retired, very low leverage, medium consumer activity.

35   Middle income males in formative households, very low leverage, medium consumer activity.

36   Low income males in young households, mainly towns, low leverage, medium consumer activity.

37   Low income females in rural, older households, very low leverage, medium consumer activity.

38   Very low income females, young households with average leverage and medium consumer activity.

39   Very high income individual in older households with very low leverage and low consumer activity

40   Low income males, in rural established households, average leverage, low consumer activity.

41   High income females in established households with very low leverage and low consumer activity.

42   Very low income females in older households, low leverage, and low consumer activity.

43   Very low income females, older households, very low leverage, and low consumer activity.

Equis Code	Description
44	Low income individuals in young households with high leverage and low consumer activity.
45	Very low income males, older households with average leverage and low consumer activity.
46	Low income males, in young rural households with low leverage and low consumer activity.
47	Low income females, young households, average leverage, and low consumer activity.
48	Low income females in young households with low leverage and low consumer activity.
49	High income females in young households with low leverage and low consumer activity.
50	Very low income males, established households, very low leverage, and low consumer activity.
51	Low income females, in young rural households, low leverage, and low consumer activity.
52	Low income males in older households with low leverage and very low consumer activity.
53	High income females in established households with very low leverage and very low consumer activity.
54	Low income males in established households with low leverage and very low consumer activity.
55	Low income females in rural formative households with low leverage and very low consumer activity.
56	Low income females in older households with very low leverage and very low consumer activity.
57	Low income males in young households with low leverage and very low consumer activity.
58	High income males in young households with low leverage and very low consumer activity.

Equis Code	Description
59	Low income males, retired, very low leverage and very low consumer activity.
60	High income females, retired, very low leverage, and very low consumer activity.
61	Middle income females, retired, very low leverage, and very low consumer activity.
62	High income males in established households with very low leverage and very low consumer activity.
63	Low income males, retired, rural with very low leverage and very low consumer activity.
64	Low Income females in rural older households with very low leverage and very low consumer activity.

APPENDIX II

PRODUCT DIRECTORIES

The product information that appears
in Appendix II has been provided
by Datapro Research Corporation,
A McGraw Hill Company.

Data Base Management Systems

Adabas

Software AG of North America, Inc.
11190 Sunrise Valley Drive
Reston, VA 22091
Telephone (703) 860-5050
(800) 843-9534.

Functions: Relational data base management system with functionally integrated set of application development and end-user tools.
Hardware: IBM System/370 architecture; Digital VAX; Wang VS.
Operating System: MVS, MVS/XA, VS1, DOS/VS(E), DOS/SP, SSX/VSE, VM/ CMS; VMS; VS.
Min. Memory: 450KB.
Source Language: ALC.
Source Listings: Not available.
Pricing: Purchase prices range from a low-end of $25,750 to a high-end of $174,000, and is determined by operating system and machine type.
Options: Also runs on Siemens 4004/45 and larger systems under PBS, BS1000, BS2000, and BS3000.
Customizing: A Customs Solutions group is available for developing customized applications with Software AG products.
Maintenance: First year included with license; annual fee of 12% charged thereafter.
Documentation: Included.
Training: Included. The Professional Services group is available for consultation on use of Software AG products.

Current users: Approximately 3,000+ Adabas users worldwide, and 500+ installations worldwide using Adabas(VMS).

Adabas (Adaptable Data Base System) is a relational data base management system with a number of utility programs. The system uses a variety of high-efficiency data management techniques. The Adabas nucleus supports concurrent batch and online processing. A data compression algorithm to load into the data base is an integral function of the system. Also featured is the separation of physical data storage from the representation of logical relationships in the data base. Adabas also includes a comprehensive security system and automatic restart/recovery capabilities.

Software AG has designed Adabas to be used by many different kinds of users with tasks varying from high-volume batch applications to simple online query programs. Adabas offers a high degree of physical and logical data independence through its three schema architecture. In addition, Adabas enhances performance by providing efficient data access at the EXCP level. Another performance enhancement includes the Adabas data compression algorithm, which saves considerable disk storage and I/O. A unique feature of Adabas is its "continuous processing option"—Adabas/CPO. This two-level mechanism is designed to eliminate interruptions to data base processing caused by I/O errors. Adabas/CPO creates a second copy of vital data base areas or even the complete data base. Adabas includes a comprehensive data security system, which supports security at the file, record, field, and value levels and offers data ciphering.

Adabas also provides application migration tools, which allow applications to operate in an Adabas environment without reprogramming. The Adabas migration products (Adabas/VSAM Bridge, Adabas/DL/I Bridge, Adabas/Total Bridge) deliver improved performance, improved security, data independence, automatic restart/recovery, application expandability, data compression, and encryption options.

Data dictionary facilities for Adabas are provided by Predict, an online active data dictionary system that provides facilities for maintaining information on virtually all aspects of data base management and application environments. Predict has the ability to actively capture program information at compile time. Cross-reference information includes program usage of maps, files, fields, and their usage, subroutines, other programs, and global variables.

Data communications support for distributed data base processing is provided by Net-Work/VTAM, Net-Work/CTCS (for Channel-To-Channel Links), Net-Work/VM (for IUCV links), and Net-Work/Hyperchannel.

Net-Work/VTAM provides network support between remote processors via telecommunications lines using IBM ACF/VTAM. It supports communications between different operating system environments via ACF/VTAM. Net-Work/CTCS is a mainframe-only option that provides network support between local processors via a channel-to-channel connection. Net-Work/VM provides network support between virtual machines in an IBM VM environment. It is important to note that Adabas and Net-Work/VM users can reside in any combination of DOS, VS1, MVS, or CMS machines. Net-Work/Hyperchannel provides support between local processors via a hyperchannel interface for Digital VAX and IBM.

Application interfaces to Adabas are supplied through two additional products, AdaSQL and Natural.

Adabas SQL is an SQL-based interface between Adabas and third-generation language applications written in Cobol, Fortran, or PL/1. Adabas SQL translates SQL syntax into Adabas direct calls, providing efficient access to the DBMS. In addition, Adabas SQL is integrated with Predict for cross-referencing and documentation.

Natural provides a complete application development and end user querying environment. It includes facilities for ad hoc query, report generation, screen format creation, and data entry. In addition, Software AG offers a number of Natural-based products that supplement the application development and end user computing environments. These products include: SuperNatural, Natural Security, Natural Connection, Natural Productivity Center, and Con-nect.

Review is an optional accounting and usage statistics system used to collect, summarize, and display statistics relating to the performance and efficiency of Adabas applications. It can be used by the DBA as a performance measurement and tuning device.

An in-depth Datapro report on this product is published in *Datapro Reports on Software* and *DP70*. Details include profile, management summary, competitive position, advantages and restrictions, user opinion, product description, and pricing.

CA-DATACOM/DB

Computer Associates International, Inc.
711 Stewart Avenue
Garden City, NY 11530-4787
Telephone (516) 227-3300
(800) 645-3003
telex 981393
fax (516) 227-3937.
See Tab D97 for int'l. headquarters.

Functions: Data base management.
Hardware: IBM System/370 architecture.
Operating System: DOS, DOS/VS(E), VM/CMS, MVS, MVS/XA, VM.
Source Language: Assembler.
Source Listings: Not available.
Pricing: Perpetual license: $82,500—$165,000 (MVS); $68,850—$119,340 (VSE or VM).
Maintenance: First year included with perpetual license; fixed percentage of prevailing purchase price annually thereafter; included for duration of lease options.
Documentation: Included.

Training: Included.
First Installed: 1974.

CA-DATACOM/DB is a relational data base management system designed for concurrent support of transaction processing and information center use. It is the cornerstone of integrated tools using an active data dictionary to tie these tools together. Support for SQL and CASE is included. CA-DATACOM/DB supports SQL at three levels. This three-level SQL support delivers an open architecture, enabling the DATACOM user to take advantage of a wide range of application packages and tools. CA-DATACOM/DB achieves both performance and the power of the relational model through unique features including a Smart Relational Optimizer and an advanced relational indexing system.

DB2 (Database2)

International Business Machines Corp. (IBM), Old Orchard Rd., Armonk, NY 10504. Telephone your local IBM representative.

Functions: Relational data base management.
Hardware: IBM System/370 architecture.
Operating System: MVS, MVS/XA, MVS/SP.
Min. Memory: 2.5MB
Peripherals: CICS, IMS/VS DC, and TSO.
Pricing: Contact vendor.
Maintenance: Contact vendor.
Documentation: Available.
Training: Available.
First Installed: June 1987.

DB2 (5740-XYR) is a large-system relational DBMS. It can be installed with the IMS/VS/DB hierarchical system or configured as a stand-alone DBMS. The DB2 system employs the SQL (Structured Query Language) as its host data base language, and is compatible, to some degree, with the SQL/DS relational system designed for use with the DOS/VS environment. It has IBM's SAA data base interface. SQL enhancements include date/time and single precision floating point data types and operations and extended ANSI SQL compatibility. Operational and performance enhancements include DL/1 batch support; and SQL optimization, utility improvements, and MVS/XA storage usage improvements. DB2 provides: relational file structure, views, table space, SQL, data space management, user interface, monitoring and accounting, security and authorization, and data set protection. The product features an integrated data base dictionary. All data in a DB2 data base is stored in VSAM entry sequenced data sets (ESDS), which can be defined and maintained by the user or by DB2. DB2 supports a relational data model. The data in DB2's data base is defined in terms of tables and accessed through operations on tables. Data definition, retrieval, manipulation, and control operations are supported by the SQL. SQL is a high-level data language available to users through an interactive terminal and through application programs written in APL2, Cobol, Fortran, PL/1, Basic, or Assembler language. DB2's is independent of both DASD and tape device type. Its architecture provides for data bases with up to 64 billion bytes per table. DB2 is supported by a set of data base utilities that operate online, including the Data Extract (DXT) and DB2 Performance Monitor.

Image/3000

Hewlett-Packard Co., 1820 Embarcadero Rd., Palo Alto, CA 94303. Telephone your local representative.

Functions: Data base management.
Hardware: Hewlett-Packard HP 3000.
Operating System: MPE.
Peripherals: Disk, console, magnetic tape or tape cartridge.
Source Language: Cobol, Fortran, SPL.
Source Listings: Available.
Pricing: Part of fundamental operating software and is included.
Maintenance: Available.
Documentation: Included.
Training: 5 days at $725/day.
Current users: 20,000+.
First Installed: June 1973.

Image is a Codasyl-like general-purpose data base management system. It uses a network data structure as its data base organization. Data entry selection is made using one of four access methods: Serial, Chained, Directed, and Calculated. Image allows information to be related logically between data sets, minimizing data redundancy and facilitating information retrieval. Image operates concurrently in both terminal and batch environments and consists of four components: Data Base Definition Language: to describe data items (fields), data sets, data set relationships, security, and storage requirements. Data Base Management Subsystems: to access and maintain data, a set of Image library routines is provided. The routines can be called from user-written programs to open, close, get, update, put, delete, find, lock, unlock, log, and return information about the data base being currently accessed. Data Base Utilities: can be used to create, maintain, and restructure a data base, and backup data. Data Base Enquiry Facility: designed for non-programmers to easily locate, report, and update data values within an Image data base through English-like commands. Security is provided at several levels. Up to 63 classes of users can be defined. A password is associated with each class. Sets of user classes can then be permitted "read" or "read-and-write" access to any or all data items and/or data sets, independent of the elements accessible to other user classes. Concurrency control is provided by Image 3000 at the data base, data set, and record level. The system also offers a logging and recovery system which is designed to restore data bases to a consistent state, both logically and structurally.

Ingres

Ingres Corporation
1080 Marina Village Parkway
Alameda, CA 94501-9891
Telephone (415) 769-1400
(800) 4-INGRES
telex 333476.

Functions: Distributed relational data base management application development tools.
Hardware: Alliant FX Series; Apollo Domain; AT&T 3B Systems; CCI Power Series; Data General MV Family; Digital VAX; Gould PowerNode; Hewlett-Packard; IBM System/370 architecture; NCR Tower 32; Pyramid x; Sequent Balance; Unisys U Series.
Add'l. Hardware: Apple AU/X; Apollo DN; Arete; Amdahl; British Tele.; Convergent Technologies; Compaq; Digital Micro-VAX; HP 150; IBM PC and compatibles; ICL; Sun.
Operating System: AU/X, Unix, UTS, Concentrix, Domain/IX, MS/PC-DOS, Xenix, VMS, Ultrix, HP-UX, MVS, VM/CMS, C-DOS, OSx.
Min. Memory: 1MB.
Source Language: C.
Source Listings: Not available.
Pricing: Licensed from $950 to $160,000.
Customizing: Available.
Maintenance: Included.
Documentation: Included.
Training: Three days included.
Current users: 8,500.
First Installed: June 1981.

Ingres is a full-function, relational data base management system combined with a visual programming applications development system along with knowledge management and object management extensions. It includes SQL, an English-like query language for interactive definition, protection, and manipulation of data through simple tables. The system features automatic optimization algorithms that provide access to online data bases. Routines for data validation, concurrency control, security, recovery, and transaction processing are also included. Ingres automatically stores and maintains all information about a data base and related applications in an integrated data dictionary. Ingres' knowledge management and object management extensions allow organizations to model their data upon their business model.

The Ingres Distributed SQL Relational Data Base System combines open architecture, distributed data base capability with integrated, fourth-generation application tools and high-performance SQL to provide a total solution for organizations with diverse and complex data processing needs. Application tools are completely integrated with the relational DBMS and include a fourth-generation application development environment and end-user decision support tools. Fill-in-the-forms data access, Visual Programming, and a complete fourth-generation language allow users to develop entire applications in minutes.

Ingres/Net and *Ingres/Star* offer networking and true distributed data base capabilities. Ingres provides ease of use for both end users and programmers. An integrated Data Dictionary keeps track of all applications elements. Artificial intelligence-based query optimization ensures top performance for all types of query processing. A wide selection of storage structures and indexing methods allow tuning for the best performance available in all types of applications. Companion gateways link directly to non-Ingres data bases. SQL or Quel, as well as screen control commands, can be embedded in C, Cobol, Basic, ADA, Pascal, Fortran, and PL/1 programs. The current Ingres, release 5.0, is 30% to 50% faster than its predecessor for Complex Queries and TP1. Overall, Ingres performance has increased ten times since its introduction.

Ingres' SQL data base language is compatible with IBM's DB2. Applications can be moved between Ingres and DB2 with minimal effort. As a result, Ingres can complement DB2 in an organization by running the same applications on minicomputers and microcomputers as DB2 runs on the IBM mainframe. Alternatively, organizations can choose Ingres as their single data base management system running on all computers from mainframes to micros. Ingres' SQL also complies with the ANSI Level 1 and X-Open SQL standards.

506 Appendix

INGRES INCLUDES

- Ingres/Menu
- Ingres/Query (Query-By-Forms)
- Ingres/Reports (Report-By-Forms and Report Writer)
- Ingres/Forms (Form Run-Time System and Visual-Forms-Editor)
- Ingres Interactive SQL and Quel

OPTIONAL FEATURES INCLUDE

- Ingres/Applications (Applications-By-Forms)
- Ingres/Graphics (ViGraph)
- Ingres/PClink
- Ingres for Personal Computers.
- Embedded SQL and Quel and preprocessors for C, Cobol, Fortran, Basic, Pascal, Ada, and PL/1
- Ingres/Net (Data Baase Networking Support)
- Ingres/Star (Distributed Data Manager)
- Ingres Gateways to RMS and dBase
- Ingres/Knowledge Management
- Ingres/Object Management

Ingres/Star is Ingre Corporation's open-architecture, distributed data base product. Distributed data base systems enable organizations to develop applications and access data that span a variety of computer systems with the same ease as if all information were resident on a single computer. Ingres/Star differs from data base networking products in that multiple computers can be accessed simultaneously. The user need not know where the data is located or protocols for accessing it. Both functions are handled transparently to the user by Ingres/Star. Ingres/Star's open architecture enables the distributed data base to operate over dissimilar hardware, operating systems, and networks. The product also provides gateways that will enable other vendors' data base management products to interface with the distributed environment. Ingres/Star is a major technological innovation that will help resolve the significant problem of corporate data being dispersed across a number of normally incompatible environments, often referred to as the "Islands of Information" problem.

Ingres/Net gives users distributed access to all Ingres data bases contained in a computer network, even with diverse operating environments. All Ingres tools and applications run interactively on the user's local computer, while Ingres information from remote computers can be accessed as necessary. Ingres/Net is optimized for speed in interactive applications and overall system throughput. The number and size of messages are minimized with Ingres/Net, thus reducing the cost of sending information over long distance lines.

Ingres/Applications 4GL allows users to share and manipulate information without writing, documenting, or debugging traditional programming code. Applications-By-Forms (ABF) keeps track of all elements of your application automatically. Forms, Reports, and Graphs are easily combined using Ingres' advanced Fourth-Generation concept. Ingres/4GL provides complete access to all SQL commands, forms control, flow of control (IF-THEN-ELSE, WHILE, functions, and procedures), and data manipulation (arithmetic and strings) to provide the flexibility to build any type of application. Complete, sophisticated, multiuser applications can be built in a fraction of the time required by traditional programming techniques.

Ingres/PClink provides personal computer users with a bridge to PC personal productivity tools from Ingres data bases on a host system. PC users can access information in host Ingres data bases and applications using a familiar PC-oriented Visual Query Language. The product allows personal computer users to browse through the contents of Ingres data bases on other computer systems, extract data, transfer the data across a network, and store and manipulate the data in users' personal computer files. Ingres/PClink automatically reformats data collected from host systems to conform with personal computer software packages, such as Lotus 1-2-3, dBase, Wordstar, and Multiplan.

Ingres for Personal Computers offers a high-performance SQL RDBMS with all of the features of Ingres. It provides DB2 compatibility for PCs, Lotus 1-2-3 style "ring menus." Complete data base and application portability between PC-DOS, VAX/VMS, Unix, MVS, and VM/CMS is provided. Ingres for Personal Computers shares data transparency between PCs, minis, and mainframes using the Ingres/Star distributed data base.

The *Ingres/Object Management Extension* stores objects in the DBMS server. It increases programmer productivity, ensures object integrity, improves performance on client/server networks, and provides organizations with SQL-based access to complex or unconventional data (i.e., latitude, longitude, coordinates, arrays, vectors, and bitmaps).

The *Ingres/Knowledge Management Extension* manages knowledge within the DBMS server using sophisticated rules, resource control, and access control systems. Ingres rules are procedures that automatically enforce business policies and referential integrities; the resource control system works with the query optimizer to establish server-enforced limitations on resource consumption. Special enhancements to the access control (data permissions) system include group- and application-level permissions, permissions to limit access to certain data control language (DCL) statements, and the ability to grant resource control permissions to groups or applications.

The *Ingres Gateway* product line provides an easy migration path from early generation file management systems, such as RMS and dBase, to distributed data base environments, such as Ingres.

An in-depth Datapro report on this product is published in *Datapro Reports on Software* and *DP70*. Details include profile, management summary, competitive position, advantages and restrictions, user opinion, product description, and pricing.

MAPPER

Unisys Corp.
P.O. Box 500
Blue Bell, PA 19424-0001
Telephone   your   local   Unisys
representative.
See Tab D97 for int'l. headquarters.

Functions: End-user oriented applications development environment.

Hardware: Unisys 1100/2200; Unisys A Series; Unisys U Series; Unisys V Series; Unisys System 80.
Add'l. Hardware: Unisys PC; PW2; IBM PC.
Pricing: Contact vendor.
Maintenance: Available.
Documentation: Included.
Current users: 6,500, plus PC users.

MAPPER SYSTEM

I. WHAT IS IT?

The MAPPER System is a revolutionary software offering from Unisys Corporation's Information Systems Group. It is a complete information system for business, finance, government, and education.

From the James Martin Report on High-Productivity Languages:

"The significance of the MAPPER System is that it enables end users to employ their own business experience to manipulate data and generate reports without assistance from DP. Spectacular improvements in information processing capability have been achieved by non-DP end users through the utilization of the MAPPER System. In many cases traditionally oriented DP personnel have greatly underestimated the capability of end users to access and process information. Given appropriate tools, such as the MAPPER System, end users can create information processing systems of surprising complexity. These tools permit end users to gain direct access to the data they need to solve business problems."

Its user-friendly construction allows all individuals and/or departments in business, finance, government, and educational organizations to make the computer a major tool in meeting their objectives and goals. It dramatically increases the throughput of the EDP function, while significantly reducing its cost. Specifically, it includes the following capabilities:

A. THE MAPPER SYSTEM IS A FOURTH-GENERATION LANGUAGE (4GL)...

But the MAPPER System is a dimension beyond other 4GLs in that the end user not only has all the usual 4GL features for information gathering, but has additional, powerful functions for doing things like repricing an entire inventory with the same easy interface as asking questions. No other 4GL can do that. Entire applications can be developed just as easily, too. The MAPPER System contains an online tutorial for self-teaching. And, if a user has a problem, the system automatically displays the exact point of the online documentation that deals with that particular error situation—no thumbing through books to look up cryptic message codes.

Indeed, the MAPPER System is far more than just a 4GL. In a recent study by Arthur Young & Company, the MAPPER System was compared to the most popular 4GLs. In the study, an overall conclusion is repeated several times. It is that, of all of the products studied, only the MAPPER environment serves every level of data processing need—from the simplest query to the most complex application, from decision support to day-to-day operations, from end user to DP professional, and from one individual to an entire network of users—with one product.

The MAPPER System is available in the broadest range of any product in the industry—bar none. Users can purchase time on a Unisys mainframe to use the MAPPER System with the lowest possible risk, as there is no equipment to buy. Or, the MAPPER System can be installed on a Unisys personal computer. The MAPPER System is also offered on micro, mini, and mainframe computers, serving more users as the systems grow in size. Amazingly, a user can become a reseller of MAPPER products and that shows you how powerful the MAPPER System is. No other 4GL can offer that— The MAPPER Business Program is an industry first!

. THE MAPPER SYSTEM IS A TRANSACTION PROCESSOR...

From the James Martin Report on High-Productivity Languages:

"The MAPPER System is unique in that it is specifically designed to support large numbers of end users. As the MAPPER System evolved, each design decision was based toward supporting large networks of distributed terminals. The overall objective of the MAPPER System was to provide large numbers of simultaneous users with the ability to access reports and manipulate information without assistance from DP. A measure of the success of the MAPPER System in meeting this objective is that it has been used to build the world's largest end-user-developed system."

It can support a heavily interactive, online network and achieve the quick response times normally seen only in exotic (and costly) installations. At Unisys, a MAPPER System supporting over 6,000 terminals handles 400,000 transactions per day and processes over 185 million records.

It can support a very large network of both remote and local terminals, printers, disks, and other devices.

It has extensive security features to control user access.

It is fully recoverable to the hour, minute, and second.

It has a complete built-in resource accounting system.

It can interface with other systems (on the same machine or on other machines in a network...including IBM).

C. ...A DATA BASE

Table-structure type (relational).

Can relate data by any common data item.

Has an integral language to process data.

Is fully recoverable.

Has historical archiving capability.

Highly efficient to enable fast response to users.

D. ...A REPORTING SYSTEM

Built on an easy-to-understand and maintainable data base "file cabinet approach."

Data is kept in tables—called "Reports"—and each report can have multiple formats.

These reports can be immediately updated by realtime transactions or periodically, in batch processing.

Users can update, change, delete, do arithmetic functions, consolidate information from multiple reports, etc., by using "MAPPER Functions" or "MAPPER Runs" (prestored sequences of functions).

If desired, users can request that data from reports be represented in color graphics form which optionally can be reproduced as plotter output.

E. . . .AN OFFICE-OF-THE-FUTURE SYSTEM

Provides full message switching to any CRT terminal, printer, or disk device on the network.

Provides electronic mail and calendar capabilities.

"Conference Call" via terminal.

Word Processing.

Full ASCII character set.

A spelling checker.

Ability to store, index, and retrieve documents.

Phrase locate and phrase change feature.

Model 204

Computer Corporation of America
4 Cambridge Center
Cambridge, MA 02142
Telephone (617) 492-8860
TWX 710 320-6479.
See Tab D97 for int'l. headquarters.

Functions: Data base management.
Operating System: DOS/VS(E), VS1, MVS, MVS/XA, VM/CMS, VM/IS.
Min. Memory: 670KB.
Peripherals: Teletypes or IBM 2740, 2741, 2260, 2265, or 3270, required for remote online processing.
Timesharing: Informatics, COMET, Datacrown.
Source Language: Assembler.
Source Listings: Available.
Pricing: Purchase—$40,000 to $300,000. Available on GSA schedule.
Maintenance: Fully guaranteed, on-call maintenance.

Documentation: Included with installation.
Training: Additional training available.
Current users: 400+.
First Installed: November 1969.

Model 204 is a high-performance data base management system. It provides all the facilities required for performing complete data base management functions. Model 204 provides the data manipulation features and high degree of data independence typical of relational DBMS products. In addition, it provides extensions to the relational model that allow the application developer great flexibility in data base design.

The Model 204 fourth-generation language, User Language, is a powerful developer and end-user application development tool used for query reporting and data base updates. User Language completely replaces the need to do development in third-generation languages, such as Cobol. The User Language is available for use in either online or batch mode. Model 204 files can also be accessed from Cobol, Fortran, Assembler, or PL/1 programs, through the Host Language Interface. Model 204 supports data independence, meaning that the application programmer need not know the file structures, format, or location of stored data. Fields can be added, deleted, or modified at any time without file reorganization. The system also features dynamic cross-referencing between files, and it offers a File Groups facility that permits many physically distinct files to be treated as a single logical file for processing, on either a temporary or permanent basis.

Model 204 can be used in batch mode or online with its own teleprocessing monitor, or through interfaces to CICS, TSO, or Intercomm. Model 204 also interfaces directly with VTAM, TCAM, BTAM and VM/VTAM. It is a true multithread system, that allows thousands of users to simultaneously access up to 16,383 files to the field level. Comprehensive data administration facilities include a data dictionary, nine levels of security, an audit trail, an online monitoring system, and complete restart/recovery utilities to ensure data base integrity. The system is highly modular, enabling users to select the most appropriate configurations to meet their needs.

ORACLE

Oracle Systems, Inc., 20 Davis Dr., Belmont, CA 94002. Telephone (415) 598-8000, (800) 345-3267; telex 171437.

Functions: Relational data base management systems (RDBMS) and services.

Hardware: Apollo Domain; AT&T 3B Systems; CCI Power Series; CDC Cyber Series; Concurrent Series 3200; Datapoint All; Elxsi 6400; Encore; Gould NPL; Gould PowerNode; Data General MV Family; Digital VAX; Harris H Series; Hewlett-Packard HP 3000; Honeywell Bull; IBM System/370 architecture; IBM System/88; Intergraph; NCR; Motorola Computer Systems; Pyramid x; Prime 50 Series; Sequent Balance; Stratus/32; Unisys; Wang All.

Add'l. Hardware: Altos; Apple; Amdahl; ARIX; Banyan; BBN; Convex; Cubix; DCL; Edge; Edisa; ETA; IBM RT/PC; ISI; Intel; MIPS; NEC; NTT; Nixdorf; Olivetti; Plexus; Siemens; Sun; TAB; Toshiba; UTS; Xenix.

Operating System: AIX, AOS, A/UX, Finder, HP-UX, MPE XL, MS-DOS, Multi-Finder, MVS, NOS/VE, OS/2, Primos, Unix, UTS, VM/CMS, VMS, VS, DOS/VSE, Xenix.

Min. Memory: Mainframe: not applicable; mini: 2MB; micro: 1MB.

Timesharing: Not available.

Source Language: C.

Source Listings: Not available.

Pricing: From $199 to $150,000.

Customizing: Available through Oracle Advanced Services.

Maintenance: Available.

Documentation: Included.

Training: Day and week-long sessions available.

Current users: 86,000 (all platforms).

First Installed: 1979.

ORACLE is the relational data base management system software based on SQL. It provides data definition, data manipulation, and data control facilities. ORACLE is compatible with IBM's DB2 and SQL/DS and is portable to 56 different computers and over 20 operating systems. Portability, connectability, and compatibility are the messages of the ORACLE relational data base system. ORACLE provides a common software platform to develop complete systems across a wide variety of computers and operating systems. Combining these systems into a cohesive distributed data base has never been easier. And since ORACLE is portable, applications need not be rewritten to take advantage of newer processors or be moved to smaller computers. The ORACLE kernel is a component of the SQL*Star distributed architecture, which provides distributed data base processing and the data base. The data base includes an interactive data dictionary that gives data base administrators complete control over access and resources within the data base. In addition, security audit features detect and log all unauthorized access or misuse of selected data within the system. These features are standard with ORACLE. ORACLE has the capability of both rollforward and rollback transaction recovery. And, with Version 6 with the Transaction Processing Subsystem, users realize continuous operations with a fault tolerant enterprise-wide data base. Oracle's Application Tools include: SQL*Plus is an ad hoc query processor capable of producing standard business reports; SQL*Forms allows development and running of online, screen-based applications; SQL*ReportWriter is a productivity tool geared to assist the application builder in specifying a wide range of report styles; SQL*Menu is an application tool that controls any Oracle application. It provides a common front end to both ORACLE and non-ORACLE applications. It can tie SQL*ReportWriter, SQL*Forms, or any other application into one common interface. For the professional programmer, Oracle has a complete set of tools that allow Cobol, Fortran, C Pascal, PL/1, Ada, Hypercard, and BASIC programs to directly manipulate the data base. The PRO products also allow for the extension of SQL*Forms to do special processing such as complicated formulas. PL/SQL is a comprehensive language for specifying the flow of control of SQL statements within one or more transactions being processed. PL/SQL is also a universal portable language allowing applications as diverse as SQL*Plus, SQL*Forms, and Pro*C or Pro*COBOL to invoke a common language. For example, PL/SQL can be used to customize the behavior of an SQL*Forms screen. Logic written in PL/SQL will automatically be portable to every computer which ORACLE runs on.

SUPRA

Cincom Systems, Inc., 2300 Montana Ave., Cincinnati, OH 45211. Telephone (513) 662-2300, (800) 543-3010; telex 810 461 2732 CINCOMSYSCIN. *See Tab D97 for int'l. headquarters.*

Functions: Relational data base management.
Hardware: Apollo Domain; Digital VAX; IBM System/370 architecture; Pyramid; Sequent; Amdahl, Nixdorf.
Operating System: MVS, MVS/XA, DOS/VSE, VSE/SP, VM/CMS; VMS; Unix.
Min. Memory: 3MB.
Timesharing: Not available.
Source Language: Pascal, Assembler.
Source Listings: Not available.
Pricing: $21,000 and up.
Customizing: Available.
Maintenance: Available.
Documentation: Included.
Training: 20 days included.
First Installed: January 1986.

Supra Version 2 is an advanced relational data base management system built on the ANSI-/SPARC-endorsed ''three schema architecture'' and is portable across IBM, Digital, and Unix platforms. Supra v2 also includes a productive implementation of SQL and will serve as the foundation for a single-system image implementation of a fully distributed data base management system. Supra can handle high transaction production environments and offers a complete set of productivity tools for end users, application developers, and data base administrators. Easy provides a forms-driven, language-free interface to the data base for end users. Spectra is an advanced relational query system that gives end users the capability to retrieve information quickly and nonprocedurally. Mantis is Cincom's application development tool and part of The CASE Environment, Cincom's end-to-end application development solution. Mantis allows SQL applications to be portable across operating systems and hardware platforms. Supra also provides support for multiple data base structures and access methods through the standard SQL interface. Users can access VSAM as well as Supra's own files without being aware of the source of the data. Additional DBMS support is planned for future releases of Supra.

Structured Query Language/ Data System (SQL/DS)

International Business Machines Corp. (IBM), Old Orchard Rd., Armonk, NY 10504. Telephone your local IBM representative.

Functions: Relational data management.
Hardware: IBM System/370 architecture.
Operating System: DOS/VS(E), VM/SP.
Min. Memory: 2MB.
Peripherals: One nine-track tape drive or 3480 magnetic tape unit.
Pricing: Contact vendor.
Maintenance: Contact vendor.
First Installed: December 1988.

SQL/DS (5688-004) provides online query, report writer, and end-user relational data base facilities. Features include: data base backup and archive operations, data base recovery, and error diagnosis; diagnostics for isolating data base failures; and options for handling data base recovery from system or user errors. Remote Relational Access Support (RRAS) when used with VM/SP Transparent Services Access Facility (TSAF), allows users on one CPU to access an SQL/DS data base on another locally or remotely connected CPU. Other features include: logical optimization; multiple language help text support and archive tape blocking support for VM; SQL allows users to query, manipulate, and define their data; American National Standards (ANS) compatibility; VARCHAR>254 data definition support; and Fortran preprocessor capabilities. SQL requests can be entered through CICS/VS or ICCF supported terminals as input to the SQL/DS Data Base Services utility, or can be embedded in application programs written in Cobol, PL/1, or Assembler. SQL/DS supports multiple, concurrent access from batch partitions, online environments, and interactive program execution environments. Other features include: restart and recovery; in-line catalog capabilities; a DL/1 extract facility; and relational productivity family and access generator technology. VSE Guest Sharing allows VSE users and programs running within a VSE Guest machine to access an SQL/DS data base running under VM/SP. An SQL Application Interface for VSAM allows the execution of CICS/VM transactions against the same VM/SP-SQL/DS or remote data base containing migrated MVS or VSE VSAM data sets.

dBASE IV

Ashton-Tate, 20101 Hamilton Avenue, Torrance, CA 90502-1319.
Telephone (213) 329-8000

Function: Database management.
Hardware: IBM PC/XT/AT and compatibles; IBM PS/2.
Min. Memory: 640KB RAM.
Pricing: Contact vendor.
Maintenance: Ninety days free support.
Documentation: Included.
First installed: 1988.

dBASE IV is a database management package that provides improved relational capabilities and SQL compatibility. dBASE IV offers the user a completely redesigned menu system called the Control Center, which provides a menuing system for creation and maintenance of records. Most features are accessible from the Control Center, but some are not. Database design with dBASE IV is achieved from the Command Center. To begin work, the user names the record file, defines the fields, and enters the data. The user does not have to leave the menu at any time during the creation process, and the transition from record creation to data entry is accomplished with just a few keystrokes. Reports and queries can be generated from the Control Center or from the dot prompt. Either way, the design process is the same. dBASE IV presents a file skeleton which displays the fields and files available; a view skeleton, which shows the fields that have been selected for the query; and the calculated field skeleton, which shows any temporary variables. dBASE IV supports character, numeric, floating-point, binary coded decimal, date, logical, and memo fields. Modifying a field definition is accomplished from the Control Center. Data transfer is accomplished either from the Control Center import menu or from the command line. The dBASE IV import facility permits direct import of files in the RapidFile, dBASE II, FrameWork II, Lotus 1-2-3, and PFS:File formats. The protect command provides the system administrator with three types of security control on a single system or in a networked environment. Login security and user passwords can be assigned, files and fields can be protected from unauthorized access, and files can be further protected through data encryption. dBASE IV's relational capabilities allow a user to define multiple relations per file, and to link multiple files at once, using the create query and create view commands. Linking multiple files is handled in the query by example (QBE) menu by pointing to the files and fields to be included in the query. The menu-driven dBASE IV applications generator allows the user to build and save modifiable and executable dBASE programs without actually writing the code. dBASE IV does not support EMS or expanded memory.

KnowledgeMan/2.5

Micro Data Base Systems, Inc., P.O. Box 248, Lafayette, IN 47902.
Telephone (317) 463-2581, (800) 344-5832

Function: Application developer's toolkit.
Hardware: IBM PC/XT/AT and compatibles.
Min. Memory: 512KB RAM.
Operating System: MS-DOS 2.1+, PC-DOS 2.1+, and CP/M-86.
Pricing: $695.
Maintenance: Vendor support is handled on a callback basis.
Training: $495 for a three-day session held at MDBS regional
offices.
Documentation: Included.

KnowledgeMan 2.5 is an upgrade to the SQL-based decision
support/relational database of MDBS. The 2.5 version offers an
improved menuing system, additional RAM access, IBM Enhanced Graphics Adapter (EGA) support, Hercules Graphics Card
support, 8087 math co-processor support, and a shopping list of
enhancements to programming features. Although Knowledge-
Man is considered a database package, the term "application
developer's toolkit" is more appropriate. With its programmabili-
ty and near replication of SQL, the program can be used by the
mainframe or mini user who wants to convert to local processing
with no compromise in performance.

MDBS III

MicroData Base Systems, Inc., Application Development Products, P.O. Box 248, Lafayette, IN 47902. Telephone (317) 463-
2581, (800) 344-5832.

Function: Data base management.
Hardware: IBM PC/XT/AT and compatibles; Digital MicroVAX
II; Unisys PC/IT; IBM RT PC; NCR Tower 1632.
Min. Memory: 256KB.
Operating System: MS-DOS, Xenix, and Unix.
Source language: C, Assembler; source code not available.
Pricing: License to use from about $4,000 to about $53,000,
depending on options and environments.
Optional features/pricing: Also available on Digital VAX, AT&T
3B Systems, and Unisys 5000/40/50. Other options include:
DDL/DMS (standard form)—$3,900-$15,900; DDL/DMS/RTL
(RTL form)—$7,025-$28,600; BLF—$1,000-$4080; DBRS—
$2,500-$5,100; DMU—$375-$800; IDML—$1,550-$4,760;
QRS—$1,950-$5,955; RDL—$1,950-$3,970.
Maintenance: First year included; 15% of list thereafter.
Customizing: Available, from simple consulting through complete
application development.
Documentation: Included.
Training: Three day seminars at $545 per attendee.
First installed: December 1981.
Current users: 2,500+.

MDBS III is an extended-network data base management system
that can be used to form data bases composed of up to 4.2
gigabytes. A user-password mechanism, together with an access
code mechanism, form part of the data security system. Automatic
data encryption, data compression, and range checking are supported. MDBS III is a high-end DBMS for professional developers
with applications having large volumes of data, complex data
relationships, or high performance requirements. In actual tests on
an IBM PC/AT, MDBS III retrieved records from a 60 megabyte
data base of over 500,000 records in less than ¼ second.

Paradox 3.0

Borland International, 1800 Green Hills Road, Scotts Valley, CA 95066. Telephone (408) 438-8400

Function: Relational database management system.
Hardware: IBM PC/XT/AT and compatibles; IBM PS/2.
Min. Memory: 512KB RAM.
Pricing: $725.
Maintenance: Included.
Customizing: Not available.
Documentation: Included.

Paradox 3.0 is a relational database. Paradox's Query-by-Example (QBE) lets the user ask complex questions about data without programming. Paradox 3.0 contains new enhancements to QBE, as well as multitable, multirecord forms for one-to-many and many-to-many relationships without programming, new multitable report capability, and fully integrated presentation graphics. Paradox 3.0 includes a complete programming environment. Script recording automates repetitive tasks. The Paradox Personal Programmer automatically generates PAL scripts that can later be modified or enhanced. The Paradox Application Language (PAL), a high-level structured programming language, builds on Paradox's interactive capabilities to create sophisticated applications in less time. Paradox contains a complete set of integrated facilities for working with PAL, including an interactive debugger and a script editor.

APPENDIX III

LOTUS 1-2-3® PROGRAMS

```
G1: [W2]                                                              READY


     G                    H                    I    J      K       L
 1    SITUATION 1.0
 2    **********************************************************************  *
 3    * YOU ARE PLANNING TO TEST A LIST. YOU ESTIMATE THE TRUE RESPONSE    *
 4    * RATE, SELECT A CONFIDENCE LEVEL, AND ENTER THE NUMBER OF PIECES    *
 5    * MAILED.  THE CONFIDENCE INTERVAL IS SHOWN BELOW.  YOU CAN USE THE  *
 6    * SAME SCREEN TO CALCULATE A CONFIDENCE INTERVAL AROUND ACTUAL RESPONSE *
 7    * **********************************************************************  *
 8    *                                                          TEST     *
 9    *                                                         MAILING   *
10    *                                                         --------   *
11    * o EXPECTED (OR ACTUAL) RESPONSE RATE.................    4.50%   *
12    * o CONFIDENCE LEVEL: 80%, 85%, 90% OR 95%..............   95.00%   *
13    * o SAMPLE SIZE................................         1,000    *
14    * o TWO SIDED TEST                                                 *
15    *                                                                  *
16    *                                                                  *
17    *                                                                  *
18    *                                                                  *
19    * THE EXPECTED RESPONSE RANGE IS BETWEEN..  3.22%   AND      5.78% *
20    * **********************************************************************  *
10-Jan-90  02:27 PM                                  CALC      CAPS
```

```
G21: [W2]                                                             MENU
Range  Line  Page  Options  Clear  Align  Go  Quit
Advance one line
     G                    H                    I    J      K       L
21
22                          PERCENT RESPONSE =   p =   4.50%
23                             SAMPLE SIZE =      n =   1,000
24
25                           STANDARD ERROR =    SE =   0.66%
26                          SQRT OF [p*(1-p)/N]
27                      CONFIDENCE LEVELS: =            80.00%     1.282
28                          TWO SIDED TEST             85.00%     1.440
29                                                     90.00%     1.645
30                                                     95.00%     1.960
31                            LEVEL USED =       a =    1.96
32                               a*SE =                 1.28%
33                               p+a*SE =               5.78%
34                               p-a*SE =               3.22%
35
36
37
38
39
40
10-Jan-90  02:27 PM                                  CALC      CAPS
```

DIRECT MARKETING STATISTICS -DAVID SHEPARD ASSOCIATES, INC

```
H22: [W40] "PERCENT RESPONSE =
I22: [W7] "p =
J22: (P2) [W7] +K11
H23: [W40] "SAMPLE SIZE =
I23: [W7] "n =
J23: (,0) [W7] +K13
H25: [W40] "STANDARD ERROR =
I25: [W7] "SE =
J25: (P2) [W7] @SQRT(K11*(1-K11)/J23)
H26: [W40] "SQRT OF [p*(1-p)/N]
H27: [W40] "CONFIDENCE LEVELS: =
J27: (P2) [W7] 0.8
H28: [W40] "TWO SIDED TEST
J28: (P2) [W7] 0.85
J29: (P2) [W7] 0.9
J30: (P2) [W7] 0.95
H31: [W40] "LEVEL USED =
I31: [W7] "a =
J31: [W7] @VLOOKUP(K12,J27..K30,1)
H32: [W40] "a*SE =
J32: (P2) [W7] (J25*J31)
H33: [W40] "p+a*SE =
J33: (P2) [W7] +J22+J32
H34: [W40] "p-a*SE =
J34: (P2) [W7] +J22-J32
```

```
N1: [W37]  'SITUATION 2.0                                              READY


    M                   N                  O       P       Q       R     S
1      SITUATION 2.0
2    * *********************************************************************  *
3    * YOU HAVE AN ESTIMATED RESPONSE RATE FOR AN UPCOMING MAILING.          *
4    * THE QUESTION IS HOW MANY PIECES SHOULD YOU MAIL GIVEN THAT YOU        *
5    * WANT TO DEVELOP A CONFIDENCE INTERVAL OF PLUS OR MINUS SOME           *
6    * PERCENT AROUND THE EXPECTED RESPONSE RATE                             *
7    * *********************************************************************  *
8    *                                                                       *
9    * o PERCENT RESPONSE.........................    3.50%                   *
10   * o CONFIDENCE LEVEL: 80%, 85%, 90% OR 95%....   95.00%                  *
11   * o ALLOWABLE PERCENTAGE ERROR...PRECISION....   0.20%                   *
12   * o CONFIDENCE INTERVAL                          3.30%   TO    3.70%  *
13   *                                                                       *
14   * o TWO SIDED TEST                                                      *
15   *                                                                       *
16   *                                                                       *
17   *                                                                       *
18   *                                                                       *
19   * ANSWER: THE QUANTITY MAILED SHOULD BE:        32,438                  *
20   * *********************************************************************  *
10-Jan-90  02:29 PM                                CALC           CAPS



    N21: [W37]                                                         READY


    M                   N                  O       P       Q       R     S
21
22                          PERCENT RESPONSE     p =      3.50%
23                          DESIRED PRECISION      =      0.20%
24                          CONFIDENCE LEVELS:           80.00%1.282
25                                                       85.00%1.440
26                                                       90.00%1.645
27                                                       95.00%1.960
28                   CONFIDENCE LEVEL USED a =            1.96
29                   DESIRED PRECISION = (a*SE) =       .0020
30                          SE= (a*SE)/a       =       .00102041
31                          SE(SQUARED)=              0.0000010
32                          p*(1-p)=                  0.033775
33   SAMPLE SIZE = N = SE*SE/(p-(1-p)=     N =          32,438
34    from se = sqrt of [{p*(1-p)}/n]
35
36
37
38
39
40
10-Jan-90  02:29 PM                                CALC           CAPS
```

DIRECT MARKETING STATISTICS -DAVID SHEPARD ASSOCIATES, INC

```
N22: [W37] "PERCENT RESPONSE
O22: [W7] "p =
P22: (P2) [W10] +P9
N23: [W37] "DESIRED PRECISION
O23: [W7] "=
P23: (P2) [W10] +P11
N24: [W37] "CONFIDENCE LEVELS:
P24: (P2) [W10] 0.8
P25: (P2) [W10] 0.85
P26: (P2) [W10] 0.9
P27: (P2) [W10] 0.95
N28: [W37] "CONFIDENCE LEVEL USED
O28: [W7] 'a =
P28: [W10] @VLOOKUP(P10,P25..Q27,1)
N29: [W37] "DESIRED PRECISION
O29: [W7] '(a*SE)
P29: (F4) [W10] +P23
N30: [W37] "SE= (a*SE)/a
P30: (F8) [W10] +P29/P28
N31: [W37] "SE(SQUARED)=
P31: (F7) [W10] +P30*P30
N32: [W37] "p*(1-p)=
P32: [W10] (P22)*(1-P22)
N33: [W37] 'SAMPLE SIZE = N = SE*SE/(p-(1-p)=
O33: [W7] 'N =
P33: (,0) [W10] +P32/P31
N34: [W37] ' from se = sqrt of [{p*(1-p)}/n]
```

T1: [W2]   READY

```
    T              U                  V       W        X      Y
1   SITUATION 3.0 -- IS IMPROVEMENT IN RESPONSE SIGNIFICANT
2   * ************************************************************** *
3   * IS THE IMPROVEMENT IN THE TEST PACKAGE STATISTICALLY DIFFERENT *
4   * FROM THE RESPONSE TO THE CONTROL PACKAGE, OR                   *
5   * IS THE DIFFERENCE IN RESPONSE BETWEEN LIST A AND LIST B        *
6   * STATISTICALLY SIGNIFICANT                                      *
7   * ************************************************************** *
8   *                                          CONTROL      TEST     *
9   *                                          LIST A       LIST B   *
10  *                                          --------     --------  *
11  * o PERCENT RESPONSE........................ 3.50%      4.50%    *
12  * o CONFIDENCE LEVEL: 80%, 85%, 90% OR 95%... 95.00%             *
13  * o SAMPLE SIZE............................ 1,000      1,200     *
14  * o ONE SIDED TEST                                               *
15  *                                                                *
16  *                                                                *
17  *                                                                *
18  *                                                                *
19  * ANSWER: DIFFERENCE IN RESPONSE RATE IS.....NOT SIGNIFICANT     *
20  * ************************************************************** *
10-Jan-90  02:32 PM                            CALC        CAPS
```

```
U35: [W34] 'DIFFERENCE BETWEEN TWO SAMPLE                                    MENU
Range  Line  Page  Options  Clear  Align  Go  Quit
Advance to top of page
      T              U                    V        W         X        Y
 21   WORKSHEET
 22                     CONTROL PROPORTION =        c      3.50%
 23                        TEST PROPORTION =        t      4.50%
 24                     ABSOLUTE DIFFERENCE =       d      1.00%
 25   CONFIDENCE LEVELS: ONE SIDED TEST =                 80.00%    0.842
 26                                                       85.00%    1.036
 27                                                       90.00%    1.282
 28                                                       95.00%    1.645
 29                          LEVEL USED =            a     1.645
 30                  SAMPLE SIZE CONTROL =         n(c)    1,000
 31                     SAMPLE SIZE TEST =         n(t)    1,200
 32   ESTIMATE OF POPULATION VALUE OF %             p     0.04045
 33   [{n(c)*c}+{n(t)*t}]/[n(c)+n(t)]
 34   ESTIMATED STANDARD ERROR OF THE             Sc-t    0.008436
 35   DIFFERENCE BETWEEN TWO SAMPLE
 36   PERCENTAGES -ESTIMATED FROM THE
 37   SAMPLES THEMSELVES
 38   sqrt[p(1-p)*{n(c)+n(t)}/{n(c)*n(t)}]
 39
 40   DECISION PARAMETER
10-Jan-90  02:34 PM                                    CALC       CAPS
```

```
U55: [W34]                                                                   READY


      T              U                    V        W         X        Y
 41   (c-t)/Sc-t                          dp  1.185394324
 42
 43   DECISION RULE:
 44   if @ABS(dp)>a then significant, if dp<a not           0
 45                              TABLE =                     0 NOT SIGNIFICANT
 46                                                          1 SIGNIFICANT
 47                             ANSWER =          NOT SIGNIFICANT
 48
 49
 50
 51
 52
 53
 54
 55
 56
 57
 58
 59
 60
10-Jan-90  02:34 PM                                    CALC       CAPS
```

DIRECT MARKETING STATISTICS -DAVID SHEPARD ASSOCIATES, INC

```
U21: [W34] 'WORKSHEET
U22: [W34] "CONTROL PROPORTION =
V22: [W9] "c
W22: (P2) [W12] +W11
U23: [W34] "TEST PROPORTION =
V23: [W9] "t
W23: (P2) [W12] +X11
U24: [W34] "ABSOLUTE DIFFERENCE =
V24: [W9] "d
W24: (P2) [W12] +W23-W22
U25: [W34] "CONFIDENCE LEVELS: ONE SIDED TEST =
W25: (P2) [W12] 0.8
X25: [W12] 0.842
W26: (P2) [W12] 0.85
X26: (F3) [W12] 1.036
W27: (P2) [W12] 0.9
X27: [W12] 1.282
W28: (P2) [W12] 0.95
X28: [W12] 1.645
U29: [W34] "LEVEL USED =
V29: [W9] "a
W29: [W12] @VLOOKUP(W12,W25..X28,1)
U30: [W34] "SAMPLE SIZE CONTROL =
V30: [W9] "n(c)
W30: (,0) [W12] +W13
U31: [W34] "SAMPLE SIZE TEST =
V31: [W9] "n(t)
W31: (,0) [W12] +X13
U32: [W34] 'ESTIMATE OF POPULATION VALUE OF %
V32: [W9] "p
W32: (F5) [W12] ((W22*W30)+(W23*W31))/(W30+W31)
U33: [W34] '[{n(c)*c}+{n(t)*t}]/[n(c)+n(t)]
U34: [W34] 'ESTIMATED STANDARD ERROR OF THE
V34: [W9] "Sc-t
W34: (F6) [W12] @SQRT(W32*(1-W32)*(W30+W31)/(W30*W31))
U35: [W34] 'DIFFERENCE BETWEEN TWO SAMPLE
U36: [W34] 'PERCENTAGES -ESTIMATED FROM THE
U37: [W34] 'SAMPLES THEMSELVES
U38: [W34] 'sqrt[p(1-p)*{n(c)+n(t)}/{n(c)*n(t)}]
U40: [W34] 'DECISION PARAMETER
U41: [W34] '(c-t)/Sc-t
V41: [W9] "dp
W41: [W12] +W24/W34
U43: [W34] 'DECISION RULE:
U44: [W34] "if @ABS(dp)>a then significant, if dp<a not
W44: [W12] @IF(@ABS(W41)>=W29,1,0)
U45: [W34] "TABLE =
W45: [W12] 0
X45: [W12] 'NOT SIGNIFICANT
W46: [W12] 1
X46: [W12] 'SIGNIFICANT
U47: [W34] "ANSWER =
W47: [W12] @VLOOKUP(W44,W45..X46,1)
```

INDEX